Praise for *The Success Principles*™

Canfield's principles are simple, but the results you'll achieve will be extraordinary!
—Anthony Robbins, author of *Awaken the Giant Within* and *Unlimited Power*

If you could only read one book this year, you have it in your hands.
—Harvey Mackay, author of the *New York Times* number one best seller
Swim with the Sharks without Being Eaten Alive

When Jack Canfield writes, I listen. This is Jack's finest piece of writing and will impact your life forever.
—Pat Williams, senior vice president of the NBA's Orlando Magic

Jack Canfield is a Master of his medium, giving people who are hungry for more life the wisdom, insights, understanding, and inspiration they need to achieve it. Great book, great read, great gift for anyone committed to becoming a Master of Life!
—Michael E. Gerber, author of *The E-Myth* books

In one book, *The Success Principles* gives you the basic strategies for success plus the advanced strategies that will help you become a success master. I have personally learned a lot from Jack Canfield and I trust you will too.
—John Gray, Ph.D., author of *Men Are from Mars, Women Are from Venus*

Before you can change your life, you must first change your thinking. Jack and Janet have created an inspirational and motivational road map for your personal success! My real estate home study course has helped thousands become confident, successful real estate investors. I am convinced *The Success Principles* will change the way you think, the way you act, and help you change your life in ways you never dreamed possible! I would not only recommend this book to my students, but also to anyone committed to being successful—beyond their wildest dreams! I urge you to read this wonderful book. It will absolutely help you to change your life for the better!
—Carleton Sheets, creator of the "No Down Payment Real Estate"
home study course

Canfield and Switzer have put their methods to success in an illuminating and easy-to-read book. Jack's teaching is highly effective and this new book will be the gift to give this year.
—Ken Blanchard, coauthor of *The One Minute Manager*® and *Customer Mania!*®

In *The Success Principles,* Jack Canfield reveals the specific methodology and results-oriented principles required for success and ultimate achievement. Whether you need to boost sales at the office, expand creativity, or create more balance in your life, this book will pave the way to achieving your highest success!
—Peter Vidmar, two-time Olympic gold medalist in gymnastics and
member of the U.S. Olympic Hall of Fame

The Success Principles will inspire and empower you to lead a more fulfilling life. Get ready for some changes with this book!
—Kathy Smith, a leading force in American fitness and wellness

Jack's message is simple, powerful, and practical. If you work the principles, the principles work. A must-read for those who want to create the successful life about which they dream.　　　　—Andrew Puzder, president and CEO of CKE Restaurants, Inc., Carl's Jr., Hardee's, and La Salsa

What a great book! Jack Canfield's *The Success Principles* is a reference book for everyone who is interested in actually having the life they have dreamed about. Keep this book with you, use it as a guide and inspiration to help you achieve your highest potential and the inner peace that you desire. You need this book.
　　　　—Marilyn Tam, former president of Reebok Apparel Products Group and author of *How to Use What You've Got to Get What You Want*

If you thought you knew everything about how to be successful in business, wait until you read what's inside *The Success Principles*. From start-up entrepreneurs to the world's most powerful CEOs, this book can and will teach anyone how to be more successful and much happier doing what they love to do.
　　　　—John Assaraf, RE/MAX Indiana, *New York Times,* and *Wall Street Journal* best-selling author of *The Street Kid's Guide to Having It All*

Page for page the best system for achieving anything you want. Get ready for the ride of your life. I couldn't put it down!
　　　　—Marcia Martin, former vice president of est and transformational coach

Jack Canfield's amazing ability to be extremely articulate, understandable, and approachable makes *The Success Principles* not only an amazing blueprint for success, but also a pure joy to read.　　　　—Jim Tunney, Ed.D., former NFL referee, educator, and author of *It's the Will, Not the Skill*

I have witnessed firsthand Jack Canfield's tenacity in using the principles within this book. It is because of this determination and his beliefs in these principles that the *Chicken Soup for the Soul*® book series was born. *The Success Principles* is not only an amazing book that will give you the guide to outstanding achievement, but it in itself is proof that the principles work.
　　　　—Peter Vegso, president of Health Communications, Inc., and publisher of *Chicken Soup for the Soul*®

Most of us know what we want out of life, but only a handful of us have learned how to get it. Now *The Success Principles* not only gives you the road map, it hands you the keys to the ignition and puts gas in your tank! Get yourself some cookies and don't put this book down till you've mastered its message.
　　　　—Wally Amos, author of *The Cookie Never Crumbles*

My good friend Jack Canfield is one of the most insightful speakers and teachers in the world today. After you have spent time with him, internalizing his ideas and insights, you will be changed in a positive way for the rest of your life.
　　　　—Brian Tracy, one of America's leading authorities on the development of human potential and personal effectiveness and author of *Success Is a Journey, Million Dollar Habits,* and *The Traits of Champions*

By bringing your actions in line with Jack's core principles and values you can achieve any success you seek, including inner peace. Jack has written the road map to that end in *The Success Principles*. All you have to do is follow it.
—Hyrum W. Smith, vice chairman and founder of FranklinCovey

In today's super-competitive marketplace, high achievers are those people who follow a systematic approach to their success. Now in the best success classic to come along in decades, *The Success Principles* catalogs and explains these systems in simple language with step-by-step instructions, and features inspiring stories of others who have traveled the path before you. If your goal is greater accomplishment, more money, more free time, and less stress, read and apply the proven principles in this book.
—Les Brown, author of *Live Your Dreams* and *Conversations on Success*

What a great collection of "successful" thoughts and ideas . . . some simple, some profound, and all "essential" in today's complex world . . . a must-read!
—Steven Stralser, Ph.D., managing director of and clinical professor at the Global Entrepreneurship Center, Thunderbird: The Garvin School of International Management, and author of *MBA in a Day: What You Would Learn in Top-Tier Schools of Business—If You Only Had the Time*

After you read *The Success Principles,* you will approach your short- and long-term goals in a completely new and exciting fashion. This book outlines the tools you need to get everything you want out of life and more! Canfield and Switzer's own success is evidence that these principles work and can be easily applied to any goal.
—Rita Davenport, president of Arbonne International

Success is something almost everyone wants, and many spend a lifetime hoping for. Some never find it while others realize it early in life. No matter where you are in your life, stop and read this magnificent book by Jack Canfield and Janet Switzer. Maybe you're already there, or are trying to get there, or are lost somewhere between the desire for and the realization of personal success. When you've finished *The Success Principles: How to Get from Where You Are to Where You Want to Be,* you'll immediately know where you are, where you want to be, and how to get there. This is a work that should become a textbook and required reading before earning "adulthood."
—Dave Liniger, chairman of the board of RE/MAX International

Jack Canfield has done it again! In *The Success Principles,* he explains with great ease and compassion the time-tested techniques employed by high achievers from every walk of life—techniques that can take you as far as you dare to dream. No matter what your definition of "success" is, this book is going to get you there!
—Jeff Liesener, president of High Achievers Network

If you've ever wanted Jack Canfield to personally mentor you in achieving your highest vision, this book is the next best thing to having him as your personal guide. It's packed with information, inspiration, and—most importantly—understanding. Along with his proven strategies, Jack's support, compassion, and integrity shine through.
—Marshall Thurber, cofounder of the Accelerated Business School and Money and You

The success principles in this book are so simple to follow but at the same time so powerful. They are essential to achieving your goals. Jack has a way of making learning entertaining and fun. This book is a true winner!

> —Kathy Coover, cofounder and senior VP of sales and marketing of Isagenix International

In a world filled with dubious paths to success, *The Success Principles* identifies the proven steps today's biggest names and brightest stars use to achieve their ideal future. I can't think of a better way to get from where you are to where you want to be.

> —Bill Harris, director, Centerpointe Research

If you have a big vision and big plans, read *The Success Principles* and take action on what you learn. After all, you deserve to have more of what you want out of life.

> —H. Ronald Hulnick, Ph.D., president of the University of Santa Monica

A unique blend of lessons and techniques with true-life anecdotes and humor make *The Success Principles* a great read. Educational, humorous, and very down-to-earth, this book uses Jack Canfield's ability to motivate and inspire without an overly "hyped" attitude. These success principles offer great value to any reader.

> —Christen Brown, president of On Camera Entertainment and author of *Star Quality*

No matter what your idea of success is, Jack Canfield can help you get there. *The Success Principles* is life's reference book for the young and old alike. Transform your dreams of success into reality. Buy this book today.

> —Gary T. Van Brunt, CEO of Discount Tire Co.

The Success Principles proves once and for all that personal achievement is not an accident of birth or privilege. Rather, it's the result of thinking, and of doing—of planning, and of follow-through. But most importantly, the power to achieve is a *skill* that can be *taught*—and no one teaches it more superbly than Jack Canfield.

> —Catherine B. Reynolds, chairman of the board of the Catherine B. Reynolds Foundation

This book is a must-read! Canfield and Switzer explain the specific, step-by-step formulas all of us can use to achieve more success in our careers and personal lives. If making more money, playing a bigger game, and achieving your dream lifestyle are what you want, *The Success Principles* delivers it masterfully.

> —Gay Hendricks, Ph.D., author of *Conscious Living* and coauthor (with Dr. Kathlyn Hendricks) of *Conscious Loving*

No matter where you are with your life, *The Success Principles* gives you proven strategies and time-tested systems to create a brighter future. Join the ranks of today's highest achievers in reading and applying what this impressive new success classic tells you. Then plan to get a copy for a friend.

> —Paul R. Scheele, author of *Natural Brilliance, Genius Code, Abundance for Life,* and *The PhotoReading Whole Mind System*

This book is a brilliantly written, masterful distillation of the leading principles and processes available today for creating real success in your life.

> —Hale Dwoskin, author of the *New York Times* best seller *The Sedona Method: Your Key to Lasting Happiness, Success, Peace, and Emotional Well-being*

Success in all areas of your life can be yours! Follow Jack Canfield's principles and strategies to achieve any goal! *The Success Principles* offers a detailed yet understandable guide to achieving more of what YOU want. It's enjoyable and effective. Read it today!
—Erin Saxton, The Idea Network

I have made the studies of success a lifetime pursuit. Thank you so much, Jack, for putting together an easy-to-understand book on success that readers of all ages and backgrounds will understand and benefit from. The powerful lessons and stories within *The Success Principles* are truly life-changing!
—James Arthur Ray, author of *The Science of Success* and
Stop the World: 29 Principles to Realize Your Infinite Self

Reading *The Success Principles* is as close as possible to having Jack Canfield as your personal coach. Jack has the ability to blend intelligence and compassion, making the book very approachable. The book's principles and stories of others who have used these principles is effective and inspiring. This dynamic book will be spoken of for years to come! —George R. Walther, author of *Heat Up Your Cold Calls*

If you are looking for a magic bullet to improve your life, your career, and your relationships, *The Success Principles* delivers it in spades. But don't just buy this impressive new classic and put it on a shelf. Read its proven strategies, apply its time-tested systems, then get ready to join the ranks of the world's highest achievers!
—Raymond Aaron, Canada's number one business and investment coach

What a great collection of "successful" thoughts and ideas . . . some simple, some profound, and all "essential" in today's complex world. A must-read! I used the principles in this book to propel my Web site from 100 visitors a month to over 5,000 visitors a month. —Zev Saftlas, author of *Motivation That Works* and
founder of empoweringmessages.com

Jack Canfield's *The Success Principles* intertwines strategies for success with proven examples and stories. The book should be a must-read for everyone who is looking to attain new heights in his or her life. Is there a way to make this required reading for future generations? I wish I had this information twenty years ago!
—Arielle Ford, author of *Hot Chocolate for the Mystical Soul*

Canfield and Switzer have created a book that is alive with intellect, compassion, and humor. This is one of the best books on success I have ever read! If you have a dream that you have not yet attained, let Jack Canfield lead the way. You will be happy you did. —Bill Cirone, superintendent of Santa Barbara County
Office of Education

If expanding your opportunities, creating new alliances, helping more people, and getting more out of every minute of your life are your goals, *The Success Principles* can bring you these results. I loved it!
—John Demartini, CEO of Demartini Seminars and
founder of the Concourse of Wisdom

Successful people know the most significant investment you can make is in yourself. *The Success Principles* helps you master the skill sets that will attract great people, great opportunities, and great fortune into your life. Let this investment pay off for you.

—Cynthia Kersey, author of *Unstoppable* and *Unstoppable Women*

If ever there was a book that uncovered the secret strategies of today's highest achievers, *The Success Principles* is it. Easy, understandable, applicable. It's the best success tool to come along in years.

—Bill Bauman, Ph.D., Bill Bauman Seminars and Mentoring

Finally, a book that lives up to what it claims. *The Success Principles* really does take your life to the next level and helps you achieve anything you've ever dreamed of. Using the principles that have made Jack Canfield and the many other successful men and women within this book, you too can attain amazing achievement. Read this book today!

—Tom Hill, founder of the Eagle Institute and author of *Living at the Summit: A Life Plan*

If you're looking for a winning plan for success, look no further than Jack Canfield's *Success Principles*.

—Suzanne de Passe, television producer

Jack Canfield is a true master. He understands what it takes to lead a successful life, and in *The Success Principles* he puts all the key elements together in one place for the rest of the world to see.

—T. Harv Eker, author of *Secrets of the Millionaire Mind*

I have been a student of Jack Canfield for over a decade and have used the principles he teaches in this book to accelerate my own success and the success of the people I train and manage at the Henry Ford Museum. This book has my highest recommendation. It will change your life.

—Jim Van Bochove, director of workforce development at The Henry Ford: America's Greatest History Attraction

Jack Canfield's *Success Principles* brilliantly and succinctly imparts the tried and true formula for living a successful, fulfilled life. You will find inspiration and motivation on every page.

—Debbie Ford, number one *New York Times* best-selling author of *The Dark Side of the Light Chasers* and *The Best Year of Your Life*

Jack Canfield has, with diamond-like clarity, crafted the ultimate success manual. It's the manual I wish I'd had when I began my quest for the best.

—Master Mary Louise Zeller, "Ninja Grandma," twelve-time national and five-time international gold medalist in Olympic-style tae kwon do

Whether you are a budding entrepreneur, have been in business for decades, or have just graduated high school, Jack Canfield's *The Success Principles* is a must-read. The book takes you step-by-step through the stages of success and achievement and will propel you to your next level (and most likely far beyond that too)! Jack's down-to-earth style and straightforward language allow the everyday person to enjoy this incredibly thorough, comprehensive, and intelligent book.

—Linda Distenfield, president, and Ira Distenfield, CEO of We The People

THE
Success
Principles™

THE Success Principles ™

HOW TO GET FROM WHERE YOU ARE TO WHERE YOU WANT TO BE

Jack Canfield

Cocreator of the
Chicken Soup for the Soul® Series

WITH

Janet Switzer

A HarperResource Book
An Imprint of HarperCollins*Publishers*

HarperCollins books may be purchased for educational, business, or sales promotional use. For information, please write: Special Markets Department, HarperCollins Publishers, Inc., 10 East 53rd Street, New York, NY 10022.

FIRST EDITION

Designed by Ellen Cipriano

Library of Congress Cataloging-in-Publication Data

Canfield, Jack, 1944–
    The success principles : how to get from where you are to where you want to be / by Jack Canfield with Janet Switzer.
      p. cm.
    Includes bibliographical references and index.
    ISBN 0-06-059488-8
    1. Success—Psychological aspects.   I. Switzer, Janet, 1963– II. Title.

BF637.S8C2777 2005
158—dc22

2004054259

05 06 07 08 09 WBC/RRD 10 9 8 7 6 5 4 3 2 1

ACKNOWLEDGMENTS

This book, like everything else I have created in my life, is the result of a huge team effort. I extend my deepest gratitude and thanks to:

Janet Switzer, without whose Herculean efforts this book would never have been completed. Thank you for your incredible support, deep insights, and long days (and nights!) spent in the original conception of this book, coauthoring a world-class book proposal, boiling my endless production of written words down into a manageable manuscript, keeping me focused, developing the Success Principles Web site, and creating such an amazing marketing plan for reaching millions of people with the message of this book. You are truly awesome!

Bonnie Solow, my literary agent. You are more than an agent. You were there every step of the way with your editorial insights, emotional support, enthusiastic encouragement, and authentic friendship. I admire your integrity, your professionalism, your commitment to excellence, your sincere desire to make a difference, and your love for life.

Steve Hanselman, my brilliant, supportive, and insightful editor and publisher at HarperCollins. Thanks for your boundless energy, your beautiful spirit, and your dedication to educating and uplifting humanity through the written word.

Mary Ellen Curley, who oversaw the marketing and production of the book from start to finish. I appreciate your professionalism and tireless efforts on behalf of the book and its message. Jane Friedman, president & CEO of HarperCollins, who championed this book from the beginning. Thanks for the inspiring job you do of running a company aligned with the principles described in this book. It is an honor to be working with you.

Katharine O'Moore-Klopf, who copyedited the manuscript. Your eagle eye and attention to detail are awesome. Thanks for a wonderful job.

Andrea Brown, who designed the book cover. I love it!

Deborah Feingold, who took the cover photo. It was fun working with you in the studio. You are a kick!

Brian Grogan, Veronica Gonzalez, Ana Maria Allessi, Andrea Rosen, Paul Olsewski, Shelby Meizlik, Nina Olmsted, Josh Marwell, and all of the others at HarperCollins who have worked so diligently on getting this book (and the audio version) onto the shelves in the bookstores and into the hands of the readers. You are the best at what you do.

Patty Aubery, president of Chicken Soup for the Soul Enterprises, for "making" me write this book. Thanks for overseeing the whole project and especially for helping get all of the endorsements. You are an awesome friend and business partner. Words can never convey how much I appreciate your support in bringing out the best in me.

Russell Kamalski, chief operating officer at Chicken Soup for the Soul Enterprises. Thanks for your calm, easygoing demeanor that helps keep it all together in the midst of the tornado-like frenzy we often find ourselves in. You're a true gentleman.

Veronica Romero, my executive assistant, who has kept my life in order with very little support from me during the last year of being buried under the weight of this project. Thanks for scheduling all of the interviews and for overseeing getting all of the necessary permissions for this book. Thanks for keeping me, my travel, and my speaking career alive and well during this time. Your tireless efforts, your attention to detail, and your commitment to excellence are awesome. Thanks so much!

Mike Foster, my other executive assistant, thanks for your help in keeping the wolves at bay so I could have the space to work on this book with a minimum of interruptions, your research support, your long hours, your sense of humor, and your shared vision. Your commitment above and beyond the call of duty to keeping our seminars filled and our computers working is also awesome. Thanks for your dedication and your love.

Jesse Ianniello, for all of her endless hours of transcribing the hundreds of hours of interviews I recorded, and for all of the other endless clerical tasks that were required to complete this book. You consistently make the difficult look easy. You are a wonder.

Robin Yerian, for looking after me in so many areas of my life, especially making sure we stay on budget so that we always have enough money to do the things we need to do.

Teresa Esparza, for managing to coordinate all my speaking engagements and keeping all of our clients happy during this "year of the book." D'ette Corona for brilliantly overseeing the *Chicken Soup for the Soul*® production schedule while I was diverted by this project. You, too, are awesome!

Heather McNamara, Nancy Mitchell Autio, Leslie Riskin, Stephanie

Thatcher, Barbara Lomonaco, and Tasha Boucher, who handled all of the details of getting *Chicken Soup* books completed and out the door during this time. And all the other people who work at Self-Esteem Seminars and Chicken Soup for the Soul Enterprises.

Erick Baldwin, Kristen Craib, Lauren Edelstein, Devon Foster, Anna Giardina, Chris Muirhead, and Danielle Schlapper, our fabulous interns from the University of California, Santa Barbara, for your typing, editing and research skills.

Gail Miller, Janet's director of training programs, who manages Janet's company so brilliantly and who continually creates the space Janet needs to help develop *The Success Principles* book and training products. Your intelligence and the results you produce are truly impressive.

Marci Shimoff, who took a week out of her life to come and help restructure the book and offered such valuable feedback. Thanks for your generosity of spirit. The depth of your friendship is astonishing.

Rick Frischman, David Hahn, and Jared Sharpe at Planned Television Arts for their world-class support in getting the word out to the folks in radio and television land. I love working with you guys!

Hale Dwoskin, Marshall Thurber, and Barbara DeAngelis, for their constant encouragement and offers of support throughout the writing of this book.

The following people who allowed me to interview them, and whose stories and anecdotes appear in this book: Raymond Aaron, Robert Allen, Jeff Arch, John Assaraf, Madeline Balletta, Marty Becker, Arthur Benjamin, Tom Boyer, Lee Brower, Stephen J. Cannell, Frank Corbo, D.C. Cordova, John Demartini, Ira and Linda Distenfeld, Hale Dwoskin, Harv Eker, Tim Ferriss, Ruben Gonzales, Greg Haven, Mike Kelley, Marilyn Kentz, Rick Kinmon, Julie Laippley, Dave Liniger, Debbie Macomber, Fabrizio Mancini, Marcia Martin, John McPherson, Mike Milliorn, David Morris, Chad Pregracke, Monty Roberts, Rudy Ruettiger, Scott Schilling, Jana Stanfield, Joe Sugarman, Marilyn Tam, Marshall Thurber, Diana Von Welanetz Wentworth, Pat Williams, and Wyland.

The following people who allowed me to interview them, and though because of space constrictions and last-minute editing, their stories don't appear in this book, their ideas, insights, and spirit are woven throughout: Jennifer Allen, John Anderson, Janet Atwood, Russell Bishop, Stan Dale, Bob Danzig, Roger Dawson, John Dealy, Kent and Kyle Healy, Orrin C. Hudson, Teresa Huggins, Tony O'Donnell, Kevin Ross, Michael Russo, Barry Spilchuk, and Gary Tuerack.

The hundreds of people who offered to be interviewed for the book—you know who you are—but whom I simply couldn't get to because of time, which I regret, because conducting the interviews was the most exciting part of creating this book. This project taught me once again just how much valuable information we all have to share with each other. I hope someday to be able to take all of you up on your offers for a future book.

The following people who read the manuscript and provided much-needed feedback: Patty Aubery, Tom Boyer, Mark Donnelly, Eldon Edwards, Mike Foster, Andrew Holmes, Russ Kamalski, Veronica Romero, Zev Saftlas, LeAnn Thieman, Marci Shimoff, and Robin Yerian. Thank you for taking time out of your busy schedules—and on such short notice—to provide your valuable comments. I appreciate you all a lot!

The following people, who have directly influenced my thinking about and achievement of success in their workshops, seminars, and coaching programs, over the years: W. Clement Stone, Og Mandino, Norman Vincent Peale, Marshall Thurber, Mark Victor Hansen, Phil Laut, Leonard Orr, Stewart Emery, Martha Crampton, Russell Bishop, Jim Newman, Lou Tice, John Gray, Tim Piering, Tracy Goss, Martin Rutte, Wayne Dyer, Bob Proctor, Lee Pulos, Brian Tracy, Jim Rohn, Anthony Robbins, Michael Gerber, Dan Sullivan, Les Hewitt, Robert Allen, Hale Dwoskin, and John Assaraf. Thanks for your brilliant minds, your courage to live on the cutting edge, and your generosity of spirit.

Dr. Jack Dawson and Dr. Bruno Wildhaber, my two chiropractors, and Wayne Darling, my massage therapist, for all the great body work that kept my body and soul together during these past stress-filled months.

The members of my mastermind group: John Assaraf, Lee Brower, Declan Dunn, Liz Edlic, and Marshall Thurber. I appreciate being part of such a loving and visionary band of brothers and sisters.

Mark Victor Hansen and Patty Hansen for their love, friendship, and partnership on the *Chicken Soup for the Soul®* journey, which has been the greatest adventure of my life.

Peter Vegso and Gary Seidler at Health Communications Inc., for believing in the dream long before anyone else did, and without whose support over the years this book would have never been created. Thanks, guys! And everyone else at HCI who has worked to make *Chicken Soup for the Soul®* a worldwide publishing phenomenon.

All my family for their love, support, and understanding during what has been unquestionably the greatest professional challenge of my career. Thanks for understanding the long hours, the sacrificed weekends, and the two canceled vacations that were required to finish this project on time. I love and appreciate you all so much. Inga, my wife, whom I adore for how much she understands me and what I am about, and for her unceasing love, support, humor, and encouragement. Christopher, my 14-year-old son, for putting up with my obsession around this book. I hope our 2 weeks in Europe this summer make up for the time lost during the past 6 months. Riley and Travis, my two stepchildren, who continue to delight me to no end with their shenani-gans. Thanks for being so supportive. Oran and Kyle, my two older sons. Now we'll have time for that promised trip to Las Vegas!

My sister Kim, for all of her moral support and encouragement when I couldn't see the light at the end of the tunnel. It's nice having a sister who is a fellow writer and understands the process. Taylor and Mary, for taking care of Mom all these many months and years. Rick and Tana, for being such a good brother and sister-in-law. Fred Angelis, my stepfather, for taking me under his wing when I was 6 and providing me with the values and work habits that have allowed me to create the level of success that I have.

Janet's family, for their support, understanding, and good humor in the face of missed vacations and endless book-related dinner conversation. To her parents, Les and Beverly, who showed Janet early on the meaning of suc-cess and who fostered an atmosphere of achievement in their home. To her siblings, Jennifer and Jeff, for their constant support and encouragement through every new step in Janet's life and career. And most especially, thanks to Janet's niece Brianne, who not only reflects how children learn to be suc-cessful but is also a gentle reminder that the most important thing is to en-joy it.

And finally, thanks to all of the assistants and participants in my seminars and workshops these past few years for sharing their dreams, struggles, and triumphs with me. Your heroic efforts in overcoming your limiting beliefs and fears, your courage in confronting the obstacles in your paths, your per-severance in the face of adversity, and the amazing lives you have all created are the inspiration that led me to write this book and share these principles with others. Thank you for being the models of vision, purpose, and passion that the world so desperately needs. Know that you are all represented in these pages.

This book is dedicated to all those courageous men and women who have ever dared to step out of the dominant culture of resignation and mediocrity and endeavor to create the life of their dreams. I honor and salute you!

Life is like a combination lock; your job is to find the right numbers, in the right order, so you can have anything you want.

BRIAN TRACY

If we did all the things we are capable of doing, we would literally astound ourselves.

THOMAS A. EDISON

CONTENTS

II. Transform Yourself for Success

III. Build Your Success Team

IV. Create Successful Relationships

V. Success and Money

VI. Success Starts Now

THE
Success
Principles™

INTRODUCTION

*If a man for whatever reason has the opportunity to lead an
extraordinary life, he has no right to keep it to himself.*

JACQUES-YVES COUSTEAU
Legendary underwater explorer and filmmaker

*If a man writes a book, let him set down only what he knows.
I have guesses enough of my own.*

JOHANN WOLFGANG VON GOETHE
German poet, novelist, playwright, and philosopher

This is not a book of good ideas. This is a book of timeless principles used by successful men and women throughout history. I have studied these success principles for over 30 years and have applied them to my own life. The phenomenal level of success that I now enjoy is the result of applying these principles day in and day out since I began to learn them in 1968.

My success includes being the author and editor of over 60 best-selling books with over 80 million copies in print in 39 languages around the world, holding a *Guinness Book* world record for having seven books on the May 24, 1998, *New York Times* bestseller list, earning a multimillion-dollar net income every year for over the past 10 years, living in a beautiful California estate, appearing on every major talk show in America (from *Oprah* to *Good Morning America*), having a weekly newspaper column read by millions every week, commanding speaking fees of $25,000 a talk, speaking to Fortune 500 companies all over the world, being the recipient of numerous professional and civic awards, having an outrageous relationship with my amazing wife and wonderful children, and having achieved a steady state of wellness, balance, happiness, and inner peace.

I get to socialize with CEOs of Fortune 500 companies; movie, television, and recording stars; celebrated authors; and the world's finest spiritual teachers and leaders. I have spoken to the members of Congress, professional athletes, corporate managers, and sales superstars in all of the best resorts and retreat centers of the world—from the Four Seasons Resort in Nevis in the British West Indies to the finest hotels in Acapulco and Cancun. I get to ski in Idaho, California, and Utah, go rafting in Colorado, and hike in the mountains of California and Washington. And I get to vacation in the world's best resorts in Hawaii, Australia, Thailand, Morocco, France, and Italy. All in all, life is a real kick!

And like most of you reading this book, my life started out in a very average way. I grew up in Wheeling, West Virginia, where my dad worked in a florist's shop, where he made $8,000 a year. My mother was an alcoholic and my father was a workaholic. I worked during the summers to make ends meet (as a lifeguard at a pool and at the same florist's shop as my father). I went to college on a scholarship and held a job serving breakfast in one of the dorms to pay for books, clothes, and dates. Nobody handed me anything on a silver platter. During my last year of graduate school, I had a part-time teaching job that paid me $120 every 2 weeks. My rent was $79 a month, so that left $161 to cover all my other expenses. Toward the end of the month, I ate what became known as my 21-cent dinners—a 10-cent can of tomato paste, garlic salt, and water over an 11-cent bag of spaghetti noodles. I know what it is like to be scraping by on the bottom rungs of the economic ladder.

After graduate school, I started my career as a high school history teacher in an all-black school on the south side of Chicago. And then I met my mentor, W. Clement Stone. Stone was a self-made multimillionaire who hired me to work in his foundation, where he trained me in the fundamental success principles that I still operate from today. My job was to teach these same principles to others. Over the years, I have gone on from my time with Stone to interview hundreds of successful people—Olympic and professional athletes, celebrated entertainers, best-selling authors, business leaders, political leaders, successful entrepreneurs, and top salespeople. I have read literally thousands of books (I average one every 2 days), attended hundreds of seminars, and listened to thousands of hours of audio programs to uncover the universal principles for creating success and happiness. I then applied those principles to my own life. The ones that worked I have taught in my speeches, seminars, and workshops to well over 1 million people in all 50 U.S. states . . . and in 20 countries around the world.

These principles and techniques have not only worked for me but they have also helped hundreds of thousands of my students achieve breakthrough success in their careers, greater wealth in their finances, greater aliveness and joy in their relationships, and greater happiness and fulfillment in their lives. My students have started successful businesses, become self-made millionaires, achieved athletic stardom, received lucrative recording contracts, starred in movie and television roles, won political offices, had huge impact in their communities, written best-selling books, been named teacher of the year in their school districts, broken all the sales records in their companies, written award-winning screenplays, become presidents of their corporations, been recognized for their outstanding philanthropic contributions, created highly successful relationships, and raised unusually happy and successful children.

THE PRINCIPLES ALWAYS WORK IF
YOU WORK THE PRINCIPLES

All of these same results are also possible for you. I know for a fact that you, too, can attain unimagined levels of success. Why? Because the principles and techniques always work—all you have to do is put them to work for you.

A few years ago, I was on a television show in Dallas, Texas. I had made the claim that if people would use the principles I was teaching, they could double their income and double their time off in less than 2 years. The woman interviewing me was highly skeptical. I told her that if she used the principles and techniques for 2 years and she didn't double her income and double her time off, I would come back on her show and write her a check for $1,000. If they did work, she had to ask me back and tell her viewers the principles had worked. A short 9 months later, I ran into her at the National Speakers Association convention in Orlando, Florida. She told me that not only had she *already* doubled her income but she had also moved to a bigger station with a substantial pay increase, had started a public speaking career, and had already finished and sold a book—all in just 9 months!

The fact is that anyone can consistently produce these kinds of results on a regular basis. All you have to do is decide what it is you want, believe you deserve it, and practice the success principles in this book.

The fundamentals are the same for all people and all professions—even if you're currently unemployed. It doesn't matter if your goals are to be the top salesperson in your company, become a leading architect, get all A's in school, lose weight, buy your dream home, or become a world-class professional athlete, a rock star, an award-winning journalist, a multimillionaire, or a successful entrepreneur—the principles and strategies are the same. And if you learn them, assimilate them, and apply them with discipline every day, they will transform your life beyond your wildest dreams.

"YOU CAN'T HIRE SOMEONE ELSE TO DO YOUR PUSH-UPS FOR YOU"

As motivational philosopher Jim Rohn has so aptly put it, "You can't hire someone else to do your push-ups for you." You must do them yourself if you are to get any value out of them. Whether it is exercising, stretching, meditating, reading, studying, learning a new language, creating a mastermind group, setting measurable goals, visualizing success, repeating affirmations, or practicing a new skill, *you* are going to have to do it. No one else can do these things for you. I will give you the road map, but you will have to drive the car. I will teach you the principles, but you will have to apply them. If you choose to put in the effort, I promise you the rewards will be well worth it.

HOW THIS BOOK IS STRUCTURED

To help you quickly learn these powerful principles, I have organized this book into six sections. Section I, "The Fundamentals of Success," contains 25 chapters that are the absolute basics you must do to get from where you are to where you want to be. You'll start by exploring the absolute necessity of taking 100% responsibility for your life and your results. From there, you'll learn how to clarify your life purpose, your vision, and what you truly want. Next we'll look at how to create an unshakable belief in yourself and your dreams. Then I'll help you turn your vision into a set of concrete goals and an action plan for achieving them. I'll even teach you how to harness the incredible power of affirmations and visualization—one of the success secrets of all Olympic athletes, top entrepreneurs, world leaders, and others.

The next few chapters have to do with taking those necessary but sometimes scary action steps that are required to make your dreams come true. You'll learn to ask for what you want, reject rejection, solicit and respond to feedback, and persevere in the face of what can sometimes seem like insurmountable obstacles.

Section II, "Transform Yourself for Success," addresses the important inner work you'll need to do—work that will help you remove any mental and emotional blocks you may have to success. It's not enough to *know* what to do. There are many books that will tell you that. You also need to understand the importance of and the methodology for removing self-defeating beliefs, fears, and habits that are holding you back. Like driving your car with the emergency brake on, these blocks can significantly slow your progress. You must learn how to release the brakes, or you will always experience life as a struggle and fall short of your intended goals. What will you learn in Section II? You'll learn how to surround yourself with successful people and how to acknowledge the positive past and release the negative past, face what isn't working in your life, embrace change, and make a commitment to lifelong learning. We'll look at how to clean up any physical and emotional messes you have created and complete all the "incompletes" in your life robbing you of valuable energy that could be better used in the achievement of your goals. I'll also teach you how to transform your inner critic into an inner coach and develop valuable success habits that will change your life forever.

Section III, "Build Your Success Team," reveals how and why to build different kinds of support teams so you can spend your time focusing exclusively on your core genius. You'll also learn how to redefine time, find a personal coach, and access your own inner wisdom—an untapped but ultrarich resource for most people.

In Section IV, "Create Successful Relationships," I'll teach you a number of principles, as well as some very practical techniques, for building and maintaining successful relationships. In this day of strategic alliances and power networks, it's literally impossible to build large-scale, long-lasting success without world-class relationship skills.

Finally, because so many people equate success with money, and because money is vital to our survival and the quality of our life, Section V is entitled "Success and Money." I'll teach you how to develop a more positive money consciousness, how to ensure that you have plenty of money to live the lifestyle you want, both now and after you retire, and the importance of tithing and service in guaranteeing your financial success.

Section VI, "Success Starts Now," consists of two short chapters on the importance of getting started now and empowering others in the process. Reading these chapters will jump-start you in creating the life you've always dreamed of but up until now may not have fully known how to create.

HOW TO READ THIS BOOK

Believe nothing. No matter where you read it, or who said it, even if I have said it, unless it agrees with your own reason and your own common sense.

BUDDHA

Everyone learns differently, and you probably know how you learn best. And though there are many ways that you can read this book, I'd like to make a few suggestions that may be helpful.

You may want to read this book through once just to get a feel for the total process before you start the work of creating the life you truly want, The principles are presented in an order that builds one upon the other. They are like the numbers in a combination lock—you need all the numbers, and you need them in the right order. It doesn't matter what color, race, gender, or age you are. If you know the combination, the lock has to open for you.

As you are reading, I strongly encourage you to underline and highlight everything that feels important to you. Make notes in the margin about the things you'll put into action. Then review those notes and highlighted sections again and again. Repetition is the key to real learning. Every time you reread portions of this book, you'll literally "re-mind" yourself of what you need to do to get from where you are to where you want to be. As you'll discover, it takes repetitive exposure to a new idea before it becomes a natural part of your way of thinking and being.

You may also discover that you're already familiar with some of the principles here. That's great! But ask yourself, *Am I currently practicing them?* If not, make a commitment to put them into action—now!

Remember, the principles only work if you work the principles.

The second time you read through this book, you'll want to read one chapter at a time, then take whatever time necessary to put it into practice. If you're already doing some of these things, keep doing them. If not, start now.

Like many of my past students and clients, you, too, may find yourself resisting taking some of the suggested action steps. But my experience has shown that the ones you most resist are the ones you need to most embrace. Remember, reading this book is not the same as doing the work, any more than reading a book on weight loss is the same as actually eating fewer calories and exercising more.

You might find it useful to connect with one or two other people who would like to join you as accountability partners and ensure that each of you actually implements what you learn. True learning only occurs when you assimilate and apply the new information—when there is a *change in your behavior*.

A WARNING

Of course, any change requires sustained effort to overcome years' worth of internal and external resistance. Initially you may find yourself getting very excited about all this new information. You may feel a newfound sense of hope and enthusiasm for the new vision of your life as it can be. This is good. But be forewarned that you may also begin to experience other feelings as well. You may feel frustration at not knowing about all of this earlier, anger at your parents and teachers for not teaching you these important concepts at home and at school, or anger at yourself for having already learned many of these things and not having acted on them.

Just take a deep breath and realize that this is all part of the process of your journey. Everything in the past has actually been perfect. Everything in your past has led you to this transformative moment in time. Everyone—including you—has always done the best they could with what they knew at the time. Now you are about to know more. Celebrate your new awareness! It is about to set you free.

You may also find that there will be times when you wonder, *Why isn't all of this working faster? Why haven't I already achieved my goal? Why aren't I rich already? Why don't I have the man or woman of my dreams by now? When am I going to achieve my ideal weight?* Success takes time, effort, perseverance, and patience. If you apply all of the principles and techniques covered in this book you *will* achieve your goals. You will realize your dreams. But it won't happen overnight.

It's natural in the achievement of any goal to come upon obstacles, to feel temporarily stuck on a plateau. This is normal. Anyone who has ever played a musical instrument, participated in a sport, or practiced a martial art knows that you hit plateaus where it seems as if you are making no progress whatsoever. That's when the uninitiated often quit, give up, drop out, or take up another instrument or sport. But the wise have discovered if they just keep practicing their instrument, sport, or martial art (or, in your case, the success principles in this book), eventually they make what feels like a sudden leap to a higher level of proficiency. Be patient. Hang in there. Don't give up. You *will* break through. The principles *always* work.

Okay, let's get started.

It's time to start living the life you've imagined.

HENRY JAMES

American-born author of 20 novels, 112 stories, and 12 plays

PART ONE

The Fundamentals of Success

Learn the fundamentals
of the game and stick to them.
Band-Aid remedies never last.

JACK NICKLAUS
Legendary professional golfer

TAKE 100% RESPONSIBILITY FOR YOUR LIFE

You must take personal responsibility. You cannot change the circumstances, the seasons, or the wind, but you can change yourself.

JIM ROHN
America's foremost business philosopher

One of the most pervasive myths in the American culture today is that we are *entitled* to a great life—that somehow, somewhere, someone (certainly not us) is responsible for filling our lives with continual happiness, exciting career options, nurturing family time, and blissful personal relationships simply because we exist.

But the real truth—and the one lesson this whole book is based on—is that there is only one person responsible for the quality of the life you live.

That person is *you*.

If you want to be successful, you have to take 100% responsibility for everything that you experience in your life. This includes the level of your achievements, the results you produce, the quality of your relationships, the state of your health and physical fitness, your income, your debts, your feelings—everything!

This is not easy.

In fact, most of us have been conditioned to blame something outside of ourselves for the parts of our life we don't like. We blame our parents, our bosses, our friends, the media, our coworkers, our clients, our spouse, the weather, the economy, our astrological chart, our lack of money—anyone or anything we can pin the blame on. We never want to look at where the real problem is—ourselves.

There is a wonderful story told about a man who is out walking one night and comes upon another man down on his knees looking for something under a streetlamp. The passerby inquires as to what the other man is looking for. He answers that he is looking for his lost key. The passerby offers to help and gets down on his knees and helps him search for the key. After an hour of fruitless searching, he says, "We've looked everywhere for it and we haven't found it. Are you sure that you lost it here?"

The other man replies, "No, I lost it in my house, but there is more light out here under the streetlamp."

It is time to stop looking outside yourself for the answers to why you haven't created the life and results you want, for it is you who creates the quality of the life you lead and the results you produce.

You—no one else!

To achieve major success in life—to achieve those things that are most important to you—you must assume 100% responsibility for your life. Nothing less will do.

ONE HUNDRED PERCENT RESPONSIBILITY
FOR EVERYTHING

As I mentioned in the introduction, back in 1969—only 1 year out of graduate school—I had the good fortune to work for W. Clement Stone. He was a self-made multimillionaire worth $600 million at the time—and that was long before all the dot-com millionaires came along in the '90s. Stone was also America's premier success guru. He was the publisher of *Success Magazine*, author of *The Success System That Never Fails*, and coauthor with Napoleon Hill of *Success Through a Positive Mental Attitude*.

When I was completing my first week's orientation, Mr. Stone asked me if I took 100% responsibility for my life.

"I think so," I responded.

"This is a yes or no question, young man. You either do or you don't."

"Well, I guess I'm not sure."

"Have you ever blamed anyone for any circumstance in your life? Have you ever complained about anything?"

"Uh . . . yeah . . . I guess I have."

"Don't guess. Think."

"Yes, I have."

"Okay, then. That means you don't take one hundred percent responsibility for your life. Taking one hundred percent responsibility means you acknowledge that you create everything that happens to you. It means you understand that *you* are the cause of all of your experience. If you want to be really successful, and I know you do, then you will have to give up blaming and complaining and take total responsibility for your life—that means all your results, both your successes *and* your failures. That is the prerequisite for creating a life of success. It is only by acknowledging that you have created everything up until now that you can take charge of creating the future you want.

"You see, Jack, if you realize that you have created your current conditions, then you can uncreate them and re-create them at will. Do you understand that?"

"Yes, sir, I do."

"Are you willing to take one hundred percent responsibility for your life?"

"Yes, sir, I am!"

And I did.

YOU HAVE TO GIVE UP ALL YOUR EXCUSES

*Ninety-nine percent of all failures come from
people who have a habit of making excuses.*

GEORGE WASHINGTON CARVER
Chemist who discovered over 325 uses for the peanut

If *you* want to create the life of your dreams, then *you* are going to have to take 100% responsibility for your life as well. That means giving up all your excuses, all your victim stories, all the reasons why you can't and why you haven't up until now, and all your blaming of outside circumstances. You have to give them all up forever.

You have to take the position that you have always had the power to make it different, to get it right, to produce the desired result. For whatever reason—ignorance, lack of awareness, fear, needing to be right, the need to feel safe—you chose not to exercise that power. Who knows why? It doesn't matter. The past is the past. All that matters now is that from this point forward you choose—that's right, it's a choice—you choose to act as if (that's all that's required—to act as if) you are 100% responsible for everything that does or doesn't happen to you.

If something doesn't turn out as planned, you will ask yourself, "How did I create that? What was I thinking? What were my beliefs? What did I say or not say? What did I do or not do to create that result? How did I get the other person to act that way? What do I need to do differently next time to get the result I want?"

A few years after I met Mr. Stone, Dr. Robert Resnick, a psychotherapist in Los Angeles, taught me a very simple but very important formula that made this idea of 100% responsibility even clearer to me. The formula is:

$$E + R = O$$
(Event + Response = Outcome)

The basic idea is that every outcome you experience in life (whether it is success or failure, wealth or poverty, health or illness, intimacy or estrangement, joy or frustration) is the result of how you have responded to an earlier event or events in your life.

If you don't like the outcomes you are currently getting, there are two basic choices you can make.

1. **You can blame the event (E) for your lack of results (O).** In other words, you can blame the economy, the weather, the lack of money, your lack of education, racism, gender bias, the current administration in Washington, your wife or husband, your boss's attitude, the lack of support, the political climate, the system or lack of systems, and so on. If you're a golfer, you've probably even blamed your clubs and the course you played on. No doubt all these factors do exist, but if they were *the* deciding factor, nobody would ever succeed.

   Jackie Robinson would never have played major league baseball, Sidney Poitier and Denzel Washington would have never become movie stars, Dianne Feinstein and Barbara Boxer would never have become U.S. senators, Erin Brockovich would never have uncovered PG&E's contamination of the water in Hinkley, California, Bill Gates would never have founded Microsoft, and Steve Jobs would never have started Apple Computers. For every reason why it's not possible, there are hundreds of people who have faced the same circumstances and succeeded.

   Lots of people overcome these so-called limiting factors, so it can't be the limiting factors that limit you. It is not the external conditions and circumstances that stop you—it is you! We stop ourselves! We think limiting thoughts and engage in self-defeating behaviors. We defend our self-destructive habits (such as drinking and smoking) with indefensible logic. We ignore useful feedback, fail to continuously educate ourselves and learn new skills, waste time on the trivial aspects of our lives, engage in idle gossip, eat unhealthy food, fail to exercise, spend more money than we make, fail to invest in our future, avoid necessary conflict, fail to tell the truth, don't ask for what we want—and then wonder why our lives don't work. But this, by the way, is what most people do. They place the blame for everything that isn't the way they want it on outside events and circumstances. They have an excuse for everything.

2. **You can instead simply change your responses (R) to the events (E)—the way things are—until you get the outcomes (O) you want.** You can change your thinking, change your communication, change the pictures you hold in your head (your images of yourself and the world)—and you can change your behavior—the things you do. That is all you really have any control over anyway. Unfortunately, most of us are so run by our habits that we never change our behavior. We get stuck in our conditioned responses—to our spouses and our children, to our colleagues at work, to our customers and our clients, to our students, and to the world at large. We are a bundle of conditioned reflexes that operate outside of our control. You have to regain control of your thoughts, your images, your dreams and daydreams, and your behavior. Everything you think, say, and do needs to become intentional and aligned with your purpose, your values, and your goals.

IF YOU DON'T LIKE YOUR OUTCOMES, CHANGE YOUR RESPONSES

Let's look at some examples of how this works.

Do you remember the Northridge earthquake in 1994? Well, I do! I lived through it in Los Angeles. Two days later, I watched as CNN interviewed people commuting to work. The earthquake had damaged one of the main freeways leading into the city. Traffic was at a standstill, and what was normally a 1-hour drive had become a 2- or 3-hour drive.

The CNN reporter knocked on the window of one of the cars stuck in traffic and asked the driver how he was doing.

He responded angrily, "I hate California. First there were fires, then floods, and now an earthquake! No matter what time I leave in the morning, I'm going to be late for work. I can't believe it!"

Then the reporter knocked on the window of the car behind him and asked the second driver the same question. This driver was all smiles. He replied, "It's no problem. I left my house at five AM. I don't think under the circumstances my boss can ask for more than that. I have lots of music cassettes

**"What do we make where I work?
Mostly we make excuses."**

and my Spanish-language tapes with me. I've got my cell phone. I have coffee in a thermos, my lunch—I even brought a book to read. So I'm fine."

Now, if the earthquake or the traffic were really the deciding variables, then everyone should have been angry. But everyone wasn't. It was their individual *response* to the traffic that gave them their particular *outcome*. It was thinking negative thoughts or thinking positive thoughts, leaving the house prepared or leaving the house unprepared that made the difference. It was all a matter of attitude and behavior that created their completely different experiences.

I'VE HEARD THERE'S GOING TO BE A RECESSION; I'VE DECIDED NOT TO PARTICIPATE

A friend of mine owns a Lexus dealership in Southern California. When the Gulf War broke out, people stopped coming in to buy Lexuses (or Lexi, for any fellow Harvard graduates and Latin students out there). They knew that if they didn't change their response (R) to the event (E) of nobody coming into the showroom, they were going to slowly go out of business. Their normal response (R) would have been to continue placing ads in the newspaper and on the radio, then wait for people to come into the dealership. But that wasn't working. The outcome (O) they were getting was a steady decrease in sales. So they tried a number of new things. The one that worked was driving a fleet of new cars out to where the rich people were—the country clubs, marinas, polo grounds, parties in Beverly Hills and Westlake Village—and then inviting them to take a spin in a new Lexus.

Now think about this . . . have you ever test-driven a new car and then got back into your old car? Remember that feeling of dissatisfaction you felt as you compared your old car to the new car you had just driven? Your old car was fine up until then. But suddenly you knew there was something better— and you wanted it. The same thing happened with these folks. After test-driving the new car, a high percentage of the people bought or leased a new Lexus.

The dealership had changed their response (R) to an unexpected event (E)—the war—until they got the outcome (O) they wanted . . . increased sales. They actually ended up selling more cars per week than before the war broke out.

EVERYTHING YOU EXPERIENCE TODAY IS THE RESULT OF CHOICES YOU HAVE MADE IN THE PAST

Everything you experience in life—both internally and externally—is the result of how you have responded to a previous event.

Event: You are given a $400 bonus.
Response: You spend it on a night on the town.
Outcome: You are broke.

Event: You are given a $400 bonus.
Response: You invest it in your mutual fund.
Outcome: You have an increased net worth.

You only have control over three things in your life—the thoughts you think, the images you visualize, and the actions you take (your behavior). How you use these three things determines everything you experience. If you don't like what you are producing and experiencing, you have to change your responses. Change your negative thoughts to positive ones. Change what you daydream about. Change your habits. Change what you read. Change your friends. Change how you talk.

IF YOU KEEP ON DOING WHAT YOU'VE ALWAYS DONE, YOU'LL KEEP ON GETTING WHAT YOU'VE ALWAYS GOT

Twelve-step programs such as Alcoholics Anonymous define *insanity* as "continuing the same behavior and expecting a different result." It ain't gonna happen! If you are an alcoholic and you keep on drinking, your life is not going to get any better. Likewise, if you continue your current behaviors, your life is not going to get any better either.

The day you change your responses is the day your life will begin to get better! If what you are currently doing would produce the "more" and "better" that you are seeking in life, the more and better would have already shown up! If you want something different, you are going to have to *do* something different!

YOU HAVE TO GIVE UP BLAMING

All blame is a waste of time. No matter how much fault you find with another, and regardless of how much you blame him, it will not change you.

WAYNE DYER
Coauthor of *How to Get What You Really, Really, Really, Really Want*

You will never become successful as long as you continue to blame someone or something else for your lack of success. If you are going to be a winner, you have to acknowledge the truth—it is *you* who took the actions, thought the thoughts, created the feelings, and made the choices that got you to where you now are. It was you!

You are the one who ate the junk food.
You are the one who didn't say no!
You are the one who took the job.
You are the one who stayed in the job.
You are the one who chose to believe them.
You are the one who ignored your intuition.
You are the one who abandoned your dream.
You are the one who bought it.
You are the one who didn't take care of it.
You are the one who decided you had to do it alone.

You are the one who trusted him.
You are the one who said yes to the dogs.

In short, you thought the thoughts, you created the feelings, you made the choice, you said the words, and that's why you are where you are now.

YOU HAVE TO GIVE UP COMPLAINING

*The man who complains about the way the ball bounces
is likely the one who dropped it.*

LOU HOLTZ
The only coach in NCAA history to lead six different college teams to
postseason bowl games, and winner of a national championship and
"coach of the year" honors

Let's take a moment to really look at complaining. In order to complain about something or someone, you have to believe that something better exists. You have to have a reference point of something you prefer that you are not willing to take responsibility for creating. Let's look at that more closely.

If you didn't believe there was something better possible—more money, a bigger house, a more fulfilling job, more fun, a more loving spouse—you couldn't complain. So you have this image of something better and you know you would prefer it, but you are unwilling to take the risks that would be required to create it.

Think about this . . . people only complain about things they can do something about. We don't complain about the things we have no power over. Have you ever heard anyone complain about gravity? No, never. Have you ever seen an elderly person all bent over with age walking down the street complaining about gravity? Of course not.

But why not? If it weren't for gravity, people wouldn't fall down the stairs, planes wouldn't fall out of the sky, and we wouldn't break any dishes. But nobody complains about it. And the reason is because gravity just exists. There is nothing anyone can do about gravity, so we just accept it. We know that complaining will not change it, so we don't complain about it. In fact, because it just is, we use gravity to our advantage. We build aqueducts down mountainsides to carry water to us, and we use drains to take away our waste.

Even more interesting is that we choose to play with gravity, to have fun with it. Almost every sport we play uses gravity. We ski, sky-dive, high-jump, throw the discus and the javelin, and play basketball, baseball, and golf—all of which require gravity.

The circumstances you complain about are, by their very nature, situations you can change—but you have chosen not to. You can get a better job, find a more loving partner, make more money, live in a nicer house, live in a better neighborhood, and eat healthier food. But all of these things would require you to change.

If you refer to the list found earlier in this chapter, you could

Learn to cook healthier food.
Say no in the face of peer pressure.
Quit and find a better job.
Take the time to conduct due diligence.
Trust your own gut feelings.
Go back to school to pursue your dream.
Take better care of your possessions.
Reach out for help.
Ask others to assist you.
Take a self-development class.
Sell or give away the dogs.

But why don't you simply do those things? It's because they involve risks. You run the risk of being unemployed, left alone, or ridiculed and judged by others. You run the risk of failure, confrontation, or being wrong. You run the risk of your mother, your neighbors, or your spouse disapproving of you. Making a change might take effort, money, and time. It might be uncomfortable, difficult, or confusing. And so, to avoid risking any of those uncomfortable feelings and experiences, you stay put and complain about it.

As I stated before, complaining means you have a reference point for something better that you would prefer but that you are unwilling to take the risk of creating. Either accept that you are making the choice to stay where you are, take responsibility for your choice, and stop complaining . . . or . . . take the risk of creating your life exactly the way you want it.

If you want to get from where you are to where you want to be, of course you're going to have to take that risk.

So make the decision to stop complaining, to stop spending time with complainers, and get on with creating the life of your dreams.

YOU'RE COMPLAINING TO THE WRONG PERSON

Have you ever noticed that people almost always complain to the wrong people—to people who can't do anything about their complaint? They go to work and complain about their spouse; then they come home and complain to their spouse about the people at work. Why? Because it's easier; it's less risky. It takes courage to tell your spouse that you are not happy with the way things are at home. It takes courage to ask for a behavioral change. It also takes courage to ask your boss to plan better so that you don't end up working every weekend. But only your boss can do anything about that. Your spouse can't.

Learn to replace complaining with making requests and taking action that will achieve your desired outcomes. That is what successful people do. That is what works. If you find yourself in a situation you don't like, either work to make it better or leave. Do something to change it or get the heck out. Agree to work on the relationship or get a divorce. Work to improve working conditions or find a new job. Either way, you will get a change. As the old adage says, "Don't just sit there (and complain), do something." And remember, it's up to you to make the change, to do something different. The world doesn't owe you anything. You have to create it.

YOU EITHER CREATE OR ALLOW EVERYTHING
THAT HAPPENS TO YOU

To be powerful, you need to take the position that you create or allow everything that happens to you. By *create*, I mean that you directly cause something to happen by your actions or inactions. If you walk up to a man in a bar who is bigger than you, has obviously been drinking for a long time, and say to him, "You are really ugly and stupid," and he jumps off the bar stool, hits you in the jaw, and you end up in the hospital—you created that. That's an easy-to-understand example.

Here's one that may be harder to swallow: You work late every night. You come home tired and burned out. You eat dinner in a coma and then sit down in front of the television to watch a basketball game. You're too tired and stressed out to do anything else—like go for a walk or play with the kids. This goes on for years. Your wife asks you to talk to her. You say, "Later!" Three years later, you come home to an empty house and a note that she has left you and taken the kids. You created that one, too!

Other times, we simply allow things to happen to us by our inaction and our unwillingness to do what is necessary to create or maintain what we want:

- You didn't follow through on your threat to take away privileges if the kids didn't clean up after themselves, and now the house looks like a war zone.
- You didn't demand he join you in counseling or leave the first time he hit you, so now you're still getting hit.
- You didn't attend any sales and motivational seminars because you were too busy, and now the new kid just won the top sales award.
- You didn't take the time to take the dogs to obedience training, and now they're out of control.
- You didn't take time to maintain your car, and now you're sitting by the side of the road with your car broken down.
- You didn't go back to school, and now you are being passed over for a promotion.

Realize that you are not the victim here. You stood passively by and let it happen. You didn't say anything, make a demand, make a request, say no, try something new, or leave.

YELLOW ALERTS

Be aware that nothing ever just "happens" to you. Just like the "yellow alerts" in the old *Star Trek* television series, you almost always receive advance warnings—in the form of telltale signs, comments from others, gut instinct, or intuition—that alert you to the impending danger and give you time to prevent the unwanted outcome.

You are getting yellow alerts all the time. There are *external* yellow alerts:

He keeps coming home later and later with alcohol on his breath.
The client's first check bounced.
He screamed at his secretary.
His mother warned you.
Your friends told you.

And there are *internal* yellow alerts:

That feeling in your stomach
That inkling you had
That fleeting thought that just maybe . . .
That intuition
That fear that emerged
That dream that woke you up in the middle of the night

We have a whole language that informs us:

Clues, inklings, suspicions
The handwriting on the wall
I had a feeling that . . .
I could see it coming for a mile.
My gut feeling told me.

These alerts give you time to change your response (R) in the E + R = O equation. However, too many people ignore the yellow alerts because paying attention to them would require them to do something that is uncomfortable. It is uncomfortable to confront your spouse about the cigarettes in the ashtray that have lipstick on them. It is uncomfortable to speak up in a staff meeting when you are the only one who feels that the proposed plan won't work. It is uncomfortable to tell someone you don't trust them.

So you pretend not to see and not to know because it is easier, more convenient and less uncomfortable, avoids confrontation, keeps the peace, and protects you from having to take risks.

LIFE BECOMES MUCH EASIER

Successful people, on the other hand, face facts squarely. They do the uncomfortable and take steps to create their desired outcomes. Successful people don't wait for disasters to occur and then blame something or someone else for their problems.

Once you begin to respond quickly and decisively to signals and events as they occur, life becomes much easier. You start seeing improved outcomes both internally and externally. Old internal self-talk such as "I feel like a victim; I feel used; nothing ever seems to work out for me" is replaced with "I feel great; I am in control; I can make things happen."

External outcomes such as "Nobody ever comes to our store; we missed our quarterly goals; people are complaining that our new product doesn't work" are transformed into "We have more money in the bank; I lead the division in sales; our product is flying off the shelves."

IT'S SIMPLE

The bottom line is that you are the one who is creating your life the way it is. The life you currently live is the result of all of your past thoughts and actions. You are in charge of your current thoughts and your present feelings. You are in charge of what you say and what you do. You are also in charge of what goes into your mind—the books and magazines you read, the movies and television shows you watch, and the people you hang out with. Every action is under your control. To be more successful, all you have to do is act in ways that produce more of what you want.

That's it. It's that simple!

SIMPLE ISN'T NECESSARILY EASY

Though this principle is simple, it is not necessarily easy to implement. It requires concentrated awareness, dedicated discipline, and a willingness to experiment and take risks. You have to be willing to pay attention to what you are doing and to the results you are producing. You have to ask yourself, your family, your friends, your colleagues, your managers, your teachers, your coaches, and your clients for feedback. "Is what I'm doing working? Could I be doing it better? Is there something more I should be doing that I am not? Is there something I am doing that I should stop doing? How do you see me limiting myself?"

Don't be afraid to ask. Most people are afraid to ask for feedback about how they are doing because they are afraid of what they are going to hear. There is nothing to be afraid of. The truth is the truth. You are better off knowing the truth than not knowing it. And once you know, you can do something about it. You cannot improve your life, your relationships, your game, or your performance without feedback.

Slow down and pay attention. Life will always give you feedback about the effects of your behavior if you will just pay attention. If your golf ball is always slicing to the right, if you're not making sales, if you're getting C's in all your college courses, if your children are mad at you, if your body is tired and weak, if your house is a mess, or if you're not happy—this is all feedback. It is telling you that something is wrong. This is the time to start paying attention to what is happening.

Ask yourself: *How am I creating or allowing this to happen? What am I doing that's working that I need to be doing more of? (Should I do more practicing, meditating, delegating, trusting, listening, asking questions, keeping my eye on the ball, advertising, saying "I love you," controlling my carbohydrate intake?)*

What am I doing that's not working? What do I need to be doing less of? (Am I talking too much, watching too much television, spending too much money, eating too much sugar, drinking too much, being late too often, gossiping, putting other people down?)

What am I not doing that I need to try on to see if it works? (Do I need to listen more, exercise, get more sleep, drink more water, ask for help, do more marketing, read, plan, communicate, delegate, follow through, hire a coach, volunteer, or be more appreciative?)

This book is full of proven success principles and techniques you can immediately put into practice in your life. You will have to suspend judgment, take a leap of faith, act as if they are true, and try them out. Only then will you have firsthand experience about their effectiveness for your life. You won't know if they work unless you give them a try. And here's the rub—no one else can do this for you. Only you can do it.

But the formula is simple—do more of what is working, do less of what isn't, and try on new behaviors to see if they produce better results.

PAY ATTENTION . . . YOUR RESULTS DON'T LIE

The easiest, fastest, and best way to find out what is or isn't working is to pay attention to the results you are currently producing. You are either rich or you are not. You either command respect or you don't. You are either golfing par or you are not. You are either maintaining your ideal body weight or you are not. You are either happy or you are not. You either have what you want or you don't. It's that simple. Results don't lie!

You have to give up the excuses and justifications and come to terms with the results you are producing. If you are under quota or overweight, all the great reasons in the world won't change that. The only thing that will change your results is to change your behavior. Prospect more, get some sales training, change your sales presentation, change your diet, consume fewer calories, and exercise more frequently—these are things that will make a difference. But you have to first be willing to look at the results you are producing. The only starting point that works is reality.

So start paying attention to what is so. Look around at your life and the people in it. Are you and they happy? Is there balance, beauty, comfort, and ease? Do your systems work? Are you getting what you want? Is your net worth increasing? Are your grades satisfactory? Are you healthy, fit, and pain free? Are you getting better in all areas of your life? If not, then something needs to happen, and only you can make it happen.

Don't kid yourself. Be ruthlessly honest with yourself. Take your own inventory.

BE CLEAR WHY
YOU'RE HERE

*Learn to get in touch with the silence within yourself and
know that everything in life has a purpose.*

ELISABETH KUBLER-ROSS, M.D.
Psychiatrist and author of the classic *On Death and Dying*

I believe each of us is born with a life purpose. Identifying, acknowledging, and honoring this purpose is perhaps the most important action successful people take. They take the time to understand what they're here to do—and then they pursue that with passion and enthusiasm.

WHAT WERE YOU PUT ON THIS EARTH TO DO?

I discovered long ago what I was put on this earth to do. I determined my true purpose in life, my "right livelihood." I discovered how to inject passion and determination into every activity I undertake. And I learned how purpose can bring an aspect of fun and fulfillment to virtually everything I do.

Now I'd like to help uncover the same secret for you.

You see, without a purpose in life, it's easy to get sidetracked on your life's journey. It's easy to wander and drift, accomplishing little.

But with a purpose, everything in life seems to fall into place. To be "on purpose" means you're doing what you love to do, doing what you're good at and accomplishing what's important to you. When you truly are on purpose, the people, resources, and opportunities you need naturally gravitate toward you. The world benefits, too, because when you act in alignment with your true life purpose, all of your actions automatically serve others.

SOME PERSONAL LIFE PURPOSE STATEMENTS

My life purpose is *to inspire and empower people to live their highest vision in a context of love and joy.* I inspire people to live their highest vision (see Principle 3, "Decide What You Want") by collecting and disseminating inspiring stories through the *Chicken Soup for the Soul®* series and in my inspirational keynote speeches. I empower people to live their dreams by writing practical self-help books like this one, *The Power of Focus,* and *The Aladdin Factor;* designing courses for high school students; and conducting seminars and workshops for adults that teach powerful tools for creating one's ideal life.

Here are the life purpose statements of some of my friends. It is important to note that they have all become self-made millionaires through the fulfillment of their life purpose.

- To inspire and empower people to achieve their destiny[1]
- To uplift humanity's consciousness through business[2]
- To humbly serve the Lord by being a loving, playful, powerful, and passionate example of the absolute joy that is available to us the moment we rejoice in God's gifts and sincerely love and serve all of his creations[3]
- To leave the world a better place than I found it, for horses and for people, too[4]
- To create and inspire one million millionaires who each give $1 million to their church or charity[5]
- To educate and inspire people to live their highest self based in courage, purpose, and joy, versus fear, need, and obligation[6]

Decide upon your major definite purpose in life and then organize all your activities around it.

BRIAN TRACY
One of America's leading authorities on the development
of human potential and personal effectiveness

---

1. Robert Allen, coauthor of *The One Minute Millionaire.*
2. D.C. Cordova, cofounder of the Excellerated Business School.
3. Anthony Robbins, author of *Personal Power* and *Get the Edge,* entrepreneur, and philanthropist.
4. Monty Roberts, author of *The Man Who Listens to Horses.*
5. Mark Victor Hansen, coauthor of the *Chicken Soup for the Soul®* series.
6. T. Harv Eker, CEO of Peak Potentials and creator of the "Millionaire Mind" seminar.

Once you know what your life purpose is, you can organize all of your activities around it. Everything you do should be an expression of your purpose. If an activity doesn't fit that formula, you wouldn't work on it. Period.

WHAT'S THE "WHY" BEHIND EVERYTHING YOU DO?

Without purpose as the compass to guide you, your goals and action plans may not ultimately fulfill you. You don't want to get to the top of the ladder only to find out you had it leaning up against the wrong wall.

When Julie Laipply was a child, she was a very big fan of animals. As a result, all she ever heard growing up was "Julie, you should be a vet. You're going to be a great vet. That's what you should do." So when she got to Ohio State University, she took biology, anatomy, and chemistry, and started studying to be a vet. A Rotary Ambassadorial Scholarship allowed her to spend her senior year studying abroad in Manchester, England. Away from the family and faculty pressures back home, she found herself one dreary day sitting at her desk, surrounded by biology books and staring out the window, when it suddenly hit her: *You know what? I'm totally miserable. Why am I so miserable? What am I doing? I don't want to be a vet!*

Julie then asked herself, *What is a job I would love so much that I'd do it for free but that I could actually get paid for? It's not being a vet. That's not the right job.* Then she thought back over all the things she'd done in her life and what had made her the most happy. And then it hit her—it was all of the youth leadership conferences that she had volunteered at, and the communications and leadership courses she had taken as elective courses back at Ohio State. *How could I have been so ignorant? Here I am at my fourth year at school and just finally realizing I'm on the wrong path and not doing the right thing. But it's been here in front of me the whole time. I just never took the time to acknowledge it until now.*

Buoyed by her new insight, Julie spent the rest of her year in England taking courses in communications and media performance. When she returned to Ohio State, she was eventually able to convince the administration to let her create her own program in "leadership studies," and while it took her 2 years longer to finally graduate, she went on to become a senior management consultant in leadership training and development for the Pentagon. She also won the Miss Virginia USA contest, which allowed her to spend much of 2002 speaking to kids all across Virginia, and more recently she has created the Role Models and Mentors for Youth Foundation, which teaches kids how to be better role models for one another. By the way, Julie is only 26 years old—a testament to the power that clarity of purpose can create in your life.

The good news is that you don't have to go all the way to England for a year abroad to get away from the daily pressures of your life long enough to create the space to discover what you are really here to do. You can simply take the time to complete two simple exercises that will help you clarify your purpose.

YOUR INNER GUIDANCE SYSTEM IS YOUR JOY

It is the soul's duty to be loyal to its own desires. It must abandon itself to its master passion.

DAME REBECCA WEST
Best-selling author

You were born with an inner guidance system that tells you when you are on or off purpose by the amount of joy you are experiencing. The things that bring you the greatest joy are in alignment with your purpose. To begin to home in on your purpose, make a list of the times you have felt most joyful and alive. What are the common elements of these experiences? Can you figure out a way to make a living doing these things?

Pat Williams is the senior vice-president of the Orlando Magic basketball team. He has also written 36 books and is a professional speaker. When I asked him what he felt the greatest secret to success was, he replied, "Figure out what you love to do as young as you can, and then organize your life around figuring out how to make a living at it." For young Pat, it was sports—more specifically, baseball. When his father took him to his first baseball game in Philadelphia, he fell in love with the game. He learned to read by reading the sports section of the *New York Times*. He knew he wanted to grow up and have a career in sports. He devoted almost every waking moment to it. He collected baseball cards, played sports, and wrote a sports column for the school newspaper.

Pat went on to have a career in the front office of the Philadelphia Phillies baseball team, then with the Philadelphia 76ers basketball team. When the NBA considered granting an expansion team franchise to Orlando, Pat was there to lead the fight. Now in his sixties, Pat has enjoyed 40-plus years doing what he loves, and he has enjoyed every minute of it. Once you are clear about what brings you the greatest joy, you will have a major insight into your purpose.

This second exercise is a simple but powerful way to create a compelling statement of your life purpose to guide and direct your behavior. Take time now to complete the following exercise.

THE LIFE PURPOSE EXERCISE[7]

1. List two of your unique personal qualities, such as *enthusiasm* and *creativity*.

   _____   _____

2. List one or two ways you enjoy expressing those qualities when interacting with others, such as *to support* and *to inspire*.

   _____   _____

3. Assume the world is perfect right now. What does this world look like? How is everyone interacting with everyone else? What does it feel like? Write your answer as a statement, in the present tense, describing the ultimate condition, the perfect world as you see it and feel it. Remember, a perfect world is a fun place to be.

   EXAMPLE: *Everyone is freely expressing
   their own unique talents. Everyone is working in harmony.
   Everyone is expressing love.*

   _____

   _____

   _____

4. Combine the three prior subdivisions of this paragraph into a single statement.

   EXAMPLE: *My purpose is to use my creativity and enthusiasm to
   support and inspire others to freely express their talents in
   a harmonious and loving way.*

   _____

   _____

   _____

---

7. There are many ways to approach defining your purpose. I learned this version of the life purpose exercise from Arnold M. Patent, spiritual coach and author of *You Can Have It All*. His most recent book is *The Journey*. You can visit his Web site at www.arnoldpatent.com.

STAYING ON PURPOSE

Once you have determined and written down your life purpose, read it every day, preferably in the morning. If you are artistic or strongly visual by nature, you may want to draw or paint a symbol or picture that represents your life purpose and then hang it somewhere (on the refrigerator, opposite your desk, near your bed) where you will see it every day. This will keep you focused on your purpose.

As you move forward in the next few chapters to define your vision and your goals, make sure they are aligned with and serve to fulfill your purpose.

Another approach to clarifying your purpose is to set aside some time for quiet reflection—time for a period of meditation. (See Principle 47, "Inquire Within"). After you become relaxed and enter into a state of deep self-love and peacefulness, ask yourself, *What is my purpose for living?* or *What is my unique role in the universe?* Allow the answer to simply come to you. Let it be as expansive as you can imagine. The words that come need not be flowery or poetic; what is important is how inspired the words make you feel.

3

DECIDE WHAT YOU WANT

*The indispensable first step to getting the things
you want out of life is this: decide what you want.*

BEN STEIN
Actor and author

Once you have decided why you are here, you have to decide what you want
to do, be, and have. What do you want to accomplish? What do you want to
experience? And what possessions do you want to acquire? In the journey
from where you are to where you want to be, you have to decide where you
want to be. In other words, what does success look like to you?

One of the main reasons why most people don't get what they want is
they haven't decided what they want. They haven't defined their desires in
clear and compelling detail.

EARLY CHILDHOOD PROGRAMMING OFTEN GETS
IN THE WAY OF WHAT YOU WANT

Inside of every one of us is that tiny seed of the "you" that you were meant
to become. Unfortunately, you may have buried this seed in response to
your parents, teachers, coaches, and other adult role models as you were
growing up.

You started out as a baby knowing exactly what you wanted. You knew
when you were hungry. You spit out the foods you didn't like and avidly de-
voured the ones you did. You had no trouble expressing your needs and
wants. You simply cried loudly—with no inhibitions or holding back—until
you got what you wanted. You had everything inside of you that you needed
to get fed, changed, held, and rocked. As you got older, you crawled around
and moved toward whatever held the most interest for you. You were clear
about what you wanted, and you headed straight toward it with no fear.

So what happened?
Somewhere along the way, someone said . . .

Don't touch that!
Stay away from there.
Keep your hands off that.
Eat everything on your plate whether you like it or not!
You don't really feel that way.
You don't really want that.
You should be ashamed of yourself.
Stop crying. Don't be such a baby.

As you got older, you heard . . .

You can't have everything you want simply because you want it.
Money doesn't grow on trees.
Can't you think of anybody but yourself?!
Stop being so selfish!
Stop doing what you are doing and come do what I want you to do!

DON'T LIVE SOMEONE ELSE'S DREAMS

After many years of these kinds of sanctions, most of us eventually lost touch
with the needs of our bodies and the desires of our hearts and somehow got
stuck trying to figure out what other people wanted us to do. We learned how
to act and how to be to get *their* approval. As a result, we now do a lot of
things we don't want to do but that please a lot of other people:

- We go to medical school because that is what Dad wanted for us.
- We get married to please our mother.
- We get a "real job" instead of pursuing our dream career in the arts.
- We go straight into graduate school instead of taking a year off and
  backpacking through Europe.

In the name of being sensible, we end up becoming numb to our own desires. It's no wonder that when we ask many teenagers what they want to do
or be, they honestly answer, "I don't know." There are too many layers of
"should's," "ought to's," and "you'd better's" piled on top of and suffocating
what they really want.

So how do you reclaim yourself and your true desires? How do you get back to what you really want with no fear, shame, or inhibition? How do you reconnect with your real passion?

You start on the smallest level by honoring your preferences in every situation—no matter how large or small. Don't think of them as petty. They might be inconsequential to someone else, but they are not to you.

STOP SETTLING FOR LESS THAN YOU WANT

If you are going to reown your power and get what you really want out of life, you will have to stop saying, "I don't know; I don't care; it doesn't matter to me"—or the current favorite of teenagers, "Whatever." When you are confronted with a choice, no matter how small or insignificant, act as if you have a preference. Ask yourself, *If I did know, what would it be? If I did care, which would I prefer? If it did matter, what would I rather do?*

Not being clear about what you want and making other people's needs and desires more important than your own is simply a habit. You can break it by practicing the opposite habit.

THE YELLOW NOTEBOOK

Many years ago, I took a workshop with self-esteem and motivational expert Chérie Carter-Scott, author of *If Life Is a Game, These Are the Rules.* As the 24 of us entered the training room on the first morning, we were directed to take a seat in one of the chairs facing the front of the room. There was a spiral-bound notebook on every chair. Some were blue, some were yellow, some were red. The one on my chair was yellow. I remember thinking, *I hate yellow. I wish I had a blue one.*

Then Chérie said something that changed my life forever: "If you don't like the color of the notebook you have, trade with someone else and get the one you want. You deserve to have everything in your life exactly the way you want it."

Wow, what a radical concept! For 20-some years, I had not operated from that premise. I had settled, thinking I couldn't have everything I wanted.

So I turned to the person to my right and said, "Would you mind trading your blue notebook for my yellow one?"

She responded, "Not at all. I prefer yellow. I like the brightness of the color. It fits my mood." I now had my blue notebook. Not a huge success in the greater scheme of things, but it was the beginning of reclaiming my birthright to acknowledge my preferences and get exactly what I want. Up until then, I would have discounted my preference as petty and not worth acting on. I would have continued to numb out my awareness of what I wanted. That day was a turning point for me—the beginning of allowing myself to know and act on my wants and desires in a much more powerful way.

MAKE AN "I WANT" LIST

One of the easiest ways to begin clarifying what you truly want is to make a list of 30 things you want to do, 30 things you want to have, and 30 things you want to be before you die. This is a great way to get the ball rolling.

Another powerful technique to unearth your wants is to ask a friend to help you make an "I Want" list. Have your friend continually ask, "What do you want? What do you want?" for 10 to 15 minutes, and jot down your answers. You'll find the first wants aren't all that profound. In fact, most people usually hear themselves saying, "I want a Mercedes. I want a big house on the ocean." And so on. However, by the end of the 15-minute exercise, the real you begins to speak: "I want people to love me. I want to express myself. I want to make a difference. I want to feel powerful" . . . wants that are true expressions of your core values.

IS WORRYING ABOUT MAKING A LIVING
STOPPING YOU?

What often stops people from expressing their true desire is they don't think they can make a living doing what they love to do.

"What I love to do is hang out and talk with people," you might say.

Well, Oprah Winfrey makes a living hanging out talking with people. And my friend Diane Brause, who is an international tour guide, makes a living hanging out talking with people in some of the most exciting and exotic locations in the world.

Tiger Woods loves to play golf. Ellen DeGeneres loves to make people laugh. My sister loves to design jewelry and hang out with teenagers. Donald Trump loves to make deals and build buildings. I love to read and share what I have learned with others in books, speeches, and workshops. It's possible to make a living doing what you love.

Make a list of 20 things you love to do, and then think of ways you can make a living doing some of those things. If you love sports, you could play sports, be a sportswriter or photographer, or work in sports management as an agent or in the front office of a professional team. You could be a coach, a manager, or a scout. You could be a broadcaster, a camera operator, or a team publicist. There are myriad ways to make money in any field that you love.

For now just decide what you would like to do, and in the following chapters I'll show you how to be successful and make money at it.

CLARIFY YOUR VISION OF YOUR IDEAL LIFE

The theme of this book is how to get from where you are to where you want to be. To accomplish this, you have to know two things—where you are and where you want to get to. Your vision is a detailed description of where you want to get to. It describes in detail what your destination looks like and feels like. To create a balanced and successful life, your vision needs to include the following seven areas: work and career, finances, recreation and free time, health and fitness, relationships, personal goals, and contribution to the larger community.

At this stage in the journey, it is not necessary to know exactly how you are going to get there. All that is important is that you figure out where there is. If you get clear on the what, the how will be taken care of.

YOUR INNER GLOBAL POSITIONING SYSTEM

The process of getting from where you are to where you want to be is like using the navigational system with GPS (Global Positioning System) technology in a newer-model car. For the system to work, it simply needs to know where you are and where you want to go. The navigation system figures out where you are by the use of an onboard computer that receives signals from three satellites and calculates your exact position. When you type in your destination, the navigational system plots a perfect course for you. All you have to do is follow the instructions.

Success in life works the same way. All you have to do is decide where you want to go by clarifying your vision, lock in the destination through goal-setting, affirmations, and visualization, and start moving in the right direction. Your inner GPS will keep unfolding your route as you continue to move forward. In other words, once you clarify and stay focused on your vision (and I'll be teaching lots of ways to do that), the exact steps will keep appearing along the way. Once you are clear about what you want and keep your mind constantly focused on it, the how will keep showing up—sometimes just when you need it and not a moment earlier.

© 2001 Randay Glasbergen.   www.glasbergen.com

GLASBERGE,

**"I'm wealthy beyond my wildest dreams!
Unfortunately, my dreams were never very wild."**

HIGH ACHIEVERS HAVE BIGGER VISIONS

*The greater danger for most of us is not that our aim is too high and
we miss it, but that it is too low and we reach it.*

MICHELANGELO

I want to encourage you not to limit your vision in any way. Let it be as big as it is. When I interviewed Dave Liniger, the CEO of RE/MAX, the country's largest real estate company, he told me, "Always dream big dreams. Big dreams attract big people." General Wesley Clark recently told me, "It doesn't take any more energy to create a big dream than it does to create a little one." My experience is that one of the few differences between the superachievers and the rest of the world is that the superachievers simply dream bigger. John F. Kennedy dreamed of putting a man on the moon. Martin Luther King Jr. dreamed of a country free of prejudice and injustice. Bill Gates dreams of a world in which every home has a computer that is connected to the Internet. Buckminster Fuller dreamed of a world where everybody had access to electrical power.

These high achievers see the world from a whole different perspective—as a place where amazing things can happen, where billions of lives can be improved, where new technology can change the way we live, and where the world's resources can be leveraged for the greatest possible mutual gain. They believe anything is possible, and they believe they have an integral part in creating it.

When Mark Victor Hansen and I first published *Chicken Soup for the Soul®*, what we call our "2020 vision" was also a big one—to sell 1 billion *Chicken Soup* books and to raise $500 million for charity through tithing a portion of all of our profits by the year 2020. We were and are very clear about what we want to accomplish.

---

*If you limit your choices only to what seems possible or reasonable,
you disconnect yourself from what you truly want,
and all that is left is a compromise.*

ROBERT FRITZ
Author of *The Path of Least Resistance*

DON'T LET ANYONE TALK YOU OUT OF YOUR VISION

There are people who will try to talk you out of your vision. They will tell you that you are crazy and that it can't be done. There will be those who will laugh at you and try to bring you down to their level. My friend Monty Roberts, the author of *The Man Who Listens to Horses*, calls these people dream-stealers. Don't listen to them.

When Monty was in high school, his teacher gave the class the assignment to write about what they wanted to do when they grew up. Monty wrote that he wanted to own his own 200-acre ranch and raise Thoroughbred racehorses. His teacher gave him an F and explained that the grade reflected that he deemed his dream unrealistic. No boy who was living in a camper on the back of a pickup truck would ever be able to amass enough money to buy a ranch, purchase breeding stock, and pay the necessary salaries for ranch hands. When he offered Monty the chance of rewriting his paper for a higher grade, Monty told him, "You keep the F; I'm keeping my dream."

Today Monty's 154-acre Flag Is Up Farms in Solvang, California, raises Thoroughbred racehorses and trains hundreds of horse trainers in a more humane way to "join up" with and train horses.[8]

---

8. To learn more about Monty and his work, go to www.montyroberts.com or read one of his books: *The Man Who Listens to Horses, Shy Boy, Horse Sense for People,* and *From My Hands to Yours.*

THE VISION EXERCISE

Create your future from your future, not your past.

WERNER ERHARD
Founder of EST training and the Landmark Forum

The following exercise is designed to help you clarify your vision. Although you could do this as a strictly mental exercise by just thinking about the answers and then writing them down, I want to encourage you to go deeper than that. If you do, you'll get deeper answers that serve you better.

Start by putting on some relaxing music and sitting quietly in a comfortable environment where you won't be disturbed. Then, close your eyes and ask your subconscious mind to give you images of what your ideal life would look like if you could have it exactly the way you want it, in each of the following categories:

1. First, focus on the financial area of your life. What is your annual income? What does your cash flow look like? How much money do you have in savings and investments? What is your total net worth?

   Next ... what does your home look like? Where is it located? Does it have a view? What kind of yard and landscaping does it have? Is there a pool or a stable for horses? What color are the walls? What does the furniture look like? Are there paintings hanging in the rooms? What do they look like? Walk through your perfect house, filling in all of the details.

   At this point, don't worry about how you'll get that house. Don't sabotage yourself by saying, "I can't live in Malibu because I don't make enough money." Once you give your mind's eye the picture, your mind will solve the "not enough money" challenge.

   Next, visualize what kind of car you are driving and any other important possessions your finances have provided.

2. Next, visualize your ideal job or career. Where are you working? What are you doing? With whom are you working? What kind of clients or customers do you have? What is your compensation like? Is it your own business?

3. Then, focus on your free time, your recreation time. What are you doing with your family and friends in the free time you've created

for yourself? What hobbies are you pursuing? What kinds of vacations do you take? What do you do for fun?

4. Next, what is your ideal vision of your body and your physical health? Are you free of all disease? How long do you live to? Are you open, relaxed, in an ecstatic state of bliss all day long? Are you full of vitality? Are you flexible as well as strong? Do you exercise, eat good food, and drink lots of water?

5. Then move on to your ideal vision of your relationships with your family and friends. What is your relationship with your family like? Who are your friends? What is the quality of your relationships with your friends? What do those friendships feel like? Are they loving, supportive, empowering? What kinds of things do you do together?

6. What about the personal arena of your life? Do you see yourself going back to school, getting training, attending workshops, seeking therapy for a past hurt, or growing spiritually? Do you meditate or go on spiritual retreats with your church? Do you want to learn to play an instrument or write your autobiography? Do you want to run a marathon or take an art class? Do you want to travel to other countries?

7. Finally, focus on the community you live in, the community you've chosen. What does it look like when it is operating perfectly? What kinds of community activities take place there? What about your charitable work? What do you do to help others and make a difference? How often do you participate in these activities? Who are you helping?

You can write down your answers as you go, or you can do the whole exercise first and then open your eyes and write them down. In either case, make sure you capture everything in writing as soon as you complete the exercise.

Every day, review the vision you have written down. This will keep your conscious and subconscious minds focused on your vision, and as you apply the other principles and tools in the book, you will begin to manifest all the different aspects of your vision.

SHARE YOUR VISION FOR MAXIMUM IMPACT

When you've finished writing down your vision, share your vision with a good friend whom you can trust to be positive and supportive. You might be afraid that your friend will think your vision is too outlandish, impossible to achieve, too idealistic, unrealistic, or materialistic. Almost all people have these thoughts when they think about sharing their vision. But the truth is, most people, deep down in their hearts, want the very same things you want. Everyone wants financial abundance, a comfortable home, meaningful work they enjoy, good health, time to do the things they love, nurturing relationships with their family and friends, and an opportunity to make a difference in the world. But too few of us readily admit it.

You'll find that when you share your vision, some people will want to help you make it happen. Others will introduce you to friends and resources that can help you. You'll also find that each time that you share your vision, it becomes clearer and feels more real and attainable. And most importantly, every time you share your vision, you strengthen your own subconscious belief that you can achieve it.

BELIEVE IT'S POSSIBLE

*The number one problem that keeps people from winning in the
United States today is lack of belief in themselves.*

ARTHUR L. WILLIAMS
Founder of A.L. Williams Insurance Company, which was sold to Primerica
for $90 million in 1989

Napoleon Hill once said, "Whatever the mind can conceive and believe, it can achieve." In fact, the mind is such a powerful instrument, it can deliver to you literally everything you want. But you have to *believe* that what you want is possible.

YOU GET WHAT YOU EXPECT

Scientists used to believe that humans responded to information flowing into the brain from the outside world. But today, they're learning instead that we respond to what the brain, on the basis of previous experience, expects to happen next.

Doctors in Texas, for example—studying the effect of arthroscopic knee surgery—assigned patients with sore, worn-out knees to one of three surgical procedures: scraping out the knee joint, washing out the joint, or doing nothing.

During the "nothing" operation, doctors anesthetized the patient, made three incisions in the knee as if to insert their surgical instruments, and then pretended to operate. Two years after surgery, patients who underwent the pretend surgery reported the same amount of relief from pain and swelling as those who had received the actual treatments. The brain *expected* the "surgery" to improve the knee, and it did.

Why does the brain work this way? Neuropsychologists who study expectancy theory say it's because we spend our whole lives becoming conditioned. Through a lifetime's worth of events, our brain actually learns what to expect next—whether it eventually happens that way or not. And because our brain expects something will happen a certain way, we often achieve exactly what we anticipate.

This is why it's so important to hold positive expectations in your mind. When you replace your old negative expectations with more positive ones— when you begin to believe that what you want is possible—your brain will actually take over the job of accomplishing that possibility for you. Better than that, your brain will actually expect to achieve that outcome.[9]

"YOU GOTTA BELIEVE"

You can be anything you want to be, if only you believe with sufficient conviction and act in accordance with your faith; for whatever the mind can conceive and believe, the mind can achieve.

NAPOLEON HILL
Best-selling author of *Think and Grow Rich*

When Philadelphia Phillies pitcher Tug McGraw—father of legendary country singer Tim McGraw—struck out batter Willie Wilson to earn the Phillies the 1980 World Series title, *Sports Illustrated* captured an immortal image of elation on the pitcher's mound—an image few people knew was played out *exactly as McGraw had planned it.*

When I had the opportunity to meet Tug one afternoon in New York, I asked him about his experience on the mound that day.

"It was as if I'd been there a thousand times before," he said. "When I was growing up, I would pitch to my father in the backyard. We would always get to where it was the bottom of the ninth in the World Series with two outs and three men on base. I would always bear down and strike them out." Because Tug had conditioned his brain day after day in the backyard, the day eventually arrived where he was living that dream for real.

McGraw's reputation as a positive thinker had begun 7 years earlier during the New York Mets' 1973 National League championship season, when Tug coined the phrase "You gotta believe" during one of the team's meetings. That Mets team, in last place in the division in August, went on to win the

---

9. Adapted from "Placebos Prove So Powerful Even Experts Are Surprised: New Studies Explore the Brain's Triumph Over Reality" by Sandra Blakeslee. *New York Times*, October 13, 1998, section F, page 1.

National League pennant and reach game 7 of the World Series, where they finally succumbed to the Oakland A's.

Another example of his always optimistic "you gotta believe" attitude was the time, while he was a spokesman for the Little League, that he said, "Kids should practice autographing baseballs. This is a skill that's often overlooked in Little League." And then he smiled his infectious smile.

BELIEVE IN YOURSELF AND GO FOR IT

Sooner or later, those who win are those who think they can.

RICHARD BACH
Best-selling author of *Jonathan Livingston Seagull*

Tim Ferriss believed in himself. In fact, he believed so strongly in his abilities that he won the national San Shou kickboxing title just 6 weeks after being introduced to the sport.

As a prior all-American and judo team captain at Princeton, Tim had always dreamed of winning a national title. He had worked hard. He was good at his sport. But repeated injuries over multiple seasons had continually denied him his dream.

So when a friend called one day to invite Tim to watch him in the national Chinese kickboxing championships 6 weeks away, Tim instantly decided to join him at the competition.

Because he had never been in any kind of striking competition before, he called USA Boxing and asked where the best trainers could be found. He traveled to a tough neighborhood in Trenton, New Jersey, to learn from boxing coaches who had trained gold medalists. And after 4 grueling hours a day in the ring, he put in more time conditioning in the weight room. To make up for his lack of time in the sport, Tim's trainers focused on exploiting his strengths instead of making up for his weaknesses.

Tim didn't want to merely compete. He wanted to win.

When the competition day at last arrived, Tim defeated three highly acclaimed opponents before making it to the finals. As he anticipated what he would have to do to win in the final match, he closed his eyes and visualized defeating his opponent in the very first round.

Later, Tim told me that most people fail not because they lack the skills or aptitude to reach their goal but because they simply don't believe they can reach it. Tim believed. And won.

IT HELPS TO HAVE SOMEONE ELSE
BELIEVE IN YOU FIRST

When 20-year-old Ruben Gonzalez showed up at the U.S. Olympic Training Center in Lake Placid, New York, he had in his pocket the business
card of a Houston businessman who believed in his Olympic dream.
Ruben was there to learn the sport of luge, a sport that 9 of 10 aspirants give
up after the first season. Almost everyone breaks more than one bone before mastering this 90-mile-per-hour race against time in an enclosed mile-
long downhill track of concrete and ice. But Ruben had a dream, passion, a
commitment not to quit, and the support of his friend, Craig, back in
Houston.

When Ruben got back to his room after the first day of training, he called
up Craig.

"Craig this is nuts! My side hurts. I think I broke my foot. That's it. I am
going back to soccer!"

Craig interrupted him. "Ruben, get in front of a mirror!"

"What?"

"I said, 'Get in front of a mirror!' "

Ruben got up, stretched the phone cord, and stood in front of a full-
length mirror.

"Now repeat after me: No matter how bad it is, and how bad it gets, I'm
going to make it!"

Ruben felt like an idiot staring at himself in the mirror, so in the most
wimpy, wishy-washy way possible, he said, "No matter how bad it is, and
how bad it gets, I'm going to make it!"

"C'mon! Say it right. You're Mr. Olympic Man! That's all you ever talk
about! Are you going to do it or not?"

Ruben started getting serious. "No matter how bad it is, and how bad it
gets, I'm going to make it!"

"Again!"

"No matter how bad it is, and how bad it gets, I'm going to make it!"

And again and again and again.

About the fifth time Ruben said it, he thought, *Hey, this feels kind of good. I'm
standing a little bit straighter.* By the tenth time he said it, he jumped up in the air
and shouted, "I don't care what happens. I'm going to make it. I can break
both legs. Bones heal. I'll come back and I will make it. I *will* be an Olympian!"

It's amazing what happens to your self-confidence when you get eyeball
to eyeball with yourself and you forcefully tell yourself what you're going to

do. Whatever your dream is, look at yourself in the mirror and declare that you are indeed going to achieve it—no matter what the price.

Ruben Gonzales made that declaration, and it changed his life. He went on to compete in three separate winter games in the luge—Calgary in 1988, Albertville in 1992, and Salt Lake City in 2002. And he's currently training for the 2006 Torino Winter Olympics, where he will be 43 years old, competing against athletes half his age.

BELIEVE IN YOURSELF

You weren't an accident. You weren't mass produced.
You aren't an assembly-line product. You were
deliberately planned, specifically gifted, and lovingly
positioned on the Earth by the Master Craftsman.

MAX LUCADO
Best-selling author

If you are going to be successful in creating the life of your dreams, you have to believe that you are capable of making it happen. You have to believe you have the right stuff, that you are able to pull it off. You have to believe in yourself. Whether you call it self-esteem, self-confidence, or self-assurance, it is a deep-seated belief that you have what it takes—the abilities, inner resources, talents, and skills to create your desired results.

BELIEVING IN YOURSELF IS AN ATTITUDE

Believing in yourself is a choice. It is an attitude you develop over time. Although it helps if you had positive and supportive parents, the fact is that most of us had run-of-the-mill parents who inadvertently passed on to us the same limiting beliefs and negative conditioning they grew up with.

But remember, the past is the past. There is no payoff for blaming them for your current level of self-confidence. It's now *your* responsibility to take charge of your own self-concept and your beliefs. You must choose to believe that you can do anything you set your mind to—anything at all—because, in fact, you can. It might help you to know that the latest brain research now indicates that with enough positive self-talk and positive visualization combined with the proper training, coaching, and practice, anyone can learn to do almost anything.

Of the hundreds of supersuccessful people I have interviewed for this and other books, almost every one of them told me, "I was not the most gifted or talented person in my field, but I chose to believe anything was possible. I studied, practiced, and worked harder than the others, and that's how I got to where I am." If a 20-year-old Texan can take up the luge and become an Olympic athlete, a college dropout can become a billionaire, and a dyslexic student who failed three grades can become a best-selling author and television producer, then you, too, can accomplish anything if you will simply believe it is possible.

If you assume in favor of yourself and act as if it is possible, then you will do the things that are necessary to bring about the result. If you believe it is impossible, you will not do what is necessary, and you will not produce the result. It becomes a self-fulfilling prophecy.

THE CHOICE OF WHAT TO BELIEVE IS UP TO YOU

Stephen J. Cannell failed first, fourth, and tenth grades. He couldn't read and comprehend like other kids in his class could. He would spend 5 hours with his mother studying for a test and then fail it. When he asked his friend who got an A how long he had studied for the test, he replied, "I didn't." Stephen concluded that he just wasn't intelligent.

"But I simply decided, as an act of will, to put it out of my mind," he told me. "I simply refused to think about it. Instead I focused my energies on what I was good at, and that was football. If it hadn't been for football, which I excelled at, I don't know what would have happened to me. I got my self-esteem from playing sports."

Putting all his energy into football, he earned interscholastic honors as a running back. From football, he learned that if he applied himself, he could achieve excellence.

Later he was able to transfer that belief in himself to his career, which oddly enough turned out to be writing scripts for television. Eventually he formed his own production studio, where he created, produced, and wrote over 350 scripts for 38 different shows, including *The A-Team*, *The Rockford Files*, *Baretta*, *21 Jump Street*, *The Commish*, *Renegade*, and *Silk Stalkings*. At the height of his studio career, he had over 2,000 people on his payroll. And if that isn't enough, after he sold his studio he went on to write 11 best-selling novels.

Stephen is a prime example of the fact that it is not what life hands you but how you respond to it, mentally and physically, that matters most.

*I am looking for a lot of men who have an infinite capacity
to not know what can't be done.*

HENRY FORD

YOU HAVE TO GIVE UP "I CAN'T"

The phrase I can't *is the most powerful force of negation
in the human psyche.*

PAUL R. SCHEELE
Chairman, Learning Strategies Corporation

If you are going to be successful, you need to give up the phrase "I can't" and all of its cousins, such as "I wish I were able to." The words *I can't* actually disempower you. They actually make you weaker when you say them. In my seminars, I use a technique called kinesiology to test people's muscle strength as they say different phrases. I have them put their left arm out to their side, and I push down on it with my left hand to see what their normal strength is. Then I have them pick something they think they can't do, such as *I can't play the piano*, and say it out loud. I then push down on their arm again. It is always weaker. Then I have them say, "I can do it," and their arm is stronger.

Your brain is designed to solve any problem and reach any goal that you give it. The words you think and say actually affect your body. We see that in toddlers. When you were a toddler, there was no stopping you. You thought you could climb up on anything. No barrier was too big for you to attempt to overcome. But little by little, your sense of invincibility is conditioned out of you by the emotional and physical abuse that you receive from your family, friends, and teachers, until you no longer believe you can.

You must take responsibility for removing *I can't* from your vocabulary. In the '80s, I attended a Tony Robbins seminar in which we learned to walk on burning coals. When we began, we were all afraid that we would not be able to do it—that we would burn the soles of our feet. As part of the seminar, Tony had us write down every other *I can't* that we had—*I can't find the perfect job, I can't be a millionaire, I can't find the perfect mate*—and then we threw them onto the burning coals and watched them go up in flames. Two hours later, 350 of us walked on the burning coals without anybody getting burned. That night we all learned that just like the belief that we couldn't walk on burning coals without getting burned was a lie, every other limiting belief about our abilities was also a lie.

DON'T WASTE YOUR LIFE BELIEVING YOU CAN'T

In 1977, in Tallahassee, Florida, Laura Shultz, who was 63 at the time, picked up the back end of a Buick to get it off her grandson's arm. Before that time, she had never lifted anything heavier than a 50-pound bag of pet food.

Dr. Charles Garfield, author of *Peak Performance* and *Peak Performers*, interviewed her after reading about her in the *National Enquirer*. When he got to her home, she kept resisting any attempts to talk about what she called "the event." She kept asking Charlie to eat breakfast and call her Granny, which he did.

Finally he got her to talk about "the event." She said she didn't like to think about it because it challenged her beliefs about what she could and couldn't do, about what was possible. She said, "If I was able to do this when I didn't think I could, what does that say about the rest of my life? Have I wasted it?"

Charlie convinced her that her life was not yet over and that she could still do whatever she wanted to do. He asked her what she wanted to do, what her passion was. She said she had always loved rocks. She had wanted to study geology, but her parents hadn't had enough money to send both her and her brother to college, so her brother had won out.

At 63, with a little coaching from Charlie, she decided to go back to school to study geology. She eventually got her degree and went on to teach at a local community college.

Don't wait until you are 63 to decide that you can do anything you want. Don't waste years of your life. Decide that you are capable of doing anything you want and start working toward it now.

IT'S ALL ABOUT ATTITUDE

When baseball great Ty Cobb was 70, a reporter asked him, "What do you think you'd hit if you were playing these days?"

Cobb, who had a lifetime batting average of .367, said, "About .290, maybe .300."

The reporter replied, "That's because of the travel, the night games, the artificial turf, and all the new pitches like the slider, right?"

"No," said Cobb, "it's because I am seventy."

Now that's believing in yourself!

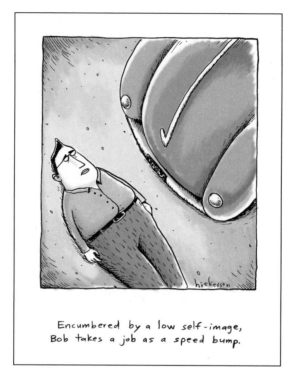

Encumbered by a low self-image,
Bob takes a job as a speed bump.

DON'T ASSUME YOU NEED A COLLEGE DEGREE

Here's another statistic showing that belief in yourself is more important than knowledge, training, or schooling: 20% of America's millionaires never set foot in college, and 21 of the 222 Americans listed as billionaires in 2003 never got their college diplomas; *2 never even finished high school!* So although education and a commitment to lifelong learning are essential to success, a formal degree isn't a requirement. This is true even in the high-tech world of the Internet. Larry Ellison, CEO of Oracle, dropped out of the University of Illinois and at the time of this writing was worth $18 billion. And Bill Gates dropped out of Harvard and later founded Microsoft. Today he is considered one of the richest men in the world, with a net worth of over $46 billion.

Even Vice President Dick Cheney dropped out of college. When you realize that the vice president, the richest man in America, and many $20 million–a–movie actors, as well as many of our greatest musicians and athletes, are all college dropouts, you see that you can start from anywhere and create a successful life for yourself.[10]

---

10. From "Some Billionaires Choose School of Hard Knocks," June 29, 2000; Forbes.com, 2003 Forbes 400 Richest People in America. Statistics were revised based on the 2003 edition of the Forbes 400 Richest People in America.

WHAT OTHERS THINK ABOUT YOU
IS NONE OF YOUR BUSINESS

You have to believe in yourself when no one else does.
That's what makes you a winner.

VENUS WILLIAMS
Olympic gold medalist and professional tennis champion

If having others believing in you and your dream was a requirement for success, most of us would never accomplish anything. You need to base your decisions about what *you* want to do on *your* goals and desires—not the goals, desires, opinions, and judgments of your parents, friends, spouse, children, and coworkers. Quit worrying what other people think about you and follow your heart.

I like Dr. Daniel Amen's 18/40/60 Rule: When you're 18, you worry about what everybody is thinking of you; when you're 40, you don't give a darn what anybody thinks of you; when you're 60, you realize nobody's been thinking about you at all.

Surprise, surprise! Most of the time, nobody's thinking about you at all! They are too busy worrying about their own lives, and if they are thinking about you at all, they are wondering what you are thinking about them. People think about themselves, not you. Think about it—all the time you are wasting worrying about what other people think about your ideas, your goals, your clothes, your hair, and your home could all be better spent on thinking about and doing the things that will achieve *your* goals.

6

BECOME AN INVERSE PARANOID

I've always been the opposite of a paranoid.
I operate as if everyone is part of a plot to
enhance my well-being.

STAN DALE
Founder of the Human Awareness Institute and author of *Fantasies Can Set You Free*

My earliest mentor, W. Clement Stone, was once described as an inverse paranoid. Instead of believing the world was plotting to do him harm, he chose to believe the world was plotting to do him good. Instead of seeing every difficult or challenging event as a negative, he saw it for what it could be—something that was meant to enrich him, empower him, or advance his causes.

What an incredibly positive belief!

Imagine how much easier it would be to succeed in life if you were constantly expecting the world to support you and bring you opportunity.

Successful people do just that.

In fact, there is growing research that the vibrations of positive expectation that successful people give off actually attract to them the very experiences they believe they are going to get.

Suddenly, obstacles and negatives are seen not as just another example of "Gee, the world hates me," but as opportunities to grow and change and succeed. If your car suddenly breaks down on the side of the road, instead of imagining a serial rapist pulling over to take advantage of you, think of the possibility that the guy who stops to help you will be the man you fall in love with and marry. If your company downsizes you out of a job, suddenly the chances are good that you'll find your dream job with more opportunity at much better pay. If you develop cancer, the possibility exists that in the process of reorganizing your life to effect a cure, you'll create a more healthy balance in your life and rediscover what's important to you.

Think about it.

Was there a time in your life when something terrible happened that later became a blessing in disguise?

Every negative event contains within it the seed
of an equal or greater benefit.

NAPOLEON HILL
Author of the success classic *Think and Grow Rich*

The big blessing for me came in the 1970s when they closed the Job Corps Center in Clinton, Iowa, where I worked as a curriculum development specialist pioneering radical new learning systems for teaching underachieving students. I had unlimited support from the administration, I was working with an exciting team of bright young people who shared the same vision of making a difference, and I really enjoyed my work.

Then, out of the blue, the government decided to relocate the center. It meant I would lose my job for at least 6 months. At first I was upset at the decision, but while attending a workshop at the W. Clement & Jesse V. Stone Foundation in Chicago, I shared my predicament with the leader, who happened to be the vice president of the foundation. As a result, he offered me a job. "We'd love to have someone like you who has experience with inner-city black and Hispanic kids. Come work for us." They gave me more money, an unlimited budget, the ability to attend any workshop, training, or convention that I wanted—and I was now working directly with W. Clement Stone, who had introduced me to these success principles to begin with.

And yet, when they first announced the relocation of the Job Corps Center and my being laid off, I was angry, scared, and despondent. I thought it was the end of the world. I thought it was a bad thing. Instead, it turned out to be the major turning point of my life. In less than 3 months, my life had gone from good to great. For 2 years, I worked with some of the most amazing people I have ever met before I left to enter a doctoral program in psychological education at the University of Massachusetts.

Now, when anything "bad" happens, I remember that *everything* that ever happens to me has within it the seed of something better. I look for the upside rather than the downside. I ask myself, "Where's the greater benefit in this event?"

I'm sure that you, too, can think back to several times in your life when you thought what had happened was the end of the world—you flunked a class, lost your job, got divorced, experienced the death of a friend or a business failure, had a catastrophic injury or illness, your house burned down—and later you realized it was a blessing in disguise. The trick is to realize that whatever you are going through now is going to turn out better in the future as well. So look for the lemonade in the lemons. The more you begin to look for the good, the sooner and more often you will find it. And if you take the attitude that it is coming, the less upset and discouraged you'll get while you're waiting for it.

HOW DO I USE THIS EXPERIENCE
TO MY ADVANTAGE?

When life hands you a lemon, squeeze it and make lemonade.

W. CLEMENT STONE
Self-made multimillionaire and former publisher of *Success Magazine*

Captain Jerry Coffee was a pilot who was shot down during the Vietnam War. He spent 7 years as a prisoner of war in some of the most hellish conditions known to humankind. He was beaten, became malnourished, and was kept in solitary confinement for years. But if you ask him how he feels about that experience, he would tell you that it was the most powerful transformational experience of his life. As he entered his cell for the first time, he realized he would be spending a lot of time alone. He asked himself, *How can I use this experience to my advantage?* He told me that he decided to see it as an opportunity rather than as a tragedy—an opportunity to get to know both himself and God—the only two beings he'd be spending time with—better.

Captain Coffee spent many hours each day reviewing every interaction he had ever had with anyone in his life. Slowly he began to see the patterns of what had worked and what hadn't worked in his life. Over time, he slowly psychoanalyzed himself. Eventually he came to totally know himself at the deepest levels. He fully accepted every aspect of his being, developed a profound sense of compassion for himself and all of humanity, and came to fully understand his true nature. As a result, he is one of the most wise, humble, and peaceful men I have ever met. He literally radiates love and spirituality. Though he admits that he would never want to have to do it again, he also says that he would not trade his experience as a prisoner of war for anything, for it has made him who he is today—a deeply spiritual and happy family man, a successful author, and one of the most moving inspirational speakers you could ever hope to hear.

LOOK FOR THE OPPORTUNITY IN EVERYTHING

What if you, too, were to greet every interaction in your life with the question "What's the potential opportunity that this is?" The supersuccessful approach every experience as an opportunity. They enter every conversation with the idea that something good will come from it. And they know that what they seek and expect, they will find.

If you take the approach that "good" is not an accident—that everyone and everything that shows up in your life is there for a reason—and that the universe is moving you toward your ultimate destiny for learning, growth, and achievement, you'll begin to see every event—no matter how difficult or challenging—as a chance for enrichment and advancement in your life.

Make a small sign or poster with the words *What's the opportunity that this is?* and put it on your desk or above your computer, so you will be constantly reminded to look for the good in every event.

You might also want to start each day by repeating the phrase, "I believe the world is plotting to do me good today. I can't wait to see what it is." And then look for the opportunities and the miracles.

HE SAW THE OPPORTUNITY

Mark Victor Hansen, my partner and coauthor on all of the *Chicken Soup for the Soul*® books, sees every encounter as an opportunity. He teaches everyone to say, "I'd like to be your partner on that. I can see many ways to expand your idea, reach more people, sell more, and make more money." That's how he became my partner on the *Chicken Soup* books. We were having breakfast one day, and he asked me, "What are you up to? What are you excited about?" I told him that I had decided to take all of the motivational and inspirational stories that I had been using in my talks and put them into a book without all of the other prescriptions for living that most self-help books contained. It would just be a book of stories that people could use in any way they wanted. After I described the book to him, he said, "I want to be your partner on this book. I want to help you write it."

I replied, "Mark, the book is already half written. Why would I let you be my partner at this stage of the project?"

"Well," he replied, "a lot of the stories you tell, you learned from me. I have a lot more you have never heard, I know I can get great stories from lots of other motivational speakers, and I can help you market the book to people and places you've probably never even thought of."

As we continued to talk, I realized Mark would be a great asset to the project. He is the consummate salesperson, and his dynamic energy and tireless promotional style would be a huge plus. So we struck a deal. That one conversation has been worth tens of millions in book royalties and licensing income to Mark.

You see, when you approach every encounter as an opportunity, you treat it like an opportunity. Mark saw my book project—as he sees every project he encounters—as an opportunity, and he approached the conversation from that perspective. The result has been a wonderful and profitable 12-year business relationship for both of us.

GOD MUST HAVE SOMETHING BETTER
IN STORE FOR ME

In 1987, along with 412 other people, I applied to the state government to be part of the 30-member California State Task Force to Promote Self-Esteem and Personal and Social Responsibility. Fortunately, I was selected; however, my longtime friend Peggy Bassett, the popular minister of a 2,000-member church, was not. I was surprised because I thought she would have been a perfect member. When I asked her how she felt about not being selected, she answered with a phrase that has stuck with me. I have since used it many times in my own life. She smiled and said, "Jack, I feel fine about it. It just means that *God has something better in store for me*." She knew in her heart of hearts that she was always being led to the right experiences for her. Her positive expectancy and her certainty that all was in divine order were an inspiration to everyone who knew her. That's why her church had grown so large. It was one of the core principles of her success.

UNLEASH THE POWER
OF GOAL-SETTING

If you want to be happy, set a goal that commands your thoughts,
liberates your energy, and inspires your hopes.

ANDREW CARNEGIE
The richest man in America in the early 1900s

Once you know your life purpose, determine your vision, and clarify what your true needs and desires are, you have to convert them into specific, measurable goals and objectives and then act on them with the certainty that you will achieve them.

Experts on the science of success know the brain is a goal-seeking organism. Whatever goal you give to your subconscious mind, it will work night and day to achieve.

HOW MUCH, BY WHEN?

To make sure a goal unleashes the power of your subconscious mind, it must meet two criteria. It must be stated in a way that you and anybody else could measure it. *I will lose 10 pounds* is not as powerful as *I will weigh 135 pounds by 5 PM on June 30*. The second is clearer, because anybody can show up at 5 o'clock on June 30 and look at the reading on your scale. It will either be 135 pounds or less or not. Notice that the two criteria are *how much* (some measurable quantity such as pages, pounds, dollars, square feet, or points) and *by when* (a specific time and date).

Be as specific as possible with all aspects of your goals—include the make, model, color, year, and features . . . the size, weight, shape, and form . . . and any other details. Remember, vague goals produce vague results.

A GOAL VERSUS A GOOD IDEA

When there are no criteria for measurement, it is simply something you want, a wish, a preference, a *good idea*. To engage your subconscious mind, a goal or objective has to be measurable. Here are a few examples to give you more clarity:

GOOD IDEA	GOAL OR OBJECTIVE
I would like to own a nice home on the ocean.	I will own a 4,000-square-foot house on Pacific Coast Highway in Malibu, California, by noon, April 30, 2007.
I want to lose weight.	I will weigh 185 pounds by 5 PM, January 1, 2006.
I need to treat my employees better.	I will acknowledge a minimum of six employees for their contribution to the department by 5 PM this Friday.

WRITE IT OUT IN DETAIL

One of the best ways to get clarity and specificity on your goals is to write them out in detail—as if you were writing specifications for a work order. Think of it as a request to God or to the universal mind. Include every possible detail.

If there is a certain house you want to own, write down its specifics in vivid colorful detail—the location, landscaping, furniture, artwork, sound system, and floor plan. If a picture of the house is available, get a copy of it. If it's an ideal fantasy, take the time to close your eyes and fill in all of the details. Then provide a date by which you expect to own it.

When you write it all down, your subconscious mind will know what to work on. It will know which opportunities to hone in on to help you reach your goal.

LOOK, LADY—YOU'RE THE ONE WHO ASKED FOR A FAMOUS MOVIE STAR WITH DARK HAIR, STRONG NOSE AND DEEP SET EYES...

YOU NEED GOALS THAT STRETCH YOU

When you create your goals, be sure to write down some big ones that will stretch you. It pays to have goals that will require you to grow to achieve them. It's a good thing to have some goals that make you a little uncomfortable. Why? Because the ultimate goal, in addition to achieving your material goals, is to become a *master* at life. And to do this, you will need to learn new skills, expand your vision of what's possible, build new relationships, and learn to overcome your fears, considerations, and roadblocks.

CREATE A BREAKTHROUGH GOAL

In addition to turning every aspect of your vision into a measurable goal, and all the quarterly and weekly and daily goals that you routinely set, I also encourage you to set what I call a breakthrough goal that would represent a quantum leap for you and your career. Most goals represent incremental improvements in our life. They are like plays that gain you 4 yards in the game of football. But what if you could come out on the first play of the game and throw a 50-yard pass? That would be a quantum leap in your progress. Just as there are plays in football that move you far up the field in one move, there are plays in life that will do the same thing. They include things such as losing 60 pounds, writing a book, publishing an article, getting on *Oprah*, winning a gold medal at the Olympics, creating a killer Web site, getting your master's or doctoral degree, getting licensed, opening your own spa, getting elected president of your union or professional association, or hosting your own radio show. The achievement of that one goal would change everything.

Wouldn't that be a goal worth pursuing with passion? Wouldn't that be something to focus on a little each day until you achieved it?

If you were an independent sales professional and knew you could get a better territory, a substantial bonus commission, and maybe even a promotion once you landed a certain number of customers, wouldn't you work day and night to achieve that goal?

If you were a stay-at-home mom whose entire lifestyle and finances would change if you earned an extra $1,000 a month through participating in a network marketing company, wouldn't you pursue every possible opportunity until you achieved that goal?

That's what I mean by a breakthrough goal. Something that changes your life, brings you new opportunities, gets you in front of the right people, and takes every activity, relationship, or group you're involved in to a higher level.

What would a breakthrough goal be for you? My youngest brother, Taylor, is a special-education teacher in Florida. He just completed a 5-year process to get his school administrator's credential, which over time will ultimately mean almost an additional $25,000 a year in income for him. That's a major leap that will significantly increase his salary and his level of influence in the school system!

Writing a best-selling book was a breakthrough goal for me and Mark Victor Hansen. *Chicken Soup for the Soul*® took us from being known in a couple of narrow fields to being recognized internationally. It created greater demand for our audio programs, speeches, and seminars. The additional income it produced allowed us to improve our lifestyle, secure our retirement, hire more staff, take on more projects, and have a larger impact in the world.

REREAD YOUR GOALS THREE TIMES A DAY

Once you've written down all your goals, both large and small, the next step on your journey to success is to activate the creative powers of your subconscious mind by reviewing your list two or three times every day. Take time to read your list of goals. Read the list (out loud with passion and enthusiasm if you are in an appropriate place) one goal at a time. Close your eyes and picture each goal as if it were already accomplished. Take a few more seconds to feel what you would feel if you had already accomplished each goal.

Following this daily discipline of success will activate the power of your desire. It increases what psychologists refer to as "structural tension" in your brain. Your brain wants to close the gap between your current reality and the vision of your goal. By constantly repeating and visualizing your goal as already achieved, you will be increasing this structural tension. This will increase your motivation, stimulate your creativity, and heighten your awareness of resources that can help you achieve your goal.

Make sure to review your goals at least twice a day—in the morning upon awakening, and again at night before going to bed. I write each of mine on a 3" × 5" index card. I keep the pack of cards next to my bed and then I go through the cards one at a time in the morning and again at night. When I travel, I take them with me.

Put a list of your goals in your daily planner or your calendar system. You can also create a pop-up or screen saver on your computer that lists your goals. The objective is to constantly keep your goals in front of you.

When Olympic decathlon gold medalist Bruce Jenner asked a roomful of Olympic hopefuls if they had a list of written goals, everyone raised their hands. When he asked how many of them had that list with them right that moment, only one person raised their hand. That person was Dan O'Brien. And it was Dan O'Brien who went on to win the gold medal in the decathlon at the 1996 Olympics in Atlanta. Don't underestimate the power of setting goals and constantly reviewing them.

CREATE A GOALS BOOK

Another powerful way to speed up the achievement of your goals is to create a Goals Book. Buy a three-ring binder, a scrapbook or an 8½" × 11" journal. Then create a separate page for each of your goals. Write the goal at the top of the page and then illustrate it with pictures, words, and phrases that you cut out of magazines, catalogues, and travel brochures that depict your goal as already achieved. As new goals and desires emerge, simply add them to your list and your Goals Book. Review the pages of your Goals Book every day.

CARRY YOUR MOST IMPORTANT GOAL
IN YOUR WALLET

When I first started working for W. Clement Stone, he taught me to write my most important goal on the back of my business card and carry it in my wallet at all times. Every time I would open my wallet, I would be reminded of my most important goal.

When I met Mark Victor Hansen, I discovered that he, too, used the same technique. After finishing the first *Chicken Soup for the Soul*® book, we

wrote "I am so happy selling 1.5 million copies of *Chicken Soup for the Soul*®
by December 30, 1994." We then signed each other's cards and carried them
in our wallets. I still have mine in a frame behind my desk.

Though our publisher laughed and told us we were crazy, we went on to
sell 1.3 million copies of the book by our target date. Some might say, "Well,
you missed your goal by 200,000 copies." Perhaps, but not by much . . . and
that book went on to sell well over 8 million copies in over 30 languages
around the world. Believe me . . . I can live with that kind of "failure."

ONE GOAL IS NOT ENOUGH

If you are bored with life, if you don't get up every morning with a
burning desire to do things—you don't have enough goals.

LOU HOLTZ
The only coach in NCAA history to ever lead six different college teams
to postseason bowl games, and a man who also won a national championship
and "coach of the year" honors

Lou Holtz, the legendary football coach of Notre Dame, is also a legendary
goal-setter. His belief in goal-setting comes from a lesson he learned in 1966
when he was only 28 years old and had just been hired as an assistant coach at
the University of South Carolina. His wife, Beth, was 8 months pregnant
with their third child and Lou had spent every dollar he had on a down payment on a house. One month later, the head coach who had hired Lou resigned, and Lou found himself without a job.

In an attempt to lift his spirits, his wife gave him a book—*The Magic of
Thinking Big*, by David Schwartz. The book said that you should write down
all the goals you want to achieve in your life. Lou sat down at the dining-
room table, turned his imagination loose, and before he knew it, he had listed
107 goals he wanted to achieve before he died. These goals covered every
area of his life and included having dinner at the White House, appearing on
the *Tonight Show* with Johnny Carson, meeting the pope, coaching at Notre
Dame, leading his team to a national championship, and shooting a hole in
one in golf. So far Lou has achieved 81 of those goals, including shooting a
hole in one—not once, but twice!

Take the time to make a list of 101 goals you want to achieve in your life.
Write them in vivid detail, noting where, when, how much, which model,
what size, and so on. Put them on 3" × 5" cards, on a goals page, or in a Goals
Book. Every time you achieve one of your goals, check it off and write *victory*

next to it. I made a list of 101 major goals that I wanted to achieve before I died, and I have already achieved 58 of them in only 14 years, including traveling to Africa, flying in a glider, learning to ski, attending the summer Olympic games, and writing a children's book.

BRUCE LEE'S LETTER

Bruce Lee, arguably the greatest martial artist to have ever lived, also understood the power of declaring a goal. If you ever get a chance to visit Planet Hollywood in New York City, look for the letter hanging on the wall that Bruce Lee wrote to himself. It is dated January 9, 1970, and it is stamped "Secret." Bruce wrote, "By 1980 I will be the best known Oriental movie star in the United States and will have secured $10 million dollars. . . . And in return I will give the very best acting I could possibly give every single time I am in front of the camera and I will live in peace and harmony."

Bruce made three films, and then in 1973 filmed *Enter the Dragon*, which was released that same year after his untimely death at age 33. The movie was a huge success and achieved worldwide fame for Bruce Lee.

WRITE YOURSELF A CHECK

Around 1990, when Jim Carrey was a struggling young Canadian comic trying to make his way in Los Angeles, he drove his old Toyota up to Mulholland Drive. While sitting there looking at the city below and dreaming of his future, he wrote himself a check for $10 million, dated it Thanksgiving 1995, added the notation "for acting services rendered," and carried it in his wallet from that day forth. The rest, as they say, is history. Carrey's optimism and tenacity eventually paid off, and by 1995, after the huge box office success of *Ace Ventura: Pet Detective*, *The Mask*, and *Dumb & Dumber*, his asking price had risen to $20 million per picture. When Carrey's father died in 1994, he placed the $10 million check into his father's coffin as a tribute to the man who had both started and nurtured his dreams of being a star.

CONSIDERATIONS, FEARS, AND ROADBLOCKS

It's important to understand that as soon as you set a goal, three things are going to emerge that stop most people—but not you. If you know that these three things are part of the process, then you can treat them as what they are—just things to handle—rather than letting them stop you.

These three obstacles to success are *considerations, fears,* and *roadblocks*.

Think about it. As soon as you say you want to double your income next year, within moments considerations such as *I'll have to work twice as hard* or *I won't have time for my family* or *My wife's going to kill me* begin to emerge. You might have thoughts such as *My territory is maxed out—I can't see how I could possibly get the buyers on my current route to buy any more product from me.* If you say you're going to run a marathon, you might hear a voice in your head say, *You could get hurt,* or *You'll have to get up two hours earlier every day.* It might even suggest that you're too old to start running. These thoughts are called *considerations*. They are all the reasons why you shouldn't attempt the goal—all the reasons why it is impossible.

But surfacing these considerations is a good thing. They are how you have been subconsciously stopping yourself all along. Now that you have brought them into conscious awareness, you can deal with them, confront them, and move past them.

Fears, on the other hand, are feelings. You may experience a fear of rejection, a fear of failure, or a fear of making a fool of yourself. You might be afraid of getting physically or emotionally hurt. You might be afraid that you will lose all the money you have already saved. These fears are not unusual. They are just part of the process.

Finally, you'll become aware of *roadblocks*. These are purely external circumstances—well beyond just thoughts and feelings in your head. A roadblock may be that nobody wants to join you on your project. A roadblock might be that you don't have all the money you need to move forward. Perhaps you need other investors. Roadblocks might be that your state or national government has rules or laws that prohibit what you want to do. Maybe you need to petition the government to change the rules.

Stu Lichtman, a business turnaround expert, took over a well-known shoe company in Maine that was in such bad shape financially, it was virtually doomed to go out of business. The business owed millions of dollars to creditors and was short the $2 million needed to pay them. As part of the proposed turnaround, Stu negotiated the sale of an unused plant near the Canadian border that would bring the company $600,000. But the state of Maine had a lien on the plant that would have taken all of the proceeds. So Stu went to the governor of Maine to inform him of the company's dilemma. "We can either go bankrupt," he said, "in which case nearly one thousand Maine residents will soon be out of work and on the unemployment rolls, costing the government millions of dollars." Or the company and the government could together pursue Stu's plan of keeping the company alive, helping to keep the state's economy going, keeping nearly 1,000 people employed, and turning the company around in preparation for a takeover by another company. But the only way to achieve that goal was to overcome—you guessed it—the *roadblock* of the state's lien on the plant. Instead of letting that lien stop him, Stu decided to talk to the person who could remove the roadblock. In the end, the governor decided to cancel the lien.

Of course, you may not encounter roadblocks that require you to approach a governor—but then again, depending on how large your goal is, you very well might!

Roadblocks are simply obstacles that the world throws at you—it rains when you're trying to put on an outdoor concert, your wife doesn't want to move to Kentucky, you don't have the financial backing you need, and so on. Roadblocks are simply real-world circumstances that you need to deal with in order to move forward. They simply exist out there and always will.

Unfortunately, when these considerations, fears, and roadblocks come up, most people see them as a stop sign. They say, "Now that I'm thinking that, feeling this, and finding out about that, I think I won't pursue this goal after all." But I'm telling you not to see considerations, fears, and roadblocks as stop signs but rather as a normal part of the process that will always appear. When you remodel your kitchen, you resign yourself to a little dust and disturbance as part of the price you will have to pay. You simply learn to deal with it. The same is true of considerations, fears, and roadblocks. You just learn to deal with them.

In fact, they're supposed to appear. If they don't, it means you haven't set a goal that's big enough to stretch you and grow you. It means there's no real potential for self-development.

I always welcome considerations, fears, and roadblocks when they appear, because many times they are the very things that have been holding me back in life. Once I can see these subconscious thoughts, feelings, and obstacles, once I am aware of them, I can face them, process them, and deal with them. When I do, I become better prepared for the next venture I want to undertake.

MASTERY IS THE GOAL

You want to set a goal that is big enough that in the process of achieving it you become someone worth becoming.

JIM ROHN
Self-made millionaire, success coach, and philosopher

Of course, the ultimate benefit of overcoming these considerations, fears, and roadblocks is not the material rewards that you enjoy but the personal development that you achieve in the process. Money, cars, houses, boats, attractive spouses, power, and fame can all be taken away—sometimes in the blink of an eye. But what can never be taken away is who you have become in the process of achieving your goal.

To achieve a big goal, you are going to have to become a bigger person. You are going to have to develop new skills, new attitudes, and new capabilities. You are going to have to stretch yourself, and in so doing, you will be stretched forever.

On October 20, 1991, a devastating fire roared through the scenic hills above Oakland and Berkeley, California, igniting one building every 11 seconds for over 10 hours, completely destroying 2,800 homes and apartments. A friend of mine who is also an author lost everything he owned, including his entire library, files full of research, and a nearly complete manuscript of a book he was writing. Though he was certainly devastated for a short period of time, he soon realized that although everything he owned was indeed lost in the fire, who he had become inside—everything he had learned and all the skills and self-confidence he had developed writing and promoting his books—was all still inside of him and could never be burned up in a fire.

You can lose the material things, but you can never lose your *mastery*— what you learn and who you become in the process of achieving your goals.

I believe that part of what we're on Earth to do is become masters of many skills. Christ was a master who turned water into wine, who healed people, who walked on water, and who calmed storms. He said that you and I, too, could do all these things *and more*. We definitely have that potential.

Even today, in a town square in Germany, stands a statue of Christ, its hands blown off during the intensive bombing of World War II. Though the townspeople could have restored the statue decades ago, they learned this more important lesson, instead placing a plaque underneath that reads "Christ hath no hands but yours." God needs our hands to complete His tasks on Earth. But to become masters and do this great work, we all have to be willing to go through the considerations, fears, and roadblocks.

DO IT NOW!

Take the time now before you go on to the next chapter to make a list of goals you want to accomplish. Make sure you have measurable (how much, by when) goals for every aspect of your vision. Then decide on a breakthrough goal, write it on the back of a business card, and put it in your wallet. And then create a list of 101 goals you want to achieve before you die. Being clear about your purpose, vision, and goals will put you in the top 3% of the world's achievers. To move into the top 1% of achievers, all you have to do is write down some specific action steps that will help you accomplish your goals on your daily to-do list. Then make sure to take those actions.

Think of it this way. If you are clear where you are going (goals) and you take several steps in that direction every day, you eventually have to get there. If I head north out of Santa Barbara and take five steps a day, eventually I have to end up in San Francisco. So decide what you want, write it down, review it constantly, and each day do something that moves you toward those goals.

CHUNK IT DOWN

*The secret of getting ahead is getting started. The secret of
getting started is breaking your complex, overwhelming tasks
into small manageable tasks, and then starting on the first one.*

MARK TWAIN
Celebrated American author and humorist

Sometimes our biggest life goals seem so overwhelming. We rarely see them as a series of small, achievable tasks, but in reality, breaking down a large goal into smaller tasks—and accomplishing them one at a time—is exactly how any big goal gets achieved. So after you have decided what you really want and set measurable goals with specific deadlines, the next step is to determine all of the individual action steps you will need to take to accomplish your goal.

HOW TO CHUNK IT DOWN

There are several ways to figure out the action steps you will need to take to accomplish any goal. One is to consult with people who have already done what you want to do and ask what steps they took. From their experience, they can give you all of the necessary steps as well as advice on what pitfalls to avoid. Another way is to purchase a book or manual that outlines the process. Yet another way is to start from the end and look backward. You simply close your eyes and imagine that it is now the future and you have already achieved your goal. Then just look back and see what you had to do to get to where you now are. What was the last thing you did? And then the thing before that, and then the thing before that, until you arrive at the first action you had to start with.

Remember that it is okay not to know how to do something. It's okay to ask for guidance and advice from those who do know. Sometimes you can get it free, and sometimes you have to pay for it. Get used to asking, "Can you tell me how to go about . . . ?" and "What would I have to do to . . . ?" and "How did you . . . ?" Keep researching and asking until you can create a realistic action plan that will get you from where you are to where you want to go.

What will you need to do? How much money will you need to save or raise? What new skills will you need to learn? What resources will you need to mobilize? Who will you need to enroll in your vision? Who will you need to ask for assistance? What new disciplines or habits will you need to build into your life?

A valuable technique for creating an action plan for your goals is called mind mapping.

USE MIND MAPPING

Mind mapping is a simple but powerful process for creating a detailed to-do list for achieving your goal. It lets you determine what information you'll need to gather, who you'll need to talk to, what small steps you'll need to take, how much money you'll need to earn or raise, which deadlines you'll need to meet, and so on—for each and every goal.

When I began creating my first educational audio-cassette album—a breakthrough goal that led to extraordinary gains for me and my business—I used mind mapping to help me "chunk down" that very large goal into all the individual tasks I would need to complete to produce a finished album.[11]

The original mind map I created for my audio album is on page 64. To mind-map your own goals, follow these steps as illustrated in the example:

1. **Center circle:** In the center circle, jot down the name of your stated goal—in this case, *Create an Audio Educational Program*.
2. **Outside circles:** Next, divide the goal into the major categories of tasks you'll need to accomplish to achieve the greater goal—in this case, *Title, Studio, Topics, Audience*, and so on.
3. **Spokes:** Then, draw spokes radiating outward from each minicircle and label each one (such as *Write Copy, Color Picture for Back Cover*, and *Arrange Lunch*.) On a separate line connected to the minicircle, write every single step you'll need to take. Break down each one of the more detailed task spokes with action items to help you create your master to-do list.

---

11. For the best primer on mind mapping, see *The Mind Map Book: How to Use Radiant Thinking to Maximize Your Brain's Untapped Potential*, by Tony Buzan and Barry Buzan (New York: Penguin Plume, 1996).

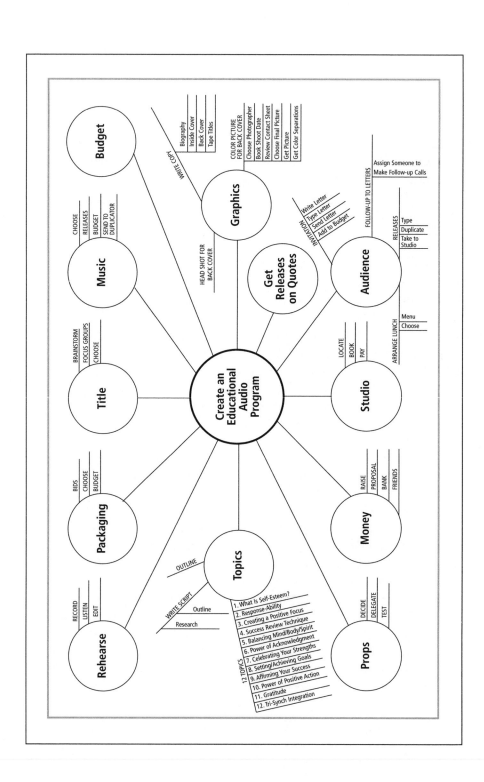

NEXT, MAKE A DAILY TO-DO LIST

Once you've completed a mind map for your goal, convert all of the to-do items into daily action items by listing each one on your daily to-do lists and committing to a completion date for each one. Then schedule them in the appropriate order into your calendar and do whatever it takes to stay on schedule.

DO FIRST THINGS FIRST

The goal is to stay on schedule and complete the most important item first. In his excellent book, *Eat That Frog! 21 Great Ways to Stop Procrastinating and Get More Done in Less Time*, Brian Tracy reveals not just how to conquer procrastination but also how to prioritize and complete all of your action items.

In his unique system, Brian advises goal-setters to identify the one to five things you must accomplish on any given day, and then pick the one you absolutely must do first. This becomes your biggest and ugliest frog. He then suggests you accomplish that task first—in essence, eat that frog first—and, by so doing, make the rest of your day much, much easier. It's a great strategy. But unfortunately, most of us leave the biggest and ugliest frog for last, hoping it will go away or somehow become easier. It never does. However, when you accomplish your toughest task early in the day, it sets the tone for the rest of your day. It creates momentum and builds your confidence, both of which move you farther and faster toward your goal.

PLAN YOUR DAY THE NIGHT BEFORE

One of the most powerful tools high achievers use for chunking things down, gaining control over their life, and increasing their productivity is to plan their next day the night before. There are two major reasons why this is such a powerful strategy for success:

1. If you plan your day the night before—making a to-do list and spending a few minutes visualizing exactly how you want the day to go—your subconscious mind will work on these tasks all night long. It will think of creative ways to solve any problem, overcome any obstacle, and achieve your desired outcomes. And if we can believe some of the newer theories of quantum physics, it will also

send out waves of energy that will attract the people and resources to you that you need to help accomplish your goals.[12]

2. By creating your to-do list the night before, you can start your day running. You know exactly what you're going to do and in what order, and you've already pulled together any materials you need. If you have five telephone calls to make, you would have them written down in the order you plan to make them, with the phone numbers next to the person's name and all the support materials at hand. By midmorning, you would be way ahead of most people, who waste the first half hour of the day clearing their desk, making lists, finding necessary paperwork—in short, just *getting ready* to work.

USE THE ACHIEVERS FOCUSING SYSTEM

A valuable tool that will really keep you focused on achieving all of your goals in the seven areas we explained in your vision (see pages 32–33) is the Achievers Focusing System developed by Les Hewitt of the Achievers Coaching Program. It is a form you can use to plan and hold yourself accountable for 13 weeks of goals and action steps. You can download a copy of the form and instructions on how to use it for free at www.thesuccessprinciples.com.

---

12. See *The Seven Spiritual Laws of Success: A Practical Guide to the Fulfillment of Your Dreams*, by Deepak Chopra (San Rafael, Calif.: Amber-Allen, 1995); *The Spontaneous Fulfillment of All Desire: Harnessing the Infinite Power of Coincidence*, by Deepak Chopra (New York: Harmony Books, 2003); *The Power of Intention: Learning to Co-Create Your World Your Way*, by Wayne W. Dyer (Carlsbad, Calif.: Hay House, 2004); and *The 11th Element: The Key to Unlocking Your Master Blueprint for Wealth and Success*, by Robert Scheinfeld (Hoboken, N.J.: John Wiley & Sons, 2003).

SUCCESS LEAVES CLUES

Success leaves clues.

ANTHONY ROBBINS
Author of *Unlimited Power*

One of the great things about living in today's world of abundance and opportunity is that almost everything you want to do has already been done by someone else. It doesn't matter whether it's losing weight, running a marathon, starting a business, becoming financially independent, triumphing over breast cancer, or hosting the perfect dinner party—someone has already done it *and left clues* in the form of books, manuals, audio and video programs, university classes, online courses, seminars, and workshops.

WHO'S ALREADY DONE WHAT YOU WANT TO DO?

If you want to retire a millionaire, for instance, there are hundreds of books, ranging from *The Automatic Millionaire* to *The One Minute Millionaire*, and workshops ranging from Harv Eker's "Millionaire Mind" to Marshall Thurber and D.C. Cordova's "Money and You."[13] There are resources on how to make millions investing in real estate, investing in stocks, starting your own business, becoming a supersalesperson, and even marketing on the Internet.

If you want to have a better relationship with your spouse, you can read John Gray's *Men Are from Mars, Women Are from Venus*; attend a couples workshop; or take Gay and Kathlyn Hendricks' online course "The Conscious Relationship."

---

13. Contact information for all of the books, seminars, and coaching programs mentioned throughout these pages can be found in "Suggested Reading and Additional Resources for Success," starting on page 441. You can also access an updated and ever-expanding list of these kinds of resources at www.thesuccessprinciples.com.

For virtually everything you want to do, there are books and courses on how to do it. Better yet, just a phone call away are people who've already successfully done what you want to do and who are available as teachers, facilitators, mentors, advisors, coaches, and consultants.

When you take advantage of this information, you'll discover that life is simply a connect-the-dots game, and all the dots have already been identified and organized by somebody else. All you have to do is follow the blueprint, use the system, or work the program that they provide.

WHY PEOPLE DON'T SEEK OUT CLUES

When I was preparing to go on a morning news show in Dallas, I asked the station's makeup artist what her long-term goals were. She said she'd always thought about opening her own beauty salon, so I asked her what she was doing to make that happen.

"Nothing," she said, "because I don't know how to go about it."

I suggested she offer to take a salon owner to lunch and ask how she had opened her own salon.

"You can do that?" the makeup artist exclaimed.

You most certainly can. In fact, you have most probably thought about approaching an expert for advice but rejected the idea with thoughts such as *Why would someone take the time to tell me what they did? Why would they teach me and create their own competition?* Banish those thoughts. You will find that most people love to talk about how they built their business or accomplished their goals.

But unfortunately, like the makeup artist in Dallas, most of us don't take advantage of all the resources available to us. There are several reasons why we don't:

- It never occurs to us. We don't see others using these resources, so we don't do it either. Our parents didn't do it. Our friends aren't doing it. Nobody where we work is doing it.
- It's inconvenient. We'd have to go to the bookstore, library, or local college. We'd have to drive across town to a meeting. We'd have to take time away from television, family, or friends.
- Asking others for advice or information puts us up against our fear of rejection. We are afraid to take the risk.
- Connecting the dots in a new way would mean change, and change—even when it is in our best interest—is uncomfortable. Who wants to be uncomfortable?
- Connecting the dots means hard work, and frankly, most people don't want to work that hard.

SEEK OUT CLUES

Here are three ways you can begin to seek out clues:

1. Seek out a teacher, coach, mentor; a manual, book, or audio program; or an Internet resource to help you achieve one of your major goals.
2. Seek out someone who has already done what you want to do, and ask the person if you can interview him or her for a half hour on how you should best proceed.
3. Ask someone if you can shadow them for a day and watch them work. Or offer to be a volunteer, assistant, or intern for someone you think you can learn from.

PRINCIPLE

10

RELEASE THE BRAKES

Everything you want is just outside your comfort zone.

ROBERT ALLEN
Coauthor, *The One Minute Millionaire*

Have you ever been driving your car and suddenly realized you had left the emergency brake on? Did you push down harder on the gas to overcome the drag of the brake? No, of course not. You simply released the brake . . . and with no extra effort you started to go faster.

Most people drive through life with their psychological emergency brake on. They hold on to negative images about themselves or suffer the effects of powerful experiences they haven't yet released. They stay in a comfort zone entirely of their own making. They maintain inaccurate beliefs about reality or harbor guilt and self-doubt. And when they try to achieve their goals, these negative images and preprogrammed comfort zones always cancel out their good intentions—no matter how hard they try.

Successful people, on the other hand, have discovered that instead of using increased willpower as the engine to power their success, it's simply easier to "release the brakes" by letting go of and replacing their limiting beliefs and changing their self-images.

GET OUT OF YOUR COMFORT ZONE

Think of your comfort zone as a prison you live in—a largely self-created prison. It consists of the collection of *can'ts, musts, must nots,* and other unfounded beliefs formed from all the negative thoughts and decisions you have accumulated and reinforced during your lifetime.

Perhaps you've even been *trained* to limit yourself.

DON'T BE AS DUMB AS AN ELEPHANT

A baby elephant is trained at birth to be confined to a very small space. Its trainer will tie its leg with a rope to a wooden post planted deep in the ground. This confines the baby elephant to an area determined by the length of the rope—the elephant's comfort zone. Though the baby elephant will initially try to break the rope, the rope is too strong, and so the baby elephant learns that it can't break the rope. It learns that it has to stay in the area defined by the length of the rope.

When the elephant grows up into a 5-ton colossus that could easily break the same rope, it doesn't even try because it learned as a baby that it couldn't break the rope. In this way, the largest elephant can be confined by the puniest little rope.

Perhaps this also describes you—still trapped in a comfort zone by something as puny and weak as the small rope and stake that controls the elephant, except your rope is made up of the limiting beliefs and images that you received and took on when you were young. If this describes you, the good news is that you can change your comfort zone. How? There are three different ways:

1. You can use affirmations and positive self-talk to affirm already having what you want, doing what you want, and being the way you want.
2. You can create powerful and compelling new internal images of having, doing, and being what you want.
3. You can simply change your behavior.

All three of these approaches will shift you out of your old comfort zone.

STOP RE-CREATING THE SAME EXPERIENCE OVER AND OVER!

An important concept that successful people understand is that you are never *stuck*. You just keep re-creating the same experience over and over by thinking the same thoughts, maintaining the same beliefs, speaking the same words, and doing the same things.

Too often, we get stuck in an endless loop of reinforcing behavior, which keeps us stuck in a constant downward spiral. Our limiting thoughts create images in our mind, and those images govern our behavior, which in turn reinforces that limiting thought. Imagine thinking that you are going to forget your lines when you have to give a presentation at work. The thought stimulates a picture of you forgetting a key point. The image creates an experience of fear. The fear clouds your clear thinking, which makes you forget one of your key points, which reinforces your self-talk that you can't speak in front of groups. *See, I knew I would forget what I was supposed to say. I can't speak in front of groups.*

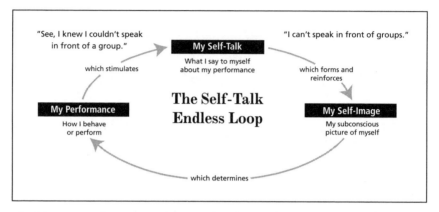

As long as you keep complaining about your present circumstances, your mind will focus on it. By continually talking about, thinking about, and writing about the way things are, you are continually reinforcing those very same neural pathways in your brain that got you to where you are today. And you are continually sending out the same vibrations that will keep attracting the same people and circumstances that you have already created.

To change this cycle, you must focus instead on thinking, talking, and writing about the reality you want to create. You must flood your unconscious with thoughts and images of this new reality.

The significant problems we face cannot be solved by the same level of thinking that created them.

ALBERT EINSTEIN
Winner, Nobel Prize for Physics

WHAT'S YOUR FINANCIAL TEMPERATURE?

Your comfort zone works the same way the thermostat in your home works. When the temperature in the room approaches the edge of the thermal range you have set, the thermostat sends an electrical signal to the furnace or the air conditioner to turn it on or off. As the temperature in the room begins to change, the electrical signals continue to respond to the changes and keep the temperature within the desired range.

Similarly, you have an internal psychological thermostat that regulates your level of performance in the world. Instead of electrical signals, your internal performance regulator uses discomfort signals to keep you within your comfort zone. As your behavior or performance begins to approach the edge of that zone, you begin to feel uncomfortable. If what you are experiencing is outside the self-image you unconsciously hold, your body will send signals of mental tension and physical discomfort to your system. To avoid the discomfort, you unconsciously pull yourself back into your comfort zone.

My stepfather, who was a regional sales manager for NCR, noticed that each of his salespeople had a self-image of themselves as a salesperson. They were a $2,000 a month salesperson or a $3,000 a month salesperson.

If a salesperson's self-image was that he earned $3,000 a month in commissions, then whenever he earned that much in commissions in the first week of the month, he would slack off for the rest of the month.

On the other hand, if it were near the end of the month and he had only earned $1,500 in commissions, he would put in 16-hour days, work weekends, create new sales proposals, and do everything possible to get to the $3,000 level for that month.

No matter what the circumstance, a person with a $36,000 self-image would always produce a $36,000 income. To do anything else would make them uncomfortable.

I remember one year my stepfather was out selling cash registers on New Year's Eve. He was out well past midnight with the intention of selling two more cash registers so that he would qualify for the annual trip to Hawaii awarded to all salesmen who hit their yearly quota. He had earned the trip for several years running, and his self-image would not allow him to lose out that year. He sold those machines and made the trip. It would have been outside of his comfort zone to do anything less.

Imagine the same scenario in relation to your savings account. Some people are comfortable as long as they have $2,000 in their savings account. Others are uncomfortable if they have any less than 8 months' income—let's say $32,000—salted away. Still others are comfortable with no savings and credit card debt of $25,000.

If the person needing $32,000 in savings to feel comfortable is hit with an unexpected medical expense of $16,000, he will curtail his spending, work overtime, have a garage sale—whatever it takes to get his savings back up to $32,000. Likewise, if he suddenly inherits money, he is likely to spend enough of it to stay in that $32,000 savings comfort zone.

No doubt you have heard that most lottery winners lose, spend, squander, or give away all of their newfound money within a few years of winning it. In fact, 80% of lottery winners in the United States file bankruptcy within 5 years! The reason is because they failed to develop a millionaire mind-set. As a result, they subconsciously re-create the reality that matches their previous mind-set. They feel uncomfortable with so much money, so they find some way to get back to their old familiar comfort zone.

We have a similar comfort zone for the kinds of restaurants we eat in, the hotels we stay in, the kind of car we drive, the houses we live in, the clothes we wear, the vacations we take, and the type of people we associate with.

If you have ever walked down Fifth Avenue in New York or Rodeo Drive in Beverly Hills, you have probably experienced walking into a store and immediately feeling as if you didn't belong there. The store was just too upscale for you. You felt out of place. That's your comfort zone in operation.

CHANGE YOUR BEHAVIOR

When I first moved to Los Angeles in 1981, my new boss took me shopping for clothes at a very upscale men's shop in Westwood. The most I had previously ever paid for a dress shirt was $35 at Nordstrom. The cheapest shirt in this store was $95! I was stunned and broke out in a cold sweat. While my boss purchased many things that day, I bought one Italian designer shirt for $95. I was so far out of my comfort zone, I could hardly breathe. The next week, I wore the shirt and was amazed by how much better it fit, how much better it felt, and how much better I looked wearing it. After a couple more weeks of wearing it once a week, I really fell in love with it. Within a month, I bought another one. Within a year, shirts like that were all I wore. Slowly my comfort zone had changed because I'd gotten used to something better even though it cost more.

When I was on the faculty of the Million Dollar Forum and Income Builders International—two organizations dedicated to teaching people how to become millionaires—all of the trainings were held at the Ritz-Carlton Hotel in Laguna Beach, California, the Hilton Hotel on the big island of Hawaii, and other high-end luxury resort hotels. The reason was to get the participants used to being treated in a first-class way. It was part of stretching their comfort zones—changing the image of who they thought they were. Every training concluded with a black-tie dinner dance. For many of the participants, it was the first time they had ever attended a black-tie affair—another comfort zone stretch.

CHANGE YOUR SELF-TALK WITH AFFIRMATIONS

I've always believed in magic. When I wasn't doing anything in this town, I'd go up every night, sit on Mulholland Drive, look out at the city, stretch out my arms, and say, "Everybody wants to work with me. I'm a really good actor. I have all kinds of great movie offers." I'd just repeat these things over and over, literally convincing myself that I had a couple of movies lined up. I'd drive down that hill, ready to take the world on, going, "Movie offers are out there for me, I just don't hear them yet." It was like total affirmations, antidotes to the stuff that stems from my family background.[14]

JIM CARREY
Actor

One way to stretch your comfort zone is to bombard your subconscious mind with new thoughts and images—of a big bank account, a trim and healthy body, exciting work, interesting friends, memorable vacations—of all your goals as already complete. The technique you use to do this is called *affirmations*. An affirmation is a statement that describes a goal in its already completed state, such as "I am enjoying watching the sunset from the lanai of my beautiful beachfront condo on the Ka'anapali coast of Maui" or "I am celebrating feeling light and alive at my perfect body weight of one thirty-five."

THE NINE GUIDELINES FOR CREATING EFFECTIVE AFFIRMATIONS

To be effective, your affirmations should be constructed using the following nine guidelines:

1. **Start with the words *I am*.** The words *I am* are the two most powerful words in the language. The subconscious takes any sentence that starts with the words *I am* and interprets it as a command—a directive to make it happen.

---

14. From an interview in *Movieline*, July 1994.

2. **Use the present tense.** Describe what you want as though you already have it, as though it is already accomplished.

Wrong: I am going to get a new red Porsche 911 Carrera.
Right: I am enjoying driving my new red Porsche 911 Carrera.

3. **State it in the positive. Affirm what you want, not what you don't want.** State your affirmations in the positive. The unconscious does not hear the word no. This means that the statement "Don't slam the door" is heard as "Slam the door." The unconscious thinks in pictures, and the words "Don't slam the door" evoke a picture of slamming the door. The phrase "I am no longer afraid of flying" evokes an image of being afraid of flying, while the phrase "I am enjoying the thrill of flying" evokes an image of enjoyment.

Wrong: I am no longer afraid of flying.
Right: I am enjoying the thrill of flying.

4. **Keep it brief.** Think of your affirmation as an advertising jingle. Act as if each word costs $1,000. It needs to be short enough and memorable enough to be easily remembered.

5. **Make it specific.** Vague affirmations produce vague results.

Wrong: I am driving my new red car.
Right: I am driving my new red Porsche 911 Carrera.

6. **Include an action word ending with *-ing*.** The active verb adds power to the effect by evoking an image of doing it right now.

Wrong: I express myself openly and honestly.
Right: I am confidently expressing myself openly and honestly.

7. **Include at least one dynamic emotion or feeling word.** Include the emotional state you would be feeling if you had already achieved the goal. Some commonly used words are *enjoying, joyfully, happily, celebrating, proudly, calmly, peacefully, delighted, enthusiastic, lovingly, secure, serenely,* and *triumphant.*

Wrong: I am maintaining my perfect body weight of 178 pounds.
Right: I am feeling agile and great at 178!

Note that the last one has the ring of an advertising jingle. The subconscious loves rhythm and rhymes. That's why we are able to more easily remember things such as "Sticks and stones will break my bones, but names will never hurt me" and "*I* before *e* except after *c*, and when sounded like *a* as in *neighbor* and *weigh*."

8. **Make affirmations for yourself, not others.** When you are constructing your affirmations, make them describe your behavior, not the behavior of others.

Wrong: I am watching Johnny clean up his room.
Right: I am effectively communicating my needs and desires to Johnny.

9. **Add *or something better*.** When you are affirming getting a specific situation (job, opportunity, vacation), material object (house, car, boat), or relationship (husband, wife, child), always add the words "or something (someone) better." Sometimes our criteria for what we want come from our ego or from our limited experience. Sometimes there is someone or something better that is available for us, so let your affirmations include this phrase when it is appropriate.

Example: I am enjoying living in my beautiful beachfront villa on the Ka'anapali coast of Maui or somewhere better.

A SIMPLE WAY TO CREATE AFFIRMATIONS

1. Visualize what you would like to create. See things just as you would like them to be. Place yourself inside the picture and see things through your eyes. If you want a car, see the world from inside the car as you are driving it.
2. Hear the sounds you would be hearing if you had already achieved your vision.
3. Feel the feeling you want to feel when you have created what you want.
4. Describe what you are experiencing in a brief statement, including what you are feeling.
5. If necessary, edit your affirmation to make it meet all of the above guidelines.

HOW TO USE AFFIRMATIONS AND VISUALIZATION

1. Review your affirmations one to three times a day. The best times are first thing in the morning, in the middle of the day to refocus yourself, and around bedtime.
2. If appropriate, read each affirmation out loud.
3. Close your eyes and visualize yourself as the affirmation describes. See it as if you were looking out at the scene from inside of yourself. In other words, don't see yourself standing out there in the scene; see the scene as if you were actually living it.
4. Hear any sounds you might hear when you successfully achieve what your affirmation describes—the sound of the surf, the roar of the crowd, the playing of the national anthem. Include other important people in your life congratulating you and telling you how pleased they are with your success.
5. Feel the feelings that you will feel when you achieve that success. The stronger the feelings, the more powerful the process. (If you have difficulty creating the feelings, you can affirm "I am enjoying easily creating powerful feelings in my effective work with affirmations.")
6. Say your affirmation again, and then repeat this process with the next affirmation.

OTHER WAYS TO USE AFFIRMATIONS

1. Post 3" × 5" cards with your affirmations around your home.
2. Hang pictures of the things you want around your house or your room. You can put a picture of yourself in the picture.
3. Repeat your affirmations during "wasted time" such as waiting in line, exercising, and driving. You can repeat them silently or out loud.
4. Record your affirmations and listen to them while you work, drive, or fall asleep. You can use endless loop tapes, an MP3 player, or an iPod.
5. Have one of your parents record a tape of encouraging things you would like to have heard from them or words of encouragement and permission you would currently like to hear.
6. Repeat your affirmations in the first person ("I am . . ."), second person ("You are . . ."), and third person ("He/she is . . .").
7. Put your affirmations on your screen saver on your computer, so you'll see them every time you use your computer.

AFFIRMATIONS WORK

I first learned about the power of affirmations when W. Clement Stone challenged me to set a goal so far beyond my current circumstances it would literally astound me if I achieved it. Though I thought Stone's challenge had merit, I didn't really apply it to my life in a serious way until several years later when I decided to make the jump from earning $25,000 a year to making $100,000 or more.

The first thing I did was to craft an affirmation after one I'd seen by Florence Scovell Shinn. My affirmation was

God is my infinite supply and large sums of money come to me quickly and easily under the grace of God for the highest good of all concerned. I am happily and easily earning, saving, and investing $100,000 a year.

Next, I created a huge replica of a $100,000 bill, which I affixed to the ceiling above my bed. On awakening, I would see the bill, close my eyes, repeat my affirmation, and visualize what I would be enjoying if I were living a $100,000-a-year lifestyle. I envisioned the house I would live in, the furnishings and artwork I would own, the car I would drive, and the vacations I would take. I also created the feelings I would experience once I had already attained that lifestyle.

Soon I awoke one morning with my first $100,000 idea. It occurred to me that if I could sell 400,000 copies of my book, *100 Ways to Enhance Self-Concept in the Classroom*, on which I received a 25¢-per-copy royalty, I would earn a $100,000 income. I added to my morning visualizations the image of my book flying off bookstore shelves and my publisher writing me a $100,000 check. Not long after, a freelance journalist approached me and wrote an article about my work for the *National Enquirer*. As a result, thousands of additional copies of my book were sold that month.

Almost daily, more and more money-making ideas flowed into my mind. For instance, I took out small ads and sold the book on my own—making $3.00 per copy instead of just 25¢. I started a mail-order catalog of other books on self-esteem and made even more money from these same buyers. The University of Massachusetts saw my catalog and invited me to sell books at a weekend conference, helping me generate more than $2,000 in 2 days—and introducing me to another strategy for making $100,000 a year.

At the same time I was visualizing greater book sales, I also got the idea to generate more income from my workshops and seminars. When I asked a friend who did similar work how I could charge higher fees, he revealed he was *already* charging more than double what I was being paid! With his encouragement, I instantly tripled my rates and discovered the schools that were hiring me to speak had budgets even higher than that.

My affirmation was paying off big time. But if I hadn't set the goal to make $100,000 and been diligent about affirming and visualizing it, I never would have raised my speaking fees, started a mail-order bookstore, attended a major conference, or been interviewed for a major publication.

As a result, my income that year skyrocketed from $25,000 to over $92,000!

Of course, I missed my $100,000 goal by $8,000, but I can assure you I wasn't depressed about it. On the contrary, I was ecstatic. I had almost quadrupled my income in less than 1 year, using the power of visualization and affirmations coupled with the willingness to act when I had an "inspired idea."

After our $92,000 year, my wife asked me, "If affirmations worked for $100,000, do you think they would also work for $1 million?" Using affirmations and visualization, we went on to achieve that goal as well and have continued to make $1 million or more every year since.

SEE WHAT YOU WANT,
GET WHAT YOU SEE

Imagination is everything. It is the preview
of life's coming attractions.

ALBERT EINSTEIN
Winner, Nobel Prize for Physics

Visualization—or the act of creating compelling and vivid pictures in your mind—may be the most underutilized success tool you possess because it greatly accelerates the achievement of any success in three powerful ways.

1. Visualization activates the creative powers of your subconscious mind.
2. Visualization focuses your brain by programming its *reticular activating system* (RAS) to notice available resources that were always there but were previously unnoticed.
3. Visualization magnetizes and attracts to you the people, resources, and opportunities you need to achieve your goal.

When you perform any task in real life, researchers have found, your brain uses the same identical processes it would use if you were only vividly visualizing that activity. In other words, your brain sees no difference whatsoever between visualizing something and actually doing it.

This principle also applies to learning anything new. Harvard University researchers found that students who visualized in advance performed tasks with nearly 100% accuracy, whereas students who didn't visualize achieved only 55% accuracy.

Visualization simply makes the brain achieve more. And though none of us were ever taught this in school, sports psychologists and peak performance experts have been popularizing the power of visualization since the

1980s. Almost all Olympic and professional athletes now employ the power of visualization.

Jack Nicklaus, the legendary golfer with more than 100 tournament victories and over $5.7 million in winnings, once said, "I never hit a shot, not even in practice, without having a very sharp, in-focus picture of it in my head. It's like a color movie. First I 'see' where I want it to finish, nice and white and sitting high on the bright green grass. Then the scene quickly changes, and I 'see' the ball going there: its path, trajectory, and shape, even its behavior on landing. Then there's sort of a fade-out, and the next scene shows me making the kind of swing that will turn the previous images into reality."

HOW VISUALIZATION WORKS TO ENHANCE PERFORMANCE

When you visualize your goals as already complete each and every day, it creates a conflict in your subconscious mind between what you are visualizing and what you currently have. Your subconscious mind tries to resolve that conflict by turning your current reality into the new, more exciting vision.

This conflict, when intensified over time through constant visualization, actually causes three things to happen:

1. It programs your brain's RAS to start letting into your awareness anything that will help you achieve your goals.
2. It activates your subconscious mind to create solutions for getting the goals you want. You'll start waking up in the morning with new ideas. You'll find yourself having ideas in the shower, while you are taking long walks, and while you are driving to work.
3. It creates new levels of motivation. You'll start to notice you are unexpectedly doing things that take you to your goal. All of a sudden, you are raising your hand in class, volunteering to take on new assignments at work, speaking out at staff meetings, asking more directly for what you want, saving money for the things that you want, paying down a credit card debt, or taking more risks in your personal life.

Let's take a closer look at how the RAS works. At any one time, there are about 8 million bits of information streaming into your brain—most of which you cannot attend to, nor do you need to. So your brain's RAS filters most of them out, letting into your awareness only those signals that can help you survive and achieve your most important goals.

So how does your RAS know what to let in and what to filter out? It lets in anything that will help you achieve the goals you have set and *constantly* visualize and affirm. It also lets in anything that matches your beliefs and images about yourself, others, and the world.

The RAS is a powerful tool, but it can only look for ways to achieve the exact pictures you give it. Your creative subconscious doesn't think in words—it can only think in pictures. So how does this help your effort to become successful and achieve the life of your dreams?

When you give your brain specific, colorful, and vividly compelling pictures to manifest—it will seek out and capture all the information necessary to bring that picture into reality for you. If you give your mind a $10,000 problem, it will come up with a $10,000 solution. If you give your mind a $1 million problem, it will come up with a $1 million solution.

If you give it pictures of a beautiful home, an adoring spouse, an exciting career, and exotic vacations, it will go to work on achieving those. By contrast, if you are constantly feeding it negative, fearful, and anxious pictures—guess what?—it will achieve those, too.

THE PROCESS FOR VISUALIZING YOUR FUTURE

The process of visualizing for success is really quite simple. All you have to do is close your eyes and see your goals as already complete.

If one of your objectives is to own a nice house on the lake, then close your eyes and see yourself walking through the exact house you would like to own. Fill in all of the details. What does the exterior look like? How is it landscaped? What kind of view does it have? What do the living room, kitchen, master bedroom, dining room, family room, and den look like? How is it furnished? Go from room to room and fill in all of the details.

Make the images as clear and bright as possible. This goes for any goal you make—whether it's in the area of work, play, family, personal finances, relationships, or philanthropy. Write down each of your goals and objectives, then review them, affirm them, and visualize them every day.

Then, each morning when you awake and each night before you go to bed, read through the list of goals out loud, pausing after each one to close your eyes and re-create the visual image of that completed goal in your mind. Continue through the list until you have visualized each goal as complete and fulfilled. The whole process will take between 10 and 15 minutes, depending on how many goals you have. If you meditate, do your visualization right after you finish meditating. The deepened state you have achieved in meditation will heighten the impact of your visualizations.

ADDING SOUNDS AND FEELINGS
TO THE PICTURES

To multiply the effect many times over, add sound, smells, tastes, and feelings to your pictures. What sounds would you be hearing, what smells would you be smelling, what tastes would you be tasting, and—most importantly—what emotions and bodily sensations would you be feeling if you had already achieved your goal?

If you were imagining your dream house on the beach, you might add in the sound of the surf lapping at the shore outside your home, the sound of your kids playing on the sand, and the sound of your spouse's voice thanking you for being such a good provider.

Then add in the feelings of pride of ownership, satisfaction at having achieved your goal, and the feeling of the sun on your face as you sit on your deck looking out over the ocean at a beautiful sunset.

"Don't disturb Daddy. He's busy visualizing unparalleled success in the business world and, by extension, a better life for us all."

FUEL YOUR IMAGES WITH EMOTION

By far, these emotions are what propel your vision forward. Researchers know that when accompanied by intense emotions, an image or scene can stay locked in the memory forever.

I'm sure you remember exactly where you were when John F. Kennedy was assassinated in 1963 or when the World Trade Center collapsed on September 11, 2001. Your brain remembers it all in great detail because not only did your brain filter information you needed for survival under these tense moments but also the images themselves were created with intense emotion. These intense emotions actually stimulate the growth of additional spiny protuberances on the dendrites of brain neurons, which ultimately creates more neural connections, thus locking in the memory much more solidly. You can bring this same emotional intensity to your own visualizations by adding inspiring music, real-life smells, deeply felt passion, even loudly shouting your affirmations with exaggerated enthusiasm. The more passion, excitement, and energy you can muster, the more powerful will be the ultimate result.

VISUALIZATION WORKS

Olympic gold medalist Peter Vidmar describes his use of visualization in his successful pursuit of the gold:

> To keep us focused on our Olympic goal, we began ending our workouts by visualizing our dream. We visualized ourselves actually competing in the Olympics and achieving our dream by practicing what we thought would be the ultimate gymnastics scenario.
>
> I'd say, "Okay, Tim, let's imagine it's the men's gymnastics team finals of the Olympic Games. The United States team is on its last event of the night, which just happens to be the high bar. The last two guys up for the United States are Tim Daggett and Peter Vidmar. Our team is neck and neck with the People's Republic of China, the reigning world champions, and we have to perform our routines perfectly to win the Olympic team gold medal."
>
> At that point we'd each be thinking, *Yeah, right. We're never going to be neck and neck with those guys. They were number one at the Budapest world championships, while our team didn't even win a medal. It's never going to happen.*
>
> But what if it did happen? How would we feel?
>
> We'd close our eyes and, in this empty gym at the end of a long day, we'd

visualize an Olympic arena with 13,000 people in the seats and another 200 million watching live on television. Then we'd practice our routines. First, I'd be the announcer. I'd cup my hands around my mouth and say, "Next up, from the United States of America, Tim Daggett." Then Tim would go through his routine as if it were the real thing.

Then Tim would go over to the corner of the gym, cup his hands around his mouth, and, in his best announcer voice, say, "Next up, from the United States of America, Peter Vidmar."

Then it was my turn. In my mind, I had one chance to perfectly perform my routine in order for our team to win the gold medal. If I didn't, we'd lose.

Tim would shout out, "Green light," and I'd look at the superior judge, who was usually our coach Mako. I'd raise my hand, and he'd raise his right back. Then I'd turn, face the bar, grab hold, and begin my routine.

Well, a funny thing happened on July 31, 1984.

It was the Olympic Games, men's gymnastics team finals in Pauley Pavilion on the UCLA campus. The 13,000 seats were all filled, and a television audience in excess of 200 million around the world tuned in. The United States team was on its last event of the night, the high bar. The last two guys up for the United States just happened to be Tim Daggett and Peter Vidmar. And just as we visualized, our team was neck and neck with the People's Republic of China. We had to perform our high bar routines perfectly to win the gold medal.

I looked at Coach Mako, my coach for the past 12 years. As focused as ever, he simply said, "Okay, Peter, let's go. You know what to do. You've done it a thousand times, just like every day back in the gym. Let's just do it one more time, and let's go home. You're prepared."

He was right. I had planned for this moment and visualized it hundreds of times. I was prepared to perform my routine. Rather than seeing myself actually standing in the Olympic arena with 13,000 people in the stands and 200 million watching on television, in my mind I pictured myself back in the UCLA gym at the end of the day with two people left in the gym.

When the announcer said, "From the United States of America, Peter Vidmar," I imagined it was my buddy Tim Daggett saying it. When the green light came on, indicating it was time for the routine, I imagined that it wasn't really a green light but that it was Tim shouting, "Green light!" And when I raised my hand toward the superior judge from East Germany, in my mind I was signaling my coach, just like I had signaled him every day at the end of hundreds of workouts. In the gym, I always visualized I was at the Olympic finals. At the Olympic finals, I visualized I was back in the gym.

I turned, faced the bar, jumped up, and grabbed on. I began the same routine I had visualized and practiced day after day in the gym. I was in memory mode, going yet again where I'd already gone hundreds of times.

I quickly made it past the risky double-release move that had harpooned my chances at the world championships. I moved smoothly through the rest of my routine and landed a solid dismount, where I anxiously waited for my score from the judges.

With a deep voice the announcement came through the speaker, "The score for Peter Vidmar is 9.95." "Yes!" I shouted. "I did it!" The crowd cheered loudly as my teammates and I celebrated our victory.

Thirty minutes later, we were standing on the Olympic medal platform in the Olympic arena with 13,000 people in the stands and over 200 million watching on television, while the gold medals were officially draped around our necks. Tim, me, and our teammates stood proudly wearing our gold medals as the national anthem played and the American flag was raised to the top of the arena. It was a moment we visualized and practiced hundreds of times in the gym. Only this time, it was for real.

WHAT IF I DON'T SEE ANYTHING WHEN I VISUALIZE?

Some people are what psychologists refer to as *eidetic visualizers*. When they close their eyes, they see everything in bright, clear, three-dimensional Technicolor images. Most of us, however, are noneidetic visualizers. That means you don't really *see* an image as much as you just *think* it. This is perfectly okay. It still works just as well. Do the visualization exercise of imagining your goals as already complete twice a day, every day, and you will still get the same benefit as those people who claim to actually see the image.

USE PRINTED PICTURES TO HELP YOU

If you have trouble seeing your goals, use pictures, images, and symbols you collect to keep your conscious and subconscious mind focused on your goals. For example, if one of your goals is to own a new Lexus LS-430, you can take your camera down to your local Lexus dealer and ask a salesperson to take a picture of you sitting behind the wheel.

If your goal is to visit Paris, find a poster of the Eiffel Tower—then cut out a picture of you and place it at the base of the Eiffel Tower as if it were a photograph taken of you in Paris. Several years ago I did this with a picture of the Sydney Opera House, and within a year I was in Sydney, Australia, standing in front of it.

If your goal is to be a millionaire, you might want to write yourself a check for $1,000,000 or create a bank statement that shows your bank account or your stock portfolio with a $1,000,000 balance.

Mark Victor Hansen and I created a mock-up of the *New York Times* Best-Seller List with the original *Chicken Soup for the Soul®* in the number-one spot. Within 15 months, that dream became a reality. Four years later, we made a *Guinness* world record for having seven books on the *New York Times* Best-Seller List at the same time.

Once you have created these images, you can place them—one to a page—in a three-ring binder that you review every day. Or you could make a dream board or treasure map—a collage of all these images on a bulletin board, wall, or a refrigerator door—somewhere where you will see them every day.

When NASA was working on putting a man on the moon, they had a huge picture of the moon covering the entire wall, from floor to ceiling, of their main construction area. Everyone was clear on the goal, and they reached that goal 2 years ahead of schedule!

VISION BOARDS AND GOAL BOOKS
MADE THEIR DREAMS COME TRUE

In 1995 John Assaraf created a vision board and put it up on the wall in his home office. Whenever he saw a materialistic thing he wanted or a trip he wanted to take, he'd get a photo of it and glue it to the board. Then he'd see himself already enjoying the object of his desire.

In May 2000, having just moved into his new home in Southern California a few weeks earlier, he was sitting in his office at 7:30 AM when his 5-year-old son Keenan came in and sat on a couple of boxes that had been in storage 4 years. Keenan asked his father what was in the boxes. When John told him his vision boards were in the boxes, Keenan replied, "Your vision whats?"

John opened one of the boxes to show Keenan a vision board. John smiled as he looked at the first board and saw pictures of a Mercedes sports car, a watch, and some other items, all of which he had acquired by then.

But as he pulled out the second board, he began to cry. On that board was a picture of the house he had just bought and was living in! Not a house *like* it but *the* house! The 7,000-square-foot house that sits on 6 acres of spectacular views, with a 3,000-square-foot guest house and office complex, a tennis court, and 320 orange trees—that very home was a home he had seen in a picture that he had cut out of *Dream Homes* magazine 4 years earlier!

Caryl Kristensen and Marilyn Kentz—better known as "The Mommies" because they make their living joking about kids, family life, and the stresses of motherhood—know the power of creating goal pictures to make their dreams come true. They started their friendship as well as their careers in the small farm town of Petaluma, California, where they were neighbors. Once they decided to become performers and create shows, they made a Goals Book, in which they listed all the things they wanted to achieve, and then illustrated them with pictures. Without exception, everything they put in the book came true!

Their achievements include *The Mommies*, an NBC sitcom that aired between 1993 and 1995, the *Caryl & Marilyn Show*, a talk show that aired on ABC between 1996 and 1997, Showtime and Lifetime cable specials, and their highly successful book, *The Mother Load*.

Because Caryl and Marilyn are both illustrators, drawing their goals seemed the easiest way to go about it, but you don't have to have drawing skills to make your own Goals Book. They worded their goals in the present tense, added feeling phrases such as "I'm feeling content and grateful," "I feel relaxed and joyful," and "Living in this wonderful house is so much fun," and they always finished off their page with this phrase: "This or something better is manifesting itself for the good of all concerned."

And this or something better always happened.

START NOW

Set aside time each and every day to visualize every one of your goals as already complete. This is one of the most vital things you can do to make your dreams come true. Some psychologists are now claiming that one hour of visualization is worth 7 hours of physical effort. That's a tall claim, but it makes an important point—visualization is one of the strongest tools in your success toolbox. Make sure you use it.

You don't need to visualize your future achievements for a whole hour. Just 10 to 15 minutes is plenty. Azim Jamal, a prominent speaker in Canada, recommends what he calls "the Hour of Power"—20 minutes of visualization and meditation, 20 minutes of exercise, and 20 minutes of reading inspirational or informational books. Imagine what would happen to your life if you did this every day.

ACT AS IF

Believe and act as if it were impossible to fail.

CHARLES F. KETTERING
Inventor with over 140 patents and honorary doctorates
from nearly 30 universities

One of the great strategies for success is to act as if you are *already where you want to be.* This means thinking like, talking like, dressing like, acting like, and feeling like the person who has already achieved your goal. Acting as if sends powerful commands to your subconscious mind to find creative ways to achieve your goals. It programs the reticular activating system (RAS) in your brain to start noticing anything that will help you succeed, and it sends strong messages to the universe that this end goal is something you really want.

START ACTING AS IF

The first time I noticed this phenomenon was at my local bank. There were several tellers working there, and I noticed that one in particular always wore a suit and tie. Unlike the other two male tellers who just wore a shirt and a tie, this young man looked like an executive.

A year later, I noticed he had been promoted to his own desk where he was taking loan applications. Two years later, he was a loan officer, and later he became the branch manager. I asked him about this one day, and he replied that he always knew he would be a branch manager, so he studied how the manager dressed and started dressing that way. He studied how the manager treated people and started interacting with people the same way. He started acting as if he were a branch manager long before he ever became one.

To fly as fast as thought, to be anywhere there is, you must first begin
by knowing that you have already arrived.

RICHARD BACH
Author of *Jonathan Livingston Seagull*

BECOMING AN INTERNATIONAL CONSULTANT

In the late '70s, I met a seminar leader who had just returned from Australia. I decided that I, too, wanted to travel and speak around the globe. I asked myself what I would need to become an international consultant. I called the passport office and asked them to send me an application. I purchased a clock that showed all the international time zones. I had business cards printed with the words *international consultant* on them. Finally, I decided that Australia would be the first place I would like to go, so I went to a travel agency and got a huge travel poster featuring the Sydney Opera House, Ayers Rock, and a kangaroo-crossing sign. Every morning while I ate my breakfast, I looked at that poster on my refrigerator and imagined being in Australia.

Less than a year later, I was invited to conduct seminars in Sydney and Brisbane. As soon as I started acting as if I were an international consultant, the universe responded by treating me like one—the powerful Law of Attraction at work.

The Law of Attraction simply states that like attracts like. The more you create the vibration—the mental and emotional states—of already having something, the faster you attract it to you. This is an immutable law of the universe and critical to accelerating your rate of success.

ACTING AS IF IN THE PGA

Fred Couples and Jim Nantz were two kids who loved golf and had very large dreams. Fred's goal was to someday win the Masters Tournament, and Jim's was to someday work for CBS Sports as an announcer. When Fred and Jim were suitemates at the University of Houston in the late '70s, they used to playact the scene where the winner of the Masters is escorted into Butler Cabin to receive his green jacket and be interviewed by the CBS announcer. Fourteen years later, the scene they had rehearsed many times in Taub Hall at the University of Houston played out in reality as the whole world was watching. Fred Couples won the Masters and was taken by tournament officials into Butler Cabin, where he was interviewed by none other than CBS

Sports announcer Jim Nantz. After the cameras stopped rolling, the two embraced each other with tears in their eyes. They always knew it was going to be the Masters that Fred won, and that Jim would be there to cover it for CBS—the amazing power of acting as if with unwavering certainty.

THE MILLIONAIRE COCKTAIL PARTY

In many of my seminars we do an exercise called the Millionaire Cocktail Party. Everyone stands up and socializes with the other participants as if they were all at an actual cocktail party. However, they must act as if they have already achieved all of their financial goals in life. They act as if they already have everything they want in life—their dream house, their vacation home, their dream car, their dream career—as well as if they have achieved any personal, professional, or philanthropic goals that are important to them.

Everyone suddenly becomes more animated, alive, enthusiastic, and outgoing. People who seemed shy a few minutes earlier reach out and assertively introduce themselves to others. The energy and volume level of the room soars. People excitedly tell each other about their achievements, invite each other to their vacation homes in Hawaii and the Bahamas, and discuss their recent safaris in Africa and their philanthropic missions to Third World countries.

After about 5 minutes, I stop the exercise and ask people to share how they are feeling. People report feeling excited, passionate, positive, supportive, generous, happy, self-confident, and content.

I then ask them to look at the fact that their inner feelings—both emotional and physiological—were different, even though in reality their outer circumstances were still the same. They had not actually become millionaires in the real world, but they had begun to feel like millionaires simply by acting as if they were.

BE, DO, AND HAVE EVERYTHING YOU WANT . . .
STARTING NOW

You can begin right now to act as if you have already achieved any goal you desire, and that outer experience of acting as if will create the inner experience—the millionaire mind-set, as it were—that will take you to the actual manifestation of that experience.

Once you choose what it is you want to be, do, or have, all you have to do is start acting as if you already are being, doing, or having it. How would you act if you already were a straight-A student, top salesperson, highly paid consultant, rich entrepreneur, world-class athlete, best-selling author, internationally acclaimed artist, sought-after speaker, or celebrated actor or musician? How would you think, talk, act, carry yourself, dress, treat other people, handle money, eat, live, travel, and so forth?

Once you have a clear picture of that, start being it—now!

Successful people exude self-confidence, ask for what they want, and say what they don't want. They think anything is possible, take risks, and celebrate their successes. They save a portion of their income and share a portion with others. You can do all of those things now before you ever become rich and successful. These things don't cost money, just intention. And as soon as you start acting as if, you will start drawing to you the very people and things that will help you achieve it in real life.

Remember, the proper order of things is to start now and *be* who you want to be, then *do* the actions that go along with being that person, and soon you will find that you easily *have* everything you want in life—health, wealth, and fulfilling relationships.

THE PARTY THAT COULD CHANGE YOUR LIFE

In 1986 I attended a party given by Diana von Welanetz and the Inside Edge that deeply impacted the lives of all of us who attended. It was a "come as you will be in 1991 party" held on the *Queen Mary* in Long Beach, California. Those of us who attended were to envision where we would like to be in 1991—5 years into the future. After we had created our ideal vision, we were to then stretch our imaginations even further, to make our vision even bigger still.

When we attended the party, we were to act as if it really were 1991 and our vision had already come true. We were to dress the part, talk the part, and bring any props that demonstrated that our dream had already come true— books written, awards earned, and large paychecks received. We were to spend the evening bragging about our accomplishments, celebrating our successes and the successes of others, talking about how happy and fulfilled we were, and discussing what we were going to do next. We were to stay in character the entire night.

When we arrived, we were met by 20 men and women who had been hired to play the part of adoring fans and paparazzi. Cameras flashed and fans screamed our names, asking for autographs.

I went as a best-selling author with several reviews of my number-one *New York Times* best seller to show people. A man who came as a multimillionaire dressed as a beach bum—his vision of retirement—spent the evening handing out real lottery tickets to everyone at the party. A woman brought a mock edition of *Time* magazine with her face on the cover for winning an international award for making advances in the peace movement.

A man who wanted to retire and spend his life as a sculptor showed up in a leather sculptor's apron with a hammer and chisel and safety goggles and pictures of sculptures he had made. Another gentleman who wanted to become a successful stock trader spent the entire evening answering his cell phone, talking animatedly and then commanding, "Buy five thousand shares" or "Sell ten thousand shares." He had actually hired someone to call him every 15 minutes during the party just to carry off his "act as if"!

A movie producer arrived dressed in a tuxedo, having envisioned winning an award for his first coproduction with the Russians. His wife, who was just embarking on a writing career and had yet to sell a book, arrived carrying mock-ups of three books she had written. In the spirit of everyone supporting everyone else's dream, people told her that they had seen her on *Oprah, Sally Jesse Raphael*, and the *Today* show. Others congratulated her for making the best-seller lists and for winning a Pulitzer prize. And so it went all evening long. (Many of you now know this author, Susan Jeffers, who did go on from that transformational evening to publish 17 successful books, including the internationally acclaimed best-selling classic *Feel the Fear and Do It Anyway*.)

And as you know if you've read this far, the same thing happened to me. I went on to write, compile, and edit over 80 books, including 11 number-one *New York Times* best sellers. That party, where we maintained our future personas for over 4 hours, flooded our subconscious minds with powerful images of already having achieved our aspirations. These vivid experiences, infused with the positive emotions generated by the events of the evening, strengthened the positive neural pathways in our brains that in some cases forged, and in other cases deepened, our new self-images of being supersuccessful.

But most importantly, it worked. All those who attended that party have gone on to realize the dreams they acted out that night and much, much more.

Make the commitment to throw a "come as you will be" party for your closest circle of friends, your company, your business associates, your graduating class, or your mastermind group. Why not build it into your annual convention or sales meeting? Think of the creative energy, awareness, and support it will release.

You can use the following invitation:

COME AS YOU WILL BE ... IN 2010!

∎

*Join us for a celebration that will stretch your imagination
and catapult you into your own future.*

∎

When: _____

Where: _____

Given by: _____

RSVP to: _____

Arrive as who you will be 5 years from now. Dress in your very best. Speak only in the present tense the entire evening, as if it were already 2010, all your goals have been achieved, and all your dreams have already come true.

You will be videotaped as you arrive. Bring props to show everyone what you have achieved in the years between, such as best-selling books you've written, magazine covers you've been on, awards you've won, and photographs or scrapbooks of your achievements. Throughout the evening, you will have the opportunity to applaud others in their achievements and to receive congratulations.

AND THE PARTY CONTINUES

A few years after the party in Long Beach, I appeared on the *Caryl & Marilyn Show* on ABC and shared my experience on the *Queen Mary*. They immediately recognized the power of the idea and decided to throw a similar party for all of their crew and friends. Here is what Marilyn wrote about it 6 years later in her book *Not Your Mother's Midlife*:

> I giggle whenever I think about our Five-Year Party. Caryl and I went all out with fake paparazzi, *Entertainment Tonight* interviews, and a red-carpet entrance. I had sent telegrams to the party house from famous people congratulating everyone on their accomplishments. Caryl and I carried around copies of our new *Mommy Book*. I'd made mock books with a cover using this crazy picture of us wearing plastic flamingos on our heads—the only photo I could drum up that afternoon. At that time we didn't even have an outline, let alone a book deal.
>
> Two years later HarperCollins released our book *The Mother Load*, and by pure coincidence, out of all the head shots we submitted for the jacket, the photograph they decided to use was the same one I used on the "fake" book jacket. The book did very well—went through three hardcover printings and eventually also sold as a paperback. . . .
>
> Six years ago my daughter was ten and in elementary school. Because I was afraid she'd be a horrid, naughty, sassy teenager within the next five years, I hired a young fifteen-year-old to play my darling, loving, "good yet normal" teenage daughter. I provided her with a script. She burst into the house and kissed my cheek, exclaiming how great it was that we had this special relationship where we talked about everything and hardly ever fought. She said she couldn't stay long because she was on her way to a party with her designated driver and, while she was quite a healthy, normal teenager, I really had nothing to worry about because she never got carried away with drinking alcohol or smoking pot. I also had to throw this in: She explained that she was going to see Denzel Washington's son at the party. The whole bit got lots of laughs.
>
> Fast-forward six years. First of all, my daughter and I have that special relationship I dreamed about. I don't know why, but we do talk about everything. (Okay, I'm not dumb . . . certain things are saved for best friends and siblings.) We rarely ever fight, she's a wise and moderate teenager, and she actually goes to parties with Denzel's son. It's true! When I'd made up that little scenario I'd had no idea if Denzel lived here in Los Angeles or in New York: I didn't even know if he had kids. What are the

chances that my daughter would end up in the same high school as his son? What a crazy Five-Year Party![15]

The purpose of the "come as you will be party" is to create an emotionally charged experience of what it will be like when you have made it—when you have achieved your dreams. When you spend an evening living out the lifestyle you want and deserve, you lay down powerful blueprints in your subconscious mind that will later support you in perceiving opportunities, creating powerful solutions, attracting the right people, and taking the necessary actions to achieve your dreams and goals.

Be clear that one party like this is not enough by itself to change your entire future. You will still have to do other things to make it happen. However, it is one more piece in an overall system of powerful "acting as if" strategies that will support you in the creation of your desired future.

---

15. *Not Your Mother's Midlife: A Ten-Step Guide to Fearless Aging,* by Nancy Alspaugh and Marilyn Kentz. Kansas City, Mo.: Andrews McMeel Universal, 2003, pages 180–181.

13

TAKE ACTION

*Things may come to those who wait, but only the things
left by those who hustle.*

ABRAHAM LINCOLN
Sixteenth president of the United States

*What we think or what we know or what we believe is, in the end,
of little consequence. The only consequence is what we do.*

JOHN RUSKIN
English author, art critic, and social commentator

The world doesn't pay you for what you know; it pays you for what you do. There's an enduring axiom of success that says, "The universe rewards action." Yet as simple and as true as this principle is, it's surprising how many people get bogged down in analyzing, planning, and organizing when what they really need to do is take action.

When you take action, you trigger all kinds of things that will inevitably carry you to success. You let those around you know that you are serious in your intention. People wake up and start paying attention. People with similar goals become aligned with you. You begin to learn things from your experience that cannot be learned from listening to others or from reading books. You begin to get feedback about how to do it better, more efficiently, and more quickly. Things that once seemed confusing begin to become clear. Things that once appeared difficult begin to be easier. You begin to attract others who will support and encourage you. All manner of good things begin to flow in your direction once you begin to take action.

TALK IS CHEAP!

Over the years of teaching and coaching people in my company and in my seminars, I have found that the one thing that seems to separate winners from losers more than anything else is that winners take action. They simply get up and do what has to be done. Once they have developed a plan, they start. They get into motion. Even if they don't start perfectly, they learn from their mistakes, make the necessary corrections, and keep taking action, all the time building momentum, until they finally produce the result they set out to produce . . . or something even better than they conceived of when they started.

To be successful, you have to do what successful people do, and successful people are highly action-oriented. I have already covered how to create a vision, set goals, break them down into small steps, anticipate obstacles and plan how to deal with them, visualize and affirm your success, and believe in yourself and your dreams. Now it's time to take action. Enroll in the course, get the necessary training, call the travel agent, start writing that book, start saving for the down payment on your home, join the health club, sign up for those piano lessons, or write that proposal.

NOTHING HAPPENS UNTIL YOU TAKE ACTION

If your ship doesn't come in, swim out to meet it.

JONATHAN WINTERS
Grammy Award–winning comedian, actor, writer, and artist

To demonstrate the power of taking action in my seminars, I hold up a $100 bill and ask, "Who wants this $100 bill?" Invariably, most of the people in the audience will raise their hands. Some will wave their hands vigorously back and forth; some will even shout out "I want it" or "I'll take it" or "Give it to me." But I just stand there calmly holding out the bill until they *get it*. Eventually, someone jumps out of her seat, rushes to the front of the room, and takes the bill from my hand.

After the person sits down—now $100 richer for her efforts—I ask the audience, "What did this person do that no one else in the room did? She got off her butt and took action. She did what was necessary to get the money. And that is exactly what you must do if you want to succeed in life. You must take action, and, in most cases, the sooner the better." I then ask, "How many of you thought about getting up and just coming and taking the money but stopped yourselves?"

I then ask them to remember what they told themselves that stopped them from getting up.

The usual answers are

"I didn't want to look like I wanted or needed it that badly."
"I wasn't sure if you would really give it to me."
"I was too far back in the room."
"Other people need it more than I do."
"I didn't want to look greedy."
"I was afraid I might be doing something wrong and then people would judge me or laugh at me."
"I was waiting for further instructions."

I then point out that whatever things they said to stop themselves are the same things that they say to stop themselves in the rest of their lives.

One of the universal truths in life is "How you do anything is how you do everything." If you are cautious here, you are probably cautious everywhere. If you hold yourself back for fear of looking foolish here, you probably hold yourself back for fear of looking foolish elsewhere. You have to identify those patterns and break through them. It's time to stop holding yourself back and just go for the gold.

RUBEN GONZALEZ GOES FOR OLYMPIC GOLD

Ever since third grade, Ruben Gonzalez had wanted to be an Olympic athlete. He respected the Olympians because they were an example of what he believed in—they are willing to commit to a goal, risk adversity in the pursuit of it, and fail and keep trying until they succeed.

But it was not until he was in college and saw Scott Hamilton compete in the 1984 Sarajevo Games that he actually made the decision to train for the Olympics. Ruben said to himself, *If that little guy can do it, I can do it too! I'm going to be in the next Olympics! It's a done deal. I just have to find a sport.*

After doing a little research on Olympic sports, Ruben decided he needed to pick a sport that would build on his strengths. He knew that he was a good athlete but not a great athlete. His strength was perseverance. He never quit anything. In fact, he had earned the nickname Bulldog in high school. He figured he had to find a sport so tough, a sport with so many broken bones, that there would be lots of quitters. That way maybe he could rise to the top on the attrition rate! He finally settled on the luge.

Next he wrote *Sports Illustrated* (this was before the Internet) and asked, "Where do you go to learn how to luge?" They wrote back, "Lake Placid, New York. That's where they had the Olympics in 1936 and 1980. That's where the track is." Ruben picked up the phone and called Lake Placid.

"I'm an athlete in Houston and I want to learn how to luge so I can be in the Olympics in four years. Will you help me?"

The guy who answered the phone asked, "How old are you?"

"Twenty-one years old."

"Twenty-one? You're way too old. You're ten years too late. We start them when they're ten years old. Forget it."

But Ruben couldn't forget it, and he started to tell the man his life story to buy some time until he thought of something. Along the way he happened to say that he was born in Argentina.

All of a sudden, the man on the other end of the phone got excited. "Argentina? Why didn't you say so? If you'll go for Argentina, we'll help you." It turns out the sport of luge was in danger of being dropped from the Olympics because there weren't enough countries competing on the

"I wondered why there was such a bad smell in here."

international level. "If you'll go for Argentina and somehow we can get you into the top fifty ranked lugers in the world in four years, which is what you'll need to make it into the Olympics, it would add one more country to the sport of luge, and that would make it a stronger sport. If you make it, you'd be helping the U.S. team." Then he added, "Before you come all the way to Lake Placid, you have to know two things. Number one: if you want to do it at your age and you want to do it in only four years, it will be brutal. Nine out of every ten guys quit. Number two: expect to break some bones."

Ruben thought, *Great! This works right into my plan. I'm not a quitter. The harder it is, the easier it is for me.*

A few days later Ruben Gonzalez was walking down Main Street in Lake Placid looking for the U.S. Olympic Training Center. A day later, he was in a beginner's class with 14 other aspiring Olympians. The first day was miserable, and he even thought of quitting, but with the help of a friend he recommitted to his Olympic dream and, though all 14 of the other aspirants eventually quit before the end of the first season, Ruben finished the summer training.

Four grueling years later, Ruben Gonzalez realized his dream when he walked into the opening ceremonies of the 1988 Calgary Winter Olympics. He returned again in Albertville in 1992 and Salt Lake City for the 2000 Winter Games. Ruben Gonzalez, because he took immediate and persistent action on his dream, will always be a "three-time Olympian."

SUCCESSFUL PEOPLE HAVE A BIAS FOR ACTION

Most successful people I know have a low tolerance for excessive planning and talking about it. They are antsy to get going. They want to get started. They want the games to begin. A good example of this is my friend Bob Kriegel's son Otis. When Otis came home for the summer with his new girlfriend after his freshman year in college, they both began looking for jobs. While Otis just picked up the phone and started calling around to see who might need someone, his girlfriend spent the first week writing and rewriting her résumé. By the end of the second day, Otis had landed a job. His girlfriend was still rewriting her résumé. Otis just got into action. He figured if someone asked for a résumé, he'd deal with it then.

Planning has its place, but it must be kept in perspective. Some people spend their whole lives waiting for the perfect time to do something. There's rarely a "perfect" time to do anything. What is important is to just get started. Get into the game. Get on the playing field. Once you do, you will start to get feedback that will help you make the corrections you need to make to be successful. Once you are in action, you will start learning at a much more rapid rate.

READY, FIRE, AIM!

Most people are familiar with the phrase "Ready, aim, fire!" The problem is that too many people spend their whole life aiming and never firing. They are always getting ready, getting it perfect. The quickest way to hit a target is to fire, see where the bullet landed, and then adjust your aim accordingly. If the hit was 2 inches above the target, lower your aim a little. Fire again. See where it is now. Keep firing and keep readjusting. Soon you are hitting the bull's-eye. The same is true for anything.

When we started marketing the first *Chicken Soup for the Soul*® book, it occurred to me that it would be a good idea to give away free excerpts from the book to small and local newspapers in exchange for them printing a box at the end of the story telling people that the story was excerpted from *Chicken Soup for the Soul*®, which was available at their local bookstore or by calling our 800 number. I had never done this before, so I wasn't sure if there was a correct way to submit a story to a newspaper or magazine, so I just sent off a story from the book entitled "Remember, You Are Raising Children, Not Flowers!" that I had written about my neighbor and his son, along with a cover letter to the editor of *L.A. Parent* magazine. The letter read:

September 13, 1993

Jack Bierman
L.A. Parent

Dear Jack,

  I would like to submit this article for publication in *L.A. Parent*. I have enclosed a brief bio. I would like you to print the little blurb I included on my new book *Chicken Soup for the Soul*® with my article. If you would like a copy of the book, I would be more than happy to send one to you!

  Thank you for your time.

Sincerely,
Jack Canfield

Encl: article "Remember, You Are Raising Children, Not Flowers!"

A few weeks later, I received the following letter back:

Dear Jack:

I was annoyed by your fax. How dare you tell me to include "the little blurb on your book." How could you assume I'd be interested in this little bit of unsolicited word processing. Then I read the article. Needless to say, I'll run your little blurb and then some!

I was moved by this exercise and am sure it will touch the hearts of our 200,000 plus readers from here to San Diego.

Has it ever appeared anywhere in my demographic? If so, where? I look forward to working with you on raising children, not flowers.

Best regards,

Jack Bierman, Editor in Chief

I had not known how to submit a proper query letter to an editor. There was an accepted format that I was unaware of. But I took action anyway. In a subsequent phone call, Jack Bierman generously taught me the correct way to submit an article to a magazine. He gave me feedback on how to do it better next time. Now I was in the game and I was learning from my experience. Ready, fire, aim!

Within a month I had submitted that same article to over 50 local and regional parenting magazines all across the United States. Thirty-five of them published it, introducing *Chicken Soup for the Soul®* to over 6 million parents.

QUIT WAITING

It's time to quit waiting for

Perfection
Inspiration
Permission
Reassurance
Someone to change
The right person to come along
The kids to leave home
A more favorable horoscope
The new administration to take over
An absence of risk
Someone to discover you
A clear set of instructions

More self-confidence
The pain to go away

Get on with it already!

SATISFACTION COMES FROM ENOUGH ACTION

Have you ever noticed that the last six letters in the word *satisfaction* are
a-c-t-i-o-n? In Latin, the word *satis* means "enough." What the ancient Romans
understood clearly was that enough action ultimately produces satisfaction.

DO IT NOW!

My mentor, W. Clement Stone, used to hand out lapel pins that said "Do it
now." When you have an inspired impulse to take action, do it now. Ray
Kroc, the founder of McDonald's, said, "There are three keys to success: 1.
Being at the right place at the right time. 2. Knowing you are there. 3. Taking
action."

On March 24, 1975, Chuck Wepner, a relatively unknown 30-to-1 un-
derdog, did what no one thought he could do—he went 15 rounds with the
world heavyweight champion Muhammad Ali. In the ninth round, he
reached Ali's chin with a right hand, knocking the champion to the ground—
shocking both Ali and the fans watching the fight. Wepner was only seconds
away from being the world's heavyweight champion. However, Ali went on
to win the 15-round bout and retain his title.

Over a thousand miles away, a struggling actor named Sylvester Stallone watched the fight on a newly purchased television set. Though Stallone
had contemplated the idea of writing a screenplay about a down-and-out
fighter getting a title shot before he saw the Ali–Wepner fight, he didn't
think it was plausible. But after seeing Wepner, whom most people didn't
know, fighting the most well-known fighter of all time, all he thought was
Get me a pencil. He began to write that night, and 3 days later, he had completed the script for *Rocky*, which went on to win three Oscars, including
one for best picture, thus launching Stallone's multimillion-dollar movie
career.

GIVE ME A BREAK!

A story is told of a man who goes to church and prays, "God, I need a break. I need to win the state lottery. I'm counting on you, God." Having not won the lottery, the man returns to church a week later and once again prays, "God, about that state lottery . . . I've been kind to my wife. I've given up drinking. I've been really good. Give me a break. Let me win the lottery."

A week later, still no richer, he returns to pray once again. "God, I don't seem to be getting through to you on this state lottery thing. I've been using positive self-talk, saying affirmations, and visualizing the money. Give me a break, God. Let me win the lottery."

Suddenly the heavens open up, white light and heavenly music flood into the church, and a deep voice says, "My son, give me a break! Buy a lottery ticket!"

FAIL FORWARD

No man ever became great or good except
through many and great mistakes.

WILLIAM E. GLADSTONE
Former prime minister of Great Britain

Many people fail to take action because they're afraid to fail. Successful people, on the other hand, realize that failure is an important part of the learning process. They know that failure is just a way we learn by trial and error. Not only do we need to stop being so afraid of failure but we also need to be willing to fail—even eager to fail. I call this kind of instructive failure "failing forward." Simply get started, make mistakes, listen to the feedback, correct, and keep moving forward toward the goal. Every experience will yield up more useful information that you can apply the next time.

This principle is perhaps demonstrated most compellingly in the area of start-up businesses. For instance, venture capitalists know that most businesses fail. But in the venture capital industry, a new statistic is emerging. If the founding entrepreneur is 55 years or older, the business has a 73% better chance of survival. These older entrepreneurs have already learned from their mistakes. They're simply a better risk because through a lifetime of learning from their failures, they have developed a knowledge base, a skill set, and a self-confidence that better enables them to move through the obstacles to success.

You can never learn less; you can only learn more. The reason I know
so much is because I have made so many mistakes.

BUCKMINSTER FULLER
Mathematician and philosopher who never graduated from college
but received 46 honorary doctorates

One of my favorite stories is about a famous research scientist who had made several very important medical breakthroughs. He was being interviewed by a newspaper reporter, who asked him why he thought he was able to achieve so much more than the average person. In other words, what set him so far apart from others?

He responded that it all came from a lesson his mother had taught him when he was 2 years old. He'd been trying to take a bottle of milk out of the refrigerator, when he lost his grip and spilled the entire contents on the kitchen floor. His mother, instead of scolding him, said, "What a wonderful mess you've made! I've rarely seen such a huge puddle of milk. Well, the damage is already done. Would you like to get down and play in the milk before we clean it up?"

Indeed, he did. And, after a few minutes, his mother continued, "You know, whenever you make a mess like this, eventually you have to clean it up. So, how would you like to do that? We could use a towel, sponge, or mop. Which do you prefer?"

After they were finished cleaning up the milk, she said, "What we have

Frank and Ernest

©1990 Thaves. Reprinted with permission. Newspaper dist. by NEA, Inc.

here is a failed experiment in how to carry a big bottle of milk with two tiny hands. Let's go out in the backyard, fill the bottle with water, and see if you can discover a way to carry it without dropping it." And they did.

What a wonderful lesson!

The scientist then remarked that it was at that moment that he knew he didn't have to be afraid to make mistakes. Instead, he learned that *mistakes are just opportunities for learning something new*—which, after all, is what scientific experiments are all about.

That bottle of spilled milk led to a lifetime of learning experiences— experiences that were the building blocks of a lifetime of world-renowned successes and medical breakthroughs!

14

JUST LEAN INTO IT

You can't cross a sea by merely staring into the water.

RABINDRANATH TAGORE
1913 Nobel laureate for literature

Oftentimes, success happens when you just lean into it—when you make yourself open to opportunities and are willing to do what it takes to pursue it further—without a contract, without a promise of success, without any expectation whatsoever. You just start. You lean into it. You see what it feels like. And you find out if you want to keep going—instead of sitting on the sidelines deliberating, reflecting, and contemplating.

LEANING INTO IT CREATES MOMENTUM

One of the most extraordinary benefits of just leaning into it is that you begin creating momentum—that unseen energy force that brings more opportunity, more resources, and more people who can help you into your life at seemingly just the right time for you to benefit the most from them.

Many of the best-known acting careers, entrepreneurial pursuits, philanthropic projects, and other "overnight successes" happened because someone responded favorably to the question "Have you ever considered . . . ?" or "Could I convince you to . . . ?" or "Would you be willing to take a look at . . . ?" They leaned into it.

BE WILLING TO START WITHOUT SEEING
THE WHOLE PATH

Take the first step in faith. You don't have to see the whole staircase.
Just take the first step.

MARTIN LUTHER KING JR.
Legendary civil rights leader

Of course, just leaning into a project or opportunity also means you must be willing to start without necessarily seeing the entire pathway from the beginning. You must be willing to lean into it and see how it unfolds.

Often we have a dream and because we can't see how we're going to achieve it, we are afraid to start, afraid to commit ourselves because the path is unclear and the outcome is uncertain. But leaning into it requires that you be willing to explore—to enter unknown waters, trusting that a port will appear.

Simply start, then keep taking what feel like logical next steps, and the journey will ultimately take you to where you want to go—*or even someplace better.*

SOMETIMES, YOU DON'T EVEN HAVE TO
HAVE A CLEAR DREAM

From as early as she could remember, Jana Stanfield wanted to be a singer. She didn't know where her dream would eventually lead her, but she knew she had to find out. She leaned into it and took some singing lessons—then eventually got a job singing weekends at the local country club. She leaned into it a little more, and at 26 years old, she packed her bags for Nashville, Tennessee, to pursue her dream of becoming a songwriter and recording artist.

Three long years she lived and worked in Nashville, seeing hundreds of more brilliant, talented, and deserving performers than there were record deals to be had. Jana began to see the music industry as a room full of slot machines that paid out just enough to keep you playing. A producer loves your work, an artist considers your song for her next album, and maybe a record company tells you you're great—but rarely do the slot machines pay off with the big jackpot, the coveted recording contract.

After several years of working at a record promotion company to learn the business "from the inside out," Jana had to face facts: There were no guarantees—she could play the slots forever and grow old in Nashville.

Finally, she admitted to herself that continuing to try to get a record deal was like pounding her head against a wall. She didn't realize at the time that often when you lean into it, roadblocks are put in your path to force you onto a different path—a path that may be truer to your real purpose.

For every failure, there's an alternative course of action. You just have to find it. When you come to a roadblock, take a detour.

MARY KAY ASH
Founder of Mary Kay Cosmetics

LOOKING FOR HER UNDERLYING MOTIVATION

Jana had learned what many achievers have: that even when you can't move forward, you can turn right or you can turn left, but you have to keep moving. She discovered through some personal development courses that sometimes, in the rush to fulfill our dreams, we get caught up in what we think is the only form that will satisfy that dream—in Jana's case, a recording contract.

But as Jana would soon learn, there are many ways to accomplish your goal if you know what you're really pursuing. Because underneath her desire to land a record deal was a deeper motivating need, the real motivation for her dream—to use her music to uplift, inspire, and offer hope to people.

I want to combine music, comedy, storytelling, and motivation with what I'm here for, she wrote in her journal. *I am an artist and my art is unfolding before me. The roadblock that blocked my path has been lifted.*

Emboldened by this new insight, Jana began to play anywhere people would let her. "Where two or more are gathered, I will bring my guitar" became her motto. She played in living rooms, driveways, schools, churches, anywhere she could.

"I'M NOT LOST, I'M JUST EXPLORING"

But Jana was still at a loss to figure out how to combine her talents in a way that would be helpful to people and pay her a modest income. There was no one out there already doing what she wanted to do—combining music, comedy, storytelling, and motivation. There was no career path already laid out to follow, no footsteps to walk in. She was charting new territory. She didn't know where she was going or what form it would ultimately take, but she kept leaning into it.

KEEP LEANING AND THE PATH WILL APPEAR

Jana began to work odd jobs—always leaning into it—trying to figure out how to turn her passion for her art and her desire to help people into something she could make a living from. *I'm willing to use my gifts to make this world a better place,* she wrote in her journal. *I don't know exactly how to use my gifts to do this, but I have let God know that I am ready.*

Again she leaned into it. Jana called churches, saying, "If you would let me come and sing two songs in your service, it will give you a chance to get to know me and how I might be helpful. Then in a few months, maybe you'd like to have me come back and do a concert in the afternoon."

THE TURNING POINT

After just two or three songs, church members would approach her and ask if she had her songs on tape. There was one song, "If I Had Only Known," that people requested more than any other. They'd say, "I noticed a lot of people crying when you played that song. I've had a loss that's so painful that I can't cry here at church because I don't know if I can put myself back together once I start. Would you make me a copy of this song so I can have it when I'm alone and really feel the feelings you're bringing to me?"

Jana spent a lot of time making cassettes and mailing them to people, but all the while, her friends kept telling her to make an album. "You've got all these demos of songs you recorded when you were trying to get a record deal," they said. "Just take your demos and make an album."

Jana thought, *Oh, I couldn't do that. It wouldn't be a real album with a real record company. It wouldn't really count. It would just show what a failure I've been.* But her friends kept after her, and eventually Jana leaned into it one more time.

She paid an engineer $100 to put together 10 of her songs, which she playfully referred to as "a compilation of my top 10 most rejected songs." She made the covers at Kinko's, and reproduced 100 cassettes, which she now laughingly recalls she thought would be "a lifetime supply." As she traveled from living room to living room and tiny church to tiny church, she set out her cassettes on a card table and sold them after her performance.

Then came the turning point.

"My husband went with me to a church in Memphis," Jana recalls. "They didn't feel comfortable having a card table with my cassettes inside the church, so they put my card table out on their new parking lot. It had just been repaved—and in 95-degree weather, the asphalt was hot and black and gooey. After the parking lot finally emptied, we got in the car and turned on the air-conditioning and began counting what we'd earned."

To Jana's amazement, she had sold $300 worth of cassettes—$50 more than she earned all week working a freelance TV job she had taken to help make ends meet. Holding that $300 in her hand made Jana realize, for the first time, that she *could* support herself doing what she loved to do.

Today, Jana's company Keynote Concerts[16] produces more than 50 motivational concerts a year for groups all over the world. She started her own recording company, Relatively Famous Records, which produced eight of Jana's CDs and has sold over 100,000 copies. Jana's songs have been recorded by Reba McEntire, Andy Williams, Suzy Bogguss, John Schneider, and Megon McDonough. She's opened for Kenny Loggins and toured with author Melody Beatty. Her "heavy mental" music has been featured on *Oprah, 20/20, Entertainment Tonight,* and radio stations coast to coast, as well as in the movie *8 Seconds.*

Jana Stanfield achieved her dream of becoming a songwriter and recording star—all because she leaned into it and trusted the path that appeared. You, too, can get from where you are to where you want to be if you'll just trust that if you lean into it, the path will appear. Sometimes it will be like driving through the fog, where you can only see the road 10 yards ahead of you. But if you keep moving forward, more of the road will be revealed, and eventually, you will arrive at the goal.

Pick an area of your life—career, financial, relationship, health and fitness, recreation, hobby, or contribution—that you would like to explore and just lean into it.

---

16. You can learn more about Jana's work and her CDs at www.janastanfield.com.

15

FEEL THE FEAR AND
DO IT ANYWAY

*We come this way but once. We can either tiptoe through life and
hope that we get to death without being too badly bruised
or we can live a full, complete life achieving our goals and
realizing our wildest dreams.*

BOB PROCTOR
Self-made millionaire, radio and TV personality, and success trainer

*I have insecurities. But whatever I'm insecure about,
I don't dissect it, but I'll go after it and say, "What am I afraid of?"
I bet the average successful person can tell you
they've failed so much more than they've had success.
I've had far more failures than I've had successes.
With every commercial I've gotten, there were 200 I didn't get.
You have to go after what you're afraid of.*

KEVIN SORBO
Actor who starred in the television series *Hercules: The Legendary Journeys*

As you move forward on your journey from where you are to where you want
to be, you are going to have to confront your fears. Fear is natural. Whenever
you start a new project, take on a new venture, or put yourself out there, there
is usually fear. Unfortunately, most people let fear stop them from taking the
necessary steps to achieve their dreams. Successful people, on the other hand,
feel the fear along with the rest of us but don't let it keep them from doing
anything they want to do—*or have to do*. They understand that fear is something to be acknowledged, experienced, and taken along for the ride. They
have learned, as author Susan Jeffers suggests, to feel the fear and do it anyway.

WHY ARE WE SO FEARFUL?

Millions of years ago, fear was our body's way of signaling us that we were out of our comfort zone. It alerted us to possible danger, and gave us the burst of adrenaline we needed to run away. Unfortunately, though this response was useful in the days when saber-toothed tigers were chasing us, today most of our threats are not all that life-threatening.

Today, fear is more of a signal that we must stay alert and cautious. We can feel fear, but we can still move forward anyway. Think of your fear as a 2-year-old child who doesn't want to go grocery shopping with you. You wouldn't let a 2-year-old's mentality run your life. Because you must buy groceries, you'll just have to take the 2-year-old along with you. Fear is no different. In other words, acknowledge that fear exists but don't let it keep you from doing important tasks.

YOU HAVE TO BE WILLING TO FEEL THE FEAR

Some people will do anything to avoid the uncomfortable feeling of fear. If you are one of those people, you run an even bigger risk of never getting what you want in life. Most of the good stuff requires taking a risk. And the nature of a risk is that it doesn't always work out. People do lose their investments, people do forget their lines, people do fall off mountains, people do die in accidents. But as the old adage so wisely tells us, "Nothing ventured, nothing gained."

When I interviewed Jeff Arch, who wrote the screenplay for the movie *Sleepless in Seattle*, he told me:

> I am about to launch the biggest gamble of my life—writing and directing a two-million-dollar comedy, when I have never directed before, and using my own money plus raising other money to fund it—and I really need to succeed at this. Really, it's an all-or-nothing situation. And the thing that I'm experiencing right now, which I think is really important and that a lot of people who write about success leave out, is you've got to be willing to be terrified. Because I am terrified about what I'm about to do. But it's not immobilizing. It's a good terrified; it's a terrified that keeps you on your toes.
>
> I know I have to do this because I had a very clear vision, and I am willing to stand alone without agreement from the industry, which I learned you have to do from when I was pitching *Sleepless in Seattle*. Believe me, when you start pitching an idea about a love story where the lead characters don't meet, you are alone. Everybody told me, "You're out of your freaking

mind." And one thing I discovered is when everyone says you're out of your mind, you just might be on to something. So, I had these reference points from my past experience. I was alone back then. And I was right. I've learned you have to believe in your dream. Because even if everyone is telling you you're wrong, that still might not mean anything—you just might be right.

You reach a point where you say, "This is it. I'm throwing everything into this. And it's got to succeed." It's like the Spanish conquistador Hernando Cortez in 1519. To prevent any thought of retreating from his mission, after he landed in Mexico, he burned all of his ships. Well, I've rented new ships just for the sake of burning them. I took out loans on ships that weren't even mine. I'm throwing money, credibility—every single thing there is—into my new project. And it's either going to be a home run or a strikeout—not a single or a double.

I know there's a terror in doing this, but there's also this confidence. It isn't going to kill me. It might make me broke, it might leave me in debt, it might make me lose credibility, and it might make the journey back a whole lot harder. But unlike Cortez, I'm not in a business where they kill you if you goof up. I think one of the secrets to my success is that I'm willing to be terrified, and I think a lot of people are not willing to be scared to death. And that's why they don't achieve the big dream.

FANTASIZED EXPERIENCES APPEARING REAL

Another important aspect to remember about fear is that, as humans, we've also evolved to the stage where almost all of our fears are now self-created. We frighten ourselves by fantasizing negative outcomes to any activity we might pursue or experience. Luckily, because we are the ones doing the fantasizing, we are also the ones who can stop the fear and bring ourselves into a state of clarity and peace by facing the actual facts, rather than giving in to our imaginations. We can choose to be sensible. Psychologists like to say that *fear* means

Fantasized
Experiences
Appearing
Real

To help you better understand how we actually bring unfounded fear into our lives, make a list of the things you are afraid to *do*. This is not a list of things you are afraid *of*, such as being afraid *of* spiders, but things you're afraid to *do*, such as being afraid to pick up a spider. For example, *I am afraid to*

- Ask my boss for a raise
- Ask Sally out for a date
- Go skydiving
- Leave my kids home alone with a sitter
- Leave this job that I hate
- Take 2 weeks away from the office
- Ask my friends to look at my new business opportunity
- Delegate any part of my job to others

Now go back and restate each fear using the following format:

I want to _____, and I scare myself by imagining _____.

The key words are *I scare myself by imagining*. All fear is self-created by imagining some negative outcome in the future. Using some of the same fears listed above, the new format would look like this:

- I want to ask my boss for a raise, and I scare myself by imagining he would say no and be angry with me for asking.
- I want to ask Sally out for a date, and I scare myself by imagining that she would say no and I would feel embarrassed.
- I want to go skydiving, and I scare myself by imagining that my parachute wouldn't open and I would be killed.
- I want to leave my kids home with a sitter, and I scare myself by imagining that something terrible would happen to them.
- I want to leave this job I hate to pursue my dream, and I scare myself by imagining I would go bankrupt and lose my house.
- I want to ask my friends to look at my new business opportunity, and I scare myself by imagining they will think I am only interested in making money off of them.

Can you see that you are the one creating the fear?

HOW TO GET RID OF FEAR

*I have lived a long life and had many troubles,
most of which never happened.*

MARK TWAIN
Celebrated American author and humorist

One way to actually *disappear* your fear is to ask yourself what you're imagining that is scary to you, and then replace that image with its positive opposite.

When I was flying to Orlando recently to give a talk, I noticed the woman next to me was gripping the arms of her seat so tightly her knuckles were turning white. I introduced myself, told her I was a trainer, and said I couldn't help but notice her hands. I asked her, "Are you afraid?"

"Yes."

"Would you be willing to close your eyes and tell me what thoughts or images you are experiencing in your head?"

After she closed her eyes, she replied, "I just keep imagining the plane not getting off the runway and crashing."

"I see. Tell me, what are you headed to Orlando for?"

"I'm going there to spend four days with my grandchildren at Disney World."

"Great. What's your favorite ride at Disney World?"

"It's a Small World."

"Wonderful. Can you imagine being at Disney World in one of the gondolas with your grandchildren in the It's a Small World attraction?"

"Yes."

"Can you see the smiles and the looks of wonder on your grandchildren's faces as they watch all the little puppets and figures from the different countries bobbing up and down and spinning around?"

"Uh-huh."

At that point I started to sing, "It's a small world after all; it's a small world after all . . ."

Her face relaxed, her breathing deepened, and her hands released their grip on the arms of the seat.

In her mind, she was already at Disney World. She had replaced the catastrophic picture of the plane crashing with a positive image of her desired outcome, and instantly her fear disappeared.[17]

You can use this same technique to disappear any fear that you might ever experience.

REPLACE THE PHYSICAL SENSATIONS FEAR BRINGS

Another technique that works for relieving fear is to focus on the *physical sensations* you're currently feeling—sensations you're probably just identifying as fear. Next, focus on those feelings you would *like* to be experiencing instead—courage, self-confidence, calm, joy.

Fix these two different impressions firmly in your mind's eye, then slowly shuttle back and forth between the two, spending about 15 seconds in each one. After a minute or two, the fear will dissipate and you will find yourself in a neutral, centered place.

REMEMBER WHEN YOU TRIUMPHED
IN THE FACE OF FEAR

Did you ever learn to dive off a diving board? If so, you probably remember the first time you walked to the edge of the board and looked down. The water looked a lot deeper than it really was. And considering the height of the board and the height of your eyes above the board, it probably looked like a *very* long way down.

You were scared. But did you look at your mom or dad or the diving instructor and say, "You know, I'm just too afraid to do this right now. I think I'll go do some therapy on this, and if I can get rid of my fear, I'll come back and try again . . ."?

No! You didn't say that.

You felt the fear, somehow mustered up courage from somewhere, and jumped into the water. You felt the fear and did it anyway.

When you surfaced, you probably swam like crazy to the side of the pool and took a few well-earned deep breaths. Somewhere, there was a little rush of adrenaline, the thrill of having survived a risk, plus the thrill of jumping through the air into the water. After a minute, you probably did it again, and

---

17. Ron Nielsen, Tim Piering, and I have used this same technique to create a new program to help fearful flyers overcome their fear of flying. For more information or to purchase a copy of *Chicken Soup for the Soul's Fearless FlightKit*™ for yourself or a friend, go online to www.fearless-flight.com.

then again and again—enough to where it got to be really fun. Pretty soon, all of the fear was gone and you were doing cannonballs to splash your friends and maybe even learning how to do a backflip.

If you can remember that experience or the first time you drove a car or the first time you kissed someone on a date, you've got the model for everything that happens in life. New experiences will always feel a little scary. They're supposed to. That's the way it works. But every time you face a fear and do it anyway, you build up that much more confidence in your abilities.

SCALE DOWN THE RISK

Anthony Robbins says, "If you can't, you must, and if you must, you can." I agree. It is those very things that we are most afraid to do that provide the greatest liberation and growth for us.

If a fear is so big that it paralyzes you, scale down the amount of risk. Take on smaller challenges and work your way up. If you're starting your first job in sales, call on prospects or customers you think will be the easiest to sell to first. If you're asking for money for your business, practice on those lending sources whom you wouldn't want to get a loan from anyway. If you're anxious about taking on new responsibilities at work, start by asking to do parts of a project you're interested in. If you're learning a new sport, start at lower levels of skill. Master those skills you need to learn, move through your fears, and then take on bigger challenges.

WHEN YOUR FEAR IS REALLY A PHOBIA

Some fears are so strong that they can actually immobilize you. If you have a full-blown phobia, such as fear of flying or fear of being in an elevator, it can seriously inhibit your ability to be successful. Fortunately there is a simple solution for most phobias. The Five-Minute Phobia Cure, developed by Dr. Roger Callahan, is easy to learn and can be self-administered as well as facilitated by a professional.

I learned about this magical technique from Dr. Callahan's book and video and have used it successfully in my seminars for more than 15 years. The process uses a simple but precise pattern of tapping on various points of the body while you simultaneously imagine the object or experience that stimulates your phobic reaction. It acts in much the same way as a virus in a computer program by permanently interrupting the "program" or sequence of events that occur in the brain between the initial sighting of the thing you are afraid of (such as seeing a snake or stepping into an airplane) and the physical response (such as sweating, shaking, shallow breathing, or weak knees) you experience.

When I was leading a seminar for real estate agents, a woman revealed that she had a phobia about walking up stairs. In fact, she had experienced it that very morning, when in response to her request for directions to the seminar, the bellman had pointed to a huge staircase leading to the grand ballroom. Fortunately, there was also an elevator, so she made it to the seminar. If there hadn't been, she would have turned around and driven home. She admitted that she had never been on the second floor of any home she had ever sold. She would pretend she had already been up there, tell the prospective buyers what they would find on the second floor, on the basis of her reading of the listing sheet, and then let them explore it on their own.

I did the Five-Minute Phobia Cure with her and then took all 100 people out to the same hotel stairway that had petrified her earlier in the day. With no hesitation, heavy breathing, or drama, she walked up and down the stairs twice. It is that simple.[18]

TAKE A LEAP!

Come to the edge, He said.
They said: We are afraid.
Come to the edge, He said.
They came. He pushed them,
And they flew . . .

GUILLAUME APOLLINAIRE
Avant-garde French poet

All the successful people I know have been willing to take a chance—a leap of faith—even though they were afraid. Sometimes they were terrified, but they knew if they didn't act, the opportunity would pass them by. They trusted their intuition and they simply went for it.

---

18. If you have a phobia that is holding you back, visit Roger Callahan's Web site at www.tftrx.com or call 800-359-2873 and order the *Five-Minute Phobia Cure* videotape or schedule a phone session with Dr. Callahan. You can also go to any Internet search engine, type in "five-minute phobia cure" or "Thought Field Therapy," and look for a practitioner near you.

Progress always involves risk; you can't steal second base
and keep your foot on first.

FREDERICK WILCOX

Mike Kelley lives in paradise and owns several companies under the umbrella of Beach Activities of Maui. With only a year of college under his belt (he never did return to get his degree), Mike left Las Vegas at age 19 for the islands of Hawaii and ended up selling suntan lotion by the pool at a hotel in Maui. From these humble beginnings, Mike went on to create a company with 175 employees and over $5 million in annual revenues that provides recreational experiences (catamaran and scuba diving excursions) for tourists and concierge services and business centers for many of the island's hotels.

Mike credits much of his success to always being willing to take a leap when needed. When Beach Activities of Maui was attempting to expand its business, there was an important hotel whose business he wanted, but a competitor had held the contract for over 15 years. To maintain a competitive edge, Mike always reads the trade journals and keeps an ear open to what is happening in his business. One day he read that this hotel was changing general managers, and the new general manager who would be coming in lived in Copper Mountain, Colorado. This got Mike to thinking: Because it is so hard to get through all of the gatekeepers to secure a meeting with a general manager, maybe he should try to contact him before he actually moved to Hawaii. Mike wrestled with what would be the best way to contact him. Should he write a letter? Should he call him on the phone? As he pondered these options, his friend Doug suggested, "Why don't you just hop on a plane and go see him?"

Always one to take action and take it now, Mike quickly put together a pro forma and a proposal and hopped on a plane the next night. After flying all night, he arrived in Colorado, rented a car and drove the 2 hours out to Copper Mountain, and showed up unannounced at the new general manager's office. He explained who he was, congratulated him on his new promotion, told him that he looked forward to having him in Maui, and asked for a few moments to tell him about his company and what it could do for his hotel.

Mike didn't get the contract during that first meeting, but the fact that a young kid was so confident in himself and his services that he would take a leap of faith to jump on a plane and fly all the way to Denver and drive out into the middle of Colorado on the off chance that he would be able to get together with him left such a huge impression on the general manager that when he did finally get to Hawaii, Mike secured the contract, which, over the ensuing 15 years, has been worth hundreds of thousands of dollars to Mike's bottom line.

TAKING A LEAP CAN TRANSFORM YOUR LIFE

Authority is 20% given and 80% taken . . . so take it!

PETER UEBERROTH
Organizer of the 1984 Summer Olympics and commissioner of
Major League Baseball, 1984–1988

Multimillionaire Dr. John Demartini is a resounding success by anyone's standards. He's married to a beautiful and brilliant woman—Athena Star-woman, the world-famous astrologer who consults and writes for 24 well-known magazines, including *Vogue*. Together, they own several homes in Australia. And they spend over 60 days a year together circumnavigating the globe in their $3 million luxury apartment onboard the $550 million ocean liner *World of ResidenSea*—a residence they purchased after selling their Trump Tower apartment in New York City.

The author of 54 training programs and 13 books, John spends the year traveling the world speaking and conducting his courses on financial success and life mastery.

But John didn't start out rich and successful. At age 7, he was found to have a learning disability and was told that he would never read, write, or communicate normally. At 14, he dropped out of school, left his Texas home, and headed for the California coast. By 17, he had ended up in Hawaii, surfing the waves of Oahu's famed North Shore, where he almost died from strychnine poisoning. His road to recovery led him to Dr. Paul Bragg, a 93-year-old man who changed John's life by giving him one simple affirmation to repeat: "I am a genius and I apply my wisdom."

Inspired by Dr. Bragg, John went to college, earned his bachelor's degree from the University of Houston and later his doctoral degree from the Texas College of Chiropractic.

When he opened his first chiropractic office in Houston, John started with just 970 square feet of space. Within 9 months, he'd more than doubled that and was offering free classes on healthy living. When attendance grew, John was ready to expand again. It was then he took a leap that changed his career forever.

"It was Monday," John said. "The shoe store next door had vacated over the weekend." *What a perfect lecture hall,* John thought as he quickly phoned the leasing company.

When no one called him back, John concluded they weren't going to rent the space soon, so he took a leap.

"I called a locksmith to come out and open up the place," John said. "I thought the worst thing they would do was charge me rent."

He quickly transformed the space into a lecture hall and within days was holding free talks there on a nightly basis. Because the space was located right next to a movie theater, he added a loudspeaker so moviegoers could hear his lectures as they walked to their cars. Hundreds began attending classes and eventually became patients.

John's practice grew rapidly. Yet nearly 6 months went by before the property manager came to investigate.

"You've got a lot of courage," the manager said. "You remind me of me." In fact, he was so impressed with John's daring, he even gave John 6 months' free rent! "Anybody that has the courage to do what you did deserves it," he told him. The manager later invited John down to his office, where he offered him a quarter of a million dollars a year to come work for him. John turned it down because he had other plans, but it was a huge validation of his courage to act.

Taking a leap helped John build a thriving practice, which he later sold to begin consulting full time with other chiropractors.

"Taking that leap opened up a doorway for me," John said. "If I'd held back . . . if I had been cautious . . . I wouldn't have made the breakthrough that gave me the life I live today."

OH, WHAT THE HECK—JUST GO FOR IT!

Do you want to be safe and good,
or do you want to take a chance and be great?

JIMMY JOHNSON
Coach who led the Dallas Cowboys football team to two consecutive
Super Bowl championships in 1992 and 1993

When Richard Paul Evans wrote his first book, *The Christmas Box*, it was simply a gift of love to his two young daughters. Later, he made photocopies for family and friends, and word spread quickly about this heartwarming tale. Spurred on by this positive reaction, Rick sought a publisher for the book. When there were no takers, Rick decided to publish it himself.

To promote the book, he took a booth at a regional American Book-

sellers Association conference, where, among other activities, celebrity authors were signing books at one end of the exhibit hall. Rick noticed these
celebrity authors were the only ones getting attention from the press. He also
noticed that when the next group of celebrities arrived for their scheduled
time, one author had failed to arrive.

With his fear being crowded out by his courage and commitment to his
dream, Rick decided to take a leap. He picked up two boxes of books, walked
toward the empty chair, sat down, and began to sign.

Seeing him at the table, a woman from the show approached him to ask him
to leave. Undaunted, Evans looked up and before she could speak said, "Sorry
I'm late." The stunned woman just looked at him and asked, "Can I get you
something to drink?" The next year, Evans was the premier author at the show
as his book climbed to number 1 on the *New York Times* Best-Seller List. Since
then, *The Christmas Box* has sold more than 8 million copies in 18 languages and
has been made into an Emmy Award–winning CBS television movie. The
book, which had been previously rejected by several major publishing houses,
was eventually purchased by Simon & Schuster for a record $4.2 million.

Living at risk is jumping off the cliff and
building your wings on the way down.

RAY BRADBURY
Author of more than 500 literary works

BE WILLING TO PUT IT ALL ON THE LINE
FOR YOUR DREAM

Only those who dare to fail greatly can ever achieve greatly.

ROBERT F. KENNEDY
Former attorney general and U.S. senator

In January of 1981, real estate investor Robert Allen took a challenge—putting
it all on the line—that would make or break his new career as an author and
seminar leader. He was looking for ways to promote his new book *Nothing
Down: How to Buy Real Estate with Little or No Money Down*. Frustrated with the
ad his publisher's public relations department had created, Bob found himself
spouting off the top of his head what he felt needed to be said in the ad. "We
need to demonstrate that someone can buy property with nothing down."

His publisher responded, "What do you mean?"

Bob said, "I don't know. You could take me to a city, take away my wallet and give me a hundred bucks, and I'd buy a property."

"How long would it take you?"

"I don't know, maybe a week, maybe three or four days—seventy-two hours."

"Can you do that?"

Bob found himself looking at the abyss, realizing he'd never done that before and not knowing for sure if he could do it now. His head was saying no and his heart was saying yes.

Bob went with his heart and said, "Yeah, I probably can do that."

"Well, if you can do that, that's the title of the ad we're going to run: 'So then he said he'd take away my wallet, give me a hundred-dollar bill, and send me out to buy a piece of real estate using none of my own money.'"

Bob said, "Okay, let it rip," and they ran the ad, which was very successful. Within a few months after being released, the book was number one on the *Time* magazine best seller list and it ended up being on the *New York Times* Best-Seller List for 46 weeks.

Later that year Bob got a call from a reporter at the *Los Angeles Times* who said, "We don't think you can do what you say you can do."

Bob replied, "Well, I'd be glad to be challenged," and then quipped, "How about a date sometime in 2050?" But the *Times* was serious—serious about taking Bob down. The reporter said, "I am going to take you down. We don't like your ad. We think you're a fraud, and you're going down." Scared, but determined he had to take the challenge, Bob set it up for 4 weeks later.

On January 12, 1981, the reporter from the *Times* met him at the Marriott Hotel just east of Los Angeles International Airport. Bob hadn't slept much the night before. In fact, he hadn't slept much for the entire month before. He lay awake at night wondering if he could really pull it off in such a short time. Taking the challenge had felt like the right thing to do, but he still didn't know if he could do it.

Together they boarded a plane and flew to San Francisco, and Bob hit the ground running. He immediately went to a real estate office and started writing no-money-down offers, and they promptly escorted them out of the office, which Bob recalls "was not a good way to start."

Bob started thinking, *Uh-oh, I'm in deep trouble now. I'm going to lose it all. It's gone. I'm not going to be able to pull this off. What was I thinking?* Was he scared? "Oh yeah, I was terrified." But he just made call after call after call and finally, toward the end of the first day, he started running into some success and found a property that somebody was willing to sell him. By the next morning, he had a signed offer.

So it had been just a little over 24 hours and he had bought his first property. Then Bob said, "We're not done yet. You gave me 72 hours. I've scheduled my life for this for the next 3 days. Let's see how many we can do." At this point, the reporter became his cheerleader. After all, the reporter had already lost the challenge, and the bigger he lost, the better the story.

Before, he was saying, "I'm going to take you down." Now it was, "Hey, Bob, go for it, boy. If you're going to beat me, beat me bad." And Bob did. He bought seven properties worth $700,000 in 57 hours and gave the reporter $20 back out of the $100 he had started with.

The subsequent article, which was syndicated by the *Los Angeles Times* and picked up by dozens of newspapers across the country, launched Bob's career. He had risked it all, and he had won big time! His book *Nothing Down* went on to sell over a million copies and became the eleventh best-selling hardcover book of the 1980s.[19]

THE CHALLENGE

If you want to achieve a high goal,
you're going to have to take some chances.

ALBERTO SALAZAR
Winner of three consecutive New York City Marathons in 1980,
1981, and 1982, and now a spokesperson for Nike

Robert Allen's life seems to have been built on leaping into the void to prove that his methods can and do work—for everyone, no matter their status—to produce wealth and abundance in their lives. Even after his stunning success of buying seven houses in 72 hours with no money down in San Francisco, the press still hounded him with, "Well, sure, *you* can do it, but the average person couldn't do it." Bob's message was that *anybody* could buy property with no money down, but the press kept countering with "Well, you're not just anybody."

Bob told me, "I became so infuriated with the press that I said, 'You can send me to any unemployment line'—and I remember stuff just coming out of my mouth, not knowing where it was coming from—'let me select someone who's broke, out of work, and discouraged, and in two days time I'll teach him the secrets of wealth. And in ninety days he'll be back on his feet with five

---

19. If you're interested in real estate investing, you can check out Robert's latest book, *Nothing Down for the 2000s: Dynamic New Wealth Strategies in Real Estate* (New York: Simon & Schuster, 2004).

thousand dollars cash in the bank, and he'll never set foot in an unemployment line again.'"

Bob went to St. Louis, asked the ex-mayor to oversee the project, went to the unemployment office, and handed out 1,200 flyers offering to teach people how to become financially independent. Expecting the room to be filled to the rafters, he had the room set up for 300 chairs, but only 50 people showed up—and half those people left at the first break as soon as they heard how much work was going to be involved. After an extensive interview process, only three couples remained. He worked with those three couples. Though all of them did deals in the first 90 days, technically only one of them made the $5,000 cash in the 3-month period. All of them did more deals that year and changed their lives in a variety of different ways. The couple that made the $5,000 cash in the first 90 days also went on to make over $100,000 in the next 12 months. Once again, by taking a huge risk, by leaping into the void, Bob had proved his point and finally made the press back off.

He went on to write a book about the experience called *The Challenge*.[20] While it was his least successful book, selling only 65,000 copies, it became his most profitable because it was the first book he ever put his name, address, and phone numbers in. Over 4,000 of the people who read that book called Bob's office and eventually paid $5,000 to attend Bob's ongoing training program. That's $20 million—not bad for being willing to pay the price of putting his butt on the line one more time.

The secret to my success is that I bit off more than I could chew
and chewed as fast as I could.

PAUL HOGAN
Actor who portrayed Crocodile Dundee

HIGH INTENTION . . . LOW ATTACHMENT

If you want to remain calm and peaceful as you go through life, you have to have high intention and low attachment. You do everything you can to create your desired outcomes, and then you let it go. Sometimes you don't get the intended result by the date that you want. That is life. You just keep moving in the direction of your goal until you get there. Sometimes the universe has other plans, and often they are better than the ones you had in mind. That is why I recommend adding the phrase "this or something better" to the end of your affirmations.

---

20. *The Challenge*, by Robert Allen (New York: Simon & Schuster, 1987).

When I was vacationing with my family on a cruise in Tahiti two summers ago, my son Christopher and my stepson Travis, both 12 at the time, and I set out on a guided bicycle tour around the island of Bora-Bora with some other members from our cruise ship. My intention for the day was a bonding experience with my two sons. The wind was blowing really hard that day and the trip was a difficult one. At one point, Stevie Eller, who was struggling along with her 11-year-old grandson, took a nasty fall and badly cut her leg. Because there were only a few others in the back of the pack with us, we stayed behind to help her. There were no homes or stores and virtually no traffic on the far side of the island, meaning that there was no way to call for help, so after attempting some crude first aid, we decided to all push on together. Bored with the slow pace, my boys took off ahead, and I spent the next several hours pedaling and walking next to my new friend until we eventually reached a hotel where she called for a taxi and I rejoined my sons, who had stopped for a swim, for the rest of the trip around the island. That night Stevie and her husband, Karl, asked us to join their family for dinner.

It turned out that they were on the nominating committee for the 2004 International Achievement Summit sponsored by the Academy of Achievement, whose mission was to "inspire youth with new dreams of achievement in a world of boundless opportunity" by bringing together over 200 university and graduate student delegates from around the world to interact with contemporary leaders who have achieved the difficult or impossible in service to their fellow humans. After our time together, they decided to nominate me to become a member of the academy and receive their Golden Plate Award, joining previous recipients such as former president Bill Clinton, Placido Domingo, George Lucas, New York mayor Rudolph Giuliani, U.S. senator John McCain, former prime minister of Israel Shimon Peres, and Archbishop Desmond Tutu. Because my nomination was accepted, I was able to attend the annual 4-day event with some of the brightest young future leaders and some of the most interesting and accomplished people in the world in 2004 and will be able to attend every year for the rest of my life—and I can even bring my sons to a future meeting!

Had I been totally attached to my original outcome of a day with my two sons and left Stevie to the care of others, I would have missed an even bigger opportunity that spontaneously came my way. I have learned over the years that whenever one door seemingly closes, another door opens. You just have to keep positive, stay aware, and look to see what it is. Instead of getting upset when things don't unfold as you anticipated, always ask yourself the question "What's the possibility that this is?"

16

BE WILLING TO PAY THE PRICE

If people knew how hard I had to work to gain my mastery,
it wouldn't seem wonderful at all.

MICHELANGELO
Renaissance sculptor and painter who spent 4 years lying on his back
painting the ceiling of the Sistine Chapel

Behind every great achievement is a story of education, training, practice, discipline, and sacrifice. You have to be willing to pay the price.

Maybe that price is pursuing one single activity while putting everything else in your life on hold. Maybe it's investing all of your own personal wealth or savings. Maybe it's the willingness to walk away from the safety of your current situation.

But though many things are typically required to reach a successful outcome, the *willingness* to do what's required adds that extra dimension to the mix that helps you persevere in the face of overwhelming challenges, setbacks, pain, and even personal injury.

PAIN IS ONLY TEMPORARY . . . THE BENEFITS
LAST FOREVER

I remember back to the 1976 Summer Olympic Games, when the men's gymnastic competition captured the attention of the world. With the roar of the crowd in the background, Japan's Shun Fujimoto landed a perfect triple-somersault twist dismount from the rings to clinch the gold medal in team gymnastics. With his face contorted in pain and his teammates holding their breath, Fujimoto followed a near-flawless routine by achieving a stunning and perfect landing—on a *broken* right knee. It was an extraordinary display of courage and commitment.

Interviewed later about the win, Fujimoto revealed that even though he had injured his knee during the earlier floor exercise, it became apparent as the competition continued that the team gold medal would be decided by the rings apparatus—his strongest event. "The pain shot through me like a knife," he said. "It brought tears to my eyes. But now I have a gold medal and the pain is gone."

What was it that gave Fujimoto his extraordinary courage in the face of excruciating pain and the very real risk of serious injury? It was a willingness to pay the price—and probably a long history of paying the price, every day, on the road to simply winning a spot to compete in the Olympics.

PRACTICE, PRACTICE, PRACTICE!

*When I played with Michael Jordan on the Olympic team,
there was a huge gap between his ability and the ability of the other great
players on that team. But what impressed me was that he was
always the first one on the floor and the last one to leave.*

STEVE ALFORD
Olympic gold medalist, NBA player, and head basketball coach
at the University of Iowa

Before Bill Bradley became a U.S. senator from New Jersey, he was an amazing basketball player. He was an all-American at Princeton University, won an Olympic gold medal in 1964, played in the NBA Championships with the New York Knicks, and was inducted into the Basketball Hall of Fame. How did he do so well at his sport? Well, for one thing, when he was in high school, he practiced for 4 hours a day every day.

In his 1996 memoir *Time Present, Time Past,* Bradley offers the following account of his self-imposed basketball-training regimen: "I stayed behind to practice after my teammates had left. My practice routine was to end by making 15 baskets in a row from each of five spots on the floor." If he missed a shot, he would start over from the beginning. He continued this practice all through his college and professional career.

He developed this strong commitment to practice when he attended summer basketball camps sponsored by the St. Louis Hawks' "Easy" Ed Macauley, where he learned the importance of practicing: "When you're not practicing, someone somewhere is. And when the two of you meet, given roughly equal ability, he will win." Bill took that advice to heart. The hours of hard work paid off. Bill Bradley scored over 3,000 points in 4 years of high school basketball.

OLYMPIC ATHLETES PAY THE PRICE

*I learned that the only way you are going to get anywhere in life is to
work hard at it. Whether you're a musician, a writer, an athlete,
or a businessman, there is no getting around it.
If you do, you'll win—if you don't, you won't.*

BRUCE JENNER
Olympic gold medalist in the decathlon

According to John Troup, writing in *USA Today*, "The average Olympian
trains four hours a day at least 310 days a year for six years before succeeding.
Getting better begins with working out every day. By 7:00 AM most athletes
have done more than many people do all day. . . . Given equal talent, the
better-trained athlete can generally outperform the one who did not give a
serious effort, and is usually more confident at the starting block. The four
years before an Olympics, Greg Louganis probably practiced each of his
dives 3000 times. Kim Zmeskal has probably done every flip in her gymnastics routine at least 20,000 times, and Janet Evans has completed more than
240,000 laps. Training works, but it isn't easy or simple. Swimmers train an
average of 10 miles a day, at speeds of 5 mph in the pool. That might not
sound fast, but their heart rates average 160 the entire time. Try running up
a flight of stairs, then check your heart rate. Then imagine having to do that
for four hours! Marathon runners average 160 miles a week at 10 mph."[21]

Although most of you reading this will never become Olympic athletes,
nor do you want to, you can become world class in whatever you do by putting in the disciplined effort to excel at your chosen trade, craft, or profession.
To win at whatever game you choose to play, you need to be willing to pay
the price.

*It's not the will to win that matters—everyone has that.
It's the will to prepare to win that matters.*

PAUL "BEAR" BRYANT
College football's winningest coach, with 323 victories, including 6 national
championships and 13 Southeastern Conference titles

---

21. John Troup, *USA Today*, July 29, 1992, page 11E.

TEN TIMES PERFECTLY

If I miss a day of practice, I know it. If I miss two days,
my manager knows it. If I miss three days, my audience knows it.

ANDRÉ PREVIN
Pianist, conductor, and composer

Today Tom Boyer is a productivity consultant who works with major corporations such as Siemens, Motorola, Polaroid, and Weyerhaeuser. But in his teens and early twenties, Tom was a dedicated clarinet player. Because he was willing to pay the price of 2 hours of practice every day—even during family vacations—he consistently won every state competition in Ohio. One year his unsuspecting high school orchestra conductor put the overture to "Semiramide" by Rossini on the state competition program because he thought that no one else would have a clarinet player that could play the clarinet solo at Tom's level. What he didn't know is that though it's only about a 20- to 30-second solo, it is unbelievably hard on every imaginable level—perhaps *the* hardest clarinet solo ever written.

When Tom walked into his next lesson with Robert Marcellus, the principal clarinet in the Cleveland Orchestra at the time, he looked at him and said, "How do I have a chance of getting this?"

Marcellus looked at him and said, "Something that hard . . . if you can play it ten times in a row without a mistake in the practice room, you have a *chance* of getting it out on stage." And then he said, "Play it." When Tom played it through correctly, he held up one finger and said, "One. Play it again." Then he held up two fingers. "Two. Play it again." Then he held up three fingers. "Play it again." And then Tom missed.

Marcellus put his forefinger and thumb together, forming a zero. "Start over. Play it again. . . . One. Play it again. . . . Two. Play it again." And on it went for 45 minutes before Tom managed to get through a 30-second solo 10 times without making a mistake. And all his teacher was doing was holding out fingers—one, two, three. . . . When Tom got to 10 times in a row without a mistake, his teacher looked at him with a little smile on his face and said, "Now tell me what you learned." Then, and only then, did he show Tom a couple of things to make playing the piece a little bit easier.

Tom went on to play the solo perfectly in the competition, and later, after 6 years in the Cleveland Institute of Music, Tom landed a spot in the Cleveland Orchestra for 2 years.

*Legendary violinist Isaac Stern was once confronted by a middle-aged
woman after a concert. She gushed, "Oh, I'd give my life to play like you!"
"Lady," said Stern acidly, "that I did!"*

DETERMINED TO BE AN ARTIST AT ANY COST

It was the 1970s and Wyland was the classic starving artist who threw everything into his dream. He painted and he hustled. He would set up art shows
at his local high school and sell original paintings for just $35, knowing that
the only way he could develop as an artist was to sell his paintings for whatever he could get to earn enough money to buy the necessary supplies he
needed to create more.

Then one day, in what was to become a defining moment for the young
artist, Wyland's mother told him, "Art really isn't a job; it's a hobby. Now go
out and get a real job." The next day she dropped him off at the Detroit Unemployment Bureau. But to Wyland's dismay, he was fired from three different jobs three days in a row. He couldn't keep his mind on the boring factory
work—he wanted to be creative and paint. A week later, he built a studio in
the basement and worked day and night creating a portfolio that eventually
won him a full scholarship to art school in Detroit.

Wyland painted every moment he could, and he managed to sell some
paintings, but for years he just managed to scrape by. But because he was determined that art was the only thing he wanted to do, he continued to work
and hone his craft.

One day, Wyland realized he had to go where other artists flourished and
where new ideas were born. His destination was the well-known art colony of
Laguna Beach, California, and with his dream fully alive, he moved into a
cramped, tiny studio where he both worked and lived for several more years.
Eventually, he was invited to participate in the annual art festival, where he
learned to talk about his work and interact with collectors. Soon after, galleries
in Hawaii discovered him but often sold his paintings without ever paying him,
claiming their overhead was high. Out of the frustration of finally selling high-
priced paintings only to have the money disappear, Wyland realized he had to
own his own galleries. In his own galleries, he could control every aspect of selling his art—from how it was framed and hung to how it was sold and who it
was sold by. Today, 26 years after opening his first gallery in Laguna Beach, he
creates as many as 1,000 works of art a year (some of which sell for $200,000
apiece), creates artistic collaborations with the folks at Disney, owns four homes
in Hawaii, California, and Florida, and lives the life he always dreamed of.

Perhaps you, like Wyland, want to turn your hobby into your career. You can become hugely successful doing what you love if you are willing to pay the price. "In the beginning, you've got to kind of suffer," Wyland says, "giving in to everybody else. But there's nothing better than eventually achieving success on your own terms."

WHATEVER IT TAKES

In 1987 a young John Assaraf moved from Toronto, Ontario, to Indianapolis, Indiana, to become partners in a fledgling RE/MAX real estate franchising operation. John was definitely willing to pay the price.

When his friends were in a bar having a drink, John was working on achieving his dream of convincing existing real estate offices to join the RE/MAX system. John approached a minimum of five real estate agents every day for 5 years.

At first people laughed John right out of their offices. Why would they give up a part of their existing income or their reputation to join a new franchise that had already failed twice? But John was passionate about his dream. In his zeal, he even tried to enroll the number-one real estate office in Indiana at the time. They thought he was nuts. But John persisted, and only 5 years later, he and his associates surpassed the $1 billion sales mark and took the lead. Today RE/MAX of Indiana's 1,500 sales associates generate over $4 billion a year in sales and earn over $100 million a year in commissions.

Today John earns a very comfortable residual income from his company in Indiana, and lives in Southern California, where he has more than ample time to play with his two sons, pursue other business interests, write books, and teach others his "success cloning" formula for success.

PUTTING IN THE TIME

Part of paying the price is the willingness to do whatever it takes to get the job done. It comes from a declaration that you are going to get it done no matter what it takes, no matter how long it takes, no matter what comes up. It's a done deal. You are responsible for the results you intend. No excuses—just a world-class performance or an outstanding result that can be counted on. Consider this:

- Michael Crichton is the Emmy and Peabody Award–winning creator of the television series *ER*. His books have sold over 100 million copies in 30 languages, and 12 have been made into films, 7 of which he directed. His books and films include *Jurassic Park, The Andromeda Strain, Congo, Coma, Twister,* and *Westworld.* He is the only person to have had, at the same time, the number-one book, the number-one movie, and the number-one television show in the United States. With all of his natural talent, Michael still says, "Books aren't written—they're rewritten. . . . It is one of the hardest things to accept, especially after the seventh rewrite hasn't quite done it."

- Ernest Hemingway rewrote *A Farewell to Arms*—39 times. This dedication to excellence would later lead him to win the Pulitzer and Nobel prizes for literature.

- M. Scott Peck only received a $5,000 advance for *The Road Less Traveled*; however, he was willing to pay the price to fulfill his dream. During the first year after it was published, he participated in 1,000 radio interviews to advertise and promote his book. He continued to do a minimum of one interview a day for the next 12 years, keeping the book on the *New York Times* Best-Seller List for over 540 weeks (a record) and selling more than 10 million copies in over 20 languages.

Talent is cheaper than table salt. What separates the talented individual from the successful one is a lot of hard work.

STEPHEN KING
Best-selling author with over 40 books in print, many of which
have been made into movies

IT'S ABOUT BUILDING MOMENTUM

When a NASA rocket takes off from Cape Canaveral, it uses up a large portion of its total fuel just to overcome the gravitational pull of the Earth. Once it has achieved that, it can virtually coast through space for the rest of its journey. Likewise, an amateur athlete often puts in full training days with Spartan self-discipline for years. But after winning a gold medal or a world championship, offers for endorsements, spokesperson contracts, speaking engagements, retail merchandise deals, and other entrepreneurial opportunities often come pouring in, allowing them to slow down a bit and take advantage of the momentum they created earlier in their career.

Likewise, in any business or profession, once you have paid the price to establish yourself as an expert, a person of integrity who delivers high-quality results on time, you get to reap the benefits of that for the rest of your life. When I started speaking, no one had ever heard of me. As I delivered more and more speeches and seminars that delivered what the client wanted, my reputation grew. I had a file full of glowing testimonial letters and a track record of credibility that was built up over many years of giving free and low-fee talks until I had honed my craft. The same was true for writing books. It took many years to get good at it.

If you are involved in network marketing, you have to put in countless hours in the beginning, not getting paid what you are worth. You may work for months with no real income, but eventually the multiplier effect of your growing downline takes effect, and eventually you are making more money than you ever imagined possible.

Creating momentum is an important part of the success process. In fact, successful people know that if you are willing to pay the price in the beginning, you can reap the benefits for the rest of your life.

GOING THROUGH THE AWKWARD STAGE

Business consultant Marshall Thurber has said, "Anything worth doing well is worth doing badly in the beginning." Remember when you first learned to drive a car, to ride a bicycle, to play an instrument, or to play a sport? You understood in advance that you were going to be very awkward at first. You assumed that awkwardness was just part of what was required to learn that new skill that you wanted.

Well, not surprisingly, this initial awkwardness applies to anything you undertake, so you have to be willing to go through that awkward stage in order to become proficient. Children give themselves permission to do this. But sadly, by the time we're adults, we are so often afraid of making a mistake that we don't let ourselves be awkward, so we don't learn the way children do. We're so afraid of doing it wrong.

I didn't learn to ski until I was in my forties, and in the beginning, I was definitely not good at it. Over time, with lessons, I got better. I didn't start playing the piano until I was 58, and it took me a long time to become proficient.

Even the first time I kissed a girl, it was awkward. But to gain a new skill or get better at *anything* you want to do, you have to be willing to keep on going in the face of looking foolish and feeling stupid for a time.

FIND OUT THE PRICE YOU HAVE TO PAY

Of course, if you don't know what the price is, you can't choose to pay it. Sometimes the first step is to investigate the steps that will be required to achieve your desired goal.

For example, many people—perhaps you—say they want to own a yacht. But have you ever researched how much money you would have to earn to buy one . . . or how much it costs to harbor the yacht in your local marina . . . or how much the monthly maintenance, fuel, insurance, and license cost? You may need to research what costs others have had to pay to achieve dreams similar to yours. You might want to make a list of several people who have already done what you want to do and interview them about what sacrifices they had to make along the way.

You may discover that some costs are more than you want to pay. You may not want to risk your health, your relationships, or your entire life savings for a certain goal. You have to weigh all of the factors. That dream job may not be worth your marriage, your kids, or a lack of balance in your life. Only you can decide what is right for you and what price *you* are willing to pay. It may be that what you want doesn't serve you in the long run. But if it does, find out what you need to do, and then set about doing it.

ASK! ASK! ASK!

*You've got to ask. Asking is, in my opinion, the world's most
powerful and neglected secret to success and happiness.*

PERCY ROSS
Self-made multimillionaire and philanthropist

History is filled with examples of incredible riches and astounding benefits people have received simply by asking for them. Yet surprisingly, asking—one of the most powerful success principles of all—is still a challenge that holds most people back. If you are not afraid to ask anybody for anything, then skip over this chapter. But if you are like most people, you may be holding yourself back by not asking for the information, assistance, support, money, and time that you need to fulfill your vision and make your dreams come true.

WHY PEOPLE ARE AFRAID TO ASK

Why are people so afraid to ask? They are afraid of many things such as looking needy, looking foolish, and looking stupid. But mostly they're afraid of experiencing rejection. They are afraid of hearing the word *no*.

The sad thing is that they're actually rejecting themselves in advance. They're saying no to themselves before anyone else even has a chance to.

When I was a graduate student at the school of education at the University of Chicago, I participated in a self-development group with 20 other people. During one of the exercises, one of the men asked one of the women if she found him attractive. I was both shocked by the boldness of the question and embarrassed for the asker—fearing what he might get as a response. As it turned out, she said that she did. Emboldened by his success, I then asked her if she found *me* attractive. After this little exercise in "bold asking," several of the women told us that they found it unbelievable how scared men were when it came to asking women for a date. She said, "You reject yourself before you even give us a chance to. Take the risk. We might say yes."

Don't assume that you are going to get a no. Take the risk to ask for whatever you need and want. If they say no, you are no worse off than when you started. If they say yes, you are a lot better off. Just by being willing to ask, you can get a raise, a donation, a room with an ocean view, a discount, a free sample, a date, a better assignment, the order, a more convenient delivery date, an extension, time off, or help with the housework.

HOW TO ASK FOR WHAT YOU WANT

There's a specific science to asking for and getting what you want or need in life, and Mark Victor Hansen and I have written a whole book about it. And though I recommend you learn more by reading our book *The Aladdin Factor*, here are some quick tips to get you started:

1. **Ask as if you expect to get it.** Ask with a positive expectation. Ask from the place that you have already been given it. It's a done deal. Ask as if you expect to get a yes.
2. **Assume you can.** Don't start with the assumption that you can't get it. If you are going to assume, assume you *can* get an upgrade. Assume you *can* get a table by the window. Assume that you *can* return it without a sales slip. Assume that you *can* get a scholarship, that you *can* get a raise, that you *can* get tickets at this late date. Don't ever assume against yourself.
3. **Ask someone who can give it to you.** Qualify the person. "Who would I have to speak to to get . . ." "Who is authorized to make a decision about . . ." "What would have to happen for me to get . . ."
4. **Be clear and specific.** In my seminars, I often ask, "Who wants more money?" I pick someone who raises a hand, and I give that person a dollar. I say, "You now have more money. Are you satisfied?"

    The person usually says, "No, I want more than that."

    So I give the person a couple of quarters, and ask, "Is that enough for you?"

    "No, I want more than that."

    "Well, just how much do you want? We could play this game of 'more' for days and never get to what you want."

    The person usually gives me a specific number, and then I point out how important it is to be specific. Vague requests produce vague results. Your requests need to be specific. When it comes to money, you need to ask for a specific amount.

Don't say: I want a raise.
Do say: I want a raise of $500 a month.

When it comes to when you want something done, don't say "soon" or "whenever it's convenient." Give a specific date and time.

Don't say: I want to spend some time with you this weekend.
Do say: I would like to go out for dinner and a movie with you on Saturday night. Would that work for you?

When it comes to a behavioral request, be specific. Say exactly what you want the person to do.

Don't say: I want more help around the house.
Do say: I want you to wash the dishes every night after dinner and take out the garbage Monday, Wednesday, and Friday nights.

5. **Ask repeatedly.** One of the most important principles of success is persistence, not giving up. Whenever you're asking others to participate in the fulfillment of your goals, some people are going to say no. They may have other priorities, commitments, and reasons not to participate. It's not a reflection on you.

Just get used to the idea that there's going to be a lot of rejection along the way to the brass ring. The key is not to give up. When someone says no, you keep on asking. Why? Because when you keep on asking—even the same person again and again—you might get a yes . . .

On a different day
When the person is in a better mood
When you have new data to present
After you've proven your commitment to them
When circumstances have changed
When you've learned how to close better
When you've established better rapport
When the person trusts you more
When you have paid your dues
When the economy is better

Kids understand this success principle perhaps better than anyone. They will ask the same person for the same thing over and over again without any hesitation. They eventually wear you down.

I once read a story in *People* magazine about a man who asked the same woman more than 30 times to marry him. No matter how many times she said no, he kept coming back—and eventually she said yes!

A TELLING STATISTIC

Herbert True, a marketing specialist at Notre Dame University, found that

- 44% of all salespeople quit trying after the first call
- 24% quit after the second call
- 14% quit after the third call
- 12% quit trying to sell their prospect after the fourth call

This means that 94% of all salespeople quit after the fourth call. But 60% of all sales are made after the fourth call. This revealing statistic shows that 94% of all salespeople don't give themselves a chance at 60% of the prospective buyers.

You may have the capacity, but you also have to have the tenacity! To be successful, you have to ask, ask, ask, ask, ask!

ASK, AND IT SHALL BE GIVEN TO YOU

In 2000, Sylvia Collins flew all the way from Australia to Santa Barbara to take one of my weeklong seminars, where she learned about the power of asking. A year later, I received this letter from her.

I have taken a detour in my career path, and I'm selling new developments on the Gold Coast with a company called Gold Coast Property. I work with a team of guys mostly in their twenties! The skills I have acquired through your seminars have helped me to perform and be an active part of a winning team! I must tell you how having self-esteem and not being afraid to ask has impacted this office!

At a recent staff meeting, we were asked what we would like to do for our once-a-month team-building day. I asked Michael, the managing director, "What target would we have to reach for you to take us to an island for a week?"

Everyone around the table just went silent and looked at me; obviously it was out of everyone's comfort zone to ask such a thing. Michael looked around and then looked at me and said, "Well, if you reach . . . (and then he set a financial target), I'll take the whole team (ten of us) to the *Great Barrier Reef*!"

Well, the next month we reached the target and off we went to Lady Elliott Island for four days—airfares, accommodations, food, and activities all paid for by the company. We had the most amazing four days—we snorkeled together, had bonfires on the beach, played tricks on each other, and had so much fun!

Afterwards, Michael gave us another target and said he would take us to Fiji if we reached it, and we reached that target in December! Even though the company is paying for these trips, Michael is miles ahead from the enormous level of increased sales!

YOU HAVE NOTHING TO LOSE AND EVERYTHING TO GAIN BY ASKING

To be successful, you have to take risks, and one of the risks is the willingness to risk rejection. Here's an e-mail I received from Donna Hutcherson, who heard me speak at her company's convention in Scottsdale, Arizona.

> My husband Dale and I heard you at the Walsworth convention in early January; . . . Dale came as one of the spouses. . . . He was particularly impressed by your mention of not having anything to lose by asking or trying. After hearing you speak, he decided to go for one of his lifetime goals (and heart's desire)—a head football coaching position. He applied for four openings within my sales territory and Sebring High School called him back the next day, encouraging him to fill out the application online. He did so right away and could hardly sleep that night. After two interviews he was chosen over 61 other applicants. Today Dale accepted the position as head football coach at Sebring High School in Sebring, Florida.
>
> Thank you for your vision and inspiration.

Here is an excerpt from another e-mail I received from Donna this past summer:

> Taking over a program that had back-to-back seasons with 1 win and 9 losses (and a reputation for giving up), Dale led the team to a winning record (with 4 "come-from-behind" wins in the last three minutes), a county championship, and only the 3rd playoff in the 78-year history of the school. He was also named County Coach of the Year and Sports Story

of the Year. Most important is that he changed the lives of the many players, staff, and students with whom he worked.

WILL YOU GIVE ME SOME MONEY?

In 1997, 21-year-old Chad Pregracke set out on a one-man mission to clean up the Mississippi River. He started with a 20-foot boat and his own two hands. Since that time, he's cleared more than 1,000 miles of the Mississippi and another 435 miles of the Illinois River, pulling more than 1 million tons of debris from the riverbanks. Using the power of asking, he's raised more than $2,500,000 in donations and enlisted more than 4,000 people to help him in his crusade.

When Chad realized he would need more barges, trucks, and equipment, he asked state and local officials for help, only to be turned down. Not to be dissuaded, Chad grabbed a phone book, turned to the business listings, and called Alcoa—"because," he said, "it started with an A."

Armed only with his passionate commitment to his dream, Chad asked to speak to the "top guy." Eventually Alcoa gave him $8,400. Later, working his way through the A's, he called Anheuser-Busch. As reported in *Smithsonian* magazine, Mary Alice Ramirez, the director of environmental outreach at Anheuser-Busch, remembers her first conversation with Chad this way:

"Will you give me some money?" Chad asked.

"Who are you?" replied Ramirez.

"I want to get rid of the garbage in the Mississippi River," Chad said.

"Can you show me a proposal?" Ramirez inquired.

"What's a proposal?" Chad replied.

Ramirez eventually invited Chad to a meeting and gave him a check for $25,000 to expand his Mississippi River Beautification and Restoration Project.[22]

More important than Chad's knowledge of fund-raising was his clear desire to make a difference, his unflagging enthusiasm, his complete dedication to the project—and his willingness to ask.

Eventually, everything Chad needed was secured through asking. He now has a board of directors made up of lawyers, accountants, and corporate officers. He has several full-time staff members and thousands of volunteers.

In the process, he has not only cleaned up miles of shoreline on the Mississippi, Illinois, Anacostia, Potomac, Missouri, Ohio, and Rock Rivers—removing over 1 million tons of trash—but he's also drawn attention to the

---

22. "Trash Talker," *Smithsonian*, April 2003, pages 116–117.

health and beauty of all rivers and the responsibility we all share in keeping them clean.[23]

START ASKING TODAY

Take time now to make a list of the things that you want that you don't ask for at home, school, or work. Next to each one, write down how you stop yourself from asking. What is your fear? Next, write down what it is costing you not to ask. Then write down what benefit you would get if you were to ask.

Take time to make a list of what you need to ask for in each of the following seven goal categories that I outlined in Principle 3 ("Decide What You Want"): financial, career, fun time and recreation, health, relationships, personal projects and hobbies, and contribution to the larger community (see pages 32–33). This might include a raise, a loan, seed money, feedback about your performance, a referral, an endorsement, time off to get additional training, someone to babysit your children, a massage, a hug, or help with a volunteer project.

---

23. For more information on the Mississippi River Beautification and Restoration Project or how to participate in Adopt a Mississippi River Mile, you can visit Chad's Web site at www. livinglandsandwaters.org, call 309-496-9848, or write Living Lands & Waters, 17615 Route 84 N., Great River Road, East Moline, IL 61244.

REJECT REJECTION

We keep going back, stronger, not weaker, because we will not allow
rejection to beat us down. It will only strengthen our resolve.
To be successful there is no other way.

EARL G. GRAVES
Founder and publisher of *Black Enterprise* magazine

If you are going to be successful, you are going to need to learn how to deal with rejection. Rejection is a natural part of life. You get rejected when you aren't picked for the team, don't get the part in the play, don't get elected, don't get into the college or graduate school of your choice, don't get the job or promotion you wanted, don't get the raise you wanted, don't get the appointment you requested, don't get the date you asked for, don't get the permission you requested, or get fired. You get rejected when your manuscript is rejected, your proposal is turned down, your new product idea is passed over, your fund-raising request is ignored, your design concept is not accepted, your application for membership is denied, or your offer of marriage is not accepted.

REJECTION IS A MYTH!

To get over rejection, you have to realize that rejection is really a myth. It doesn't really exist. It is simply a concept that you hold in your head. Think about it. If you ask Patty to have dinner with you and she says no, you didn't have anyone to eat dinner with before you asked her, and you don't have anyone to eat dinner with after you asked her. The situation didn't get worse; it stayed the same. It only gets worse if you go inside and tell yourself something extra like "See, Mother was right. No one will ever like me. I am the slug of the universe!"

If you apply to Harvard for graduate school and you don't get in, you weren't in Harvard before you applied, and you are not in Harvard after you applied. Again, your life didn't get worse; it stayed the same. You haven't really lost anything. And think about this—you have spent your whole life not going to Harvard; you know how to handle that.

The truth is, you never have anything to lose by asking, and because there is something to possibly gain, by all means ask.

SWSWSWSW

Whenever you ask anyone for anything, remember the following: SWSWSWSW, which stands for "some will, some won't; so what—someone's waiting." Some people are going to say yes, and some are going to say no. So what! Out there somewhere, someone is waiting for you and your ideas. It is simply a numbers game. You have to keep asking until you get a yes. The yes is out there waiting. As my partner Mark Victor Hansen is so fond of saying, "What you want wants you." You just have to hang in there long enough to eventually get a yes.

81 NOS, 9 STRAIGHT YESES

Because it had so dramatically changed her life, a graduate of my "Self-Esteem and Peak Performance Seminar" was volunteering in the evenings to call people to enroll them in an upcoming seminar I was conducting in St. Louis. She made a commitment to talk to three people every night for a month. Many of the calls turned into long conversations with people asking tons of questions. She made a total of 90 phone calls. The first 81 people decided not to take the seminar. The next 9 people all signed up. She had a 10% success ratio, which is a good ratio for phone enrollments, but all 9 enrollments came in the last 9 calls. What if she had given up after the first 50 people and said, "This just isn't working. It's not worth the effort. Nobody is signing up." But because she had a dream of sharing with others the life-transforming experience that she had had, she persevered in the face of a lot of rejection, knowing that it was indeed a numbers game. And her commitment to the outcome paid off—she was instrumental in helping 9 people transform their lives.

If you're committed to a cause that evokes your passion and commitment, you keep learning from your experiences, and you stay the course to the end, you will eventually create your desired outcome.

Never give up on your dream. . . . Perseverance is all important.
If you don't have the desire and the belief in yourself to keep trying after
you've been told you should quit, you'll never make it.

TAWNI O'DELL
Author of *Back Roads*, an Oprah Book Club pick

JUST SAY "NEXT!"

Get used to the idea that there is going to be a lot of rejection along the way to the gold ring. The secret to success is to not give up. When someone says no, you say, *"Next!"* Keep on asking. When Colonel Harlan Sanders left home with his pressure cooker and his special recipe for cooking Southern fried chicken, he received over 300 rejections before he found someone to believe in his dream. Because he rejected rejection over 300 times, there are now 11,000 KFC restaurants in 80 countries around the world.

If one person tells you no, ask someone else. Remember, there are over 5 billion people on the planet! Someone, somewhere, sometime will say yes. Don't get stuck in your fear or resentment. Move on to the next person. It is a numbers game. Someone is waiting to say yes.

CHICKEN SOUP FOR THE SOUL®

In the fall of 1991, Mark Victor Hansen and I began the process of selling our first *Chicken Soup for the Soul®* book to a publisher. We flew to New York with our agent, Jeff Herman, and met with every major publisher that would grant us a meeting. All of them said they weren't interested. "Collections of short stories don't sell." "There's no edge to the stories." "The title will never work." After that we were rejected by another 20 publishers who had received the manuscript through the mail. After being rejected by more than 30 publishers, our agent gave the book back to us and said, "I'm sorry; I can't sell it for you." What did we do? We said, *"Next!"*

We also knew we had to think outside of the box. After weeks of wracking our brains, we hit on an idea that we thought would work. We printed up a form that was a promise to buy the book when it was published. It included a place for people to write their name, address, and the number of books they pledged to buy.

Over a period of months, we asked everyone who attended our speeches or seminars to complete the form if they would buy a copy of the book when it was published. Eventually we had promises to buy 20,000 books.

The following spring, Mark and I attended the American Booksellers Association convention in Anaheim, California, and walked from booth to booth, talking to any publisher who would listen. Even with copies of our signed pledge forms to demonstrate the market for our book, we were turned down again and again. But again and again we said, *"Next!"* At the end of the second very long day, we gave a copy of the first 30 stories in the book to Peter Vegso and Gary Seidler, copresidents of Health Communications, Inc., a struggling publisher specializing in addiction-and-recovery books, who agreed to take it home and look it over. Later that week, Gary Seidler took the manuscript to the beach and read it. He loved it and decided to give us a chance. Those hundreds of "nexts" had paid off! After over 130 rejections, that first book went on to sell 8 million copies, spawning a series of 80 best-selling books that have been translated into 39 languages.

And those pledge forms? When the book was finally published, we stapled an announcement to the signed forms, sent them to the person at the address on the form, and waited for a check. Almost everyone who had promised to buy a book came through on his or her commitment. In fact, one entrepreneur in Canada bought 1,700 copies and gave one to every one of his clients.

This manuscript of yours that has just come back from another editor is a precious package. Don't consider it rejected. Consider that you've addressed it "to the editor who can appreciate my work" and it has simply come back stamped "not at this address." Just keep looking for the right address.

BARBARA KINGSOLVER
Best-selling author of *The Poisonwood Bible*

155 REJECTIONS DIDN'T STOP HIM

When 19-year-old Rick Little wanted to start a program in the high schools that would teach kids how to deal with their feelings, handle conflict, clarify their life goals, and learn communication skills and the values that would help them live more effective and fulfilling lives, he wrote a proposal and shopped it to over 155 foundations. He slept in the back of his car and ate peanut butter on crackers for the better part of a year. But he never gave up his dream. Eventually, the Kellogg Foundation gave Rick $130,000. (That's almost $1,000 for each no he endured.) Since that time, Rick and his team have raised over $100 million to implement the Quest program in over 30,000 schools around the world. Three million kids per year are being taught important life skills because one 19-year-old rejected rejection and kept on going until he got a yes.

In 1989 Rick received a grant for $65,000,000, the second largest grant ever given in U.S. history, to create the International Youth Foundation. What if Rick had given up after the one hundredth rejection and said to himself, *Well, I guess this just isn't supposed to be*? What a great loss to the world and to Rick's higher purpose for being.

HE KNOCKED ON 12,500 DOORS

*I take rejection as someone blowing a bugle in my ear
to wake me up and get going, rather than retreat.*

SYLVESTER STALLONE
Actor, writer, and director

When Dr. Ignatius Piazza was a young chiropractor fresh out of school, he decided he wanted to set up offices in the Monterey Bay area of California. When he approached the local chiropractic association for assistance they advised him to set up shop somewhere else. They told him he wouldn't be successful because there were already too many chiropractors in the area. Undaunted, he applied the Next Principle. For months, he went from door to door early in the morning until sunset, knocking on doors. After introducing himself as the new young doctor in town, he asked a few questions:

"Where should I locate my office?"

"What newspapers should I advertise in to reach your neighbors?"

"Should I open early in the morning or stay open into the evening for those who have nine-to-five jobs?"

"Should I call my clinic Chiropractic West or Ignatius Piazza Chiropractic?"

And finally, he asked, "When I hold my open house, would you like to receive an invitation?" If people said yes, he wrote down their names and addresses and continued on . . . day after day, month after month. By the time he was done, he had knocked on over 12,500 doors and talked to over 6,500 people. He got a lot of nos. He got a lot of nobody-homes. He even got trapped on one porch—cornered by a pit bull—for a whole afternoon! But he also received enough yeses that during his first month in practice he saw 233 new patients and earned a record income of $72,000—in an area that "didn't need another chiropractor"!

Remember, to get what you want you are going to need to ask, ask, ask, and say *next, next, next* until you get the yes(es) you are looking for! Asking is, was, and always will be a numbers game. Don't take it personally, because it isn't personal. It's just not a match until it is.

SOME FAMOUS REJECTIONS

The girl doesn't, it seems to me, have a special perception or feeling which would lift that book above the "curiosity" level.

From the rejection slip for *The Diary of Anne Frank*

Everyone who has ever made it to the top has had to endure rejections. You just have to realize that they are not personal. Consider the following:

- When Alexander Graham Bell offered the rights to the telephone for $100,000 to Carl Orton, president of Western Union, Orton replied, "What use would this company make of an electrical toy?"
- Angie Everhart, who started modeling at the age of 16, was once told by model agency owner Eileen Ford that she would never make it as a model. Why not? "Redheads don't sell." Everhart later became the first redhead in history to appear on the cover of *Glamour* magazine, had a great modeling career, and then went on to appear in 27 films and numerous TV shows.
- Novelist Stephen King almost made a multimillion-dollar mistake when he threw his *Carrie* manuscript in the garbage because he was tired of the rejections. "We are not interested in science fiction which deals with negative utopias," he was told. "They do not sell." Luckily, his wife fished it out of the garbage. Eventually *Carrie* was printed by another publisher, sold more than 4 million copies, and was made into a blockbuster film.
- In 1998, Google cofounders Sergey Brin and Larry Page approached Yahoo! and suggested a merger. Yahoo! could have snapped up the company for a handful of stock, but instead they suggested that the young Googlers keep working on their little school project and come back when they had grown up. Within 5 years, Google had an estimated market capitalization of $20 billion. At the time of this writing, they were about to launch an initial public offering auction that eventually raised $1.67 billion.

It is impossible to sell animal stories in the U.S.A.

From the rejection slip for George Orwell's *Animal Farm*

The record for the most astounding number of rejections would probably be John Creasey's. A popular British mystery writer, Creasey collected 743 rejection slips before he sold his first book! Impervious to rejection, over the next 40 years he went on to publish 562 full-length books under 28 different pseudonyms! If John Creasey can handle 743 rejections on his way to success, so can you.

19

USE FEEDBACK TO YOUR ADVANTAGE

Feedback is the breakfast of champions.

KEN BLANCHARD AND SPENCER JOHNSON
Coauthors of *The One Minute Manager*

Once you begin to take action, you'll start getting feedback about whether you're doing the right thing. You'll get data, advice, help, suggestions, direction, and even criticism that will help you constantly adjust and move forward while continually enhancing your knowledge, abilities, attitudes, and relationships. But asking for feedback is really only the first part of the equation. Once you receive feedback, you have to be willing to respond to it.

THERE ARE TWO KINDS OF FEEDBACK

There are two kinds of feedback you might encounter—negative and positive. We tend to prefer the positive—that is, results, money, praise, a raise, a promotion, satisfied customers, awards, happiness, inner peace, intimacy, pleasure. It feels better. It tells us that we are on course, that we are doing the right thing.

We tend not to like negative feedback—lack of results, little or no money, criticism, poor evaluations, being passed over for a raise or a promotion, complaints, unhappiness, inner conflict, loneliness, pain. However, there is as much useful data in negative feedback as there is in positive feedback. It tells us that we are off course, headed in the wrong direction, doing the wrong thing. That is also valuable information.

In fact, it's so valuable that one of the most useful projects you could undertake is to change how you feel about negative feedback. I like to refer to negative feedback as information about "improvement opportunities." The world is telling me where and how I can improve what I am doing. Here is a place I can get better. Here is where I can correct my behavior to get even closer to what I say I want—more money, more sales, a promotion, a better relationship, better grades, or more success on the athletic field.

To reach your goals more quickly, you need to welcome, receive, and embrace all the feedback that comes your way.

ON COURSE, OFF COURSE,
ON COURSE, OFF COURSE

There are many ways to respond to feedback, some of which work (they take you closer to your stated objectives), and some of which don't (they keep you stuck or take you even further from your goals).

When I conduct trainings on the success principles, I illustrate this point by asking for a volunteer from the audience to stand at the far side of the room. The volunteer represents the goal I want to reach. My task is to walk across the room to where he is standing. If I get to where he is standing, I have successfully reached my goal.

I instruct the volunteer to act as a constant feedback–generating machine. Every time I take a step, he is to say "On course" if I am walking directly toward him and "Off course" if I am walking even the slightest bit off to either side.

Then I begin to walk very slowly toward the volunteer. Every time I take a step directly toward him, the volunteer says, "On course." Every few steps, I purposely veer off course, and the volunteer says, "Off course." I immediately correct my direction. Every few steps, I veer off course again and then correct again in response to his "off course" feedback. After a lot of zigzagging, I eventually reach my goal . . . and give the person a hug for volunteering.

I ask the audience to tell me which the volunteer had said more often— "on course" or "off course." The answer is always "off course." And here is the interesting part. I was off course more than I was on course, and I still got there . . . just by continually taking action and constantly adjusting to the feedback. The same is true in life. All we have to do is to start to take action and then respond to the feedback. If we do that diligently enough and long enough, we will eventually get to our goals and achieve our dreams.

WAYS OF RESPONDING TO FEEDBACK
THAT DON'T WORK

Though there are many ways you can respond to feedback, some responses simply don't work:

1. **Caving in and quitting:** As part of the seminar exercise I described above, I will repeat the process of walking toward my goal; however, in this round I will purposely veer off course, and when my volunteer keeps repeating "Off course" over and over, I break down and cry, "I can't take it anymore. Life is too hard. I can't take all this negative criticism. I quit!"

   How many times have you or someone you know received negative feedback and simply caved in over it? All that does is keep you stuck in the same place.

   It's easier not to cave in when you receive feedback if you remember that feedback is simply information. Think of it as correctional guidance instead of criticism. Think of the automatic pilot system on an airplane. The system is constantly telling the plane that it has gone too high, too low, too far to the right, or too far to the left. The plane just keeps correcting in response to the feedback it is receiving. It doesn't all of a sudden freak out and break down because of the relentless flow of feedback. Stop taking feedback so personally. It is just information designed to help you adjust and get to your goal a whole lot faster.

2. **Getting mad at the source of the feedback:** Once again, I will begin walking toward the other end of the room while purposely veering off course, causing the volunteer to say "Off course" over and over. This time I put one hand on my hip, stick out my chin, point my finger, and yell, "Bitch, bitch, bitch! All you ever do is criticize me! You're so negative. Why can't you ever say anything positive?"

   Think about it. How many times have you reacted with anger and hostility toward someone who was giving you feedback that was genuinely useful? All it does is push the person and the feedback away.

3. **Ignoring the feedback:** For my third demonstration, imagine me putting my fingers in my ears and determinedly walking off course. The volunteer might be saying "Off course, off course," but I can't hear anything because my fingers are in my ears.

   Not listening to or ignoring the feedback is another response that doesn't work. We all know people who tune out everyone's point of view but their own. They are simply not interested in what other people think. They don't want to hear anything anyone else has to say. The sad thing is, feedback could significantly transform their lives, if only they would only listen.

So, as you can see, when someone gives you feedback, there are three possible reactions that don't work: (1) crying, falling apart, caving in, and giving up; (2) getting angry at the source of the feedback; and (3) not listening to or ignoring the feedback.

Crying and falling apart is simply ineffective. It may temporarily release whatever emotions you have built up in your system, but it takes you out of the game. It doesn't get you anywhere. It simply immobilizes you. Not a great success strategy! Caving in and giving up doesn't work either. It may make you feel safer and may stop the flow of "negative" feedback, but it doesn't get you the good stuff! You can't win in the game of life if you are not on the playing field!

Getting angry at the person giving you the feedback is equally ineffective! It just makes the source of the valuable feedback attack you back or simply go away. What good is that? It may temporarily make you feel better, but it doesn't help you get more successful.

On the third day of my advanced seminar, when everyone knows everybody else pretty well, I have the whole group (about 40 people) stand up, mill around, and ask as many people as possible the following question: "How do you see me limiting myself?" After doing this for 30 minutes, people sit down and record what they have heard. You'd think that this would be hard to listen to for 30 minutes, but it is such valuable feedback that people are actually grateful for the opportunity to become aware of their limiting behaviors and replace them with successful behaviors. Everyone then develops an action plan for transcending their limiting behavior.

Remember, feedback is simply information. You don't have to take it personally. Just welcome it and use it. The most intelligent and productive response is to say, "Thank you for the feedback. Thank you for caring enough to take the time to tell me what you see and how you feel. I appreciate it."

ASK FOR FEEDBACK

Most people will not voluntarily give you feedback. They are as uncomfortable with possible confrontation as you are. They don't want to hurt your feelings. They are afraid of your reaction. They don't want to risk your disapproval. So to get honest and open feedback, you are going to need to ask for it . . . and make it safe for the person to give it to you. In other words, don't shoot the messenger.

A powerful question to ask family members, friends, and colleagues is "How do you see me limiting myself?" You might think that the answers would be hard to listen to, but most people find the information so valuable that they are grateful for what people tell them. Armed with this new feedback, they can create a plan of action for replacing their limiting behaviors with more effective and productive behaviors.

THE MOST VALUABLE QUESTION
YOU MAY EVER LEARN

In the 1980s, a multimillionaire businessman taught me a question that radically changed the quality of my life. If the only thing you get out of reading this book is the consistent use of this question in your personal and business life, it will have been worth the money and time you have invested. So what is this magical question that can improve the quality of every relationship you are in, every product you produce, every service you deliver, every meeting you conduct, every class you teach, and every transaction you enter into? Here it is:

> On a scale of 1 to 10, how would you rate the quality of our relationship (service/product) during the last week (2 weeks/month/quarter/semester/season)?

Here are a number of variations on the same question that have served me well over the years:

> On a scale of 1 to 10, how would you rate the meeting we just had? me as a manager? me as a parent? me as a teacher? this class? this meal? my cooking? our sex life? this deal? this book?

Any answer less than a 10 gets the follow-up question:

> What would it take to make it a 10?

This is where the valuable information comes from. Knowing that a person is dissatisfied is not enough. Knowing in detail what will satisfy them gives you the information you need to do what is necessary to create a winning product, service, or relationship.

Make it a habit to end every project, meeting, class, training, consultation, installation, and consultation with the two questions.

MAKE IT A WEEKLY RITUAL

I ask my wife these same two questions every Sunday night. Here is a typical scenario:

"How would you rate the quality of our relationship this past week?"

"Eight."

"What would it take to make it a ten?"

"Put the kids to bed without me having to remind you that it's time to do it. Come in for dinner on time or call me and tell me you are going to be late. I hate sitting here waiting and wondering. Let me finish a joke I am telling without interrupting and taking over because you think you can tell it better. Put your dirty laundry in the clothes hamper instead of in a pile on the floor."

I also ask my assistants this question every Friday afternoon. Here is one response I received from Deborah early on in her employment:

"Six."

"Whoa! What would it take to make it a ten?"

"We were supposed to have a meeting this week to go over my quarterly review, but it got pushed aside by other matters. It makes me feel unimportant and that you don't care about me as much as the other people around here. I need to talk to you about a lot of things, and I feel really discounted. The other thing is that I feel that you are not using me enough. You are not delegating anything but the simple stuff to me. I want more responsibility. I want you to trust me more with the important stuff. I need more of a challenge. This job has become boring and uninteresting to me. I need more of a challenge, or I am not going to make it here."

This was not easy to hear, but it was true and it led to two wonderful results. It helped me delegate more "important stuff" to her and thus cleared my plate, giving me more free time—and it also created a happier assistant who was able to serve me and the company better.

BE WILLING TO ASK

Most people are afraid to ask for corrective feedback because they are afraid of what they are going to hear. There is nothing to be afraid of. The truth is the truth. You are better off knowing the truth than not knowing the truth. Once you know it, you can do something about it. You cannot fix what you don't know is broken. You cannot improve your life, your relationships, your game, or your performance without feedback.

But what's the worst part of this avoidance approach to life? You are the only one who is not in on the secret. The other person has usually already told their spouse, their friends, their parents, their business associates, and other potential customers what they are dissatisfied with. As we discussed in Principle 1 ("Take 100% Responsibility for Your Life"), most people would rather complain than take constructive action to solve their problems. The only problem is that they are complaining to the wrong person. They should be telling you, but they are unwilling to for fear of your reaction. As a result, you are being deprived of the very thing you need to improve your relationship, your product, your service, your teaching, or your parenting. You must do two things to remedy this.

First, you must intentionally and actively solicit feedback. Ask your partner, your friends, your colleagues, your boss, your employees, your clients, your parents, your teachers, your students, and your coaches. Use the question frequently. Make it a habit to always ask for corrective feedback. "What can I/we do to make this better? What would it take to make it a ten for you?"

Second, you must be grateful for the feedback. Do not get defensive. Just say, "Thank you for caring enough to share that with me!" If you are truly grateful for the feedback, you will get a reputation for being open to feedback. Remember, feedback is a gift that helps you be more effective.

Be grateful for it.

Get your head out of the sand and ask, ask, ask! Then check in with yourself to see what fits for you, and put the useful feedback into action. Take whatever steps are necessary to improve the situation—including changing your own behavior.

A few years ago, our company discontinued using a printer because another one offered us better service for a lower price. About 4 months later, our original printer called and said, "I've noticed you haven't used me for any printing lately. What would it take for you to start giving me your printing business again?"

I replied, "Lower prices, on-time turnaround, and pickup and delivery. If you can guarantee us those three things, I'll give you a small portion of our printing and try you again." Eventually, he won back most of our printing because he beat other people's prices, picked up and delivered, finished on time, and provided more than acceptable quality. Because he asked the question "What would it take . . . ," he got the information he needed to ensure his ongoing success with us.

SHE ASKED HER WAY TO SUCCESS
IN 3 SHORT MONTHS

One of the best-selling weight-loss books ever published was the book *Thin Thighs in 30 Days*. What's so interesting about it, though, is that it was developed solely using feedback. The author, Wendy Stehling, worked in an advertising agency but hated her job. She wanted to start her own agency but didn't have the money to do so. She knew she would need about $100,000, so she began asking, "What's the quickest way to raise $100,000?"

Sell a book, said the feedback.

She decided if she wrote a book that could sell 100,000 copies in 90 days—and she made $1 per book—she would raise the $100,000 she needed. But what kind of book would 100,000 people want? "Well, what are the best-selling books in America?" she asked.

Weight loss books, said the feedback.

"Yes, but how would I distinguish myself as an expert?" she asked.

Ask other women, said the feedback.

So she went out to the marketplace and asked, "If you could lose weight in only one part of your body, what part would you choose?" The overwhelming response from women was *My thighs.*

"When would you want to lose it?" she asked.

Around April or May, in time for swimsuit season, said the feedback.

So what did she do? She wrote a book called *Thin Thighs in 30 Days* and released it April 15. By June, she had her $100,000—all because she asked people what they wanted and responded to the feedback by giving it to them.

HOW TO LOOK REALLY BRILLIANT
WITH LITTLE EFFORT

Virginia Satir, the author of the classic parenting book *Peoplemaking,* was probably the most successful and famous family therapist that ever lived.

During her long and illustrious career, she was hired by the Michigan State Department of Social Services to provide a proposal on how to revamp and restructure the Department of Social Services so it would serve the client population better. Sixty days later, she provided the department with a 150-page report, which they said was the most amazing piece of work they had ever seen. "This is brilliant!" they gushed. "How did you come up with all these ideas?"

She replied, "Oh, I just went out to all the social workers in your system and I asked them what it would take for the system to work better."

LISTEN TO THE FEEDBACK

Human beings were given a left foot and a right foot to make a mistake first to the left, then to the right, left again and repeat.

BUCKMINSTER FULLER
Engineer, inventor, and philosopher

Whether we ask or not, feedback comes to us in various forms. It might come verbally from a colleague. Or it might be a letter from the government. It might be the bank refusing your loan. Or it could be a special opportunity that comes your way because of a specific step you took.

Whatever it is, it's important to listen to the feedback. Simply take a step . . . and listen. Take another step and listen. If you hear "Off course," take a step in a direction you believe may be on course . . . and listen. Listen externally to what others may be telling you, but also listen internally to what your body, your feelings, and your instincts may be telling you.

Is your mind and body saying, "I'm happy; I like this; this is the right job for me," or "I'm weary; I'm emotionally drained; I don't like this as much as I thought; I don't have a good feeling about that guy"?

Whatever feedback you get, don't ignore the yellow alerts. Never go against your gut. If it doesn't feel right to you, it probably isn't.

IS ALL FEEDBACK ACCURATE?

Not all feedback is useful or accurate. You must consider the source. Some feedback is polluted by the psychological distortions of the person giving you the feedback. For example, if your drunk husband tells you, "You are a no-good *bleep*," that is probably not accurate or useful feedback. The fact that your husband is drunk and angry, however, *is feedback you should listen to.*

LOOK FOR PATTERNS

Additionally, you should look for patterns in the feedback you get. As my friend Jack Rosenblum likes to say: "If one person tells you you're a horse, they're crazy. If three people tell you you're a horse, there's a conspiracy afoot. If ten people tell you you're a horse, it's time to buy a saddle."

The point is that if several people are telling you the same thing, there is probably some truth in it. Why resist it? You may think you get to be right, but the question you have to ask yourself is "Would I rather be right or be happy? Would I rather be right or be successful?"

I have a friend who would rather be right than be happy and successful. He got mad at anyone who tried to give him feedback. "Don't you talk to me that way, young lady." "Don't tell me how to run my business. This is my business and I'll run it the way I want to." "I don't give a hoot what you think." He was a "my way or the highway" person. He wasn't interested in anyone else's opinion or feedback. In the process, he alienated his wife, his two daughters, his clients, and all his employees. He ended up with two divorces, kids who didn't want to speak to him, and two bankrupt businesses. But he was "right." So be it, but don't *you* get caught in this trap. It is a dead-end street.

What feedback have you been receiving from your family, friends, members of the opposite sex, coworkers, boss, partners, clients, vendors, and your body that you need to pay more attention to? Are there any patterns that stand out? Make a list, and next to each item, write an action step you can take to get back on course.

WHAT TO DO WHEN THE FEEDBACK TELLS YOU YOU'VE FAILED

When all indicators say you've had a "failure experience," there are a number of things you can do to respond appropriately and keep moving forward:

1. Acknowledge you did the best you could with the awareness, knowledge, and skills you had at the time.
2. Acknowledge that you survived and that you can absolutely cope with any and all of the consequences or results.
3. Write down everything you learned from the experience. Write all of your insights and lessons down in a file in your computer or a journal called *Insights and Lessons.* Read through this file often. Ask others involved—your family, team, employees, clients, and others— what they learned. I often have my staff write "I learned that . . ." at the top of a piece of paper and then write as much as they can think of in a 5-minute period. Then we make a list under the heading of "Ways to Do It Better Next Time."
4. Make sure to thank everyone for their feedback and their insights. If someone is hostile in the delivery of their feedback, remember that it is an expression of their level of fear, not your level of incompetence or unlovability. Again, just thank them for their feedback. Explaining, justifying, and blaming are all a waste of everybody's time. Just take in the feedback, use whatever is applicable and valuable for the future, and discard the rest.
5. Clean up any messes that have been created and deliver any communications that are necessary to complete the experience— including any apologies or regrets that are due. Do not try to hide the failure.
6. Take some time to go back and review your successes. It's important to remind yourself that you have had many more successes than you have had failures. You've done many more things right than you've done wrong.

7. Regroup. Spend some time with positive loving friends, family, and coworkers who can reaffirm your worth and your contribution.

8. Refocus on your vision. Incorporate the lessons learned, recommit to your original plan, or create a new plan of action, and then get on with it. Stay in the game. Keep moving toward the fulfillment of your dreams. You're going to make a lot of mistakes along the way. Dust yourself off, get back on your horse, and keep riding.

COMMIT TO CONSTANT AND NEVER-ENDING IMPROVEMENT

We have an innate desire to endlessly learn, grow, and develop.
We want to become more than what we already are. Once we yield to
this inclination for continuous and never-ending improvement,
we lead a life of endless accomplishments and satisfaction.

CHUCK GALLOZZI

People call me a perfectionist, but I'm not. I'm a "rightist."
I do something until it's right, and then I move on to the next thing.

JAMES CAMERON
Oscar-winning director of *Titanic* and the *Terminator* series

In Japan, the word for constant and never-ending improvement is *kaizen*. Not only is this an operating philosophy for modern Japanese businesses, it is also the age-old philosophy of warriors, too—and it's become the personal mantra of millions of successful people.

Achievers—whether in business, sports, or the arts—are committed to continual improvement. If you want to be more successful, you need to learn to ask yourself, "How can I make this better? How can I do it more efficiently? How can I do this more profitably? How can we do this with greater love?"

THE MIND-NUMBING PACE OF CHANGE

In today's world, a certain amount of improvement is necessary just to keep up with the rapid pace of change. New technologies are announced nearly every month. New manufacturing techniques are discovered even more often. New words come into use anytime a trend or fad catches on. And what we learn about ourselves, about our health, and about the capacity for human thought continues almost unabated.

Improving is therefore necessary simply to survive. But to thrive, as successful people do, a more dedicated approach to improvement is required.

IMPROVE IN SMALL INCREMENTS

Whenever you set out to improve your skills, change your behavior, or better your family life or business, beginning in small, manageable steps gives you a greater chance of long-term success. Doing too much too fast not only overwhelms you (or anyone else involved in the improvement), it can doom the effort to failure—thereby reinforcing the belief that it's difficult, if not impossible, to succeed. When you start with small, achievable steps you can easily master, it reinforces your belief that you can easily improve.

DECIDE WHAT TO IMPROVE ON

At work, your goal might be for your company to improve the quality of your product or service, your customer service program, or your advertising. Professionally you might want to improve your computer skills, your typing speed, your sales skills, or your negotiating skills. At home you might want to improve your parenting skills, communication skills, or cooking skills. You could also focus on improving your health and fitness, your knowledge of investing and money management, or your piano playing. Or perhaps you want to develop greater inner peace through meditation, yoga, and prayer. Whatever your goal, decide where you want to improve and what steps you'll need to take to achieve that improvement.

Is it learning a new skill? Perhaps you can find that in a night class at the local community college. If it's improving your service to the community, perhaps you can find a way to spend an extra hour per week volunteering.

To keep yourself focused on constant and never-ending improvement, ask yourself every day, "How can I/we improve today? What can I/we do better than before? Where can I learn a new skill or develop a new competency?" If you do, you'll embark on a lifelong journey of improvement that will ensure your success.

YOU CAN'T SKIP STEPS

He who stops being better stops being good.

OLIVER CROMWELL
British politician and soldier (1599–1658)

One of life's realities is that major improvements take time; they don't happen overnight. But because so many of today's products and services promise overnight perfection, we've come to expect instant gratification—and we become discouraged when it doesn't happen. However, if you make a commitment to learning something new every day, getting just a little bit better every day, then eventually—over time—you will reach your goals.

Becoming a master takes time. You have to practice, practice, practice! You have to hone your skills through constant use and refinement. It takes years to have the depth and breadth of experience that produces expertise, insight, and wisdom. Every book you read, every class you take, every experience you have is another building block in your career and your life.

Don't shortchange yourself by not being ready when your big break appears. Make sure you have done your homework and honed your craft. Actors usually have to do a lot of preparation—acting classes, community theater, off-Broadway plays, bit parts in movies and television, more acting classes, voice lessons, accent training, dancing lessons, martial arts training, learning to ride a horse, more bit parts—until one day they are ready for the dream part that is ready for them.

Successful basketball players learn to shoot with their opposite hand, improve their foul-throw shooting, and work on their three-point shots. Artists experiment with different media. Airline pilots train for every kind of emergency in a flight simulator. Doctors go back to school to learn new procedures and obtain advanced certifications. They are all engaged in a process of constant and never-ending improvement.

Make a commitment to keep getting better and better every day in every way. If you do, you'll enjoy the feelings of increased self-esteem and self-confidence that come from self-improvement, as well as the ultimate success that will inevitably follow.

MARGIN OF GREATNESS

In the sport of professional baseball most respectable players bat an average of .250, or 1 hit for every 4 times they come to bat. If a .250 batter is also a good fielder, he can expect to do well in the majors. But anyone who hits .300, or 3 hits for every 10 times he comes to bat, is considered a star. By the end of a season, out of the thousands of players in the leagues, only about a dozen players will have achieved a .300 average. These hitters are honored as the greatest players, receive the multimillion-dollar player contracts, and land the lucrative commercial endorsements.

But consider this: The difference between the truly great ones and the average players is only 1 hit out of 20! A player who bats .250 gets 5 hits in every 20 times at bat, but a .300 hitter gets 6 hits out of those same 20 times at bat. Isn't that amazing? In the world of professional baseball, the margin of greatness is only 1 more hit out of 20! It takes only a little extra bit of performance to go from good to great.

KEEP SCORE
FOR SUCCESS

You have to measure what you want more of.

CHARLES COONRADT
Founder, The Game of Work

Remember when you were growing up and your mom or dad measured you every few months and kept track of your height on the wall near the pantry door? It was something visible that let you know where you stood in relation to the past and to your future goal (which was usually to be as tall as your mom or dad. It let you know you were making progress. It encouraged you to eat right and drink your milk to keep growing.

Well, successful people keep the same kind of measurements. They keep score of exciting progress, positive behavior, financial gain . . . anything they want more of.

In his groundbreaking book, *The Game of Work*,[24] Charles Coonradt says that scorekeeping stimulates us to create more of the positive outcomes we're keeping track of. It actually reinforces the behavior that created these outcomes in the first place.

Think about it. Your natural inclination is always to improve your score. If you were to keep score on the five things that would advance your personal and professional objectives the most, imagine how motivated you would be each time the numbers improved in your favor.

---

24. *The Game of Work: How to Enjoy Work as Much as Play*, by Charles A. Coonradt (Park City, Utah: Game of Work, 1997). Also see *Scorekeeping for Success*, by Charles A. Coonradt (Park City, Utah: Game of Work, 1999), and *Managing the Obvious: How to Get What You Want Using What You Know*, by Charles A. Coonradt with Jack M. Lyon and Richard Williams (Park City, Utah: Game of Work), 1994.

MEASURE WHAT YOU WANT, NOT
WHAT YOU DON'T WANT

We learn early in life that it's valuable to count what's valuable. We count the number of times we skip the rope, the number of jacks we pick up, the number of marbles we collect, the number of base hits we get in Little League, and the number of boxes of Girl Scout cookies we sell. Batting averages in baseball tell us the number of times we hit the ball, not the percentage of times we didn't. We keep score mostly of what is good, because that is what we want more of.

When Mike Walsh at High Performers International wanted to increase his bottom line, he started keeping track not just of the number of enrollments his company was getting but also of how many cold calls employees were making, how many face-to-face appointments they set up, and how many of those appointments they turned into enrollments. As a result of this kind of scorekeeping, Mike saw a 39% increase in revenues in just 6 months.

NOT JUST FOR BUSINESS OWNERS ANYMORE

When Tyler Williams joined a junior basketball league, his father, Rick Williams, coauthor of *Managing the Obvious*, decided to counteract the usual negative focus of youth sports by creating a "parent's scorecard" to keep track of what Tyler did right, rather than what he did wrong.

He tracked seven contributions his son could make to the team's success—points, rebounds, assists, steals, blocked shots, and so on—and awarded Tyler one point every time he made one of those positive plays. Whereas the statistics kept by the coaches centered chiefly on points and rebounds—the two traditional forms of measurement used in junior basketball—Tyler's dad's scorecard awarded points for virtually everything positive accomplished during a game.

It wasn't long before Tyler was sprinting over during timeouts to check on his contribution points. When they reached home after the game, Tyler would hustle to his bedroom, where he had a chart on the wall that plotted his progress. With a simple graph Tyler made himself, he could see where he was improving. As the season progressed, the line on his graph went steadily upward. Without a single harsh word from his coach or his dad, Tyler had turned into a better basketball player—and enjoyed the process besides.

KEEPING SCORE AT HOME

Of course, scorekeeping isn't just for business, sports, and school. It can be applied to your personal life, too. In the May 2000 issue of *Fast Company* magazine, Vinod Khosla, the founding CEO of Sun Microsystems, said

> It's great to know how to recharge your batteries. But it's even more important to make sure that you actually do it. I track how many times I get home in time to have dinner with my family; my assistant reports the exact number to me each month. I have four kids, ages 7 to 11. Spending time with them is what keeps me going.
>
> Your company measures its priorities. People also need to place metrics around their priorities. I spend about 50 hours a week at work, and I could easily work 100 hours. So I always make sure that, at the end of it all, I get home in time to eat with my kids. Then I help them with their homework and play games with them. . . . My goal is to be home for dinner at least 25 nights a month. Having a target number is key. I know people in my business who are lucky if they make it home 5 nights a month. I don't think that I'm any less productive than those people.[25]

START KEEPING SCORE TODAY

Decide where you need to keep score in order to manifest your vision and achieve your goals.

Make sure to keep score in all the areas of your life: financial, professional, school, recreation and fun time, health and fitness, family and other relationships, personal projects, and contribution to others.

Post your scores where you and any others playing the game can easily see them.

---

25. "Don't Burn Out!" *Fast Company*, May 2000, page 106.

22

PRACTICE PERSISTENCE

Most people give up just when they're about to achieve success.
They quit on the one-yard line. They give up at the last minute
of the game, one foot from a winning touchdown.

H. ROSS PEROT
American billionaire and former U.S. presidential candidate

Persistence is probably the single most common quality of high achievers. They simply refuse to give up. The longer you hang in there, the greater the chance that something will happen in your favor. No matter how hard it seems, the longer you persist the more likely your success.

IT'S NOT ALWAYS GOING TO BE EASY

Sometimes you are going to have to persist in the face of obstacles—unseen obstacles—that no amount of planning or forethought could have predicted. Sometimes, you'll encounter what seem like overwhelming odds. And sometimes, the universe will test your commitment to the goal you're pursuing. The going may be hard, requiring you to refuse to give up while you learn new lessons, develop new parts of yourself, and make difficult decisions.

History has demonstrated that the most notable winners usually
encountered heartbreaking obstacles before they triumphed.
They won because they refused to become discouraged by their defeats.

B.C. FORBES
Founder of *Forbes* magazine

Hugh Panero, chief executive at XM Satellite Radio, is an example of amazing commitment and perseverance in the corporate sector. After 2 years recruiting investors ranging from General Motors and Hughes Electronics to DIRECTV and Clear Channel Communications, Panero's dream of becoming the world's largest subscription radio service nearly collapsed at the last minute when investors threatened to back out if an acceptable deal wasn't struck by midnight, June 6, 2001. After exhausting negotiations and shuttle diplomacy, Panero and his chairman of the board, Gary Parsons, secured commitments of $225 million just minutes before the deadline.

Less than a year later, the launch of one of XM's $200 million satellites was aborted just 11 seconds before liftoff when an engineer misread a message on his computer screen, forcing the company to wait for the next available launch date 2 months later!

Still, Panero persevered and finally scheduled the debut of XM Radio's 101 channels of programming for September 12, 2001. But when terrorists attacked the World Trade Center on the morning of September 11—just a day prior to the scheduled debut—Panero was forced to cancel the satellite's launch party and pull XM's inaugural TV ad featuring a rap star rocketing past a group of towering skyscrapers.

Panero's team urged him to postpone the company's launch for another year. Yet in the end, Panero held fast to his dream and debuted the service just 2 weeks later.

Today, through all the setbacks and delays, most of which make our own daily difficulties pale by comparison, XM dominates the satellite radio business with more than 1.7 million subscribers paying every month to enjoy 68 channels of commercial-free music plus 33 channels of premier sports, talk, comedy, children's and entertainment programming, and traffic and weather information. And stock prices have risen from the original price of $12 to $25 a share.[26]

JUST ONE MORE TELEPHONE POLE

Fall down seven times, get up eight times.

JAPANESE PROVERB

Having lost his right leg to cancer, Terry Fox embarked on a cross-Canada run called the Marathon of Hope in 1980 to raise money for cancer research. His shuffle-and-hop running style took him about 24 miles per day—close to

---

26. See www.xmradio.com for more information. Stock price is as of June 1, 2004.

a complete 26-mile marathon every single day—with an artificial leg! He managed to run for 143 days and covered 3,339 miles from his starting point in St. John's, Newfoundland, to Thunder Bay, Ontario, where he was forced to abandon his run when doctors discovered cancer in his lungs. He died a few months later, but his inspiring example has left a legacy: Annual Terry Fox runs are held in Canada and around the world that so far have raised $340 million for cancer research. When asked how he kept himself going as exhaustion set in and he had thousands of miles ahead of him, he answered, "I just keep running to the next telephone pole."

FIVE YEARS

"No" is a word on your path to "Yes." Don't give up too soon.
Not even if well-meaning parents, relatives, friends, and colleagues
tell you to get "a real job." Your dreams are your real job.

JOYCE SPIZER
Author of *Rejections of the Written Famous*

When Debbie Macomber decided to pursue her dream of becoming a writer, she rented a typewriter, put it on the kitchen table, and began typing each morning after the kids went off to school. When the kids came home, she moved the typewriter and made them dinner. When they went to bed, she moved it back and typed some more. For 2½ years, Debbie followed this routine. Supermom had become a struggling writer, and she was loving every minute of it.

One night, however, her husband, Wayne, sat her down and said, "Honey, I'm sorry, but you're not bringing in any income. We can't do this anymore. We can't survive on just what I make."

That night, her heart broken and her mind too busy to let her sleep, she stared at the ceiling in their darkened bedroom. Debbie knew—with all the responsibilities of keeping up a house and taking four kids to sports, church, and scouts—that working 40 hours a week would leave her no time to write.

Sensing her despair, her husband woke up and asked, "What's wrong?"

"I really think I could've made it as a writer. I really do."

Wayne was silent for a long time, then sat up, turned on the light, and said, "All right, honey, go for it."

So Debbie returned to her dream and her typewriter on the kitchen table, pounding out page after page for another 2½ years. Her family went without vacations, pinched pennies, and wore hand-me-downs.

But the sacrifice and the persistence finally paid off. After 5 years of struggling, Debbie sold her first book. Then another. And another. Until finally, today, Debbie has published more than 100 books, many of which have become *New York Times* best-sellers and 3 of which have sold for movies. Over 60 million copies of her books are in print, and she has millions of loyal fans.

And Wayne? All that sacrifice in support of his wife paid off handsomely. He got to retire at age 50 and now spends his time building an airplane in the basement of their 7,000-square-foot mansion.

Debbie's kids got a gift far more important than a few summer camps. As adults, they realize what Debbie gave them was far more important—permission and encouragement to pursue their own dreams.

Today, Debbie still has dreams she wants to fulfill—a television series based on her books, an Emmy Award, a number-one *New York Times* best seller.

To accomplish them, she has a routine: She gets up every morning at 4:30, reads her Bible, and writes in her journal. By 6:00, she's swimming laps in the pool. And by 7:30, she's in her office answering mail. She writes between 10:00 AM and 4:00 PM, producing three new books a year with discipline and perseverance.

What could you accomplish if you were to follow your heart, practice this much daily discipline, and never give up?

NEVER GIVE UP ON YOUR HOPES AND DREAMS

Persistence and determination alone are omnipotent.
The slogan "press on" has solved and always will solve
the problems of the human race.

CALVIN COOLIDGE
Thirtieth president of the United States

Consider this:

- Admiral Robert Peary attempted to reach the North Pole seven times before he made it on try number eight.
- In its first 28 attempts to send rockets into space, NASA had 20 failures.

- Oscar Hammerstein had five flop shows that lasted less than a combined total of 6 weeks before *Oklahoma!* which ran for 269 weeks and grossed $7 million.
- Tawni O'Dell's career as a writer is a testament to her perseverance. After 13 years, she had written six unpublished novels and collected 300 rejection slips. Finally, her first novel, *Back Roads*, was published in January 2000. Oprah Winfrey chose her book for the Oprah Book Club, and the newly anointed novel rose to number two on the *New York Times* Best-Seller List, where it remained for 8 weeks.

NEVER, NEVER, NEVER GIVE UP

During the Vietnam War, Texas computer billionaire H. Ross Perot decided he would give a Christmas present to every American prisoner of war in Vietnam. According to David Frost, who tells the story, Perot had thousands of packages wrapped and prepared for shipping. He chartered a fleet of Boeing 707s to deliver them to Hanoi, but the war was at its height, and the Hanoi government said it would refuse to cooperate. No charity was possible, officials explained, while American bombers were devastating Vietnamese villages. Perot offered to hire an American construction firm to help rebuild what Americans had knocked down. The government still wouldn't cooperate. Christmas drew near, and the packages were unsent. Refusing to give up, Perot finally took off in his chartered fleet and flew to Moscow, where his aides mailed the packages, one at a time, at the Moscow central post office. They were delivered intact.[27] Can you now see why this man became the great success that he did? He simply refused to ever quit.

HANG IN THERE

It's always too soon to quit!

NORMAN VINCENT PEALE
Inspirational author

If you hang in there long enough, you will eventually reach your goal. Consider the career of major league baseball player Pat Tabler. Pat played 7 sea-

---

27. Adapted from *David Frost's Book of Millionaires, Multimillionaires, and Really Rich People*, by David Frost (New York: Random House, 1984).

sons in the minor leagues and 10 full seasons in the major leagues. He played in one World Series and one all-star game. When you look at his stats, it doesn't look like he was doing very well his first 7 years, but look at how his earnings grew over the lifetime of his career because he persevered in the pursuit of his dream.

	SALARY	BATTING AVERAGE
Minor Leagues		
1976	$2,500	.231
1977	$3,000	.238
1978	$3,500	.273
1979	$4,750	.316
1980	$5,000	.296
1981	$15,000	.301
1981	$25,000	.342
Cleveland Indians		
1983	$51,000	.291
1984	$102,000	.290
1985	$275,000	.275
1986	$470,000	.326
1987	$605,000	.307
Cleveland Indians, Kansas City Royals, and New York Mets		
1988	$800,000	.282
1989	$825,000	.259
1990	$725,000	.273
Toronto Blue Jays		
1991	$800,000	.216
1992	$800,000	.252
Total	**$5,546,750**	

HOW TO DEAL WITH OBSTACLES

For every failure, there's an alternative course of action.
You just have to find it. When you come to a roadblock, take a detour.

MARY KAY ASH
Founder, Mary Kay Cosmetics

Whenever you confront an obstacle or run into a roadblock, you need to stop and brainstorm three ways to get around, over, or through the block. For every obstacle, come up with three different strategies for handling the potential obstacle. There are any number of ways that will work, but you will find them only if you spend time looking for them. Always be solution-oriented in your thinking. Persevere until you find a way that works.

Difficulties are opportunities to better things; they are stepping-stones
to greater experience. . . . When one door closes, another always opens;
as a natural law it has to, to balance.

BRIAN ADAMS

23

PRACTICE THE RULE OF 5

Success is the sum of small efforts, repeated day in and day out.
ROBERT COLLIER
Best-selling author and publisher of *The Secret of the Ages*

When Mark Victor Hansen and I published the first *Chicken Soup for the Soul®* book, we were so eager and committed to making it a best seller that we asked 15 best-selling authors ranging from John Gray (*Men Are from Mars, Women Are from Venus*) and Barbara DeAngelis (*Real Moments*) to Ken Blanchard (*The One Minute Manager*) and Scott Peck (*The Road Less Traveled*) for their guidance and advice. We received a ton of valuable information about what to do and how to do it. Next, we visited with book publishing and marketing guru Dan Poynter, who gave us even more great information. Then we bought and read John Kremer's *1001 Ways to Market Your Book*.

After all of that, we were overwhelmed with possibilities. To tell the truth, we became a little crazy. We didn't know where to start, plus we both had our speaking and seminar businesses to run.

FIVE SPECIFIC THINGS THAT MOVE YOU
TOWARD YOUR GOAL

We sought the advice of Ron Scolastico, a wonderful teacher, who told us, "If you would go every day to a very large tree and take five swings at it with a very sharp ax, eventually, no matter how large the tree, it would have to come down." How very simple and how very true! Out of that we developed what we have called the Rule of 5. This simply means that every day, we do five specific things that will move our goal toward completion.

With the goal of getting *Chicken Soup for the Soul®* to the top of the *New York Times* Best-Seller List, it meant having five radio interviews or sending out five review copies to editors who might review the book or calling five network marketing companies and asking them to buy the book as a motivational tool for their salespeople or giving a seminar to at least five people and selling the book in the back of the room. On some days we would simply send out five free copies to people listed in the *Celebrity Address Book*—people such as Harrison Ford, Barbra Streisand, Paul McCartney, Steven Spielberg, and Sidney Poitier. As a result of that one activity, I ended up meeting Sidney Poitier—at his request—and we later learned that the producer of the television show *Touched by an Angel* required all of the people working on the show to read *Chicken Soup for the Soul*® to put them in "the right frame of mind." One day we sent copies of the book to the all jurors in the O.J. Simpson trial. A week later, we received a nice letter from Judge Lance Ito thanking us for thinking of the jurors, who were sequestered and not allowed to watch television or read the newspaper. The next day, four of the jurors were spotted reading the book by the press, and that led to some valuable public relations for the book.

We made phone calls to people who could review the book, we wrote press releases, we called in to talk shows (some at 3 AM), we gave away free copies at our talks, we sent them to ministers to use as a source of talks for their sermons, we gave free "Chicken Soup for the Soul" talks at churches, we did book signings at any bookstore that would have us, we asked businesses to make bulk purchases for their employees, we got the book into the PXs on military bases, we asked our fellow speakers to sell the book at their talks, we asked seminar companies to put it in their catalogues, we bought a directory of catalogues and asked all the appropriate ones to carry the book, we visited gift shops and card shops and asked them to carry the book—we even got gas stations, bakeries, and restaurants to sell the book. It was a lot of effort—a minimum of five things a day, every day, day in and day out—for over 2 years.

LOOK WHAT A SUSTAINED EFFORT CAN DO

Was it worth it? Yes! The book eventually sold over 8 million copies in 39 languages.

Did it happen overnight? No! We did not make a best seller list until over a year after the book came out—a year! But it was the sustained effort of the Rule of 5 for over 2 years that led to the success—one action at a time, one book at a time, one reader at a time. But slowly, over time, each reader told another reader, and eventually, like a slow-building chain letter, the word was spread and the book became a huge success—what *Time* magazine called "the publishing phenomenon of the decade." It was less of a publishing phenomenon and more of a phenomenon of persistent effort—thousands of individual activities that all added up to one large success.

In *Chicken Soup for the Gardener's Soul*, Jaroldeen Edwards describes the day her daughter Carolyn took her to Lake Arrowhead to see a wonder of nature—fields and fields of daffodils that extend for as far as the eye can see. From the top of the mountain, sloping down for many acres across folds and valleys, between the trees and bushes, following the terrain, there are rivers of daffodils in radiant bloom—a literal carpet of every hue of the color yellow, from the palest ivory to the deepest lemon to the most vivid salmon-orange. There appear to be over a million daffodil bulbs planted in this beautiful natural scene. It takes your breath away.

As they hiked into the center of this magical place, they eventually stumbled on a sign that read: "Answers to the Questions I Know You Are Asking." The first answer was "One Woman—Two Hands, Two Feet and Very Little Brain." The second was "One at a Time." The third: "Started in 1958."

One woman had forever changed the world over a 40-year period one bulb at a time. What might you accomplish if you were to do a little bit—five things—every day for the next 40 years toward the accomplishment of your goal. If you wrote 5 pages a day, that would be 73,000 pages of text—the equivalent of 243 books of 300 pages each. If you saved $5 a day, that would be $73,000, enough for four round-the-world trips! If you invested $5 a day, with compound interest at only 6% a year, at the end of 40 years, you'd have amassed a small fortune of around $305,000.

The Rule of 5. Pretty powerful little principle, wouldn't you agree?

EXCEED EXPECTATIONS

It's never crowded along the extra mile.

WAYNE DYER
Coauthor of *How to Get What You Really, Really, Really, Really Want*

Are you someone who consistently goes the extra mile and routinely overdelivers on your promises? It's rare these days, but it's the hallmark of high achievers who know that exceeding expectations helps you stand above the crowd. Almost by force of habit, successful people simply do more. As a result, they experience not only greater financial rewards for their extra efforts but also a personal transformation, becoming more self-confident, more self-reliant, and more influential with those around them.

GO THE EXTRA MILE

Seattle-based Dillanos Coffee Roasters roasts coffee beans and distributes them to coffee retailers in almost all 50 U.S. states. Dillanos' mission statement is "Help people, make friends, and have fun." The company has six core values that guide all of their activities. They are so committed to these values that the entire staff of 28 reads the list in unison at the end of every staff meeting. Number two on the list is "Provide an 'extra mile' level of service, always giving the customer more than they expect." This means they treat everyone of their customers like they'd treat a best friend—someone you'd go the extra mile for.

In 1997 one of those "friends," Marty Cox, who owned four It's a Grind Coffee Houses in Long Beach, California, was just an "average size customer," but Marty had big plans for the future. Founder and CEO David Morris wanted to help his "friend" fulfill his big dream. Dillanos shipped their beans by UPS. But in 1997 UPS went on strike, creating a threat to Marty's livelihood. How to get Marty's beans—the lifeblood of his business—from Seattle to Long Beach?

Dillanos considered the option of using the post office, but the company had heard through the grapevine that the post offices and FedEx were way overworked because of the UPS strike, and they didn't want to risk the beans arriving late. So Morris rented a trailer and drove his 800-pound coffee order to Marty's location, 2 weeks in a row. David made the 17-hour drive from Seattle to Long Beach, delivered Marty's 1-week coffee supply, drove back, got more coffee, drove down there the next week, and delivered it again. That kind of commitment to go the extra mile—literally 2,320 miles round-trip— turned Marty into a loyal long-term customer. And what has that meant to Dillanos? In just 6 years, Marty's four stores grew into a 150-store franchise with retail operations in nine states. Marty is now Dillanos' biggest customer. Going the extra mile pays off!

As a result of going the extra mile for all of their customers, Dillanos has grown from a single 25-pound roaster in one 1,600-square-foot room roasting 200 pounds of coffee beans a month in 1992 to two 800-pound roasters in a 26,000-square-foot facility delivering well over 1 million pounds of coffee beans a year, with annual sales over $10 million and a growth rate that is on track to double every 3 years.

FROM THE MAILROOM TO PRODUCER IN 4 YEARS

If you are willing to do more than you are paid to do,
eventually you will be paid to do more than you do.

SOURCE UNKNOWN

Back when television producer and screenwriter Stephen J. Cannell had 2,000 people working for him, his company would hire talented kids right out of film school to work in the mailroom and do other odd jobs. Often, Cannell would hear complaints about the $7-per-hour starting wage or all the overtime and think, *Wow, they just don't get it. That job and their wages and my company are here for just a short time in these kids' lives. While they could turn this experience into a tremendous launching pad, instead they're complaining about short-term stuff like dollars. They don't even comprehend that how high they go in life could very well be determined by how much time and effort they put in downstairs in my mailroom.*

Then one day, Cannell began hearing about an unusual new recruit. He was 40 years old and had been a rock-and-roll drummer earning over $100,000 a year in the music business. With his wife expecting a baby, he wanted off the road and was willing to take a job at minimum wage in Cannell's mailroom.

"Have you met the new guy?" people would say.

Soon everyone was talking about his work ethic, attitude, and drive. Steve Beers was one of those guys who was always looking to be of extra service, always with his ears open to projects that needed to be done.

When he was filling in for Cannell's regular limo driver one day, he overheard Cannell mention a suit he would need cleaned for an upcoming function. The next day it appeared, freshly back from the dry cleaners, on the hook in the limo. When Cannell asked him how it got there, he replied, "I got it from your wife and had it cleaned."

When he heard that a secretary needed to get checks to the bank right away, he offered to take them on his lunch hour. When kids in the mailroom fumed about having to deliver scripts to actors' homes at midnight on a night they had a date, Beers said, "Give them to me. I'll do it." Yet he never asked for extra compensation or even took credit for his efforts.

When two of Cannell's producers asked on the same day that Beers be made associate producer on their new shows, Cannell enthusiastically assigned him to *21 Jump Street*—a huge jump up from the mailroom. A year later, Cannell moved him up to producer on *21 Jump Street* and then shortly thereafter to co-executive producer on that show *and* on *Booker*, paying him over $500,000 a year.

"He's not a writer," Cannell said. "He really had none of the tools you would need to become an executive producer—except one. He was willing to work so hard that he stood head and shoulders above everybody else, which showed me exactly the kind of attitude and dedication he had."

Since becoming the co–executive producer for *21 Jump Street*, Beers has produced numerous pilots and series, including Steven Spielberg's sci-fi miniseries *Taken*. Beers is currently the co–executive producer of Showtime's hit series *Dead Like Me*. Beers's directing credits include episodes of *Dead Like Me*, *Magnificent Seven*, *Seaquest*, and, of course, *21 Jump Street*.

What was the success principle that took Steve Beers from the mailroom to the top—from $7 an hour to $500,000 a year? He was willing to go the extra mile and exceed everyone's expectations.

What could you accomplish if you were willing to go the extra mile, put in just a little extra effort, provide just a little more service? Are there circumstances in your life right now where you could do more, provide better value, overdeliver, or improve on what is asked of you? Do you have the opportunity—but also the personal initiative—to go the extra mile?

GIVE MORE THAN PEOPLE EXPECT

When Mike Kelley (whom you first met on page 122) first arrived on the island of Maui, he worked at several hotels selling suntan lotion to tourists. Mike, who would later go on to own several successful businesses in the islands, always went the extra mile for his patrons. One of his products was aloe vera gel for sunburn relief. He would show them the product, and then ask, "Are you familiar with aloe?" (This was back in the 1980s, when most Americans were not.) "I'll bring some over in a few minutes to show you." Then he would leave the hotel beach, climb to the top of a large rock that jutted out into the ocean, cut a piece of the large aloe plant that grew there, and dice it up until the jelly emerged. He would then take the aloe leaf over to them and put some of the jelly on their burn. They were so impressed by his extra effort that he almost always made a sale.

WHY GO THE EXTRA MILE?

So what's the payoff for you? When you give more than is expected, you are more likely to receive promotions, raises, bonuses, and extra benefits. You won't need to worry about job security. You'll always be the first hired and the last fired. Your business will make more money and attract lifelong loyal customers. You'll also find that you feel more satisfied at the end of each day.

But you have to start now for the rewards to begin appearing.

GIVE SOMETHING ABOVE AND BEYOND
WHAT IS EXPECTED

If you want to really excel at what you do—really become a howling success in school, business, or life—do more than is required, always giving something extra, something that is not expected. A business that goes the extra mile earns the respect, loyalty, and referrals of its customers.

When Mike Foster ran a computer store, he never let anyone walk out of the store with a box of components. He delivered the computer, printer, modems, and other components and spent 2 hours setting up the system, getting it to work perfectly and then providing training on how to use it. Mike's store dominated the Deaf Smith County, Texas, computer industry.

When Harv Eker sold a piece of exercise equipment, he would deliver it, set it up, and then train the person on how to correctly use the machinery. Harv's company grew so fast that he went from zero to millionaire in only 2 years.

If you're focused on only your own needs, you may think that giving more than is expected is unfair. Why should you give extra effort without compensation or recognition? You have to trust that eventually it will get noticed and that you will receive the compensation and recognition that you deserve. Eventually, as the old saying goes, the cream always rises to the top. So will you and your company. You will earn an impeccable reputation, and that is one of your most valuable assets.

Here are a few more examples of giving more than is expected:

- A client pays you for an oil painting and you frame it for him at no extra charge.
- You sell someone a car and you detail it and fill it up with gas before you deliver it to him.
- You sell someone a house, and when she moves in she discovers a bottle of champagne and a gift certificate for $100 to a local gourmet restaurant.
- As an employee, you not only do all of your own work but you also work on your day off when another employee calls in sick, you take on new responsibilities without demanding more pay, you offer to train a new employee, you anticipate problems before they occur and prevent them, you see something that needs to be done and you act on it without waiting to be asked, and you constantly are looking for what else you can do to make a contribution and be of service. Instead of focusing on how you can get more, you focus on how you can give more.

What can you do to go the extra mile and give more value to your boss, more service to your clients and customers, or more value to your students? One way is to surprise people with more than they expect.

I know a car dealer in Los Angeles who provides a free car wash for all of his customers every Saturday at his dealership. Nobody expects it, and everyone loves it. It gets him lots of referral business because everyone is always talking about how satisfied they are with his service.

THE FOUR SEASONS ALWAYS GOES THE EXTRA MILE

The name *Four Seasons* is synonymous with knock-your-socks-off service. The hotel chain always goes the extra mile. If you ask for directions from hotel staffers, they never just tell you—they walk you there. They always treat everybody as if they are royalty.

Dan Sullivan tells the story about the man who was taking his daughter to San Francisco for the weekend but realized that he didn't know how to braid her hair the special way her mother did it. When he called the Four Seasons to see if there was a staff person who could help him out, he was told that there was a woman on staff who was already assigned that job. It was something that management had anticipated that guests would someday need, and the hotels had it covered. Now that's going the extra mile.

Another hotel chain that is noted for its outstanding service is the Ritz-Carlton. When I arrived at my room during my last stay at the Ritz-Carlton in Chicago, there was a hot thermos of chicken noodle soup waiting on the desk. It had a little sign on it that read "Chicken Soup for Jack Canfield's Body." It was accompanied by a wonderful card from the manager saying how much he and his staff enjoyed the *Chicken Soup* books.

NORDSTROM GOES THE EXTRA MILE

Nordstrom is another chain of stores that is known for going the extra mile. Nordstrom's staff has always provided extraordinary service. Nordstrom salespeople have even been known to drop off merchandise to a customer on their way home from work.

Nordstrom also has a policy that you can return anything at any time. Does the policy get abused? Sure it does! But as a result of this policy, Nordstrom has an extraordinary reputation for quality customer service. It is part of the company's carefully guarded brand image. As a result, Nordstrom is very profitable.

Make a commitment to be world class like the Four Seasons, Ritz-Carlton, and Nordstrom by going the extra mile and exceeding expectations—starting today.

PART TWO

Transform
Yourself
for Success

*The greatest revolution of our generation is the
discovery that human beings, by changing the
inner attitudes of their minds, can change
the outer aspects of their lives.*

WILLIAM JAMES
Harvard psychologist

DROP OUT OF THE "AIN'T IT AWFUL" CLUB . . . AND SURROUND YOURSELF WITH SUCCESSFUL PEOPLE

You are the average of the five people you spend the most time with.

JIM ROHN
Self-made millionaire and successful author

When Tim Ferriss was 12 years old, an unidentified caller left the above Jim Rohn quote on his answering machine. It changed his life forever. For days, he couldn't get the idea out of his mind. At only 12 years of age, Tim recognized that the kids he was hanging out with were not the ones he wanted influencing his future. So he went to his mom and dad and asked them to send him to private school. Four years at St. Paul's School set him on a path that led to a junior year abroad in Japan studying judo and Zen meditation; 4 years at Princeton University, where he became an all-American wrestler; a national kickboxing championship; and eventually starting his own company at the age of 23. Tim knew what every parent intuitively knows—that we become like the people we hang out with.

Why else are parents always telling their kids that they don't want them hanging out with "those kids"? It's because we know that kids (and adults!) become like the people they hang out with. That is why it is so important to spend time with the people you want to become like. If you want to be more successful, you have to start hanging out with more successful people.

There are lots of places to find successful people. Join a professional association. Attend your professional conferences. Join the chamber of commerce. Join the country club. Join the Young Presidents' Organization or the Young Entrepreneurs Organization. Volunteer for leadership positions. Join civic groups like Kiwanis, Optimists International, and Rotary International. Volunteer to serve with other leaders in your church, temple, or mosque. Attend lectures, symposia, courses, seminars, clinics, camps, and retreats taught by those who have already achieved what you want to achieve. Fly first class or business class whenever you can.

YOU BECOME LIKE THE PEOPLE YOU SPEND THE MOST TIME WITH

Pay any price to stay in the presence of extraordinary people.

MIKE MURDOCK
Author of *The Leadership Secrets of Jesus*

John Assaraf is a successful entrepreneur who has seemingly done it all—including traveling the world for a year in his twenties, owning and operating a franchising company whose annual real estate revenues topped $3 billion, and helping to build Internet virtual tour pioneer Bamboo.com (now IPEX) from a team of 6 people to a team of 1,500 in just over a year, netting millions in monthly sales and completing a successful initial public offering on the NASDAQ after just 9 months.

John was a street kid who had been entangled in the world of drugs and gangs. When he landed a job working in the gym at the Jewish community center across the street from his apartment in Montreal, his life was changed by the powerful principle that you become like the people you spend the most time with. In addition to earning $1.65 an hour, he received access to the men's health club. John recounts that he got his early education in business in the men's sauna. Every night after work, from 9:15 to 10 PM, you'd find him in the steamy hot room listening to successful businessmen tell their tales of success and failure.

Many of those successful men were immigrants who had come to Canada to stake their claim, and John was fascinated as much by their setbacks as by their successes. The stories of what went wrong with their businesses, families, and health gave him inspiration, because his own family was experiencing tremendous challenges and difficulties, and John learned that it was normal to have challenges—that other families also went through similar crises and still made it to the top.

These successful people taught John to never give up on his dreams. "No matter what the failure," they told him, "try another way; try going up, over,

around, or through, but never give up. There's always a way." John also
learned from these successful men that it makes no difference where you are
born, what race or color you are, how old you are, or whether you come from
a rich family or a poor family. Many of the men in that sauna spoke broken
English; some were single and some were divorced; some were happily married and some were not; some were healthy and others were in terrible shape;
some had college degrees and some didn't. Some hadn't even been to high
school. For the first time, John realized that success is not reserved just for
those born into well-to-do families without challenges and to whom every
advantage has been given. He realized that no matter what the conditions of
your life, you could build a life of success. He was in the presence of men
from all walks of life who had done it and freely shared their wisdom and experience with him.

Every night John attended his own private business school—in a sauna in
a Jewish community center. You, too, need to be surrounded with those who
have done it; you need to be surrounded with people who have a positive attitude, a solution-oriented approach to life—people who know that they can
accomplish whatever they set out to do.

Confidence is contagious. So is lack of confidence.

VINCE LOMBARDI
Head coach of the Green Bay Packers who led them to six division titles,
five NFL championships, and two Super Bowls (I and II)

DROP OUT OF THE "AIN'T IT AWFUL" CLUB

*There are two types of people—anchors and motors. You want
to lose the anchors and get with the motors because the motors
are going somewhere and they're having more fun.
The anchors will just drag you down.*

WYLAND
World-renowned marine artist

When I was a first-year history teacher in a Chicago high school, I quickly
stopped going into the teachers' lounge, which I soon dubbed the Ain't It
Awful Club. Worse than the haze of cigarette smoke that constantly hung
over the room was the cloud of emotional negativity. "Can you believe what

they want us to do now?" "I got that Simmons kid again this year in math. He's a holy terror." "There is no way you can teach these kids. They are totally out of control." It was a constant stream of negative judgments, criticisms, blaming, and complaining. Not too long after, I discovered a group of dedicated teachers that hung out in the library and ate together at two tables in the teachers' lunchroom. They were positive and believed they could overcome and handle anything that was thrown at them. I implemented every new idea they shared with me, as well as a few more that I picked up from my weekend classes at the University of Chicago. As a result, I was selected by the students as teacher of the year in only my first year of teaching.

BE SELECTIVE

I just do not hang around anybody that I don't want to be with. Period. For me, that's been a blessing, and I can stay positive. I hang around people who are happy, who are growing, who want to learn, who don't mind saying sorry or thank you . . . and [are] having a fun time.

JOHN ASSARAF
Author, *The Street Kid's Guide to Having It All*

I'd like you to do a valuable exercise that my mentor W. Clement Stone did with me. Make a list of everyone you spend time with on a regular basis— your family members, coworkers, neighbors, friends, people in your civic organization, fellow members of your religious group, and so on.

When you've completed your list, go back and put a minus sign (−) next to those people who are negative and toxic, and a plus sign (+) next to those who are positive and nurturing. As you make a decision about each person, you might find that a pattern will begin to form. Perhaps your entire workplace is filled with toxic personalities. Or perhaps it's your friends who naysay everything you do. Or maybe it's your family members who constantly put you down and undermine your self-esteem and self-confidence.

I want you to do the same thing that Mr. Stone told me to do. Stop spending time with those people with a minus sign next to their name. If that is impossible (and remember, nothing is impossible; it is always a choice), then severely decrease the amount of time you spend with them. You have to free yourself from the negative influence of others.

Think about it. I'm sure you know people who only have to walk into the room to totally drain you of energy. I refer to these people as psychic vampires. They literally suck the life energy right out of you. Stop spending time with them.

Are there people in your life who are always complaining and blaming others for their circumstances? Are there people who are always judging others, spreading negative gossip, and talking about how bad it is? Stop spending time with them as well.

Are there people in your life who, simply by calling you on the telephone, can bring tension, stress, and disorder to your day? Are there dream-stealers who tell you that your dreams are impossible and try to dissuade you from believing in and pursuing your goals? Do you have friends who constantly attempt to bring you back down to their level? If so, then it is time for some new friends!

AVOID TOXIC PEOPLE

Until you reach the point in your self-development where you no longer allow people to affect you with their negativity, you need to avoid toxic people at all costs. You're better off spending time alone than spending time with people who will hold you back with their victim mentality and their mediocre standards.

Make a conscious effort to surround yourself with positive, nourishing, and uplifting people—people who believe in you, encourage you to go after your dreams, and applaud your victories. Surround yourself with possibility thinkers, idealists, and visionaries.

SURROUND YOURSELF WITH SUCCESSFUL PEOPLE

One of the clients who hired me to teach these success principles to their salespeople is one of the leading manufacturers of optical lenses. As I mingled with the salespeople prior to the event, I asked each person I met if he or she knew who the top five salespeople in the company were. Most answered yes and quickly rattled off their names. That night I asked my audience of 300 people to raise their hands if they knew the names of the top five salespeople. Almost everyone raised a hand. I then asked them to raise their hands again if they had ever gone up to any of these five people and asked them to share their secrets of success. Not one hand went up. Think about it! Everyone knew who the most effective people in the company were, but because of an unfounded fear of rejection, nobody had ever asked these sales leaders to share their secrets with them.

If you are going to be successful, you have to start hanging out with the successful people. You need to ask them to share their success strategies with you. Then try them on and see if they fit for you. Experiment with doing what they do, reading what they read, thinking the way they think, and so on. If the new ways of thinking and behaving work, adopt them. If not, drop them, and keep looking and experimenting.

26

ACKNOWLEDGE YOUR POSITIVE PAST

I look back on my life like a good day's work;
it is done and I am satisfied with it.

GRANDMA MOSES
American folk artist who lived 101 years

Most people in our culture remember their failures more than their successes. It's the result of the "leave 'em alone—zap 'em" approach to parenting, teaching, and management that is so prevalent in our culture. When you were a young child, your parents left you alone when you were playing and being cooperative, and then zapped you when you made too much noise, were a nuisance, or got into trouble. You probably received a perfunctory "good job" when you got A's but got a huge lecture when you got C's and D's, or, God forbid, an F. In school, most of your teachers marked the answers you got wrong with an X rather than marking the ones you got right with a check mark or a star. In sports, you got yelled at when you dropped the football or the baseball. There was almost always more emotional intensity around your errors, mistakes, and failures than there was around your successes.

Because the brain more easily remembers events that were accompanied by strong emotions, most people underestimate and underappreciate the number of successes they've had in relation to the number of failures they've had. One of the ways to counteract this phenomenon is to consciously focus on and celebrate your successes. One of the exercises I do in my corporate seminars is to have the participants each share a success they have had in the past week. It is always amazing to see how difficult this is for so many people. Many people don't think they have had any successes. They can easily tell you 10 ways they messed up in the last 7 days but have a much harder time telling you 10 victories they had.

The sad truth is that we all have many more victories than failures—it's just that we set the bar too high for what we call a success. A participant in the

GOALS (Gaining Opportunities and Life Skills) Program I developed to help get people off welfare in California[28] actually asserted that he didn't have *any* successes. When I inquired about his accent, he told us that he had left Iran when the shah was toppled in 1979. He had moved his whole family to Germany, where he had learned German and become a car mechanic. More recently he had immigrated his whole family to the United States, had learned English, and was now in a program learning to be a welder—but he didn't think he had any successes! When the group asked him what he thought a success was, he replied that it was owning a home in Beverly Hills and driving a Cadillac. In his mind, anything less than that was not an achievement. Slowly, with a little coaching, he began to see that he had many success experiences every single week. Simple things such as getting to work on time, getting into the GOALS Program, learning to speak English, providing for his family, and buying his daughter her first bicycle were all successes.

THE POKER CHIP THEORY OF
SELF-ESTEEM AND SUCCESS

So why am I making such a big deal about acknowledging your past successes? The reason it is so important is because of its impact on your self-esteem. Imagine for a moment that your self-esteem is like a stack of poker chips. Then imagine that you and I are playing a game of poker and you have 10 chips and I have 200 chips. Who do you think is going to play more conservatively in this game of poker? Yes, you are. If you lose two bets of 5 chips, you're out of the game. I can lose 5 chips 40 times before I'm out of the game, so I am going to take more risks because I can afford to take the losses. Your level of self-esteem works the same way. The more self-esteem you have, the more risks you are willing to take.

Research has shown over and over again that the more you acknowledge your past successes, the more confident you become in taking on and successfully accomplishing new ones. You know that even if you fail, it won't destroy you, because your self-esteem is high. And the more you risk, the more you win in life. The more shots you take, the more chances you have of scoring.

Knowing that you have had successes in the past will give you the self-confidence that you can have more successes in the future. So let's look at some simple but powerful ways to build and maintain a high level of confidence and self-esteem.

---

28. For information on the GOALS Program, which we developed for the state of California to help get people off welfare, contact the Foundation for Self-Esteem, 6035 Bristol Parkway, Culver City, CA 90230. Phone: 310-568-1505. So far, 355,000 people have graduated from this program.

BEGIN WITH NINE MAJOR SUCCESSES

Here is a simple way to begin an inventory of your major successes. (Consider also doing this exercise with your spouse or whole family.) Start by dividing your life into three equal time periods—for example, if you are 45 years old, your three time periods would be from birth to 15, 16 to 30, and 31 to 45. Then list three successes you've had for each time period. To help you get started, I've listed my own below:

First Third: Birth to Age 20

   1. Elected patrol leader in the Boy Scouts
   2. Caught winning touchdown pass to win city championship game
   3. Admitted to Harvard University

Second Third: Age 20 to 40

   1. Earned my master's degree in education from the University of Massachusetts
   2. Published my first book
   3. Founded the New England Center for Personal and Organizational Development

Final Third: Age 40 to 60

   1. Founded Self-Esteem Seminars
   2. *Chicken Soup for the Soul*® hit number one on the *New York Times* Best-Seller List
   3. Achieved goal of having spoken professionally in all 50 states

CAN YOU LIST 100 SUCCESSES?

To really convince yourself that you're a successful person who can continue to achieve great things, complete the next step of this exercise and list 100 or more of your life successes.

My experience is that most people do fine coming up with the first 30 or so; then it becomes a little more difficult. To come up with 100, you are going to have to list things like learning to ride a bicycle, singing a solo at church, getting your first summer job, the first time you got a hit in Little

League, making the cheerleading squad, getting your driver's license, writing an article for your school newspaper, getting an A in Mr. Simon's history class, surviving basic training, learning to surf, winning a ribbon at the county fair, modifying your first car, getting married, having your first child, and leading a fund-raising campaign for your child's school. These are all things you probably take for granted now, but they all need to be acknowledged as successes along your life's journey. Depending on your age, you may even need to resort to writing down "passed first grade, passed second grade, passed third grade," but that's okay. The goal is simply to get to 100.

CREATE A VICTORY LOG

Another powerful way to keep adding to that stack of poker chips is to keep a written record of your successes. It can be as simple as a running list in a spiral-bound notebook or a document on your computer, or it can be as elaborate as a leather-bound journal. By recalling and writing down your successes each day, you log them into your long-term memory, which enhances your self-esteem and builds your self-confidence. And later, if you need a boost of self-confidence, you can reread what you have written.

Peter Thigpen, a former vice president at Levi Strauss & Co., kept such a victory log on his desk, and every time he had a victory or a win, he wrote it down. And when he was about to do something scary, such as negotiate for a multimillion-dollar bank loan or make a speech to the board of directors, he would read his victory log to build up his self-confidence. His list included entries such as *I opened up China as a market*, *I got my teenage son to clean up his room*, and *I got the board to approve the new expansion plan*.

When most people are about to embark on some frightening task, they have a tendency to focus on all the times they tried before and didn't succeed, which undermines their self-confidence and feeds their fear that they will fail again. Keeping and referring to your victory log keeps you focused on your successes instead.

Start your own victory log as soon as possible. If you want, you can also embellish it like a scrapbook with photos, certificates, memos, and other reminders of your success.

DISPLAY YOUR SUCCESS SYMBOLS

Researchers have discovered that what you see in your environment has a psychological impact on your moods, your attitudes, and your behavior. Your environment has a great deal of influence over you. But here's an even more important fact: You have almost total control over your immediate environment. You get to choose what pictures are hung on your bedroom or office wall, what memorabilia gets taped to your refrigerator or locker door, and what mementos you place on your desk or in your cubicle at work.

A valuable technique that will help build your self-esteem and motivate you to greater future success is the practice of surrounding yourself with awards, pictures, and other objects that remind you of your successes. These might include medals from your armed services days, a picture of you scoring the winning touchdown, your wedding picture, a trophy, a framed copy of the poem you had published in the local newspaper, a letter of thanks, your college diploma, or your Eagle Scout badge or Girl Scout Gold Award.

Make a special place—a special shelf, the top of your dresser, the refrigerator door, a "victory wall" in a hallway you pass through every day—and fill it with your success symbols. Clean out that special drawer, those boxes in the closet, your files—then frame, laminate, polish, and display those symbols of your success so you will see them every day. This will have a powerful effect on your subconscious mind. It will subtly program you to see yourself as a winner—someone who has consistent successes in life! It will also convey this message to others. It will instill confidence in you and in others for you.

This is also a great thing to do for your children. Proudly display their success symbols as well—papers, ribbons, artwork, photographs of them in their baseball uniform or playing the violin, photographs of them enjoying themselves, trophies, medals, and other awards. If you have children living at home, frame their best artwork and hang it on the walls of the kitchen, their rooms, and the hallways in the house. When they see these framed and on the wall, it can be a major boost to their self-esteem.

THE MIRROR EXERCISE

You are a living magnet. What you attract into your life is in harmony with your dominant thoughts.

BRIAN TRACY
Leading authority on the development of human potential
and personal effectiveness

Just as you acknowledge your big successes, you need to acknowledge your small daily successes, too. The Mirror Exercise is based on the principle that we all need acknowledgment, but the most important acknowledgement is the acknowledgment we give ourselves.

The Mirror Exercise gives your subconscious mind the positive strokes it needs to pursue further achievements and it helps change any negative beliefs you have toward praise and accomplishment, which puts you in an achieving frame of mind. Do this exercise for a minimum of 3 months. After that, you can decide whether you want to continue. I know some very successful people who have been doing this every night for years.

Just before going to bed, stand in front of a mirror and appreciate yourself for all that you have accomplished during the day. Start with a few seconds of looking directly into the eyes of the person in the mirror—your mirror image looking back at you. Then address yourself by name and begin appreciating yourself *out loud* for the following things:

- Any achievements—business, financial, educational, personal, physical, spiritual, or emotional
- Any personal disciplines you kept—dietary, exercise, reading, meditation, prayer
- Any temptations that you did not give in to—eating dessert, lying, watching too much TV, staying up too late, drinking too much

Maintain eye contact with yourself throughout the exercise. When you're finished appreciating yourself, complete the exercise by continuing to look deep into your own eyes and saying, "I love you." Then stand there for another few seconds to really feel the impact of the experience—as if you were the one in the mirror who had just listened to all of this appreciation. The trick during this last part is to not just turn away from the mirror feeling embarrassed or thinking of yourself or the exercise as stupid or silly.

Here is an example of what your exercise might sound like:

Jack, I want to appreciate you for the following things today: First, I want to appreciate you for going to bed on time last night without staying up too late watching TV so that you got up bright and early this morning and you had a really good conversation with Inga. And then you meditated for twenty minutes before you took a shower. You helped with getting the kids' lunches together, and you ate a healthy low-fat, low-carbohydrate breakfast. You got to work on time and led a very good staff meeting with your support team. You did a great job of helping everyone listen to everybody's feelings and ideas. And you were great at drawing out the quiet ones.

Let's see . . . oh, and then you ate a really healthy lunch—soup and salad—and you didn't have the dessert that was offered. And you drank the ten glasses of water that you committed to drinking every day. And then . . . let's see . . . you finished editing the new staff orientation manual, and you got a really good start on scheduling the summer management training program. And then you filled in your Daily Success Focus Journal before you left work. Oh, and you appreciated your assistant for all of her contributions for the day. It was great to see how she just lit up.

And when you got home, you spent quality time playing with the kids, especially Christopher, and then you read a book to all of the kids. That was really special. And now you're going to bed at a good time again and not staying up all night surfing the Internet. You were great today.

And one more thing, Jack—I love you!

It's not unusual to have a number of reactions the first few times you do this. You might feel silly, embarrassed, like crying (or actually begin crying), or just generally uncomfortable. Occasionally, people have even reported breaking out in hives, feeling hot and sweaty, or feeling a little light-headed. These are natural and normal reactions, as this is a very unfamiliar thing to be doing. We are not trained to acknowledge ourselves. In fact, we are mostly trained to do the opposite: *Don't toot your own horn. Don't get a swelled head. Don't get a stuffed shirt. Pride is a sin.* As you begin to act more positive and nurturing toward yourself, it is natural to have physical and emotional reactions as you release the old negative parental wounds, unrealistic expectations, and self-judgments. If you experience any of these things—and not all people do—don't let these things stop you. They are only temporary and will pass after a few days of doing the exercise.

The first time I did this exercise, after just 40 days I noticed that all my negative internal self-talk had totally vanished, crowded out by the daily positive focus of the Mirror Exercise. I used to berate myself for things like misplacing my car keys or my glasses. That critical voice just simply disappeared. The same kind of thing can happen for you, but only if you take the time to actually do the exercise.

One note to remember: If you find yourself lying in bed realizing you haven't done the Mirror Exercise yet, get out of bed and do it. Looking at yourself in the mirror is a critical part of the exercise. And one last bit of advice: Be sure to let your spouse, children, roommate, or parents know in advance that you will be doing this exercise each evening for the next 3 months or more. You don't want them to walk in on you and think you've lost your mind!

REWARD YOUR INNER CHILD

Inside all of us are three distinct and totally separate ego states that work in concert to make up our unique personality. We have a parentlike ego, an adult ego, and a childlike ego who act much the same way parents, adults, and children do in real life.

Your adult ego state is the rational part of yourself. It gathers data and makes logical decisions devoid of emotion. It plans your schedule, balances your checkbook, figures out your taxes, and determines when to rotate your tires.

Your parentlike ego tells you to tie your shoes, brush your teeth, eat your vegetables, do your homework, exercise, meet your deadlines, and finish your projects. It is your inner critic—the part that judges you when you don't live up to its standards. But it's also the nurturing part of yourself that makes sure you're protected, taken care of, and provided for. It is also the part that validates, appreciates, and acknowledges you for doing a good job.

Your childlike ego, on the other hand, does what all children do—it whines, begs for attention, craves hugs, and acts out when it doesn't get its needs met. As we go through life, it's almost as if we have a 3-year-old holding on to us who's constantly asking, *Why are we sitting at this desk? Why aren't we having more fun? Why am I still up at three in the morning? Why am I reading this boring report?*

As the parent of this "inner child," one of your most important tasks is to engage it and reward it for behaving itself while you get your work done.

If you had a 3-year-old in real life, you might say, "Mommy has to finish this proposal in the next twenty minutes. But after Mommy's done, we'll go for an ice cream or play a video game." Your real-life 3-year-old would probably answer, "Okay; I'll be good because I know I'm going to get something good at the end of it."

Well, not surprisingly, your inner child is no different. When you ask it to be still, let you finish your work, stay up late, and so on, it will behave as long as it knows there's a reward at the end of the behaving. At some point, it needs to know it will get to read a novel, go to the movies, play with a friend, listen to music, go dancing, let loose, eat out, get a new "toy," or take a vacation.

A big part of creating more success in your life is rewarding yourself when you succeed. In reality, rewarding yourself for your successes keeps your inner child happy and compliant the next time it must behave. It knows it can trust you to eventually deliver on your promises. If you don't, just like a real child, it will start to sabotage your efforts by doing things like getting sick, having accidents, or making mistakes that cost you a promotion or even your job, so that you are *forced* to take some time off. And that will only take you further away from the success you really want.

A SENSE OF COMPLETION

Another reason to celebrate your successes is that you don't feel complete until you've been acknowledged. It gives you a sense of accomplishment and recognition. If you spend weeks producing a report and your boss doesn't acknowledge it, you feel incomplete. If you send someone a gift and get no acknowledgment, there's this little incomplete taking up attention units inside of you. Your mind needs to complete the cycle.

Of course, even more important than completing, the simple, enjoyable act of acknowledging and rewarding our successes causes our subconscious mind to say, *Hey, succeeding is cool. Every time we produce a success, we get to do something fun. Jack will buy us something we want or take us someplace neat. Let's have more of these successes, so Jack will take us out to play.*

Rewarding yourself for your wins powerfully reinforces your subconscious mind's desire to want to work harder for you. It's just basic human nature.

KEEP YOUR EYE
ON THE PRIZE

It's easy to be negative and unmotivated, but it takes some work to be positive and motivated. While there's no off button for those relentless "tapes," there are things that you can do to turn down the volume and shift your focus from the negative to the positive.

DONNA CARDILLO, R.N.
Speaker, entrepreneur, humorist, and master motivator

Successful people maintain a positive focus in life no matter what is going on around them. They stay focused on their past successes rather than their past failures, and on the next action steps they need to take to get them closer to the fulfillment of their goals rather than all the other distractions that life presents to them. They are constantly proactive in the pursuit of their chosen objectives.

THE MOST IMPORTANT 45 MINUTES OF THE DAY

An important part of any focusing regimen is to set aside time at the end of the day—just before going to sleep—to acknowledge your successes, review your goals, focus on your successful future, and make specific plans for what you want to accomplish the next day.

Why do I suggest the *end* of the day? Because whatever you read, see, listen to, talk about, and experience during the last 45 minutes of the day has a huge influence on your sleep and your next day. During the night, your unconscious mind replays and processes this late-night input up to six times more often than anything else you experienced during the day. This is why cramming for school exams late at night can work and why watching a scary movie before bed will give you nightmares. This is also why reading good bedtime stories is so important for children—not just to get them to fall asleep, but because the repeated messages, lessons, and morals of the story become part of the fabric of the child's consciousness.

As you drift off to sleep, you enter into the alpha brain wave state of consciousness—a state in which you are very suggestible. If you drift off to sleep while watching the 11 PM news, that is what you'll be imprinting into your consciousness—war, crime, automobile accidents, rape, murder, executions, gang wars, drive-by shootings, kidnappings, and scandals in the boardroom and on Wall Street.

Think how much better it would be to read an inspirational autobiography or a self-improvement book instead. Imagine the power of meditating, listening to a self-help audio program, or taking the time to plan the next day right before you go to sleep.

In addition, here are a few exercises that will keep you focused and moving forward at the end of the day.

THE EVENING REVIEW

Sit with your eyes closed, breathe deeply, and give yourself *one* of the following directions:

- Show me where I could have been more effective today.
- Show me where I could have been more conscious today.
- Show me where I could have been a better (fill in your profession—manager, teacher, etc.) today.
- Show me where I could have been more loving today.
- Show me where I could have been more assertive today.
- Show me where I could have been more (fill in any characteristic) today.

As you sit calmly in a state of quiet receptivity, you'll see that a number of events from the day will come to mind. Just observe them without any kind of judgment or self-criticism. When no more events come to mind, take each incident and replay it in your mind *the way you would have preferred to have done it* had you been more conscious and intentional at the time. This creates a subconscious image that will help form the desired behavior the next time a similar situation occurs.

THE DAILY SUCCESS FOCUS JOURNAL

Another powerful tool to keep yourself focused on the positive and your eye on the prize is the Daily Success Focus Journal. This is an advanced variation on the victory log discussed in the last chapter. If you do this exercise every day for a month, you will increase your self-confidence as well as improve your performance in all areas of your life.

At the end of every day, simply identify five things that you accomplished during the day. These can be in any area of your life—work, school, family, spirituality, finances, health, personal development, or community service.

Create a blank version of the form on the next page[29]—then, once you've identified a success, write it down in the first box under "Success." Next, consider why that accomplishment is important to you and write that reason down in the second box under the heading "Reason." Then, identify how you can make further progress in this same area listed under "Further Progress." Last, write down a specific action step that will lead to this progress and jot that down in the fourth box under "Next Action." For example, in the sample form on the next page, the first success is "I conducted a great staff meeting." The reason that is important is that "it created the team spirit we were lacking." The "Further Progress" box needs to be something else I could do to create more team spirit, which in this case is to plan and execute an off-site staff development day. A "Next Action" I could take is to form a committee with Ann and Bob to plan the day. This quick and simple process keeps me constantly moving forward in the arena of building team spirit as well as many other areas.

Once you have completed the form, transfer all of the action items in the "Next Action" column into your calendar or planner. Schedule a specific time to do each item so that you actually get them done. Get them onto your calendar or to-do list. Can you see how much forward momentum this exercise would create in your life?

If you are a manager, consider having your whole staff do this 30-day exercise with you. It will keep them focused and will build up their confidence. This also works well as an exercise for the whole family at home. I have seen many teenagers blossom after only 30 days of doing this exercise.

---

29. You can download a free 8½" × 11" version of this form at www.thesuccessprinciples.com.

THE DAILY SUCCESS FOCUS JOURNAL

Day: Monday   **Date:** 2/15/05

	SUCCESS	REASON	FURTHER PROGRESS	NEXT ACTION
1	I conducted a great staff meeting.	It created the team spirit we were lacking.	Plan an off-site staff development day.	Form a committee with Ann and Bob.
2	I booked a long weekend at the Ojai Spa and Inn for Inga and me.	We really need to get away and rejuvenate our relationship.	Start planning summer with Patty and Jeff.	Talk to Patty about best time to get together.
3	I did 30 minutes on the stair-stepper.	It's important to my health and to my weight loss goal.	Add weight lifting to my routine.	Talk to Martin about his personal trainer.
4	I had a great dinner conversation and homework session with Christopher.	It's important to deepening and sustaining our relationship.	Do it again on Wednesday.	Check my calendar and free up the time.
5	I finished editing the tech report for my boss.	It helps get the upgrade we need on the office computer systems.	Get approvals for the expenditures.	Schedule a meeting of the executive committee.

CREATE YOUR IDEAL DAY

Another powerful tool to keep you focused on creating your life exactly as you want it to be is to take a few minutes after you have planned your next day's schedule and visualize the entire day going exactly as you want it. Visualize everyone being there when you call them, every meeting starting and ending on time, all of your priorities being handled, all of your errands being completed with ease, making every sale, and so on. See yourself performing at your best in every situation you will encounter during the next day. This will give your subconscious all night to work on creating ways to make it all happen just as you have visualized it.

Get into the habit now of visualizing your ideal next day the night before. It will make a huge difference in your life.

CLEAN UP YOUR MESSES
AND YOUR INCOMPLETES

If a cluttered desk is the sign of a cluttered mind,
what is the significance of a clean desk?

LAURENCE J. PETER
American educator and author

DECIDE

COMPLETE   **PLAN**

THE CYCLE OF
COMPLETION

FINISH   **START**

CONTINUE

Take a look at the diagram above. It's called the Cycle of Completion. Each of these steps—Decide, Plan, Start, Continue, Finish, and Complete—is required to succeed at anything, to get a desired result, to finish. Yet how many of us never *complete*? We get all the way through the finishing stage—but leave one last thing undone.

Are there areas in your life where you've left uncompleted projects or failed to get closure with people? When you don't complete the past, you can't be free to fully embrace the present.

FAILING TO COMPLETE ROBS YOU
OF VALUABLE ATTENTION UNITS

When you start a project or make an agreement or identify a change you need to make, it goes into your present memory bank and takes up what I call an attention unit. We can only pay attention to so many things at one time, and each promise, agreement, or item on your to-do list leaves fewer attention units to dedicate to completing present tasks and bringing new opportunities and abundance into your life.

So why don't people complete? Often, incompletes represent areas in our life where we're not clear—or where we have emotional and psychological blocks.

For instance, you might have a lot of requests, projects, tasks, and other things on your desk you really want to say no to—but you're afraid of being perceived as the bad guy. So you put off responding to avoid saying no. Meanwhile the sticky notes and stacks of paper pile up and distract you. There may also be circumstances in which you have to make decisions that are difficult or uncomfortable. So rather than struggle with the discomfort, you let the incompletes pile up.

Some incompletions come from simply not having adequate systems, knowledge, or expertise for handling these tasks. Other incompletions pile up because of our bad work habits.

GET INTO COMPLETION CONSCIOUSNESS

Continually ask yourself, *What does it take to actually get this task completed?* Then you can begin to consciously take that next step of filing completed documents, mailing in the forms required, or reporting back to your boss that the project has been completed. The truth is that 20 things *completed* have more power than 50 things half completed. One finished book, for instance, that can go out and influence the world is better than 13 books you're in the process of writing. Rather than starting 15 projects that end up incomplete and take up space in the house, you'd be better off if you had started just 3 and completed them.

THE FOUR D'S OF COMPLETION

One way to take care of to-do items is something we've all seen in time management courses: Do it, delegate it, delay it, or dump it. When you pick up a piece of paper, decide then and there whether you'll ever do anything with it. If not, dump it. If you can take care of it within 10 minutes, do it immediately. If you still want to take care of it yourself, but know it will take longer, delay it by filing it in a folder of things to do later. If you can't do it yourself or don't want to take the time, delegate it to someone you trust to accomplish the task. Be sure to have the person report back when he or she finishes the task so that you know it is complete.

MAKING SPACE FOR SOMETHING NEW

In addition to professional incompletes, most households are also groaning under the weight of too much clutter, too many papers, worn-out clothes, unused toys, forgotten personal effects, and obsolete, broken, and unneeded items. In the United States, the entire ministorage industry has sprung up to help homeowners and small businesses store what they can't fit in their homes and offices.

But do we really need all this stuff? Of course not.

One of the ways to free up attention units is to free your living and work environment from the mental burden of this clutter. When you clear out the old, you also make room for something new.

Take a look at your clothes closet, for instance. If you've got one of those where you can't put another thing into it—where you struggle to pull out a dress or shirt—that may be one reason why you don't have more new clothes. There's nowhere to put them. If you haven't worn something in 6 months and it's not a seasonal or a special-occasion item such as an evening gown or tuxedo, get rid of it.

If there's *anything* new that you want in your life, you've got to make room for it. I mean that psychologically as well as physically.

If you want a new man in your life, you've got to let go of (forgive and forget) the last one you stopped dating 5 years ago. Because if you don't, when a new man meets you, the unspoken message he picks up is "This woman's attached to somebody else. She hasn't let go."

My good friend Martin Rutte once told me that whenever he wants to bring in new business, he thoroughly cleans his office, home, car, and garage. Every time he does, he starts getting calls and letters from people who want to work with him. Others find that doing spring cleaning helps them gain new clarity on problems, challenges, opportunities, and relationships.

When we don't throw away clutter and items we no longer need, it's as if we don't trust our ability to manifest the necessary abundance in our lives to buy new ones. But incompletes like this keep that very abundance from showing up. We need to complete the past so that our present can show up more fully.

TWENTY-FIVE WAYS TO COMPLETE BEFORE MOVING FORWARD

How many things do you need to complete, dump, or delegate before you can move on and bring new activity, abundance, relationships, and excitement into your life? Use the checklist below to jog your thinking, make a list, and then write down how you'll complete each task.

Once you've made your list, choose four items and start completing them. Choose those that would immediately free up the most time, energy, or space for you—whether it's mental space or physical space.

At minimum, I encourage you to clean up one major incomplete every 3 months. If you want to really get the ball rolling, schedule a "completion weekend," and devote 2 full days to handling as many things on the following list as possible.

1. Former business activities
2. Promises not kept, not acknowledged, or not renegotiated
3. Unpaid debts or financial commitments (money owed to others or to you)
4. Closets overflowing with clothing never worn
5. A disorganized garage crowded with old discards
6. Haphazard or disorganized tax records
7. Checkbook not balanced or accounts that should be closed
8. "Junk drawers" full of unusable items
9. Missing or broken tools
10. An attic filled with unused items
11. A car trunk or backseat full of trash
12. Incomplete car maintenance
13. A disorganized basement filled with discarded items
14. Credenza packed with completed or unrealized projects
15. Filing left undone

16. Computer files not backed up or data needing to be converted for storage
17. Desk surface cluttered or disorganized
18. Family pictures never put into an album
19. Mending, ironing, or other piles of items to repair or discard
20. Deferred household maintenance
21. Personal relationships with unstated resentments or appreciations
22. People you need to forgive
23. Time not spent with people you've been meaning to spend time with
24. Incomplete projects or projects delivered without closure or feedback
25. Acknowledgments that need to be given or asked for

WHAT'S IRRITATING YOU?

Like incompletes, daily irritants are equally damaging to your success because they, too, take up attention units. Perhaps it's the missing button on your favorite suit that keeps you from wearing it to an important meeting or the torn screen on your patio door that lets in annoying insects. One of the best things you can do to move further and faster along your success path is to fix, replace, mend, or get rid of those daily irritants that annoy you and stay on your mind.

Talane Miedaner, the author of *Coach Yourself to Success*, recommends walking through every room of your house, your garage, and all around your property, jotting down those things that irritate, annoy, and bother you and then arranging to get each one handled. Of course, none of these may be urgent to your business or life-threatening to your family. But every time you notice them and wish they were different, they pull energy from you. They are subtly subtracting energy from your life instead of adding energy to your life.

CONSIDER HIRING A PROFESSIONAL ORGANIZER TO GET YOU STARTED

The mission of the National Association of Professional Organizers (NAPO) is to help you declutter your life and build systems to ensure that things stay that way. You may need someone who has a dispassionate eye to look beyond your attachments, familiarity, and fears and be neutral in a way you can't.

Plus, NAPO members are experts in how to make things efficient and easy. It is their profession.[30]

For about the cost of several business lunches, you can hire an organizer from your local area for a day of work. Additionally, you can hire people to clean your home, as well as handle all the little irritants, maintenance chores, and other tasks you either don't want to do or aren't skilled enough to do.

If your finances don't allow for a professional organizer, ask a friend to help. Hire a neighborhood teen or the stay-at-home mom down the street. You can also read one of the many good how-to books and tackle things yourself.[31] Just remember that you don't need to get it done all at once. Choose one each month. Just as cleaning up your incompletes is important to your successful future, there is literally no excuse for enduring the disorganization in your life.

---

30. You can find organizers in your area by visiting the NAPO Web site at www.napo.net and clicking on "Find an Organizer." The following Web sites also help you locate professional organizers near you: www.organizersincanada.com and www.organizerswebring.com, which includes listings for seven countries. Martha Ringer is the productivity coach who has helped me organize my desk and my work flow. In 2 days' time, my office looked like a brand-new place, and my work flow is now clean and efficient. You can find her at www.martharinger.com.

31. Some of the best are
—*Getting Organized*, by Stephanie Winston (New York: Bantam Books, 1978).
—*Organizing from the Inside Out* (second edition), by Julie Morgenstern (New York: Henry Holt, 2004).
—*Organizing from the Inside Out for Teens*, by Julie Morgenstern and Jessi Morgenstern-Colón (New York: Henry Holt, 2002).
—*How to Be Organized in Spite of Yourself* (revised edition), by Sunny Schlenger and Roberta Roesch (New York: Signet Books, 1999).
—*Let Go of Clutter*, by Harriet Schecter (New York: McGraw-Hill, 2001).

29

COMPLETE THE PAST TO EMBRACE THE FUTURE

None of us can change our yesterdays,
but all of us can change our tomorrows.

COLIN POWELL
Secretary of state of the United States of America
under President George W. Bush

Does this sound familiar? Some people go through life as if they have a big anchor behind them, weighing them down. If they could release it, they would be able to move faster and succeed more easily. Perhaps that's you—holding on to past hurts, past incompletes, past anger or fear. Yet releasing these anchors can often be the final step you need to complete your past and embrace the future.

I have known people who have forgiven their parents and doubled their income in the ensuing few months, as well as doubled their productivity and doubled their ability to achieve things. I've known others who have forgiven their aggressors for past harm and been relieved of actual physical ailments.

The truth is . . . we need to let go of the past to embrace the future. One method I use for this is called the Total Truth Process.

THE TOTAL TRUTH PROCESS AND TOTAL TRUTH LETTER

The Total Truth Process and the Total Truth Letter are tools to help you release negative emotions from the past and come back to your natural state of love and joy in the present.[32]

The reason I call it *total* truth is that often, when we're upset, we fail to communicate *all* our true feelings to the person we're upset with. We get

---

32. I thank John Gray and Barbara DeAngelis, who first taught me this process.

stuck at the level of anger or pain and rarely move past it to emotional completion. As a result, it can be difficult to feel close to—or even at ease with—the other person after such an angry or painful confrontation.

The Total Truth Process helps us express our true feelings, so we can recapture the caring, closeness, and cooperation that is our natural state.

The process is intended not to let us dump or discharge negative emotions on another but to allow us to move through the negative emotions and release them so that we can return to the state of love and acceptance that is our natural state of being, and from which joy and creativity can flow.

The Stages of the Total Truth

The Total Truth Process can be conducted verbally or in writing. Whichever method you choose, the goal is to express the anger and hurt, and then move toward forgiveness and love.

If you participate verbally—always with the other person's permission—begin by expressing your anger, and then move through each stage all the way through to the final stage of love, compassion, and forgiveness. You can use the following prompts to keep you focused at each stage. For the process to be effective, you need to spend an equal amount of time on each of the six stages.

1. Anger and resentment
    I'm angry that . . .   I'm fed up with . . .
    I hate it when . . .   I resent . . .

2. Hurt
    It hurt me when . . .   I feel hurt that . . .
    I felt sad when . . .   I feel disappointed about . . .

3. Fear
    I was afraid that . . .   I get afraid of you when . . .
    I feel scared when . . .   I'm afraid that I . . .

4. Remorse, regret, and accountability
    I'm sorry that . . .   I'm sorry for . . .
    Please forgive me for . . .   I didn't mean to . . .

5. Wants
    All I ever want(ed) . . .   I want(ed) . . .
    I want you to . . .   I deserve . . .

6. Love, compassion, forgiveness, and appreciation
    I understand that . . .   I forgive you for . . .
    I appreciate . . .   Thank you for . . .
    I love you for . . .

If you're uncomfortable participating verbally or if the other person cannot or will not participate, put your feelings in writing using the Total Truth Letter to express your true feelings.

The Total Truth Letter

Follow these steps when writing a Total Truth Letter:

1. Write a letter to the person who has upset you, with roughly equal portions of the letter expressing each of the feelings in the Total Truth Process.
2. If the other party is not someone who is likely to agree to cooperate with this process, you may choose to simply throw the letter away once you have completed it. Remember, the main purpose here is to get you free from the unexpressed emotions, not to change the other person.
3. If the person you are upset with is willing to participate, have him or her write a Total Truth Letter to you, too. Then exchange letters. Both of you should be present when you read the letters. Then discuss the experience. Avoid trying to defend your position. Make an effort to understand where the other person is coming from.

After some practice, you may find you can go through the six stages of the process quickly and less formally, but in times of great difficulty, you will still want to use the six stages as a guideline.

FORGIVE AND MOVE ON

As long as you don't forgive, who and whatever it is will occupy rent-free space in your mind.

ISABELLE HOLLAND
Award-winning author of 28 books

Although it may seem unusual to mention forgiveness in a book on how to become more successful, the reality is that anger, resentment, and the desire for revenge can waste valuable energy that *could* be directed toward positive goal-directed action.

In light of the Law of Attraction, we have already discussed that you attract more of whatever feelings you are experiencing. Being negative, angry, and unforgiving about a past hurt only ensures that you'll attract more of the same into your life.

FORGIVE AND BRING YOURSELF
BACK TO THE PRESENT

In the world of business, in families, and in personal relationships, we, too, need to come from a place of love and forgiveness—to let go so that we can move on. You need to forgive a business partner who lied to you and hurt you financially. You need to forgive a coworker who stole credit for your work or gossiped about you behind your back. You need to forgive an ex-spouse who cheated on you, then got nasty during the divorce. You needn't condone their actions or ever trust them again. But you do need to learn whatever lessons there are, forgive, and move on.

When you do forgive, it puts you back in the present—where good things can happen to you and where you can take action to create future gains for yourself, your team, your company, and your family. Staying mired in the past uses valuable energy and robs you of the power you need to forge ahead in the creation of what you want.

BUT IT'S SO HARD TO LET GO

I know how hard it can be to forgive and let go. I've been kidnapped and assaulted by a stranger, been physically abused by an alcoholic father, been the victim of reverse racism, had employees embezzle serious amounts of money from me, been sued in some blatantly frivolous lawsuits, and been taken advantage of in a number of business dealings.

But after each experience, I did the work of processing it and forgiving the other party because I knew that if I didn't, those past hurts would eat away at me and prevent me from focusing my full attention on the future life I wanted to create.

With each experience, I also learned how to avoid letting it happen again. I learned how to better follow my intuition. I learned how I could better protect my family and my hard-earned assets. And each time I finally released the experience, I felt lighter, freer, and stronger—with more energy to focus on the more important tasks at hand. There was no more negative self-talk. No more bitter recriminations.

*Resentment is like drinking poison and then hoping
it will kill your enemies.*

NELSON MANDELA
Winner of the Nobel Peace Prize

Whatever hurts you are feeling, know that I've felt many of them, too.

But also know that *what can hurt you even more* is harboring the resentment, holding a grudge, and rerunning the same hatred over and over. The word *forgive* really means to give it up *for yourself*—not for them.

I've had people in my seminars who, when they finally *truly* forgive someone, release long-term migraine headaches within minutes, find immediate relief from chronic constipation and colitis, release their arthritis pain, improve their eyesight, and immediately experience a host of other physical benefits. One man actually lost 6 pounds in the following 2 days without changing his eating habits! I have also seen people subsequently create miracles in their careers and financial lives. Believe me, it is definitely worth the effort.

STEPS TO FORGIVING

The following steps are *all* integral to forgiving:

1. Acknowledge your anger and resentment.
2. Acknowledge the hurt and pain it created.
3. Acknowledge the fears and self-doubts that it created.
4. Own any part you may have played in letting it occur or letting it continue.
5. Acknowledge what you were wanting that you didn't get, and then put yourself in the other person's shoes and attempt to understand where he or she was coming from at that time, and what needs the person was trying to meet—however inelegantly—by his or her behavior.
6. Let go and forgive the person.

If you're paying attention, you probably noticed that these steps involve the same six stages as the Total Truth Process.

MAKE A LIST

Make a list of anyone you feel has hurt you and how:

_____ hurt me by _____.

Then one by one, taking as many days as you need, go through the Total Truth Process with each person. You can do it as a written process or a verbal process where you pretend you are talking to the person who is sitting in an empty chair across from you. Make sure you take ample time to think about what must have been going on in each person's life at the time to make him or her do whatever they did to you. It is important to remember the following truth:

All people (including you) are always doing the best they can to meet their basic needs with the current awareness, knowledge, skills, and tools they have at the time. If they could have done better, they would have done better. As they develop more awareness of how their behavior affects others, as they learn more effective and less harmful ways to meet their needs, they will behave in less harmful ways.

Think about it. No parent ever wakes up in the morning and says to his or her mate, "I've just figured out three more ways we can screw up our kid." Parents are always doing the best they can to be good parents. But the combination of their own psychological wounds, their lack of knowledge and parenting skills, and the pressures of their lives often converge and create behaviors that hurt us. It was not personal to you. They would have done the same thing to anyone who was in your shoes at that moment. The same is true for everyone else . . . all the time.

THE FORGIVENESS AFFIRMATION

One final technique for helping you forgive is to recite this affirmation several times each day:

I release myself from all the demands and judgments that have kept me limited. I allow myself to go free—to live in joy and love and peace. I allow myself to create fulfilling relationships, to have success in my life, to experience pleasure, to know that I am worthy and deserve to have what I want.

I now go free. In that process I release all others from any demands and expectations I have placed on them. I choose to be free. I allow others to be
free. I forgive myself and I forgive them. And so it is.

IF THEY CAN DO IT, YOU CAN DO IT

In my search for inspirational stories for the *Chicken Soup for the Soul®* books,
I have read many stories of forgiveness that let me know that human beings
can forgive anything—no matter how tragic or brutal.

In 1972, the Pulitzer Prize was awarded for a photograph of a young Vietnamese girl, her arms outstretched in terror and pain, running naked—her
clothes having been seared from her body—and screaming from her village,
which had just been bombed with napalm in the Vietnam War. That photo
was reprinted thousands of times around the world and can still be found in
high school history books. That day, Phan Thi Kim Phuc received third-
degree burns over more than half of her body. After 17 operations and 14
months of painful rehabilitation, Kim miraculously survived. Having overcome her painful past through a process of forgiveness, she is now a Canadian
citizen, a goodwill ambassador for the United Nations Educational and Scientific and Cultural Organization (UNESCO), and the founder of the Kim
Foundation, which helps innocent victims of war. Everyone who has ever met
Kim comments on the amazing quality of peace that radiates from her.[33]

In 1978, Simon Weston joined the Welsh Guards in Great Britain. As
part of the Falklands Task Force, he was aboard the *Sir Galahad* when it was
bombed by Argentine planes. His face was badly disfigured, as he suffered
burns over 49% of his body. He has undergone 70 operations since that fate-
ful day and will still have to endure more. It would be easy for him to spend
the rest of his life being bitter. Instead he says, "If you spend your life full of
recriminations and bitterness, then you've failed yourself, failed the surgeons
and nurses and everyone else, because you aren't giving anything back. Hatred can consume you, and it's wasted emotion."

Instead of drowning in a sea of bitterness, Simon has become an author,
a motivational speaker, and the cofounder and vice president of Weston
Spirit, a nonprofit organization that has worked with tens of thousands of
young people whose lifestyles reflect a poverty of aspiration in the United
Kingdom.[34]

Like Simon and Kim, you can transcend and triumph, too.

---

33. For more information on the work of the Kim Foundation, visit www.kimfoundation.com.
34. For more information on the work and vision of Weston Spirit, visit www.westonspirit.org.uk.

FACE WHAT ISN'T WORKING

Facts do not cease to exist because they are ignored.

ALDOUS HUXLEY
Visionary writer

*Our lives improve only when we take chances—and the first and
most difficult risk we can take is to be honest with ourselves.*

WALTER ANDERSON
Editor, *Parade* magazine

If you are going to become more successful, you have to get out of denial and
face what isn't working in your life. Do you defend or ignore how hostile and
toxic your work environment is? Do you make excuses for your bad marriage? Are you in denial about your lack of energy, your excess weight, your ill
health, or your level of physical fitness? Are you failing to acknowledge that
sales have been on a consistent downward trend for the last 3 months? Are
you putting off confronting an employee who is not delivering at an acceptable standard of performance? Successful people face these circumstances
squarely, heed the warning signs, and take appropriate action, no matter how
uncomfortable or challenging it might be.

REMEMBER THE YELLOW ALERTS

Remember the "yellow alerts" I mentioned when I taught you about E + R =
O in Principle 1 ("Take 100% Responsibility for Your Life")? Yellow alerts are
all those little signals you get that something's not right. Your teen comes
home late from school again. Strange notices show up in the company mail.
The odd comment from a friend or neighbor. Sometimes we choose to acknowledge these alerts and take action, but more often than not, we simply
choose to ignore them. We pretend not to notice that something's amiss.

To face what's not working in your life usually means you're going to have to do something uncomfortable. It means you might have to exercise more self-discipline, confront somebody, risk not being liked, ask for what you want, demand respect instead of settling for an abusive relationship, or maybe even quit your job. But because you don't want to do these uncomfortable things, you'll often defend tolerating a situation that doesn't work.

WHAT DOES DENIAL LOOK LIKE?

Though the bad situations in our lives can be uncomfortable, embarrassing, and painful, we often live with them or—worse—hide them behind myths, widely accepted views, and platitudes. We don't even realize we are in denial. We use phrases such as these:

It's just what guys do.
You can't control teenagers these days.
He's just venting his frustrations.
It's got nothing to do with me.
I keep my nose clean.
It's none of my business.
It's not my place to say.
I don't want to rock the boat.
Don't make waves.
There's nothing I can do about it.
Don't wash your dirty linen in public.
Credit card debt like this is normal.
That doesn't happen to people like us.
I'll get fired if I say anything.
Mom's church friends check on her.
Luckily it's only marijuana.
She's just at that age.
I need these to help me relax.
I have to work these long hours to get ahead.
We just have to wait it out.
I'm sure he is going to pay it back.

Occasionally, we'll even make up *reasons* why something that is not working *is working*, not realizing that if we just acknowledged the bad situation sooner, it would often be less painful to resolve. It would be cheaper, the circumstances might be more beneficial, the problems would be easier to solve, we could be more honest with everyone concerned, we would feel better about ourselves, and we would certainly have more integrity. But we have to get past our denial.

Successful people, on the other hand, are more committed to finding out why things are going wrong and fixing them than they are to defending their own position or maintaining their ignorance.

In business, they look at the hard truth in real numbers rather than recalculating the numbers to look good to the stockholders. They want to know why someone didn't use their product or service, why the ad campaign didn't work, or why expenditures are unusually high. They are rational and in touch with reality. They are willing to look at what *is* and deal with it rather than hide it and deny it.

> *Doing more of what doesn't work won't make it work any better.*
>
> CHARLES J. GIVENS
> Real estate investment strategist and author of *Wealth Without Risk*

KNOW WHEN TO HOLD THEM, KNOW WHEN TO FOLD THEM

A big part of getting out of denial is to get good at recognizing bad situations and then deciding to do something about them. It always amazes me how difficult recognition and decision is for most people—even when it comes to alcoholism and drug addiction. With many addicts, their marriages fail, their businesses fail, they lose their house, and even end up on skid row before they realize their addiction is not working for them.

Fortunately, most of our problems are less severe than drugs, but that doesn't make the recognition or decision any easier. Take your job, for instance. Are you in denial about what you would really like to be doing? Worse yet, do you constantly remark on how happy and fulfilled you are when you're not? Are you living a lie?

Workaholics are a perfect example of this kind of denial. A high-pressure schedule can't possibly work long term for anyone, but most workaholics will defend it with comments such as "I'm making great money," "This is how I support my family," "It's how I get ahead," and "I have to do it to compete at the office." As we've explored already, defending and justifying a bad situation is really just a form of denial.

DENIAL IS BASED ON FEAR

Often, denial is based on the notion that something even worse will happen once we stop denying and take action. In other words, we're afraid to face facts squarely.

Many a therapist can tell you that, in spite of overwhelming clues that their spouse is having an affair, many patients won't confront their spouse over it. They simply don't want to face the fact that the marriage might be over.

What are some of the situations *you* are afraid to deal with?

- Your teenager who is smoking or doing drugs?
- A supervisor who leaves early but dumps his or her late projects on you?
- A business partner who doesn't participate fully or spends too much?
- Your house payment or expenses that are becoming unmanageable?
- Your aging parents who need full-time care?
- Your health that is becoming a problem because of poor nutrition or lifestyle?
- A spouse who is withdrawn, disrespectful, or abusive?
- Not enough time for yourself and your children?

Though many of the situations above require drastic changes in how you live, work, and relate to others, remember that the solution to these problems isn't always to quit your job, get a divorce, fire the employee, or ground your teenager. It may be more productive to choose less extreme alternatives such as a discussion with your boss, marriage counseling, setting boundaries with your teens and siblings, scaling back your expenditures, and seeking competent professional help. Of course, these less drastic solutions still require you to face your fears and take action.

But you have to face what isn't working *first*.

The good news is that the more you face uncomfortable situations, the better you get at it. When you face just one thing that isn't working, the next time you have the slightest inkling, you are more likely to take action immediately.

TAKE ACTION NOW

Make a list of what isn't working in your life. Start with the seven major areas where you would normally set goals—financial, career or business, free time or family time, health and appearance, relationships, personal growth, and, finally, making a difference. Ask your staff, family, friends, class, group, coach, or team what they believe is not working.

Ask: *What's not working? How can we improve it? What requests can I make? What do you need from me? How can I help you? What do I/we need to do? What action steps can I/we take to get each of these situations to work the way I/we would like?*

Do you need to talk to someone? Call a repairperson? Ask someone for help? Learn a new skill? Find a new resource? Read a book? Call an expert? Make a plan to fix it?

Choose one action and do it. Then keep taking another action and another action until you get the situation resolved.

31

EMBRACE CHANGE

Change is the law of life. And those who look only to the past
or present are certain to miss the future.

JOHN F. KENNEDY
Thirty-fifth president of the United States

Change is inevitable. At this very moment, for instance, your body and cells are changing. The Earth is changing. The economy, technology, how we do business, even how we communicate is changing. And though you can resist that change and potentially be swept away by it, you can also choose to cooperate with it, adapt to it, and benefit from it.

GROW OR DIE

In 1910, Florists' Telegraph Delivery—known today as FTD—was founded by 15 American florists who began using the telegraph to exchange orders and deliver flowers to customers' loved ones thousands of miles away. Gone were the days when a daughter or sister would go to the local florist and order a small bouquet. Family members were relocating to cities and towns far from home. And FTD flourished by identifying this trend and combining it with the telegraph, which represented a change in the way we communicate.

Around the same time, the American railroad industry began to see the automobile and the airplane as new technologies designed to transport people and goods from place to place. But unlike other industries who readily embraced these new machines, the railroad industry resisted, believing instead that they were in the railroad business—not the business of transporting goods and people. They didn't realize what they were up against. They didn't grow. Though businesses focusing on the railroads might have become automobile and aircraft businesses, they didn't. As a result, they almost died out.

WHERE DO YOU NEED TO GROW?

When change happens, you can either cooperate with it and learn how to benefit from it or you can resist it and eventually get run over by it. It's your choice.

When you embrace change wholeheartedly as an inevitable part of life, looking for ways to use new changes to make your life richer, easier, and more fulfilling, your life will work much better. You will experience change as an opportunity for growth and new experiences.

A few years ago, I was hired to consult with the Naval Sea Systems Command in Washington, D.C. They had just announced they were moving the entire command to San Diego, California, which meant that a lot of civil service jobs were going to be lost in that transition. My job was to conduct a seminar for all the nonmilitary personnel who would not be moving to California. And though the Naval Sea Systems Command had offered everyone jobs and transfers to San Diego (including reimbursement of all moving expenses) or assistance in locating a new job in the Washington, D.C., area, many of the employees had become almost frozen with fear and resentment.

Though nearly all of them looked at this change as a major disaster in their lives, I encouraged them to look at it as an opportunity—as something new. I taught them about $E + R = O$ and how although the move to San Diego (E) was inevitable, their outcome—whether or not they flourished—afterward (O) was entirely dependent on their response (R) to the situation. "Perhaps you'll find a more empowering job in D.C.," I said, "or even get a job with better pay. Or maybe you would like to move to California where it's warm most of the year and new friends and adventures are awaiting you."

Slowly they began to move from panic and fear to realizing that things could indeed work out, maybe even for the better, if only they embraced this change as an opportunity to create something new and better.

HOW TO EMBRACE CHANGE

Realize that there are two kinds of change—*cyclical change* and *structural change*—neither of which you can control.

Cyclical change, such as the change we see in the stock market, happens several times a year. Prices go up and they go down. There are bull markets and corrections. We see seasonal changes in the weather, holiday spending by the American public, more travel in the summer, and so on. These are changes that happen in cycles, and frankly most of them we just accept as a normal part of life.

But there are also structural changes—such as when the computer was invented and completely changed how we live, work, get our news, and make purchases. Structural changes are the kinds of changes where there is no going back to doing things the way they were before. And these are the kinds of changes that can sweep you away if you resist them.

Like the Naval Sea Systems Command employees, FTD florists, or the railroad industry, will *you* embrace these structural changes and work to improve your life—or will you resist them?

Remember back to a time when you experienced a change but resisted. Perhaps it was a move, a job transfer, a change in suppliers, a change in technology in your company, a change in management, or even your teenager going off to college—a change you were going to have to deal with and you thought it was the worst thing in the world.

What happened once you surrendered to the change? Did your life actually eventually improve? Can you look back now and say, "Wow, I'm glad that happened. Look at the good it eventually brought me."

If you can always remember that you've been through changes in the past—and that they've largely worked out for the best—you can begin to approach each new change with the excitement and anticipation you should. To help embrace any change, ask yourself the following questions:

> What's changing in my life that I'm currently resisting?
> Why am I resisting that change?
> What am I afraid of with respect to this change?
> What am I afraid might happen to me?
> What's the payoff for my keeping things the way they are?
> What's the cost I'm paying for keeping things the way they are?
> What benefits might there be in this change?
> What would I have to do to cooperate with this change?
> What's the next step I could take to cooperate with this change?
> When will I take it?

32

TRANSFORM YOUR INNER CRITIC INTO AN INNER COACH

A man is literally what he thinks.

JAMES ALLEN
Author of *As a Man Thinketh*

Research indicates that the average person—that means you!—talks to himself or herself about 50,000 times a day. And most of that self-talk is about yourself, and according to the psychological researchers, it is 80% negative—things such as *I shouldn't have said that. . . . They don't like me. . . . I'm never going to be able to pull this off. . . . I don't like the way my hair looks today. . . . That other team is going to kill us. . . . I can't dance. . . . I'll never be a good skater. . . . I'm not a speaker. . . . I'll never lose this weight. . . . I can't ever seem to get organized. . . . I'm always late.*

Argue for your limitations, and sure enough, they're yours.

RICHARD BACH
Author of *Jonathan Livingston Seagull*

We know from the research that these thoughts have a powerful effect on us. They affect our attitude, our physiology, and our motivation to act. Our negative thoughts actually control our behavior. They make us stutter, spill things, forget our lines, break out in a sweat, breathe shallowly, feel scared—and taken to the extreme, they can even paralyze or kill us.

WORRIED HIMSELF TO DEATH

Nick Sitzman was a strong, healthy, and ambitious young railroad yardman. He had a reputation as a diligent hard worker and had a loving wife and two children and many friends.

One midsummer day, the train crews were informed that they could quit an hour early in honor of the foreman's birthday. While performing one last check on some of the railroad cars, Nick was accidentally locked in a refrigerator boxcar. When he realized that the rest of the workmen had left the site, Nick began to panic.

He banged and shouted until his fists were bloody and his voice was hoarse, but no one heard him. With his knowledge of "the numbers and the facts," he predicted the temperature to be zero degrees. Nick's thought was *If I can't get out, I'll freeze to death in here.* Wanting to let his wife and family know exactly what had happened to him, Nick found a knife and began to etch words on the wooden floor. He wrote, "It's so cold, my body is getting numb. If I could just go to sleep. These may be my last words."

The next morning, the crew slid open the heavy doors of the boxcar and found Nick dead. An autopsy revealed that every physical sign of his body indicated he had frozen to death. And yet the refrigeration unit of the car was inoperative, and the temperature inside indicated 55 degrees Fahrenheit. Nick had killed himself by the *power of his own thoughts*.[35]

You, too, if you're not careful, can kill yourself with your limiting thoughts—not all at once like Nick Sitzman, but little by little, day after day, until you have slowly deadened your natural ability to achieve your dreams.

YOUR NEGATIVE THOUGHTS AFFECT YOUR BODY

We also know from polygraph (lie-detector) tests that your body reacts to your thoughts—changing your temperature, heart rate, blood pressure, breathing rate, muscle tension, and how much your hands sweat. When you are hooked up to a lie detector and are asked a question such as "Did you take the money?" your hands will get colder, your heart will beat faster, your blood pressure will go up, your breathing will get faster, your muscles will get tighter, and your hands will sweat if you did take the money and you lie about it. These kinds of physiological changes occur not only when you are

---

35. From *The Speaker's Sourcebook*, by Glen Van Ekeren (Englewood-Cliffs, N.J.: Prentice-Hall, 1988).

lying but also in reaction to every thought you think. Every cell in your body is affected by every thought you have.

Negative thoughts affect your body negatively—weakening you, making you sweat, and making you uptight. Positive thoughts affect your body in a positive way, making you more relaxed, centered, and alert. Positive thoughts will cause the secretion of endorphins in the brain and will reduce pain and increase pleasure.

TALK TO YOURSELF LIKE A WINNER

You are today where your thoughts have brought you; you will be tomorrow where your thoughts take you.

JAMES ALLEN
Author of *As a Man Thinketh*

So what if you could learn to always talk to yourself like a winner instead of a loser? What if you could transform your negative self-talk into positive self-talk? What if you could silence your thoughts of lack and limitation and replace them with thoughts of unlimited possibility? What if you could replace any victim language in your thoughts with the language of empowerment? And what if you could transform your inner critic, who judges your every move, into a supportive inner coach who would encourage you and give you confidence as you faced new situations and risks? Well . . . all of that is possible with a little awareness, focus, and intention.

STOMP THOSE ANTS

Psychiatrist Daniel G. Amen has named the limiting thoughts we hear in our head ANTs—Automatic Negative Thoughts. And just like real ants at a picnic, your ANTs can ruin your experience of life. Dr. Amen recommends that you learn to stomp the ANTs.[36] First you have to become aware of them; next you have to shake them off and stomp them by challenging them. Finally, you have to replace them with more positive and affirming thoughts.

---

36. See *Change Your Brain, Change Your Life*, by Daniel G. Amen, M.D. (New York: Three Rivers Press, 1998), for an illuminating look into how to use brain-compatible strategies to overcome anxiety, depression, obsessiveness, anger, and impulsiveness—all of which can severely block creating the life you want. The next few pages on stomping the ANTs draw heavily on Dr. Amen's insights.

Don't believe everything you hear—even in your own mind.

DANIEL G. AMEN, M.D.
Clinical neuroscientist, psychiatrist, and specialist in attention-deficit disorders

The key to dealing with any kind of negative thinking is to realize that you are ultimately in charge of whether to listen to or agree with any thought. Just because you think it—or hear it—doesn't mean it's true.

You want to constantly ask yourself, *Is this thought helping me or hurting me? Is it getting me closer to where I want to go, or taking me further away? Is it motivating me to action, or is it blocking me with fear and self-doubt?* You have to learn to challenge and talk back to the thoughts that are not serving you in creating greater success and happiness.

To talk back to your ANTs, you first have to be aware of them. My friend Doug Bench, the author of the "Mastery of Advanced Achievement Home Study Course,"[37] recommends writing down every negative thought you think or say out loud and every negative thought you hear anyone else say—for 3 whole days! (Make sure that 2 of the days are workdays and that 1 is a weekend day.) This is the best way to heighten your awareness of your ANTs. Here are a couple of others.

Ask your spouse or partner, children, roommates, and fellow employees to catch you and impose a dollar fine every time they hear you uttering a negative thought. In a recent workshop I attended, we had to put $2 in a bowl every time we said anything that was blaming, justifying, or self-negating. It was amazing to see how fast the bowl filled up. However, as the 4 days went on, there were fewer and fewer automatic negative comments as we all became more aware and stomped the ANTs before they even came out of our mouths. (By the way, if you can enroll others to do this exercise at the same time you do, it's a lot easier.)

DIFFERENT TYPES OF ANTS

It is helpful to understand some of the different kinds of ANTs that might attack you. When you recognize these kinds of ANTs, realize they are irrational thoughts that need to be challenged and replaced. Here are some of the most common kinds of ANTs and how to stomp them.

---

37. Learn more about Doug's fascinating work applying the latest neuroscience and brain research to the achievement of advanced levels of success at his Web site: www.scienceforsuccess.com.

Always-or-Never Thinking

In reality, very few things are always or never. If you think something is always going to happen or you will never get what you want, you are doomed from the outset. When you use all-or-nothing words such as *always, never, everyone, no one, every time,* and *everything,* you are usually wrong. Here are some examples of always-or-never thinking:

> *I'll never get a raise.*
> *Everyone takes advantage of me.*
> *My employees never listen to me.*
> *I never get any time for myself.*
> *They're always making fun of me.*
> *I never get a break.*
> *No one ever cuts me any slack.*
> *Every time I take a risk, I get slammed.*
> *Nobody cares if I live or die.*

When you find yourself thinking always-or-never thoughts, replace them with what is really true. Replace *You always take advantage of me* with *I get angry when you take advantage of me, but I know that you have treated me fairly in the past and that you will again.*

Focusing on the Negative

Some people focus only on the bad and never on the good in a situation. When I was conducting trainings for high school teachers, I noticed that most of the teachers I met had a pattern of focusing on the negative. If they taught a lesson and 30 kids got it but 4 didn't, they would focus on the 4 who didn't get it and would feel bad, rather than focus on the 26 who did get it and feel good.

Learn to look for the positive. Not only will it help you feel better, but it will also be a critical component of your creating the success you want. Recently a friend of mine told me he had seen an interview with a multimillionaire on television who described the turning point in his career as the morning he asked all of his staff to talk about one good thing that had occurred during the past week. At first all that came up were more complaints, problems, and difficulties. Finally, one employee commented on the fact that the UPS driver who delivered packages to the office had told him that he had applied to college and was going to go back to school to get his degree, and on how inspired he was by the man's commitment to further his education to pursue his ultimate dream in life. Slowly, one employee and then another came up with something that was positive to share. Soon, this became a part of every meeting. Eventually, they had to end the meetings before every positive thing could be recounted. The whole attitudinal focus of the company changed from focusing on the negative to focusing on the good, and the business just took off and grew exponentially from that moment on.

Learn to play the Appreciation Game. Look for things to appreciate in every situation. When you actively seek the positive, you become more appreciative and optimistic, which is a requirement for creating the life of your dreams. Look for the good.

My wife was recently in an automobile accident. She drove through an intersection where the traffic light was inoperative because of a power outage, and hit another car turning across her lane. She could have succumbed to a multitude of ANTs—*What's wrong with me? I should have been paying better attention. I shouldn't have been out driving when the power was out.* Instead, she focused on the positive—*I'm so lucky to be alive and relatively unhurt. The other driver is alive and well. Thank God I was in such a safe car. I am so glad the police came as fast as they did. It's amazing how many people were there to help. This was a real wake-up call.*

A powerful exercise for building your appreciation muscle is to take 7 minutes every morning to write down all the things you appreciate in your life. I recommend this as a daily ritual for the rest of your life; however, if you think that is excessive, at least do it for 30 to 40 days. It will create a huge change in how you see the world.

Catastrophic Predicting

In catastrophic predicting, you create the worst possible scenario in your mind and then act as if it were a certainty. This could include predicting that your sales prospect won't be interested in your product, the person you are attracted to will reject your request to go out on a date, your boss won't give you a raise, or the plane you're flying on will crash. Replace "She'll probably laugh at me if I ask her out for a date" with "I don't know what she'll do. She might say yes."

Mind-Reading

You are mind-reading when you believe you know what another person is thinking even though he or she hasn't told you. You know you're mind-reading when you're thinking thoughts such as *He's mad at me.... She doesn't like me.... He's going to say no.... He's going to fire me.* Replace mind-reading with the truth: *I don't know what he is thinking unless I ask him. Maybe he's just having a bad day.*

Remember, unless you're a psychic living in California, you can't read anyone else's mind. You don't ever know what they're really thinking unless they tell you or you ask them. Check out your assumptions by asking, "I'm imagining you might be mad at me. Are you?" I use the phrase "When in doubt, check it out!" to keep myself on track with this one.

Guilt-Tripping

Guilt happens when you think words such as *should, must, ought to*, or *have to*. Here are some examples: *I ought to spend more time studying for my bar exam. . . . I should spend more time at home with my kids. . . . I have to exercise more*. As soon as we feel like we *should* do something, we create an internal resistance to doing it.

I will not should on myself today.

SEEN ON A POSTER

You will be more effective if you replace guilt-tripping with phrases such as *I want to . . . It supports my goals to . . . It would be smart to . . . It's in my best interest to . . .* Guilt is never productive. It will stand in the way of achieving your goals. So get rid of this emotional barrier to success.

Labeling

Labeling is attaching a negative label to yourself or someone else. It is a form of shorthand that stops you from clearly making the distinctions that would be helpful to being more effective. Some examples of negative labels are *jerk, idiot, arrogant*, and *irresponsible*. When you use a label like this, you are lumping yourself or another into a category of all the jerks or idiots you have ever known, and that makes it more difficult to deal with that person or situation as the unique person or experience they are. Challenge the thought *I am stupid* with *What I just did was less than brilliant, but I am still a smart person*.

All meaning is self-created.

VIRGINIA SATIR
Noted psychotherapist known for her contributions in the fields
of family therapy and self-esteem

Personalizing

You personalize when you invest a neutral event with personal meaning. *Kevin hasn't called me back yet. He must be mad at me.* Or *We lost the Vanderbilt account. It must be my fault. I should have spent more time on the proposal.* The truth is that there are many other possible explanations for other people's actions besides the negative reasons your ANTs come up with. For example, Kevin may not have called you back because he is sick, out of town, or overwhelmed with his own priorities. You never really know why other people do what they do.

TRANSFORMING YOUR INNER CRITIC
INTO YOUR INNER COACH

One of the most powerful exercises for retraining your inner critic is to teach it to tell you the *total* truth. (See Principle 29, "Complete the Past to Embrace the Future.") To transform your inner critic into your inner coach, you have to understand a core principle. Most self-criticism and self-judgment is motivated by love. Part of you is trying to motivate the rest of you to do something for your own good. Just like your parents, your inner critic really has your best interests in mind when it is criticizing you. It wants you to do better because it wants you to get the benefit of the better behavior. The problem is that it tells you only part of the truth.

When you were a little kid, your parents may have yelled at you and sent you to your room after you did something stupid like run out in front of a car. Their real communication was "I love you. I don't want you to get hit by a car. I want you to stay around so that I can enjoy watching you grow up into a happy and healthy adult." But they delivered only half of the message. "What's wrong with you? Were you born without a brain? You know better than to run out into the street when there are cars coming. You're grounded for the next hour. Go up to your room and think about what you just did." In their fear of losing you, they expressed only their anger. But underneath the anger were three more layers of message that never got delivered—fear, specific requests, and love. A complete message would look like this:

Anger:	I am mad at you for running out into the street without looking to see if any cars were coming.
Fear:	I am afraid that you are going to get badly hurt or killed.

Requests: I want you to pay more attention when you are playing
            near the street. Stop and look both ways before you
            walk or run out into the street.
Love: I love you so much. I don't know what I would do
            without you. You are so precious to me. I want you to
            be safe and healthy. You deserve to have lots of fun and
            stay safe so you can always enjoy life to its fullest. Do
            you understand?

What a different message! You need to train your inner critic to talk to you the same way. You can practice this on paper or as a verbal exercise in which you talk to yourself out loud. I usually imagine talking to a clone of myself sitting in an empty chair opposite me.

Make a list of all the things you say when you are judging yourself. Include all of the things that you tell yourself you should do that you don't do. A typical list might look like this:

You don't exercise enough.
You're gaining too much weight.
You're a fat slob—a real couch potato!
You drink too much alcohol and eat too many sweets.
You need to cut down on the carbs!
You need to watch less television and go to bed earlier.
If you got up earlier, you'd have more time to exercise.
You're lazy. Why don't you finish the things you start?!
You start an exercise program, but you never stick with it!
You're irresponsible. You don't keep your word.

Once you have completed your list, then practice communicating the same information using the same four-step process outlined above: (1) anger, (2) fear, (3) requests, and (4) love. Spend a minimum of 1 minute on each step. Make sure to be very specific in the requests stage. State exactly what you want yourself to do. "I want you to eat better" is too vague. Be more specific, such as "I want you to eat at least four servings of vegetables every day. I want you to cut out French fries and desserts. I want you to eat some kind of fruit for breakfast every day. I want you to eat whole grains like whole wheat and brown rice rather than white flour." The more specific you are, the more value you will receive from the exercise. If you do it out loud, which I recommend, *do it with as much emotion and passion as possible.*

Here's an example of what it might sound like using the list of judgments above:

Anger: I am angry at you for not taking better care of your
              body. You are such a lazy slob! You drink too much and
              you eat too much. You don't have any self-discipline!
              When are you going to get it together? You're lazy! All
              you do is sit around and watch TV. I can't stand how
              lazy you are. You just get fatter and more out of shape
              every year. Your clothes don't fit, and you don't look
              good. You disgust me!

Fear: If you don't change, I am afraid you are going to keep
              gaining weight until you are facing a real health risk. I
              am afraid your cholesterol is going to get so high that
              you might have a heart attack. I'm afraid that you could
              become diabetic. I am afraid that you are never going to
              change and then you are going to die young and never
              really live out your destiny. If you keep this up, you're
              never going to fulfill your dream. I'm afraid that if you
              don't start eating better and taking better care of
              yourself, no one is going to be attracted to you. You
              might end up living alone for the rest of your life.

Requests: I want you to join a health club and go at least three days
              a week. I want you to go for a twenty-minute walk the
              other four days. I want you to cut out one hour of televi-
              sion a day and devote that to exercise. I want you to stop
              eating fried foods and start eating more fresh fruits and
              vegetables. I want you to stop drinking sodas and start
              drinking more water. I want you to limit drinking
              alcohol to Friday and Saturday nights.

Love: I love you. I want you to be around for a long time. I
              want you to have a wonderful relationship. You deserve
              to look good in your clothes and to feel good about
              yourself. You deserve to have all of your dreams come
              true. I want you to feel alive and energetic rather than
              tired and lethargic all the time. You deserve to live life
              fully and enjoy every moment of it. You deserve to be
              totally happy.

Whenever you hear a part of you judging yourself, simply reply, "Thank
you for caring. What is your fear? . . . What specifically do you want me to
do? . . . How will this serve me? . . . Thank you."

The first time I experienced this inner critic–to–inner coach process 20
years ago, it changed my life. After quitting my job at another training company, I had been working as a consultant and a professional speaker, but what

I really wanted to do was start my own training company, train other trainers, open offices in other cities, and make a huge difference in the world. But it seemed like such an overwhelming commitment, and I was afraid of failure. What's worse, I had been regularly beating myself up for not having the courage to take the leap.

After completing the exercise, something shifted. I went beyond beating myself up to realizing how much I was missing out on by not taking the leap. I told myself clearly what I needed to do, and the following day, I outlined a business plan for the new company, asked my mother-in-law for a $10,000 loan, asked a friend to be my business partner, scheduled a meeting to draw up the incorporation papers, and began designing the letterhead. Less than 3 months later, I conducted my first weekend training in St. Louis for over 200 people. Less than a year later, I had offices in Los Angeles, St. Louis, Philadelphia, San Diego, and San Francisco. Since then, over 40,000 people have participated in my weekend and weeklong training programs: "Self-Esteem and Peak Performance," "Self-Esteem in the Classroom," "The Power of Focus," "Training of Trainers," "Couples Relationships," "Creating Wealth and Prosperity," "Living Your Highest Vision," and "Living the Success Principles."

By turning my inner critic into an inner coach, I was able to stop feeling like a failure and start engaging in the activities that made my dream a reality. I was able to move from someone who was using my energy against myself to someone who was using my energy to create what I wanted.

Do not let the seeming simplicity of this technique fool you. It is very powerful. But like everything else in this book, to obtain the value, you must use it. No one else can do it for you. Take 20 minutes now to turn your inner critic into an inner coach. Get all of you on your own side—working together for the greater good of your dreams and aspirations.

HOW TO SILENCE YOUR PERFORMANCE CRITIC

Have you ever taught a class, given a speech, made a sales presentation, competed in an athletic event, acted in a play, given a concert, or performed any kind of job, and then found yourself on the way home listening to that voice in your head telling you how you messed up, what you should have done differently, how you could have and should have done it better? I'm sure you have. And if you listen to that voice for very long, it can undermine your self-confidence, lower your self-esteem, and even demoralize and eventually paralyze you. Here is another simple but powerful method for redirecting the communication from one of judgment and criticism to one of correction and support.

Remembering again that the deepest underlying motivation of your inner critic is to help you be better at what you do, tell your inner critic to stop criticizing and berating you or you will stop listening to it. Tell that inner voice you are not willing to listen to any more character assassinations, name-calling, or browbeating—only specific steps you can take to do it better *the next time*. This eliminates put-downs and focuses the conversation on "improvement opportunities" for the next occasion. Now the inner critic becomes an inner coach that is simply pointing out ways to improve future results. The past is over, and there is nothing you can do to change it. You can only learn from it and improve your performance *the next time*.

Here is an example of what this might sound like taken from my own life. *IC* indicates that the inner critic/inner coach is talking.

IC: I can't believe it. What were you thinking? You tried to put way too much information in that seminar. You were talking way too fast, and you were rushed at the end. There's no way people could have assimilated all of that information! After all these years as a seminar leader, you'd think you'd know better than that!

Me: Hold on a minute. I'm not going to listen to you criticizing me. I just worked hard all day to give people the best experience that I knew how to create at the time. Now that I've done it, I am sure there are ways to improve it next time. If you have *specific* things you want me to do *next time*, then tell me. That is all I am interested in hearing about. I'm not interested in your judgments, just your ideas for how to make it better next time.

IC: All right. Next time pick just three or four major points to focus on and really drive those points home with examples, humor, and more interpersonal exercises so that people really integrate the material. You can't teach people everything you know in one day.

Me: You're right. Anything else?

IC: Yes. Make sure to include more interactive learning games in the afternoon when the energy is lower. That will make sure everyone stays alert and awake.

Me: Okay. Anything else?

IC: Yes. I think it would work better to take a ten-minute break every hour rather than a twenty-minute break every two hours. That'll help keep the energy higher and allow more time for people to integrate what they are learning.

Me: Good idea. Anything else?

IC: Yes. Make sure to integrate some physical activities throughout the day to keep the kinesthetic learners more engaged.

Me: Anything else?

IC: Yes. Make sure you give people two copies of the Achiever's Focusing Sheet next time—one to write on in the seminar and one to use as a photocopying master after they leave the seminar. Otherwise they can't really use it. You could also put a copy on your Web site that they could download for duplication.

Me: Good idea. Anything else?

IC: No. I think that's it.

Me: Okay. I've written all of that down. I will definitely incorporate these things into my next seminar. Thank you.

IC: You're welcome.

As you can see from the example, there are a lot of things that your inner coach observes about how to improve your performance in future situations. The problem—up until now!—is that it has been presenting the information as a judgment. Once you switch the conversation to a nonemotional discussion of improvement opportunities, the experience changes from a negative to a positive one.

And here's a valuable tip. Because research on memory tells us that a new idea lasts for only about 40 seconds in short-term memory and then it is gone, it is important to write these ideas down and put them in a file that you will review before your next performance. Otherwise, you may lose the benefit of the valuable feedback.

TRANSCEND YOUR LIMITING BELIEFS

Your subconscious mind does not argue with you. It accepts what your conscious mind decrees. If you say,"I can't afford it," your subconscious mind works to make it true. Select a better thought. Decree,"I'll buy it. I accept it in my mind."

DR. JOSEPH MURPHY
Author of *The Power of Your Subconscious Mind*

Many of us have beliefs that limit our success—whether they are beliefs about our own capabilities, beliefs about what it takes to succeed, beliefs about how we should relate with other people, or even common myths that modern-day science or studies have long since refuted. Moving beyond your limiting beliefs is a critical first step toward becoming successful. You can learn how to identify those beliefs that are limiting you and then replace them with positive ones that support your success.

YOU ARE CAPABLE

One of the most limiting beliefs apparent today is the notion that somehow we are not capable of accomplishing our goals. Despite the best educational materials available, and despite decades of recorded knowledge about how to accomplish any task, we somehow choose to say instead, *I can't do that. I don't know how. There's no one to show me. I'm not smart enough.* And on and on.

Where does this come from? For most of us, it's a matter of early childhood programming. Whether they knew it or not, our parents, grandparents, and other adult role models told us, *No, no, honey. That's too much for you to handle. Let me do that for you. Maybe next year you can try that.*

We take this sense of inability into adulthood, and then it gets reinforced through workplace mistakes and other "failures." But what if you decided to say instead, *I can do this. I am capable. Other people have accomplished this. If I don't have the knowledge, there's someone out there who can teach me.*

You make the shift to competence and mastery. The shift in thinking can mean the difference between a lifetime of "could haves" versus accomplishing what you really want in life.

YOU ARE CAPABLE AND WORTHY OF LOVE

Likewise, many people don't believe they are competent to handle life's challenges or worthy of love—the two main pillars of high self-esteem. Believing that you are capable of handling anything that comes up in your life means that you are no longer afraid of anything. And think about this—haven't you handled everything that has ever happened to you? Things that were far more difficult than you thought they would be? The death of a loved one, divorce, being broke? Loss of a friend, your job, your money, your reputation, your youth? These things were tough, but you handled them. And you can handle anything else that happens to you as well. Once you get that, your confidence will soar.

Believing you are worthy of love means that you believe *I deserve to be treated well—with respect and dignity. I deserve to be cherished and adored by someone. I am worthy of an intimate and fulfilling relationship. I won't settle for less than I deserve. I will do whatever it takes to create that for myself.*

YOU CAN OVERCOME ANY LIMITING BELIEF

In addition to believing we are incapable or somehow not deserving of love, we often suffer from other limiting beliefs, too. Do any of these sound familiar?

I'm not (smart, attractive, rich, old, or young) enough.
Women don't do that sort of thing.
They'd never pick me to head the new project.
Even if I don't like this job, I need the financial security.
Nothing I do is ever successful.
You can't get rich in this town.

HOW TO OVERCOME ANY LIMITING BELIEF

Here is a simple but powerful four-step process you can use to transform any limiting belief into an empowering belief.

1. Identify a limiting belief that you want to change. Start by making a list of any beliefs you have that might be limiting you. A fun way to do that is to invite two or three friends who would also like to accelerate their growth to join you to brainstorm a list of all the things you heard growing up from your parents, guardians, teachers, coaches—even well-meaning religious instructors such as the nuns in Catholic school—that might somehow still be limiting you. Here are some common ones and the limiting beliefs that grow out of them:

   > You're stupid.
   > *I'm stupid.*
   > You're not smart enough to go to college.
   > *I'm not college material.*
   > Money doesn't grow on trees.
   > *I'll never be rich.*
   > Can't you do anything right?
   > *I can't do anything right, so why even try?*
   > Eat everything on your plate. The children in China are starving.
   > *I should eat everything on my plate, even if I'm not hungry.*
   > If you're not a virgin, nobody will want to marry you.
   > *I am damaged goods and no one will ever love me.*
   > The only person you ever think about is yourself.
   > *It's not okay to focus on my own needs.*
   > Children should be seen and not heard.
   > *I need to be quiet if I want to be loved.*
   > People aren't interested in your problems.
   > *I should hide what is really going on with me.*
   > Boys don't cry.
   > *It's not okay to share my feelings, especially my sadness.*
   > Act like a lady.
   > *It's not okay to act playful (silly, sexual, spontaneously).*
   > Nobody's interested in your opinion.
   > *What I think is not important.*

When you are finished creating your list, pick a belief that you think is still limiting you and take yourself through the remaining three steps of the process.

2. Determine how the belief limits you.

3. Decide how you want to be, act, or feel.

4. Create a turnaround statement that affirms or gives you permission to be, act, or feel this new way.

For example:

1. My negative limiting belief is *I have to do everything by myself. It's not okay to ask for help. It is a sign of weakness.*

2. The way it limits me is that I don't ask for help and I end up staying up too late and not getting enough sleep.

3. The way I want to feel is that it's okay to ask for help. It does not make me weak. It takes courage to ask for help. I want to ask for help when I need it. I want to delegate some of the things I don't like doing and that are not the best use of my time to others.

4. It's okay to ask for help. I am worthy of receiving all the support I need.

Here are some other examples of turnaround statements:

Negative: It's not okay to focus on my own needs.

Turnaround: My needs are just as important as everyone else's needs.

Negative: If I express my true feelings, people will think I am weak and take advantage of me.

Turnaround: The more I express my true feelings, the more people love, respect, and support me.

Negative: I can't do anything right, so why even try?

Turnaround: I can do many things right, and each time I try something new, I learn and get better.

SUMMARY OF THE PROCESS

Remember, all your inner dialogue and outer conversation should be aimed at getting you to where you want to be. So keep replacing any thought or belief that is keeping you from achieving your goals with an empowering thought or belief that will take you closer to your goals. Use the following template to turn any limiting belief into an empowering belief.

1. My negative/limiting belief is _____.
2. The way it limits me is _____.
3. The way I want to be, act, or feel is _____.
4. My turnaround statement that affirms or gives me permission to do this is _____.

Once you have created a new belief—your turnaround statement—you will need to implant it into your subconscious mind through constant repetition several times a day for a minimum of 30 days. Use the affirmation techniques we discussed in Principle 10, "Release the Brakes."

As Claude Bristol points out in his magnificent book *The Magic of Believing*, "This subtle force of repeated suggestion overcomes our reason. It acts directly on our emotions and our feelings, and finally penetrates to the very depths of our subconscious minds. It's the repeated suggestion that makes you believe."

34

DEVELOP FOUR NEW SUCCESS HABITS A YEAR

The individual who wants to reach the top in business must appreciate the might and force of habit. He must be quick to break those habits that can break him—and hasten to adopt those practices that will become the habits that help him achieve the success he desires.

J. PAUL GETTY
Founder of Getty Oil Company, philanthropist, and, by the late 1950s,
widely regarded as the richest man in the world

Psychologists tell us that up to 90% of our behavior is habitual. Ninety percent! From the time you get up in the morning until the time you retire at night, there are hundreds of things you do the same way every day. These include the way you shower, dress, eat breakfast, read the newspaper, brush your teeth, drive to work, organize your desk, shop at the supermarket, and clean your house. Over the years, you have developed a set of firmly entrenched habits that determine how well every area of your life works, from your job and your income to your health and your relationships.

The good news is that habits help free up your mind while your body is on automatic. This allows you to plan your day while you are in the shower and talk to your fellow passengers while you are driving your car. The bad news is that you can become locked into unconscious self-defeating behavior patterns that inhibit your growth and limit your success.

Whatever habits you currently have established are producing your current level of results. More than likely, if you want to create higher levels of success, you are going to need to drop some of your habits (not returning phone calls, staying up too late watching television, making sarcastic comments, eating fast food every day, smoking, being late for appointments, spending more than you earn) and replace them with more productive habits (returning phone calls within 24 hours, getting 8 hours of sleep each day, reading for an hour a day, exercising four times a week, eating healthy food, being on time, and saving 10% of your income).

GOOD OR BAD, HABITS ALWAYS DELIVER RESULTS

Success is a matter of understanding and religiously practicing specific, simple habits that always lead to success.

ROBERT J. RINGER
Author of *Million Dollar Habits*

Your habits determine your outcomes. Successful people don't just drift to the top. Getting there requires focused action, personal discipline, and lots of energy every day to make things happen. The habits you develop from this day forward will ultimately determine how your future unfolds.

One of the problems for people with poor habits is that the results of their bad habits usually don't show up until much later in life. When you develop a chronic bad habit, life will eventually give you consequences. You may not like the consequences, but life will still deliver them. The fact is, if you keep on doing things a certain way, you will always get a predictable result. Negative habits breed negative consequences. Positive habits create positive consequences.

TAKE ACTION TO DEVELOP BETTER HABITS NOW

There are two action steps for changing your habits: The *first step* is to make a list of all the habits that keep you unproductive or that might negatively impact your future. Ask others to help you objectively identify what they believe are your limiting habits. Look for patterns. Also review the list of the most common unsuccessful habits below:

- Procrastinating
- Paying bills at the last minute
- Not delivering on promised documents and services in a timely way
- Letting receivables get overdue
- Arriving late for meetings and appointments
- Forgetting someone's name within seconds of being introduced

- Talking over others' comments, instead of listening
- Answering the telephone during family time or spouse time
- Handling the mail more than once
- Working late
- Choosing work over time with your children
- Having fast-food meals more than 2 days a week

Once you have identified your negative habits, the *second step* is to choose a better, more productive success habit and develop systems that will help support them.

For example, if your goal is to get to the gym every morning, one system you might put in place is to go to bed 1 hour earlier and set your alarm ahead. If you're in sales, you might develop a checklist of activities so that all prospects receive the same series of communications.

Maybe you want to get in the habit of completing your work by close of business Friday, so you're free to spend weekends with your spouse and children. That's an excellent habit, *but what specifically will you do to adopt that new habit?* What activities will you engage in? How will you stay motivated? Will you develop a checklist of what must be accomplished by Friday afternoon to keep you on track? Will you spend less time chatting with coworkers at the water cooler? E-mail people their promised documents as you are talking on the phone with them? Take shorter lunches?

WHAT COULD YOU ACHIEVE IF YOU TOOK ON FOUR NEW HABITS A YEAR?

If you use these strategies to develop just four new habits a year, 5 years from now you'll have 20 new success habits that could bring you all the money you want, the wonderful loving relationships you desire, a healthier, more energized body, plus all sorts of new opportunities.

Start by listing four new habits you would like to establish in the next year. Work on one new habit every quarter. If you work diligently on building one new habit every 13 weeks, you won't overwhelm yourself with an unrealistic list of New Year's resolutions . . . and research now shows that if you repeat a behavior for 13 weeks—whether it is meditating for 20 minutes a day, flossing your teeth, reviewing your goals, or writing thank-you letters to your clients—it will be yours for life. By systematically adding one behavior at a time, you can dramatically improve your overall lifestyle.

Here are a couple of hints for making sure you follow through on your commitment to your new habit. Put up signs to remind you to follow through on the new behavior. When I learned that even a little dehydration can decrease your mental acuity by as much as 30%, I decided to develop the habit that all of the health practitioners had been advising—drink ten 8-ounce glasses of water a day. I put signs that said "Drink water!" on my phone, my office door, my bathroom mirror, and my kitchen refrigerator. I also had my secretary remind me every hour. Another powerful technique is to partner up with someone, keep score (see Principle 21), and hold each other account-able. Check in with each other at least once a week to make sure you are stay-ing on track.

Perhaps the most powerful way to stay on track is to follow the "no ex-ceptions rule," which is explained in the next chapter.

99% IS A BITCH;
100% IS A BREEZE

There is a difference between interest and commitment.
When you're interested in doing something, you do it only
when it's convenient. When you're committed to something,
you accept no excuses, only results.

KEN BLANCHARD
Chief Spiritual Officer of the Ken Blanchard Companies and coauthor of
over 30 books, including the classic best seller *The One Minute Manager*

In life the spoils of victory go to those who make a 100% commitment to the outcome, to those who have a "no matter what it takes" attitude. They give it their all; they put everything they have into getting their desired result—whether it be an Olympic gold medal, the top sales award, a perfect dinner party, an A in microbiology, or their dream house.

What a simple concept this is—yet you'd be surprised how many people wake up every day and fight with themselves over whether or not to keep their commitments, stick to their disciplines, or carry out their action plans.

THE "NO-EXCEPTIONS RULE"

Successful people adhere to the "no exceptions rule" when it comes to their daily disciplines. Once you make a 100% commitment to something, there are no exceptions. It's a done deal. Nonnegotiable. Case closed! Over and out. If I make a 100% commitment to monogamy, that is it. I never have to think about it again. There are no exceptions no matter what the circumstances. It ends the discussion, closes that door, permits no other possibility. I don't have to wrestle with that decision every day. It's already been made. The die has been cast. All the bridges are burned. It makes life easier and simpler and keeps me on focus. It frees up tons of energy that would otherwise be spent internally debating the topic over and over and over, because all the energy I expend on internal conflict is unavailable to use for creating outer achievement.

If you make the 100% commitment to exercise every day for 30 minutes, no matter what, then it is settled. You simply just do it. It doesn't matter if you are traveling, if you have a 7:00 AM television interview, if it's raining outside, if you went to bed late last night, if your schedule is full, or if you simply don't feel like it. You just do it anyway.

It's like brushing your teeth before you go to bed. You always do it, no matter what. If you find yourself in bed and you have forgotten, you get out of bed and brush them. It doesn't matter how tired you are or how late it is. You just do it.

ONLY ON A FULL MOON

My mentor Sid Simon is a successful speaker, trainer, best-selling author, and poet who splits his time between Hadley, Massachusetts, in the summer and Sanibel, Florida, in the winter. When I was a graduate student at the University of Massachusetts, Sid was the most popular professor in the Department of Education.

One of Sid's highest priorities is his health and fitness. At 77 years old, he still bikes on a regular basis, takes supplements, eats healthy foods, and—oh yes—he allows himself a bowl of ice cream on the one day a month when there's a full moon.

When I attended Sid's seventy-fifth birthday celebration, over 100 of his family members, closest friends, and adoring former students came from all across the country to celebrate with him. Dessert was the standard birthday cake and ice cream. Only one problem, though—there wasn't a full moon. To cajole him into giving himself permission on this once-in-a-lifetime special occasion, four people who knew of Sid's commitment dressed as moon goddesses and entered the room carrying a huge full moon made out of cardboard and aluminum foil, so there would be a virtual full moon for Sid.

But even with all of that loving persuasion, Sid stood firm on his commitment and declined the ice cream. He knew if he broke his commitment this one time, it would be that much easier to break it the next time he was offered ice cream. It would be easier to rationalize, justify, and explain away his commitment. Sid knew that a 100% commitment is actually easier to keep, and he was unwilling to undermine years of success for other people's approval. We all learned a lot about true self-discipline that night.

© 1998 Randy Glasbergen.

"I'm going to order a broiled skinless chicken breast, but I want you to bring me lasagna and garlic bread by mistake."

NO MATTER WHAT

Dr. Wayne Dyer, internationally renowned motivational speaker and host of the PBS show *The Power of Intention*, is another friend of mine who has made a similar commitment to his health and fitness. For 22 years, Wayne ran every day for a minimum of 8 miles—every day without fail! Wayne has been known to run up and down hotel stairwells and hallways during freezing weather in New York—and even up and down airplane aisles during international flights.

Whether your discipline is to read for an hour, practice the piano 5 days a week, make two sales calls every day, learn a new language, practice typing, hit 200 golf balls, do 50 sit-ups, run 6 miles, meditate, pray, read the Bible, spend 60 quality minutes with your kids—or whatever else you need to do to achieve your goals—commit 100% to those daily disciplines that will get you there.

ONE FINAL REASON 100% IS SO IMPORTANT

This powerful 100% commitment also figures critically in other important areas—for instance, the workplace. Consider what a commitment to just 99.9% quality would mean in the following work situations. It would mean

- One hour of unsafe drinking water every month
- Two unsafe landings at O'Hare International Airport each day

- 16,000 lost pieces of mail per hour
- 20,000 incorrectly filled drug prescriptions every year
- 500 incorrect surgical operations performed each week
- 50 newborn babies dropped at birth by doctors every day
- 22,000 checks deducted from the wrong account each hour
- Your heart failing to beat 32,000 times each year!

Can you see why 100% is such an important percentage? Just think how much better your life and the whole world would work if you were committed to 100% excellence in everything you do.

LEARN MORE
TO EARN MORE

If I am through learning, I am through.

JOHN WOODEN
UCLA basketball coach who won 10 NCAA championships

People who have more information have a tremendous advantage over people who don't. And though you may think it takes years to acquire the knowledge you would need to become supersuccessful, the truth is that simple behaviors such as reading for an hour a day, turning television time into learning time, and attending classes and training programs can make it surprisingly easy to increase your knowledge—and substantially increase your level of success.

DECREASE YOUR TELEVISION TIME

The sad reality is the average American watches television 6 hours a day. If you are one of these *average* folks, by the time you are 60 years old you will have wasted 15 years of your life watching television. That's one fourth of your life! Do you really want to spend one fourth of your life watching other people—the ones on television who are working—getting rich living out their dreams while you are vegetating?

In my first meeting with my mentor, W. Clement Stone, he asked me to eliminate 1 hour of television a day. He went on to explain that cutting out just 1 hour of television a day creates an extra 365 hours per year (that's over nine additional 40-hour workweeks—2 months of additional time!) to accomplish whatever is most important to you.

I asked him what he wanted me to do with that extra hour. "Anything productive," he said. "You can learn a new language, get superfit, spend quality time with your wife or children, learn to play a musical instrument, make

more sales calls, or go back to school and get a degree. But what I most recommend is that you read for an hour a day. Read inspirational autobiographies of successful people. Read books on psychology, sales, finance, and
health. Study the principles of successful living." And that is what I did.

My good friend Marshall Thurber reads a cutting-edge business book almost every day—at least 20 books a month. Marshall is the most informed
guy I know. He has an executive summary service—ededge—that provides
subscribers with one cutting-edge business book a month, a summary of the
book, and an interview with its author—all for just a little more than the cost
of the book. And while ededge started out as a service to CEOs and corporate
executives, it's now available to all of us. For details, visit www.ededge.com.

LEADERS ARE READERS

Self-made millionaire Dr. John Demartini made a list of all the Nobel Prize
winners, then made a list of all the greats in those same fields—whether it was
poetry, science, religion, or philosophy. He then proceeded to read their
works and their biographies. Not surprisingly, John is also one of the brightest and wisest guys I have ever met. Reading pays off.

"You can't put your hand in a pot of glue without some of that glue sticking," says John. "So, too, you can't put your mind and heart into some of the
works of these masters without some of it sticking. If you read about immor-
tals, you increase the possibility of leaving an immortal effect. The result has
been enormous for me."

Jim Rohn, America's foremost motivational philosopher, also suggests
you use that 1 extra hour a day to read. He taught me that if you were to read
one book a week, in 10 years you'd have read 520 books and in 20 years,
more than 1,000 books—enough to easily put you in the top 1% of experts in
your field. Add to those the books from masters in related areas and you'd
have an edge that others simply don't have.

LEARN TO READ FASTER TO READ MORE

If you read more slowly than you'd like, consider taking a course to increase
not only your reading speed but also how fast you absorb the information.
The best resource I've found is the PhotoReading Course developed by Paul
Scheele. It's available as a weekend workshop in many cities around the world
or as a self-study course from Learning Strategies Corporation (2000 Plymouth Road, Minnetonka, MN 55305; phone: 800-735-8273). You can learn
more about the course online at www.learningstrategies.com.

A WEEKLY SYSTEM FOR GETTING SMART

Take a look at the reading list I've included on pages 441 to 451. Reading books like these will help you achieve mastery in those areas of life that are central to your happiness and fulfillment. They contain some of the best time-tested wisdom, information, methodologies, systems, techniques, and secrets of success that have ever been recorded. If you make a commitment to read one book a week, review what you have read, and apply at least one thing you learn from each book, you will be miles ahead of everyone else in creating an extraordinary life.

All of the books on this list are ones that have helped me attain the high level of success I have achieved. Many of them are timeless classics and should make up the core of your personal success library.

If you can't yet afford to purchase your own books, borrow them from friends or your local library.

STUDY THE LIVES OF GREAT PEOPLE

In addition to this list, some of the best books out there are biographies and autobiographies of great people. By reading them, you will learn how to become great yourself. Former New York Mayor Rudolph Giuliani writes, "Political biographies have long been on my reading list. John F. Kennedy's *Profiles in Courage* made a huge impression on me as a teenager. As an adult, whenever I'd hear a politician say something pandering, I would muse, 'Doesn't anyone want a chapter in *Profiles in Courage* anymore?' I consumed biographies on Lincoln and Washington with the same enthusiasm I had for those on Ruth, Gehrig, and DiMaggio."[38] When I recently heard Rudy Giuliani speak in Santa Barbara, he told us that it was what he had read earlier in biographies of Winston Churchill and how he led England through the bombings of World War II that helped him lead New York after the terrorist attacks of September 11, 2001.

A great resource for good condensed inspiration and information drawn from the biographies of the great is the Great Life Network. The company has created a series of books, software, and audio programs that bring you the success stories of more than 500 of the world's most recognized people—all in short, easy-to-understand formats. Check out their Web site at www. greatlifenetwork.com.

---

38. From *Leadership*, by Rudolph W. Giuliani, with Ken Kurson (New York: Hyperion, 2002).

A final thought: If you're going to watch television, make a point of watching *Biography* on A&E Television Networks. I am always inspired by the lives of the people the program chronicles.

ATTEND SUCCESS RALLIES, CONFERENCES, AND RETREATS

I remember the first time I attended a success rally. Thousands of people were on hand to learn from many of the greatest speakers, trainers, and motivators of our day. You, too, can access these powerful learning experiences by attending rallies, conferences, and retreats—additionally benefiting from the excitement and inspiration of your fellow attendees and the networking that goes on at these events. Keep an eye out for ads in your local paper.

BE TEACHABLE

In a humble state, you learn better. I can't find anything else
very exciting about humility, but at least there's that.

JOHN DOONER
Chairman and CEO of Interpublic, the world's largest advertising conglomerate

While I was writing this book, I sat next to Skip Barber on a flight to Las Vegas. Skip trains people to drive high-performance cars under actual racing conditions. When I asked him what distinguishes his best students, he replied, "The ones who get it are teachable. They're open to learning. The ones who don't make it think they know everything already. You can't teach them anything."

To learn and grow in life, you need to be teachable, too. You need to let go of already knowing it all and needing to be right and look good, and open yourself to being a learner. Listen to those who have earned the right to speak, who have already done what you want to do.

I'm reminded of Dr. Billy Sharp, my boss when I worked at the W. Clement and Jesse V. Stone Foundation and one of the smartest men I ever knew. Whenever I attended meetings where he visited with outside consultants, Billy was always strangely quiet. One day, I asked him why he seldom spoke in these meetings. Not only was his reply revealing but it also taught me why he knew so much. "I already know what I know," he said. "If I'm talking to impress someone else, I don't learn anything new. I want to learn what they know." And he always did.

BE PREPARED WHEN OPPORTUNITY KNOCKS

In his book *Live Your Dreams*, Les Brown tells the story of how he dreamed of becoming a popular Miami disc jockey. "When I set out," he says, "I had no idea how I would do it, but I knew life would present the opportunities if I was prepared and in a position to take advantage of them."

Les shadowed his high school drama teacher, learning as much as he could about linguistics. Together, they worked on Les's speaking voice. Soon, Les began developing his own on-air style of patter, pretending at school that he was performing on the radio. He sought out mentors who could prepare him for the opportunity of being on the air. And after high school, though Les earned his wage as a city sanitation worker, his persistence landed him a job as a late-night gofer at a prominent Miami radio station.

Les immediately took advantage of the opportunity to learn even more. He absorbed all he could—hanging around the disc jockeys and engineers and practicing what he learned in a makeshift cardboard studio he created in his bedroom. His microphone was a hairbrush. Finally, one night, a deejay couldn't finish his show and Les had his chance to get on the air.

When the chance came, not only was Les prepared to be on the radio but he was also prepared to be great on the radio. The style, patter, dialogue, and broadcasting skills he had worked so hard to develop paid off instantly—Les was an immediate hit, and he was later promoted to fill-in deejay . . . then finally became a full-time disc jockey with his own radio show.

WHAT DO YOU NEED TO DO TO GET READY?

If you're an industry expert and believe your consulting business would sky-rocket after presenting a workshop at the national convention, why not get prepared now . . . by writing your speaker's kit, joining Toastmasters, outlining and practicing your speech, and getting ready to be on the platform?

If you want a promotion at work, why not ask your boss what it takes to become promotable? Perhaps you need to go back to school and get your MBA. Or maybe you need 1 year of accounting experience. Or perhaps you need to learn the latest software programs. Do that, and when the next promotion comes around, you can say, "I'm ready!"

Do you need to learn a new foreign language? Could you develop advanced skills, more resources, or new contacts? Do you need to get your body into better physical shape? Should you expand your business skills, sales skills, or negotiating skills? Are you learning new skills on the computer—such as using

PowerPoint, PageMaker, Photoshop, or Excel? Do you need to learn golf so that you can make business deals on the golf course? Would it improve your home life and marriage by taking dancing classes with your spouse? Are you learning to sail or play tennis? Do you need to learn to play a musical instrument, take acting classes, or learn how to write better to get where you want to go?

Whatever you need to do to get ready, start now by making a list of the top 10 things you could be doing to be ready when opportunity finds you. Take classes on your own time. Read books. Get new skills. Go to your industry's trade show. Dress the part. Look like a player before you're there.

As Les Brown's story teaches us, all it takes is passion, persistence, and the belief that someday the opportunity will come. Start getting ready now.

ATTEND HUMAN-POTENTIAL TRAININGS

Nothing changes until you do.

SOURCE UNKNOWN

Imagine that you suddenly discovered you were driving with the emergency brake on. Would you push harder on the gas? No! You would simply release the brake and instantly go faster—without any additional expenditure of energy.

Most of us are going through life with the emergency brake on. It's time to release the limiting beliefs, emotional blocks, and self-destructive behaviors that are holding you back.

In addition to the techniques we've already covered in Principles 10 ("Release the Brakes"), 32 ("Transform Your Inner Critic into an Inner Coach"), and 33 ("Transcend Your Limiting Beliefs"), the two most powerful methods for releasing the brake are personal development training and individual therapy. If I were to attribute my success to any one thing, it would be the hundreds of personal development seminars I have attended over the past 40 years. All of us—including me—need outside influences to help us break through our habitual patterns and assist us in creating new ways of thinking and behaving.

Below is a short list of the organizations I've personally found most powerful in my life and the lives of my family, staff, and students. Visit their Web sites, call and talk to them, attend their guest events, and then make a decision to attend a couple a year that feel right for you. See "Suggested Reading and Additional Resources for Success" on pages 441–451 for more information on these and other training organizations.

Canfield Training Group, P.O. Box 30880, Santa Barbara, CA 93130. Phone: 805-563-2935. Fax: 805-563-2945. www.jackcanfield.com

Global Relationship Centers, 25555 Pedernales Point Drive, Spicewood, TX 78669. Phone: 512-264-3333. Fax: 512-264-2913. www.grc333.com

Hoffman Institute, 223 San Anselmo Avenue, suite 4, San Anselmo, CA 94960. Phone: 415-485-5220. Toll free: 800-506-5253. www.hoffmaninstitute.org

Insight Seminars, 2101 Wilshire Boulevard, suite 101, Santa Monica, CA 90403. Phone: 310-315-9733. www.insightseminars.org

Landmark Education—The Forum, 353 Sacramento Street, suite 200, San Francisco, CA 94111. Phone: 415-981-8850. www.landmarkeducation.com

Peak Potentials Training, 1651 Welch Street, North Vancouver, BC, Canada, V7P 3G9. Phone: 604-983-3344. www.peakpotentials.com

Sedona Training Associates, 60 Tortilla Drive, Sedona, AZ 86336. Phone: 928-282-3522. Fax: 928-203-0602. www.sedona.com

THERAPY AND COUNSELING

Although the training I've recommended above will expand your mind and help increase your possibilities in life, some of us simply need more in-depth work to remove the emotional blocks and childhood programming that are holding us back. For some, therapy and counseling are the answer.

In my experience, however, only about 20% of the therapists and counselors you will encounter are highly competent and effective. Ask around and get referrals.

Most therapists specialize in one approach or type of therapy. There are three approaches I especially recommend—Gestalt therapy, psychosynthesis, and neurolinguistic programming (more popularly known as NLP). To find a good therapist or counselor in these approaches, see "Suggested Reading and Additional Resources for Success" on pages 441 through 451.

COMMIT TO LIFELONG LEARNING

Realize that the amount of knowledge and information available in the world is growing at a mind-numbing pace. In fact, it has been said that all human knowledge has doubled in the last 10 years. Don't expect this trend to slow down.

More alarming, the information that allows you to be successful—to be on the cutting edge of your career and profession—is evolving at the same pace. That's why you *must* commit to lifelong self-improvement and learning—improving your mind, increasing your skills, and boosting your ability to assimilate and apply what you learn.

37

STAY MOTIVATED WITH THE MASTERS

A successful person realizes his personal responsibility for self-motivation. He starts with himself because he possesses the key to his own ignition switch.

KEMMONS WILSON
Founder of Holiday Inn Hotels

So many of us today are trained—by the media, by our parents, by our schools, by our culture—to have limiting, "it's not possible, I don't deserve it" beliefs. This early conditioning is often so ingrained that it takes continual external motivation to overcome the decades of negative effects and move toward more success-oriented thoughts and attitudes.

Attending a weekend workshop isn't enough. Neither is reading a book or watching a training video. What truly successful people do is listen daily to audio programs from the world's most renowned motivational masters—in the car, at home, and at the office—even if it's just for 15 minutes each day.

LEARN VIRTUALLY ANYTHING YOU WANT OR NEED TO KNOW

The average person commutes 30 minutes each way to and from work. In 5 years, that's 1,250 hours in the car—enough time to give yourself the equivalent of a college education! Whether you're commuting by car or train, riding your bike, or going for a run, listening to audio CDs can give you the edge you need to excel in virtually any area of your life. You can keep yourself motivated, learn a language, learn management skills, learn sales and marketing strategies, learn better communication, learn about holistic health, and more.

Copyrigth 2004 by Randy Glasbergen.
www.glasbergen.com

—GLASBERGEN

"I listened to some motivational tapes while you
were at work and I've decided to become a Great Dane!"

You can even discover the success secrets of the world's most powerful industrialists, business titans, real estate moguls, and entrepreneurs.

SLEEPLESS IN VIRGINIA AT 4:00 AM

Just how motivating can the masters be in your life?

To the outside world, Jeff Arch's life looked pretty good in 1989. He was
running a successful karate school and had a happy marriage and a 4-year-old
daughter and a 1-month-old son. But inside, something was missing. He had
always dreamed of being a successful playwright and screenwriter, but his
early efforts had not paid off, and so he had turned his attention to feeding his
young family.

Still awake at 4:00 AM one night, he found himself watching an infomer-
cial for Tony Robbins's Personal Power program. Sitting alone in his living
room, Jeff thought, *I have to face it—I'm doing a good job, but this is not where I
want to be. I have to admit there have been big disappointments and that they have hurt.
As a writer, I have to admit that I have failed in every possible way there is to fail—and
there is nothing more to learn from failure—so maybe now it's time to succeed, and see
what lessons are there. But this time I have to go at it like a black belt, and this time I
have to put all my attitudes aside and try these other ones—I can always go back to the
ones I had. But if they were such good attitudes, I wouldn't be sitting here at four in the
morning wondering what to do with my life, and what to tell my kids when they get a*

little older and start asking questions. "I heard you were going to be a writer, Dad—what happened?" I can't face that. I don't want to be one of those guys who give their kids all this life advice but have nothing to back it up. What authority would I have to tell them anything? How can I tell them to go after their dreams if I don't go after mine?

Jeff instantly made two decisions that would dramatically change his life. He picked up the phone and ordered the program. Then he promised himself that when the program arrived, unless it was total garbage, he would complete it, no matter what. And he would use it as his ticket back into writing.

When the program arrived, Jeff did each day's lesson just as he had promised himself. He didn't tell anyone about it because he was too self-conscious. He wanted to get results first. Fortunately, the information turned out to be just what Jeff needed. The first day he listened to the tapes, he knew he had to return to his writing, and the very next morning, after 3 years away from his typewriter, he turned in the keys of the karate school and resigned his position to pursue his dream.

"Tony was the first person—the first voice I ever heard—that didn't say, 'You're dreaming too big,'" Jeff told me. "He didn't say, 'Come on, you're asking for too much.' What he said was 'You've got to think bigger than you ever thought you could think!' Here I was, thirty-five years old, and it was the first time in my life somebody gave me permission and encouragement to dream bigger than I was already dreaming." Tony's program told Jeff, "You've got to dream even bigger!"

Inspired by Tony's suggestion and drawing on the self-confidence that earning a third-degree black belt had given him, Jeff dove back into writing screenplays. Though his earlier ones took 6 months to 3 years to write, this one was finished and ready in a month!

The script was well received, but it didn't sell. Unfortunately Jeff had written a story about the Cold War—in the fall of 1989—and the Berlin Wall came down the day he finished his script. Suddenly, after 50 years, the Russians were no longer the enemy.

Jeff could have said to himself, *When are you going to realize that you are not meant to be a writer?* and simply have given up one more time. But with his new attitude, he knew to ask a better question—*How bad do you want what you want?* Instead of giving up, he thought about how to get what he wanted. *Okay, it wasn't the writing; it was the choice of plots. What has nothing to do with current events? What kind of theme would be timeless?*

And the answer was *Love is timeless.* So he thought, *If I write a love story that has nothing to do with history, that will never change.*

The result was a screenplay for *Sleepless in Seattle*, which Jeff once again created in less than a month, and it sold less than 3 months later for a quarter of a million dollars. *Sleepless in Seattle* went on to become a megahit that garnered Jeff an Oscar nomination for best screenplay (plus two more screen-play nominations from the Writers Guild of America and the British Academy of Film and Television Arts), revitalized the genre of romantic comedy, and catapulted the careers of Meg Ryan and Tom Hanks to even higher levels.

If a motivational and educational audio program can launch a million-dollar screenwriting career worthy of an Oscar nomination, don't you owe it to yourself to take advantage of the same kind of resources that Jeff Arch did?[39]

AUDIOTAPES UNLEASHED HIS CREATIVITY

For nearly 20 years Allen Koss had enjoyed quite a successful career as a Hollywood television producer. At least it appeared to be successful from the outside. He had developed and produced a good number of shows the average viewer would consider classics in the genre, including *Concentration*, *Joker's Wild*, and *Tic Tac Dough*. The money and the titles were nice, and he certainly had the respect of his peers, but unfortunately, all the satisfaction was on the outside.

Inside, he felt as if it could all end any second. He never felt in control. He was always just reacting to what was coming at him (always at high speed) and never felt he really held the reins of his destiny. He was always stressed out, and he constantly felt as if he had just used up all his creativity and had no idea where his next creative thought would come from. Eventually, as the stress mounted, he found himself using food to salve the pain, and he gained a lot of weight—which made him feel even worse.

Finally, the seams of his life split when a long-running show he had produced went off the air. At first, he tried to create new shows to work on, but the market was tight and he met with virtually no success. He was able to get some work from other producers, but it was not enough to keep things going.

The less he worked, the more acute his anxiety became. The more anxious he became, the worse his stress—and all its symptoms—became. He was stuck in a vicious downward cycle.

After a while, his financial situation was becoming dire, his weight had ballooned, and fights with his wife and family were a regular event. He was losing friends, people in the industry seemed less willing to work with him, and he was becoming more and more isolated.

One day, as he was thumbing through a copy of *Psychology Today*, he ran across an ad for some cassette tapes containing an audio technology that

---

39. *Personal Power II* and Tony Robbins's newest program, *Get the Edge*, are available at www.anthonyrobbins.com or from Nightingale-Conant, whose contact information is listed on page 268.

claimed to alter brain wave patterns, which resulted in positive mental and emotional changes for the listener. It seemed pretty implausible, but at this point he thought, *What have I got to lose?*

So he called the Centerpointe Research Institute, and after wending his way through various secretaries, he finally managed to talk to Bill Harris, the owner. Bill told him he had created an audio cassette program built around something he called Holosync. Allen decided to order the Holosync program, and when it arrived, he put on an audiotape, sat down in his favorite easy chair, put on his headphones, sat back, and relaxed. He continued to do this for 30 minutes each day.

From the very first time he used the Centerpointe tapes, his stress level began to decrease, and the more he used them, the less stressed he became. And the less anxious he became, the easier he was to get along with, and the more people seemed to be willing to help him. Things began to turn around for him.

Allen's creativity returned, too. He saw situations from a whole new perspective, and creative solutions to his problems seemed to almost miraculously pour from his mind! And the longer he used the program, the more he seemed to know himself, in a very deep and satisfying way.

As he became involved in new projects, he did so with new clarity about exactly how he fit in, how all the pieces fit together, and how he could most successfully bring the project to completion. Instead of avoiding him, people were now seeking Allen out to work on his projects.

As his confidence returned and increased, he finally began to feel in control of his destiny. And with his stress level melting away, his weight problem melted away as well.[40]

WHERE TO GET THE BEST MOTIVATIONAL AUDIO PROGRAMS

You'll find my list of favorite motivational audio programs in "Suggested Reading and Additional Resources for Success," pages 441 through 451. Or go to www.thesuccessprinciples.com for a more complete and constantly updated list of recommended audio programs on success, wealth-building, health, relationships, and more. In addition, here are the four best producers of motivational and educational audio programs. Write or call for a catalogue or order online.

---

40. You can order the Holosync audio program from Centerpointe Research Institute by calling 800-945-2741 or visiting www.centerpointe.com.

© 1998 Randy Glasbergen.

GLASBERGEN

**"I'm going to be late for work this morning. I was listening
to my motivation tapes and suddenly found myself driving
farther and faster than I ever imagined I could!"**

Nightingale-Conant (6245 W. Howard Street, Niles, IL 60714; phone:
1-800-560-6081; www.nightingale.com) has programs by motivational giants
Tony Robbins, Zig Ziglar, Brian Tracy, Jim Rohn, Napoleon Hill, Les Brown,
Robert Allen, Wayne Dyer, Mark Victor Hansen, me, and many others, as well as
information-packed educational programs.

Learning Strategies Corporation (2000 Plymouth Road; Minnetonka, MN
55305-2335; phone: 1-800-735-8273; www.learningstrategies.com) produces
in-depth experiential courses on audio. I highly recommend their work for
producing long-lasting transformational results in your life.

Fred Pryor Seminars/CareerTrack (9757 Metcalf Avenue, Overland Park, KS 66212;
phone: 1-800-780-8476; www.pryor.com) produces audio-recorded courses that
run the full range from personal development to business development. They
have a broad and extensive catalogue.

SkillPath Seminars (P.O. Box 804441; Kansas City, MO 64180-4441; phone:
1-800-873-7545; www.ourbookstore.com) produces audio-recorded programs
covering their most in demand seminar topics, including time management,
simplifying your life, thriving in challenging situations, and also programs
designed specifically for women.

I also highly recommend four audio programs that I have produced to
help you become more successful in every area of your life: *Maximum Confidence, Self-Esteem and Peak Performance, The Aladdin Factor*, and *The Success Principles: A 30-Day Journey from Where You Are to Where You Want to Be*. They are all
available at www.jackcanfield.com.

FUEL YOUR SUCCESS
WITH PASSION
AND ENTHUSIASM

Enthusiasm is one of the most powerful engines of success.
When you do a thing, do it with all your might. Put your whole
soul into it. Stamp it with your own personality. Be active,
be energetic, be enthusiastic and faithful, and you will accomplish
your object. Nothing great was ever achieved without enthusiasm.

RALPH WALDO EMERSON
American essayist and poet

Passion is something within you that provides the continual enthusiasm, focus, and energy you need to succeed. But unlike feel-good motivation derived from external sources, true passion has a more spiritual nature. It comes from within. And it can be channeled into amazing feats of success.

FILLED WITH PASSION

The word *enthusiasm* comes from the Greek word *entheos*, which means "to be filled with God." When you are filled with spirit, you are naturally inspired and passionate. Sometimes that passion expresses itself in a dynamic and energetic way, like the hustle of a champion athlete who is "on fire." Other times it expresses itself in a more peaceful and calm way, like the passion of Mother Teresa for ministering to the needs of the dying in Calcutta.

No doubt you know or have met people who are passionate about life and enthusiastic about their work. They can't wait to get up in the morning and get started. They are eager and energetic. They are filled with purpose and totally committed to their mission. This kind of passion comes from loving and enjoying your work. It comes from doing what you were born to do. It comes from following your heart and trusting your joy as a guide. Enthusiasm and passion come as a result of caring about what you do. If you love your work, if you enjoy it, you're already a success.

YOUR SUCCESS IS GUARANTEED

My son Kyle, aka Inspector Double Negative, is a hip-hop artist in Berkeley, California. Though he's been struggling to make it financially for the last 8 years, he has already created 10 full-length CDs; performed at Woodstock '99; opened for KRS1 and Public Enemy; performed with Joan Baez, Jurrassic 5, Dilated Peoples, the Beat Junkies, Blackalicious, the Alkaholiks, Freestyle Fellowship, Babatunde Olatunji, and Masta Ace; sat in as a guest DJ for radio station KPOO in San Francisco; and taught hip-hop history, culture, and production at Richmond High School in Richmond, California.

He has doggedly pursued his dream and never given up on his art.

So even if he were never to make a lot of money or become a rap super-star outside of the Bay Area, Kyle is already successful. Because when you are happy doing what you love, you've already won. When you do something you love with passion and perseverance, you are already a success. Even if you never hit the big time, who cares? You were having fun doing what you love all the time anyway. (Kyle's CDs are available online at www.KoolKyle.com.)

A PASSION FOR HORSES

Monty Roberts is definitely a man who has found his passion. He is a horse trainer on a mission to show people that violence is never the answer. He believes that horses are trying to teach people that if they could get violence out of their lives, they would find a much happier existence. His work has produced 8 national champions in the show rings of the world and more than 300 international stakes winners in Thoroughbred racing. He's written several books, including *The Man Who Listens to Horses*, which spent 58 weeks on the *New York Times* Best-Seller List.

Monty has a unique way of tuning into his passion, which he recently described to me:

> When I was in first, second, and third grade, I discovered that whenever I think about doing something that really excites me, I get a very strong tingling sensation down low in the depth of my stomach on each side of my belt buckle.

As a child, I would most often experience this feeling while daydreaming about winning a championship or achieving a certain goal as a competitive horseman. Once I had my goals in place, this tingling in my belly also told me which direction to go at every crossroad in my life. I could just wait until the tingle came, and then I knew what the next right step was.

Knowing my goals and setting my course allowed me to follow a road map, which introduced me to a life free of work—or work as most people know it. Sure, I worked hard, but it was always to follow the tingle that set me on a course of doing exactly what I wanted most to do. This meant that I could execute the most grueling schedules imaginable without considering them to be work. I am 69 years of age, and I have a schedule that would choke down most people in their thirties and forties.

I read in many inspirational and self-help-type books that we should work hard so as to earn the right to retire young and enjoy "free time." By following my strongest desires and seeking my greatest goals, I have created an environment filled with the joy that free time and my work time are the same.

A PASSION FOR TEACHING

Hobart Elementary School is the third largest elementary school in the United States and is located in a gang- and drug-infested Los Angeles neighborhood. The fifth-grade students in teacher Rafe Esquith's classroom, who all speak English as a second language, score 50 points higher in math and reading than the students in the rest of the school. Their grasp and mastery of the English language is gained through learning and performing the plays of Shakespeare. To date, the Hobart Shakespeareans have performed 15 full-length plays to packed audiences, from the White House to the inner city. Among their passionate supporters are actors Sir Ian McKellen and Hal Holbrook.

When you walk into Rafe's classroom, you notice the large banner— THERE ARE NO SHORTCUTS—draped above the chalkboard. The nearby "Walls of Fame" feature school pennants from Stanford, Princeton, Yale, and UCLA, where many of his students have sought higher education. School officials from all over the world sit in his classroom to observe the educational miracles at work. Not only was Rafe honored as Disney's National Teacher of the Year but he is also the sole teacher in history to be presented with a National Medal of the Arts. Queen Elizabeth has given him the highest tribute bestowed on a non-British citizen—he was named a Member of the British Empire.

What has fueled this devoted, visionary public-school teacher to work 12-hour days, 6 days a week, 52 weeks a year for 21 years? Passion and enthusiasm. There's nothing he loves more than bringing the joys of literature, theater, music, science, math, and plain old fun to hundreds of kids. The results? He infuses his students with their own joy for learning, boosting their self-esteem while boosting their academic performances. As Rafe puts it, "I'm a very ordinary fellow who made one smart move. I would not allow today's educational fiasco of systemized mediocrity and uniformity to crush me into the robot so many potentially good teachers become. I kept my own spirit and personal passions alive in my class, and as a lover of Shakespeare have passed on that excitement to eager young minds. In my school's neighborhood of failure and despair, success and excellence have become the standard rather than the exception to the rule. And best of all, the kids and I have a helluva good time working so hard and climbing to great heights. It's a wonderful life."[41]

HOW TO DEVELOP PASSION

How can you develop passion in the most important areas of your life?

Let's look at your career for a moment. That's the work that occupies the majority of your week. A recent Gallup poll said a full one third of Americans would be happier in another job. Ask yourself: *Am I doing what I love to do?*

If you aren't, and you had the choice to do anything you wanted to do, what would that be? If you believe you can't make money doing that, imagine that you just won the lottery. After buying your expensive mansion, a Rolls-Royce, and all the toys and travel you wanted, what would you do with your day? *What you're doing now or something different?*

The most successful people I've met love what they do so much, they would actually do it for free. But they're successful because they've found a way to make a living doing what they love to do.

If you're not skilled enough to do the work you'd love to do, make time to educate yourself so you are. Do whatever it takes to prepare—working part time in your dream job or even volunteering as an intern—while still maintaining your current job.

Pay attention, too, to those times outside of the office when you feel the happiest, the most joyous, the most fully engaged, the most acknowledged and appreciated, and the most connected with yourself and others. What were you doing at those times? What were you experiencing? Those events are indicators of ways you can bring passion into your life outside your day-to-day work. It tells you what you would be happiest doing with your time.

---

41. If you want to read an inspirational story of passion and enthusiasm, get a copy of *There Are No Shortcuts*, by Rafe Esquith (New York: Anchor Books, 2004). Another teacher producing miracles in the inner city because of her passion for teaching and for children is Marva Collins. See *Marva Collins' Way*, by Marva Collins and Civia Tamarkin (New York: Jeremy Tarcher/Putnam, 1982).

HOW TO KEEP PASSION AND ENTHUSIASM ALIVE

Passion is a powerful tool for success and, as such, deserves to be an area you consistently work on.

Passion makes your days fly by. It helps you get more done in less time. It helps you make better decisions. And it attracts others to you. They want to be associated with you and your success.

So how can you maintain passion and enthusiasm every day? The most obvious is to spend more time doing what you love to do. As I have discussed in earlier chapters, that includes discovering your true purpose, deciding what you really want to do and have, believing you can do and have it, deliberately creating your dream career, delegating as much as you can that is not your core genius to someone else, and taking concrete steps toward the attainment of your goals.

Another key to passion and enthusiasm is to reconnect with your original purpose for doing anything that you do. When you look underneath the surface of the things that feel like have-tos rather than want-tos, you'll almost always find that there is a deeper purpose that you are passionate about. You may not love the idea of sitting in a pediatrician's waiting room with your child, but when you get underneath it, aren't you passionate about your child's health and well-being? Ask yourself, *What is the why underneath what I am doing?* If you can get in touch with that, it is a lot easier to get enthusiastic about whatever it is that you *have* to do.

You'll discover that all of the things you feel like you have to do are really choices that you are making that serve some higher purpose such as feeding your family, creating security for your future, staying out of jail, or contributing to your health and longevity. Once you realize that these are choices you are making, you realize you can make one more choice, and that is the choice of your attitude. Even if you are trapped in an elevator with three strangers, you have a choice about your attitude. You can choose to be grumpy about not getting your work done, or you can see it as an opportunity to meet some new people. The choice is up to you. Why not choose to do everything you do with joy and enthusiasm? The choice is up to you.

And here is one final thought. When you express your passion and enthusiasm, you will become a magnet to others, who will be attracted to your high level of energy. They will want to play with you, work with you, and support your dreams and goals. As a result, you will ultimately get more done in a shorter period of time.

PART THREE

Build Your Success Team

Alone we can do so little;
together we can do so much.

HELEN KELLER
American author, lecturer, and advocate for the blind

39

STAY FOCUSED ON YOUR CORE GENIUS

Success follows doing what you want to do.
There is no other way to be successful.

MALCOLM S. FORBES
Publisher of *Forbes* magazine

I believe you have inside you a core genius—some one thing that you love to do and do so well that you hardly feel like charging people for it. It's effortless for you and a whole lot of fun. And if you could make money doing it, you'd make it your lifetime's work.

Successful people believe this, too. That's why they put their core genius first. They focus on it—and delegate everything else to other people on their team.

Compare that to the other people in the world who go through life doing everything, even those tasks they're bad at or that could be done more cheaply, better, and faster by someone else. They can't find the time to focus on their core genius because they fail to delegate even the most menial of tasks.

When you delegate the grunt work—the things you hate doing or those tasks that are so painful, you end up putting them off—you get to concentrate on what you love to do. You free up your time so that you can be more productive. And you get to enjoy life more.

So why is delegating routine tasks and unwanted projects so difficult for most people?

Surprisingly, most people are afraid of looking wasteful or being judged as being above everyone else. They are afraid to give up control or reluctant to spend the money to pay for help. Deep down, most people simply don't want to let go.

Others—potentially you—have simply fallen into the *habit* of doing everything themselves. "It's too time-consuming to explain it to someone," you say. "I can do it more quickly and better myself anyway." But can you?

DELEGATE COMPLETELY

If you're a professional earning $75 per hour and you pay a neighborhood kid $10 an hour to cut the grass, you save the effort of doing it yourself on the weekend and gain 1 extra hour when you could profit by $65. Of course, though 1 hour doesn't seem like much, multiply that by at least 20 weekends in the spring and summer and you discover you've gained 20 hours a year at $65 per hour—or an extra $1,300 in potential earnings.

Similarly, if you're a real estate agent, you need to list houses, gather information for the multiple listings, attend open houses, do showings, put keys in lockboxes, write offers, and make appointments. And if you're lucky, you eventually get to close a deal.

But let's say that you're the best closer in the area.

Why would you want to waste your time writing listings, doing lead generation, placing lockboxes, and making videos of the property when you could have a staff of colleagues and assistants doing all that, thus freeing you up to do more closing? Instead of doing just one deal a week, you could be doing three deals because you had delegated what you're less good at.

One of the strategies I use and teach is complete delegation. It simply means that you delegate a task once and completely—rather than delegating it each time it needs to be done.

When I hired the gardener for my Santa Barbara estate, I said, "I want my grounds to look as close as possible to the grounds at the Four Seasons Biltmore in Montecito using the budget I'm providing you." When I go to the Four Seasons, I don't have to check whether the trees need to be trimmed or the automatic sprinklers are working. Someone else is in charge of that. Well, I want the same luxury at my home. "With that as our operating principle," I said, "here's the budget. Take charge of the grounds. If I'm ever not happy, I'll let you know. If I'm not happy a second time, I'll find someone else. Does that feel like a workable agreement?"

My landscaper was, in fact, very excited. He knew he wouldn't be micromanaged, and I knew I wouldn't have to worry about it again—and I don't. See what I mean? Complete delegation.

When my niece came to stay with us one year while she attended the local community college, we made another complete delegation—the grocery shopping. We told her she could have unlimited use of our van if she would buy the groceries every week. We provided her with a list of staples that we always want in the house (eggs, butter, milk, ketchup, and so on), and her job was to check every week and replace anything that was running low. In addition, my wife planned meals and let her know which items she wanted for the main courses (fish, chicken, broccoli, avocadoes, and so on). The task was delegated once and saved us hundreds of hours that year that could be devoted to writing, exercise, family time, and recreation.

BECOME A CON ARTIST DOING WHAT YOU LOVE TO DO

The biggest mistake people make in life is not trying to make a living at doing what they most enjoy.

MALCOLM S. FORBES

Strategic Coach Dan Sullivan once stated that all entrepreneurs are really con artists. They get other people to pay them to practice getting better at what they love to do.[42]

Think about it.

Tiger Woods loves to play golf. People pay him big money to play golf. Every time he plays, he learns more about playing better. He gets to practice and hang out with other golfers, all the while getting paid for it.

Anthony Robbins is a speaker and a trainer. He loves speaking and training. He has arranged his life so that people are constantly paying him large sums of money to do what he loves to do.

Or consider baseball great Sammy Sosa of the Chicago Cubs. It takes him about 1 second to hit a home run—as long as it takes for the ball to meet the bat. He earns $10,625,000 for about 70 seconds of batting time per year, so he has gotten really good at making the bat meet the ball. That's where he makes his money. That's where he puts all his time—practicing and getting ready for the bat to meet the ball. He has found his core genius and devotes the majority of his waking hours to perfecting his genius.

Of course, most of us are not on par with Tiger Woods, Tony Robbins, or Sammy Sosa, but the fact is that we could learn a lot from their level of focus.

Many salespeople, for example, spend more time on account administration than they do on the phone making sales, when they *could* hire a part-time administrator (or share the cost with another salesperson) to do this time-consuming detail work.

Most female executives spend too much time running their household,

---

42. I am grateful to Dan Sullivan for many of the ideas in this chapter and the next. You can learn more about his breakthrough coaching ideas at www.strategiccoach.com.

when they could easily and inexpensively delegate this task to a cleaning service or part-time mother's helper, freeing themselves to focus on their career or spend more time with their family.

Even most entrepreneurs spend less than 30% of their time focusing on their core genius and unique abilities. In fact, by the time they've launched a business, it often seems entrepreneurs are doing everything *but* the one thing they went into business for in the first place.

Don't let this be your fate. Identify your core genius, then delegate completely to free up more time to focus on what you love to do.

DO WHAT YOU LOVE—THE MONEY WILL FOLLOW

Starting out to make money is the greatest mistake in life.
Do what you feel you have a flair for doing, and if you are good
enough at it, the money will come.

GREER GARSON
Winner of the 1943 Academy Award for best actress

Diana von Welanetz Wentworth is someone who has always focused on her core genius while following her heart and has been wildly successful as a result. Her greatest pleasure was always to be cooking something and gathering people around the table to share at a deep level over food. She was always reaching for a deeper connection, what she calls "a sense of celebration at the table." So she started her career writing books about how to give a party and do everything ahead of time so you can actually be present and connect more deeply with the people you invite.

Then in May 1985, she went on a trip to the Soviet Union with a group of leaders in the human potential movement, where she noticed that, for the most part, they were all loners. Even though they were quite well known for their books and their impact in the world, they didn't know each other. When she returned, she realized that her life purpose had always been more about connection than food. She had just used food as a catalyst.

That realization led her to create the Inside Edge, an organization that hosted weekly breakfast meetings in Beverly Hills, Orange County, and San Diego, California, where nationally recognized people of vision came together to share their knowledge and wisdom on human potential, spirituality, consciousness, and world peace. Speakers included people such as Mark Victor Hansen and me, motivational expert Anthony Robbins, management consultant Ken Blanchard, actor Dennis Weaver, counselor the Reverend Leo

Booth, and authors Susan Jeffers and Dan Millman. In addition to listening to an inspirational speaker, participants would network, encourage each other to dream bigger, and support each other's projects. Eighteen years later, the Orange County chapter still continues to meet every week.[43]

Diana has gone on to write and coauthor numerous books, including *The Chicken Soup for the Soul Cookbook*, once again integrating her love of food with her love of people sharing their ideas, wisdom, and stories.

43. Go to www.insideedge.org for more information on the Inside Edge.

REDEFINE TIME

The world is entering a new time zone, and one of the most difficult adjustments people must make is in their fundamental concepts and beliefs about the management of time.

DAN SULLIVAN
Founder and president, the Strategic Coach

The most successful people I know create superior results yet still maintain a balance among work, family, and recreation in their lives. To achieve this, they use a unique planning system that structures their time into three very different kinds of days that are prescheduled to assure the highest payoff for their efforts while still allowing abundant amounts of free time to pursue their personal interests.

This system, which I call the Breakthrough Results Time System, divides all of your time into three kinds of days: Best Results Days, Preparation Days, and Rest & Recreation Days.

BEST RESULTS DAYS

A Best Results Day is a day in which you spend at least 80% of your time operating in your core genius, or primary area of expertise—interacting with people or processes that give you the highest payoffs for the time you invest. To be successful, you must schedule more Best Results Days and hold yourself accountable for producing the results.

In the previous chapter, we discussed your core genius—that one thing you love to do and do so well, you hardly feel like charging people for it. It's effortless for you and a whole lot of fun. And if you could make money doing it, you'd make it your lifetime's work. Your core genius is your natural talent, the area where you shine.

My areas of genius are speaking, conducting seminars, coaching, writing, and editing. I do these things easily and well—and when I do them in a focused way, they're the things I get paid the most money for. For me, a Best Results Day would be a day in which I spend 80% of the time speaking or leading a seminar for a fee, writing or editing a book (like this one), developing a new audio program, or coaching someone to achieve a greater level of success.

For Janet Switzer, a Best Results Day is writing and developing marketing materials, developing knowledge products, or speaking to a group of consultants and business owners about producing exponential leaps in income generation.

Your Best Results Day might be spent designing a new line of clothing, making sales calls, negotiating deals, producing a loan package to send to a mortgage lender, painting, performing, or writing a grant proposal for a non-profit organization.

PREPARATION DAYS

A Preparation Day is a day when you prepare and plan for a Best Results Day—either by learning a new skill, locating a new resource, training your support team, or delegating tasks and projects to others. Preparation Days ensure that your Best Results Days are as productive as possible.

For me, a Preparation Day might be spent taking a seminar to improve my training skills, planning how to maximize sales of our books and tapes on the Internet, rehearsing a new speech, reading potential stories for a new *Chicken Soup for the Soul®* book, or delegating a project to a member of my support team. Yours might be seeking out a mentor, developing a new sales presentation, writing a brochure, preparing your studio for a recording session, interviewing a new job candidate, training an assistant, attending an industry or professional convention, or writing an employee manual.

REST & RECREATION DAYS

A Rest & Recreation (R & R) Day extends from midnight to midnight and involves no work-related activity of any kind. It's a day completely free of business meetings, business-related phone calls, cell phone calls, e-mails, or reading work-related documents.

On a true R&R Day, you're not available to your staff, clients, or students for any kind of contact except for *true* emergencies—injury, death, flood, or fire. The truth is that most so-called emergencies aren't emergencies at all. They're simply employees, coworkers, and family members who don't have—or haven't been given—enough training, responsibility, or authority to handle the unexpected situations that arise. You have to set clear boundaries,

"It's come to my attention, Wycliff, that you're actually planning a life outside the office."

stop rescuing people, and trust that they can handle things by themselves. When you train your employer, staff, and coworkers not to bother you on your R & R Days, it forces them to become more self-reliant. It also forces them to grow in ability and self-confidence. If you are consistent over time, people will eventually get the message. This is ultimately a good thing because it frees you up to have more R & R Days *and* more Best Results Days.

R & R MEANS SOME DAYS *WITHOUT* THE KIDS, TOO

The question often arises about what to do with the children. For the most part, you need to take some time away from your children on a regular basis. If you can't afford a babysitter, ask a trusted relative to take them. We've used both aunts and uncles and our 20-year-old nieces. If they are unavailable or unwilling, trade with other parents: You take their little ones for a weekend and they take yours on a different weekend. And don't make the mistake of calling every hour to see how they're doing. Let go, trust, and take care of yourself for a change.

R & R DAYS HELP YOU WORK HARDER . . .
AND SMARTER

The value of regular R & R days is that you come back to your work refreshed and ready to tackle it with renewed vigor, enthusiasm, and creativity. To become truly successful, you need these breaks to allow yourself some distance from your normal day-to-day life—so you can become more creative in generating breakthrough ideas and solving problems.

I believe everyone's ultimate goal should be 130 to 150 days off each year. If you took every weekend off—doing no work whatsoever—you would instantly enjoy 104 vacation days. And if you found another 48 R & R Days in the form of long weekends, holiday weeks, 2-week vacations, and other opportunities, you could easily enjoy 150 R & R Days to recharge, rejuvenate, and rest—with no laptops, no e-mails, no documents, and no contact with your staff, coworkers, or boss.

It may take you a while to work up to that number, perhaps years, but the main thing is to constantly work to increase your number of R & R Days every year.

USE YOUR VACATION TIME

According to the Travel Industry Association of America, the average vacation in 1997 was 7.1 days. In 2001, it was down to 4.1 days. Even more alarming, the Families and Work Institute reports that more than one fourth of all American employees *did not even use* their vacation time. Why? They were afraid that their job might not be there when they returned.

Compare that with the concept of R & R Days, which actually makes you more rested, more productive, *and more valuable to your employer.* Jane Moyer, Xerox Business Services' role-model manager for 1996 and now at iQuantic in San Francisco, summarized perfectly the value of R & R Days in this interview with *Fast Company* magazine:

> . . . every October, I spend some time on Cape Cod. I rent a cabin that's two blocks from the ocean, and I stay there for a week. The cabin has no phone or television. I don't get in my car, I don't listen to the radio, and I don't read newspapers. For the first couple of days, I go through withdrawal, but then I adjust. I cook, I read, I walk on the beach. It's absolutely glorious. On my way home, when I start thinking about work again, I see things differently. Work seems much less cluttered. One of the amazing things about getting away is that it helps me understand what's important and what's not.[44]

---

44. From *Fast Company*, May 2000, page 101.

START SCHEDULING

The key to getting more R & R Days and Best Results Days in your life is to sit down and schedule them. By jotting down how many Best Results Days, Preparation Days, and R & R Days you spend every month right now, you can work to increase the number of Best Results Days and true 24-hour R & R Days on your calendar, and reduce the number of Preparation Days. With this kind of schedule, you'll find yourself creating greater results at work, enjoying more fulfillment in your personal life, and experiencing more balance between the two.

Here are some other steps you might want to take to begin implementing the Breakthrough Results Time System:

1. List the three Best Results Days you have ever had. Write down any common elements. This will give you valuable clues as to how to create more perfect Best Results Days. Plan for them.
2. Meet with your boss, staff, and coworkers to discuss how to create more Best Results Days where you can focus 80% of your time on using your areas of brilliance to produce your best results.
3. Meet with your friends or family and discuss how to create more true R & R Days in your life.
4. Schedule at least four vacations—they can be long weekends or longer—for the next year. These can be as simple as a weekend camping trip, a weekend in San Francisco taking in the sights, a trip to the wine country, a weekend at the shore, a fishing trip, or a week visiting friends in a nearby state, or it can include that dream-of-a-lifetime vacation you have always wanted to take to California, Hawaii, Florida, Mexico, Europe, or Asia. If you don't plan it, it won't happen, so sit down and make a plan.
5. List the three best R&R Days you have ever had and look for the common elements in those. Schedule more of those elements into your planned R & R Days.

As our world gets more complicated and more pressured, you will have to be increasingly more conscious and intentional to structure your time in a way that takes full advantage of your talents and maximizes your results and your income. Start now to control your time and your life. Remember, you are in charge.

BUILD A POWERFUL
SUPPORT TEAM
AND DELEGATE TO THEM

The ascent of Everest was not the work of one day, nor even of those
few unforgettable weeks in which we climbed. . . . It is, in fact,
a tale of sustained and tenacious endeavor by many,
over a long period of time.

SIR JOHN HUNT
Scaled Mount Everest in 1953

Every high achiever has a powerful team of key staff members, consultants, vendors, and helpers who do the bulk of the work while he or she is free to create new sources of income and new opportunities for success. The world's greatest philanthropists, athletes, entertainers, professionals, and others also have people who manage projects and handle everyday tasks—enabling them to do more for others, hone their craft, practice their sport, and so on.

THE TOTAL FOCUS PROCESS

To help you clarify what you should be spending your time on and what you should be delegating to others, do the following exercise. Your goal is to find the top one, two, or three activities that best use your core genius, bring you the most money, and produce the greatest level of enjoyment.

1. Start by listing all those activities that occupy your time ... whether they're business-related, personal, or related to your civic organizations or volunteer work. List even small tasks such as re-turning phone calls, filing, or photocopying.

2. Next, choose from this list those one, two, or three things you are particularly brilliant at, your special and unique talents, those things very few other people can do as well as you. Also choose from this list the three activities that generate the most income for you or your company. Any activities that you are brilliant at *and* that generate the most income for you or your company are the activities where you'll want to focus the most time and energy.

3. Finally, create a plan for delegating everything else to other people. Delegating takes time, training, and patience, but over time you can keep chipping away at the low-payoff, nonessential tasks on your list until you are doing less and less of those and more and more of what you are really good at. That is how you create a brilliant career.

SEEK OUT KEY "STAFF MEMBERS"

If you're a business owner—and remember, becoming an entrepreneur early in life is one of the hallmarks of the most successful individuals throughout modern history—start looking for key staff members now or train your existing staff members on the tasks you identified above. If you're a one-person business, start looking for a dynamic number-two person who could handle your projects, run your programs, book your sales transactions, and completely take over other tasks while you concentrate on what you do best. You can hire them outright as employees or have them work part time on a contract basis as your company grows. I've also seen many future achievers find a top-flight business manager months sooner than they expected, only to see their business grow exponentially once they make a deal to bring that person on board.

If philanthropic pursuits or community projects are your "business," there are volunteers you can "hire" to help you. Consider college interns, who may work solely for class credit. We use several in our company. Or perhaps a local foundation can offer you staff support for your project. You never know until you ask.

And if you are a stay-at-home mom or dad, your most valuable "staff" will be your house cleaner, the teenage helper down the street, your babysitter, and others who can help you get away for time by yourself and with your spouse. A neighbor or babysitter could also do grocery shopping, get your car washed, pick up the kids, or pick up the laundry and dry cleaning—all for $8 an hour. If you're a single parent, these folks are even more important to your successful future and should be chosen with great care.

Often you'll find that once you put the word out, the right person was already circulating in your universe—you just didn't know it.

WHY YOU NEED PERSONAL ADVISORS

Our world has become a very complex place. Just filing your tax return, planning for retirement, rewarding your employees—even buying a home—has become more complicated than ever. That's why every high achiever has a powerful team of personal advisors to turn to for assistance, advice, and support. In fact, this team is so critical, it pays to begin assembling the team early on in your success journey.

Regardless of whether you own a business, work for someone else, or stay home and raise your children, you need personal advisors to answer questions, help you plan, ensure that you make the most of life's efforts, and more. Your personal advisors can walk you through challenges and opportunities, saving you time, effort, and usually money. Your team of advisors should include your banker, your lawyers, a high-net-worth certified public accountant, your investment counselor, your doctor, nutritionist, personal trainer, and the leader of your religious organization.

In fact, if you run a business, this principle takes on a whole new meaning. Too many business owners, for example, don't even have an accountant. They run their entire business on a computer program and never have any outside expert checking their numbers. They never form relationships with outside consultants who can free them up to pursue their core competency and help them grow.

If you're a teenager or a college student, your team might be your parents, your best friends, your football coach, your counselor—people who believe in you. Often with teens, we find that their parents aren't really a part of their core group but instead are part of the enemy. Sometimes this is the teen's perception, but sometimes it's actually the way things are. If your parents are dysfunctional, alcoholic, or abusive, or if they're simply not there because they're workaholics or divorced, you need a team of friends and other adults in your corner. Often, it's a parent of another teen in your neighborhood.

If you're a working mom, your core group should include a good babysitter or day care program. Not only should you investigate them thoroughly, but you should also have a backup resource. You should have a good pediatrician, and dentist, too, plus others who can support you in raising healthy, happy children as you pursue your career.

Athletes have their coterie of coaches, chiropractors, nutritionists, and performance consultants. They have, as part of their support team, people who specialize in designing diets for their body type and for their sport. They find trustworthy advisors and build and maintain those relationships over time.

Once you determine who members of this support team are, you can begin to build and nurture those relationships. Make sure team members are clear about what you expect from them *and that you are clear about what they expect from you.* Is this a paid relationship? What kind of working relationship is preferable? How can both of you be there when the other person needs you? How can team members help you grow and succeed?

And finally, how can you keep in touch with them and best maintain this relationship? I recommend that you create a schedule of monthly, quarterly, or semiannual meetings with every member of your team.

ONCE YOU'VE CHOSEN YOUR TEAM MEMBERS, TRUST THEM

If you don't have an assistant, you are one.

RAYMOND AARON
Founder, "The Monthly Mentor"

If you have chosen with care, you can begin to offload anything and everything that takes you away from focusing on your core genius—even "personal" projects.

When Raymond Aaron sold his home and decided to move into an apartment, he delegated the entire project to his assistant. He told her to find a one-bedroom luxury apartment near his office with an exercise facility on the main floor. "Find it, negotiate the lease, and bring me the contract to sign," he said. "Then hire a moving van, get a check from my office to pay the movers, pack up the fragile items, supervise the movers, and drive behind them to my new home." He even had her hire an advance cleaning crew, arrange the furniture with the movers, unpack boxes, put everything away— and call Raymond when the move was complete.

And where was Raymond while his assistant was moving his house? On vacation in Florida!

Though we often fear that if someone else performs tasks for us, they won't be done well—the reality is there are people who *love* to do what you hate to do. And they often do a much better job than you would or *could* yourself—at a surprisingly low cost.

JUST SAY NO!

You don't have to let yourself be terrorized by other people's
expectations of you.

SUE PATTON THOELE
Author of *The Courage to Be Yourself*

Our world is a highly competitive and overstimulating place, and more and more concentration is needed every day just to stay focused on completing your daily tasks and pursuing your longer-term goals. Because of the explosion of communications technology, we are more accessible to more people than ever before. Complete strangers can reach you by telephone, cell phone, pager, fax, regular mail, express mail, and e-mail. They can e-mail and instant-message you at home, at work, and on your hand-held computer. If you're not there, they can leave messages on your answering machine or your voice mail. If you are there, they can interrupt you with call waiting.

It seems everyone wants a piece of you. Your kids want rides or to borrow the car, your coworkers want your input on projects that are not your responsibility, your boss wants you to work overtime to finish a report he needs, your sister wants you to take her kids for the weekend, your child's school wants you to bake four dozen cookies for teacher appreciation day and be a driver for next week's field trip, your mother wants you to come over and fix her screen door, your best friend wants to talk about his impending divorce, a local charity wants you to head up the annual luncheon committee, and your neighbor wants to borrow your van to pick up some lumber at Home Depot. And an endless slew of telemarketers want you to subscribe to the local newspaper, contribute to the nearby wildlife sanctuary, or transfer all of your credit card debt over to their new card. Even your pets are clamoring for more attention.

We suffer under project and productivity overload at work—taking on more than we can comfortably deliver in an unconscious desire to impress others, get ahead, and keep up with others' expectations. Meanwhile, our top priorities go unaddressed.

To be successful in achieving your goals and creating your desired lifestyle, you will have to get good at saying no to all of the people and distractions that would otherwise devour you. Successful people know how to say no without feeling guilty.

DON'T JUST DELEGATE, ELIMINATE!

If you are going to increase your results and your income as well as increase the amount of R & R Days in your life, you are going to have to eliminate those tasks, requests, and other time-stealers that don't have a high payoff.

You will have to structure your work so that you are focusing your time, effort, energies, and resources only on projects, opportunities, and people that give you a huge reward for your efforts. You are going to have to create strong boundaries about what you will and won't do.

Start by creating what Jim Collins, author of *Good to Great*, calls a "*stop* doing" list. Most of us are busy but undisciplined. We are active but not focused. We are moving, but not always in the right direction. By creating a stop-doing list as well as a to-do list, you bring more discipline and focus into your life.

Start by creating a stop-doing list as soon as possible. Then make the things on your list "policies." People respond to policies. They understand a policy as a boundary. They will respect you more for being clear about what you won't do. For example, some of my "don't do" policies on a personal level are:

- I never lend my car to anyone for any reason.
- I don't lend money. I am not a bank.
- We don't schedule outside social events on Friday night. That is our family night.
- I don't discuss charitable contributions over the phone. Send me something in writing.

On a business level, some of my "don't do" policies are:

- I don't give endorsements for books of fiction.
- I don't lend my books to other people. They rarely come back, and they are the source of my livelihood, so I don't lend them out.
- I don't schedule more than five talks in one month.
- I no longer coauthor books with first-time authors. Their learning curve is too time-consuming and expensive.
- I don't do individual counseling or coaching. There is greater leverage in working with a group.

- Except for when I am doing a new-book tour, I don't schedule more than two radio interviews in a day.
- I don't take any calls on Tuesdays and Thursdays. Those are writing days.

CONSIDER GIVING UP YOUR CELL PHONE AND YOUR E-MAIL

Today, a lot of people have taken a "drastic" approach to regaining control of their life—they've given up their cell phones and their e-mail. The technological revolution was supposed to make our lives easier. But nearly a decade after e-mail became popular and cell phones became affordable for everyone, most of us are inundated with nonessential e-mail (not to even mention spam).

Many businesspeople I know spend 3 to 4 hours a day just answering e-mail. I used to be one of them. Now my assistant opens my e-mails and only brings me the important ones (less than five a day) to respond to.

Others can't even go shopping, out to dinner, or on vacation without their cell phones going off—not once but several times. This trend is worldwide. I still carry a cell phone, but I turn it on only to make outgoing calls.

Because they provide instant communication, cell phones and e-mail also create the expectation of an instant response. People who have your cell phone number know they can instantly reach you for help with their immediate needs. E-mails are delivered within minutes—so they expect you to respond equally fast.

When you distribute your cell phone number and e-mail address, you give others implied permission to make these demands upon you. But imagine how much more time and control over your life you would have if you didn't have to react to all these immediate needs or read dozens of nonessential e-mails every day.

Just last week I was having lunch with four top people in a major publishing firm. They were all complaining about how overwhelmed they were by the amount of e-mail they were getting—as many as 150 messages a day—and most of them were being generated right inside the company.

When I asked them how much of it was essential to their job, the answer was maybe 10% to 20%. When I asked why they didn't just tell people to take them off of their general distribution list, they said they were afraid of hurting people's feelings. It seemed they would rather suffer than solve the problem. Think about the consequences of not telling the truth and changing things. If they could cut out even half of the unwanted e-mails, they would save 90 minutes per workday. That would add up to 375 hours, or just over nine 40-hour workweeks a year. That's more than 2 months of valuable time. Isn't that worth a few people being upset for a few days?

Barry Spilchuk, my close friend and coauthor of *A Cup of Chicken Soup for the Soul*, recently sent an e-mail to everyone in his address book asking them to stop forwarding him feel-good e-mails, poems, and other material. (He apologized for the bulk e-mail!) If he can do it, you can do it.

IF SAYING NO IS SO IMPORTANT, THEN WHY IS IT SO HARD TO SAY?

Why do we find it so hard to say no to everybody's requests? As children, many of us learned that *no* was an unacceptable answer. Responding with *no* was cause for discipline. Later, in our careers, *no* may have been the reason for a poor evaluation or failing to move up the corporate ladder.

Yet highly successful people say no all the time—to projects, to crazy deadlines, to questionable priorities, and to other people's crises. In fact, they view the decision to say no as equally acceptable as the decision to say yes.

Others say no but will offer to refer you to someone else for help. Still

"No, Thursday's out. How about never—is never good for you?"

others claim their calendar, family obligations, deadlines, and even finances as reasons why they must decline requests. At the office, achievers find other solutions to their coworkers' repeated emergencies, rather than becoming a victim of someone else's lack of organization and poor time management.

"IT'S NOT AGAINST YOU; IT'S FOR ME"

One response that I have found helpful in saying no to crisis appeals or time-robbing requests from people is "It's not against you; it's for me."

When the local PTA chairman calls with yet another weekend fund-raising event that needs your dedication, you can say, "You know, my saying no to you is not against you or what you are trying to do. It's a very worthy cause, but recently I realized I've been overcommitting myself outside my home. So even though I support what you're doing, the fact is I've made a commitment to spend more time with my family. It's not against you; it's for us." Few people can get angry at you for making and standing by a higher commitment. In fact, they'll respect you for your clarity and your strength.

There are lots of valuable techniques you can learn that will make it easier to say no without feeling guilty. I recommend you read one of the several good books that address this issue in greater depth than I have space for here. The two best books are *When I Say No, I Feel Guilty*, by Manuel J. Smith, and *How to Say No Without Feeling Guilty*, by Patti Breitman and Connie Hatch.

43

SAY NO TO THE GOOD SO THAT YOU CAN SAY YES TO THE GREAT

Good is the enemy of great.

JIM COLLINS
Author of *Good to Great*

What a simple concept it is, yet you'd be surprised how frequently even the world's top entrepreneurs, professionals, educators, and civic leaders get caught up in projects, situations, and opportunities that are merely good, while the great is left out in the cold, waiting for them to make room in their lives. In fact, concentrating on merely the good often prevents the great from showing up, simply because there's no time left in our schedules to take advantage of any additional opportunity.

Is this your situation—constantly chasing after mediocre prospects or pursuing misguided schemes for success when you could be holding at bay opportunities for astounding achievement?

THE PARETO PRINCIPLE: WHEN 20% EQUALS 80%

If you surveyed your life and jotted down those activities that brought you the most success, the most financial gain, the most advancement, and the most enjoyment, you would discover that about 20% of your activity produces about 80% of your success. This phenomenon is the basis for the Pareto Principle, named after the nineteenth-century economist who discovered 80% of an enterprise's revenue comes from 20% of its customers.[45]

---

45. See *The 80/20 Principle: The Secret to Success by Achieving More with Less,* by Richard Koch (New York: Currency, 1998) for an illuminating exploration of the application of the 80/20 Rule to accelerating the achievement of personal success.

STOP MAJORING IN THE MINORS

Instead of dedicating yourself—and your time—to mundane, nonproductive, time-stealing activity, imagine how rapidly you would reach your goals and improve your life if you said no to those time-wasting activities and instead focused on the 20% of activity that would bring you the most benefit?

What if instead of watching television, mindlessly surfing the Internet, running unnecessary errands, and addressing problems you could have avoided in the first place, you used the extra time to focus on your family, your marriage, your business, starting a new income stream, and other forward-motion pursuits?

SYLVESTER STALLONE'S "ROCKY" BEGINNING

Sylvester Stallone knows how to say no to the good. After finishing the very first *Rocky* screenplay, Stallone encountered several producers who were interested in making it into a movie. But even though that alone would have made Stallone a lot of money, he insisted on playing the lead role, too. Even though other actors such as James Caan, Ryan O'Neal, and Burt Reynolds were considered to play Rocky Balboa, Stallone said no, and after finding backers willing to finance a shoestring budget of under $1 million, Stallone completed filming on location in just 28 days.

Rocky went on to become the sleeper hit of 1976, earning over $225 million dollars and garnering Oscars for best picture and best director, as well as acting and writing nominations for Stallone, who took full charge of his golden opportunities and turned Rocky Balboa—and later John Rambo—into industry franchises that have grossed over $2 billion in revenues worldwide.

What could show up in your life if you said no to the good?

HOW CAN YOU DETERMINE WHAT'S TRULY GREAT, SO YOU CAN SAY NO TO WHAT'S MERELY GOOD?

1. **Start by listing your opportunities—one side of the page for *good* and the other side for *great*.** Seeing options in writing will help crystallize your thinking and determine what questions to ask, what information to gather, what your plan of attack might be, and so on. It will help you decide if an opportunity truly fits with

your overall life purpose and passion or if it's just life taking you down a side road.

2. **Talk to advisors about this potential new pursuit**. People who have traveled the road before you have vast experience to share and hard-headed questions to ask about any new life opportunity you might be contemplating. They can talk to you about expected challenges and help you evaluate the hassle factor—that is, how much time, money, effort, stress, and commitment will be required.

3. **Test the waters**. Rather than take a leap of faith that the new opportunity will proceed as you expect, conduct a small test, spending a limited amount of time and money. If it's a new career you're interested in, first seek part-time work or independent consulting contracts in that field. If it's a major move or volunteer project you're excited about, see if you can travel for a few months to your dream locale or find ways to immerse yourself in the volunteer work for several weeks.

4. **And finally, look at where you spend your time**. Determine if those activities truly serve your goals or if saying no would free up your schedule for more focused pursuits.

FIND A WING TO
CLIMB UNDER

Study anyone who's great, and you'll find that they apprenticed
to a master, or several masters. Therefore, if you want to
achieve greatness, renown, and superlative success,
you must apprentice to a master.

ROBERT ALLEN
Self-made multimillionaire and coauthor of *The One Minute Millionaire*

Despite some of the best information available on how to accomplish any task, most people still tend to ask their friends, neighbors, coworkers, and siblings for advice on key issues they may be facing. Too often, they ask the advice of others who have never triumphed over the specific hardship they are facing or who have never succeeded in their specific area of endeavor.

As I pointed out in Principle 9, success leaves clues. Why not take advantage of all the wisdom and experience that already exists by finding a mentor who has already been down the road you are traveling? All you have to do is ask.

One of the main strategies of the successful is that they constantly seek out guidance and advice from experts in their field. Make a list of the people you would like to ask to mentor you. Approach them and ask for their help.

DETERMINE IN ADVANCE WHAT YOU WANT
FROM A MENTOR

Though it may seem daunting at first to contact successful people and ask for ongoing advice and assistance, it's easier than you think to enlist the mentorship of those who are far above you in the areas in which you'd like to succeed.

What mentors do more than anything, says famed speaker and best-selling author Les Brown, is help you see possibilities. In other words, mentors help you overcome "possibility blindness" both by acting as a role model for you and by conveying a certain level of expectation as they communicate with you.

When Les started his speaking career in the early 1980s, he sent a cassette tape of his earliest keynote speech to the late Dr. Norman Vincent Peale, the world-renowned speaker and publisher of *Guideposts* magazine. That cassette tape led to a long and fruitful relationship for Les, as Dr. Peale not only took Les under his wing and counseled him on his speaking style but also quietly opened doors and helped Les get important speaking engagements. Suddenly, though Les was a virtual unknown on the circuit, speakers' bureaus began calling him for bookings, even raising his rate to $5,000 per speech from the modest $700 Les had been charging.

As Les recounts the story, Norman Vincent Peale was the first person to tell Les he could make it big in the speaking industry.

"He spoke more to my heart than to my mind," said Les. "While I was doubting myself, my abilities, my lack of education, and my background, Dr. Peale said, 'You have the right stuff. You have everything it takes. Just continue to speak from your heart and you will do well.' "

That's when Les realized the value of having a mentor. And though their relationship consisted only of brief phone conversations and Les's occasionally trailing after Dr. Peale to learn his speaking style, in the end it meant more to both men than they knew at the time.

During his last public speech at age 95, Dr. Peale used one of his protégé's oft-repeated phrases: "Shoot for the moon because even if you miss, you'll land among the stars."

Perhaps like Les, you just need someone to open doors for you. Or perhaps you need a referral to a technical expert who can help you build a new service for your company. Maybe you simply need validation that the path you're pursuing is the right one. A mentor can help you with all of these things, but you need to be prepared to ask for specific advice.

DO YOUR HOMEWORK

One of the easiest ways to research the names and backgrounds of people who have been successful in your area of interest is to read industry magazines, search the Internet, ask trade association executive directors, attend trade shows and conventions, call fellow entrepreneurs, or approach others who operate in your industry or profession.

Look for mentors who have the kind of well-rounded experience you need to tackle your goal. When you start seeing a pattern of the same few people being recommended, you know you've identified your short list of possible mentors.

Janet Switzer regularly mentors hundreds of people on how to grow their business. When Lisa Miller of CRA Management Group called Janet, she was just about to sign away a large percentage of her revenues to someone she thought would help her develop a new area of her business. Janet showed Lisa how to instantly accomplish the same goal without outside parties and even helped her land new business from existing clients, accelerating Lisa's company growth plan by 4 months and earning her hundreds of thousands of extra dollars.

To contact possible mentors like Janet and ensure a successful conversation once you do, make a list of specific points you'd like to cover in your first conversation, such as why you'd like them to mentor you and what kind of help you might be looking for. Be brief, but be confident, too.

The truth is that successful people like to share what they have learned with others. It is a human trait to want to pass on wisdom. Not everyone will take the time to mentor you, but many will if asked. You simply need to make a list of the people you would like to have as your mentor and ask them to devote a few minutes a month to you.

Some will say no, but some will say yes. Keep asking until you get a positive response.

Les Hewitt, who founded the Achievers Coaching Program, coached the owner of a small trucking company who wanted to ask one of the major players in the trucking industry to be his mentor. The mentor was delighted to be asked, and he ended up helping the young man's company grow exponentially. His original script is one you might imitate:

> Hello, Mr. Johnston, my name is Neil. We haven't met yet. And I know you're a busy man, so I'll be brief. I own a small trucking business. Over the years, you have done a fantastic job building your business into one of the largest companies in our industry. I'm sure you had some real challenges when you were first starting out. Well, I'm still in those early stages, trying to figure everything out. Mr. Johnston, I would really appreciate it if you would consider being my mentor. All that would mean is spending ten minutes on the phone with me once a month, so I could ask you a few questions. I'd really appreciate it. Would you be open to that?

If you are a small-business owner, or are contemplating starting a business, you should contact your local chapter of SCORE (Service Corps of Retired Executives). Working in partnership with the U.S. Small Business Administration, SCORE is an extensive, national network of over 10,000 retired and working volunteers providing free business counseling and advice as well as low-cost workshops as a public service to all types of businesses, in all stages of development, from idea to start-up to success. You can find one of their 389 chapter offices at www.score.org. Another source of free business advice and counseling for small-business owners is Small Business Development Centers, a service of the U.S. Small Business Administration. They have 63 offices across the country waiting to serve you. Find out more at www.sba.gov/sbdc.

TAKE ACTION ON YOUR MENTORS' ADVICE

Mentors don't like to have their time wasted. When you seek out their advice . . . *follow it*. Study their methods, ask your questions, make sure you understand the process—then, as much as is humanly possible, duplicate your mentors' efforts. You may even be able to improve on them.

VALUABLE ADVICE

Jason Dorsey was a typical college student when he unexpectedly met his first mentor, a local entrepreneur who had been asked to speak to his business class at the University of Texas. When Brad challenged the class by defining success as something greater than just making lots of money, Jason was intrigued and risked asking him to be his mentor.

During their first meeting, Brad asked Jason about his plans. He replied that he planned to finish college, work on the New York Stock Exchange, get an MBA, start his own business, and eventually retire at 40. Once retired, he planned to work with hard-to-reach youth to make sure they got a good education and a respectable job.

Hearing this, Brad asked Jason how old he would be by the time he got around to helping these young people. Jason guessed he'd be about 45. Then Brad asked a life-changing question: "Why wait twenty-five years to start doing what you really want to do? Why not start now? The longer you wait, the more difficult it might be for young people to relate to you."

Brad's observation made sense, but Jason was only 18 and living in a college dorm. He asked, "How do you think I could best help people my own age if I started now?"

"Write a book they will actually want to read," replied Brad. "Tell them your secrets for feeling good about yourself even when everyone else is so negative. Tell them what it takes to ask someone to be your mentor. Tell them why you have so many job opportunities and you're only 18 years old."

So on January 7, 1997, at 1:58 AM, Jason started writing his book. Because he didn't know he couldn't do it, he completed the first draft of *Graduate to Your Perfect Job* just 3 weeks later. Jason published the book himself, started speaking at schools, and began mentoring other young people. By the time he was 25, he had spoken to over 500,000 people, been featured on NBC's *Today* show three times, and seen his first book become a course in over 1,500 schools. Jason is such a compelling speaker and motivator that soon the schools were hiring him to train their teachers and counselors as well. His latest venture is a new company that helps executives and managers learn how to motivate and retain young employees. Best of all, Jason is still learning from his mentors—all five of them.

Now only 26 years old, Jason just won the Austin Under 40 Entrepreneur of the Year Award in the category of education. Just think, if Jason had not taken the risk to ask a stranger to be his mentor, he'd just be getting that MBA right about now.

BE PREPARED TO RETURN THE FAVOR

Be prepared to give your mentors something in return; even if it's something simple such as keeping them updated on industry information or calling with new opportunities that might benefit them, look for ways to give to your mentors. Help others, too. What a great reward to any mentor—to eventually have their former protégé out in the world helping others to grow!

HIRE A PERSONAL COACH

I absolutely believe that people, unless coached,
never reach their maximum capabilities.

BOB NARDELLI
President and CEO of Home Depot

You would never expect an athlete to reach the Olympic Games without a world-class coach. Nor would you expect a professional football team to enter the stadium without a whole team of coaches—head coach, offensive coach, defensive coach, and special teams coach. Well, today, coaching has moved into the business and personal realm to include coaches who have succeeded in your area of interest—and who can help you traverse this same path or even one far greater.

ONE OF THE BEST-KEPT SECRETS OF THE SUCCESSFUL

Of all the things successful people do to accelerate their trip down the path to success, participating in some kind of coaching program is at the top of the list. A coach will help you clarify your vision and goals, support you through your fears, keep you focused, confront your unconscious behaviors and old patterns, expect you to do your best, help you live by your values, show you how to earn more while working less, and keep you focused on your core genius.

WORTH MORE THAN MONEY

I have had many coaches who have helped me achieve my goals—business coaches, writing coaches, marketing coaches, and personal coaches. But without a doubt, the one coaching experience that most helped me leap forward in every area of my life was "The Strategic Coach Program" for entrepreneurs with Dan Sullivan.

What were the results? First and foremost, I immediately doubled my free time. I delegated more tasks, scheduled vacations rather than merely thought about them, and hired additional staff that ultimately positioned my business to earn more. And that was just in the first few months.

Not only did my business benefit but my family did, too.

For me, coaching wasn't just about making more money—although a big part of coaching is focused on making more money, managing it better, and settling on a financial plan that gives you the kind of freedom you want. It was about helping me make better decisions for myself and my business. The truth is, most coaching clients are smart—very smart. Yet they still know the value of accessing someone who can be objective, honest, and constructive about the options they are facing.

Another coach I have used with great success is Mike Foster, the CEO Tech Coach. Mike has helped me and my office upgrade all of our use of technology and computer systems. We now have one of the most advanced technological offices in the country. Most people are only utilizing about 10% of their computers' capabilities. Use a tech coach to maximize your effectiveness. (You can reach Mike at www.ceotechcoach.com.)

WHY COACHING WORKS

Executive coaches are not for the meek. They're for people who value unambiguous feedback. If coaches have one thing in common, it's that they are ruthlessly results-oriented.

FAST COMPANY MAGAZINE

Regardless of whether the program is designed to achieve a specific business goal—say, increasing your real estate listings—or whether it is specifically designed to help you simply gain more clarity and progress in all aspects of your personal and professional life, a coach can help you

- Determine your values, vision, mission, purpose, and goals
- Determine specific action steps to help you achieve those goals
- Help you sort through opportunities
- Keep you focused on your top priorities

- Achieve balance in your life while still accomplishing your business or career goals

As humans we tend to do only some of what we are required to do but virtually all of what we want to do. A personal coach can help you discover what you truly want to do—and can help you determine the steps and take the actions necessary to get there.

DIFFERENT FORMATS FOR COACHING

Coaching can be delivered privately or in groups. Most often, it's done through regularly scheduled telephone contact, although it can also be done in person, as appropriate. Over the course of the sessions, you'll work together with your coach to develop goals, strategies, and a plan of action that is positive, desirable, and realistic. Support is often provided between sessions through e-mail and other media.

Occasionally, depending on the coach, you may be coached via structured large-group teleconferences in which you listen to valuable information, and then implement what you hear on your own.

Some coaches will work with you every week and others once a month. Dan Sullivan's coaching program only met once every quarter but had so much homework that it turned out to be one of the most profound experiences of my life.

HOW TO FIND A COACH

There are literally thousands of coaches available to work with you. There are personal coaches, life coaches, and business coaches. Some are industry specific (dental, chiropractic, real estate, and speaking), some are job specific (executive coaches), and some are interest specific (strategic planning, health and wellness, finances, and career transition). You can find them on the Internet, in the phone book, and by asking around. There are organizations like Coach U and the International Coach Federation that can help you find a coach near you.[46] Check out "Suggested Reading and Additional Resources for Success," pages 441 through 451, and www.thesuccessprinciples.com for more organizations that can help connect you with a coach who can accelerate your success.

---

46. Find out more about Coach U at www.coachu.com and about the International Coach Federation at www.coachfederation.org. For information on Dan Sullivan's "Strategic Coach Program," go to www.strategiccoach.com.

MASTERMIND YOUR WAY
TO SUCCESS

*When two or more people coordinate in a spirit of harmony and
work toward a definite objective or purpose, they place
themselves in position, through the alliance, to absorb power
directly from the great storehouse of Infinite Intelligence.*

NAPOLEON HILL
Author of *Think and Grow Rich*

We all know that two heads are better than one when it comes to solving a
problem or creating a result. So imagine having a permanent group of five to
six people who meet every week for the purpose of problem solving, brainstorming, networking, and encouraging and motivating each other.

This process, called *masterminding*, is one of the most powerful tools for
success presented in this book. I don't know anybody who has become supersuccessful who has not employed the principle of masterminding.

AN OLD IDEA THAT'S NEW AGAIN

Napoleon Hill first wrote about mastermind groups in 1937 in his classic
book *Think and Grow Rich*. And all the world's richest industrialists—from
the early twentieth century to today's modern icons of business—have har-
nessed the power of the mastermind group. It's the one concept achievers reference most when they credit any one thing with helping them become a
millionaire.

Andrew Carnegie had a mastermind group. So did Henry Ford. In fact,
Ford would mastermind with brilliant thinkers such as Thomas Edison
and Harvey Firestone in a group they held at their winter mansions in Fort
Myers, Florida.

They knew, as millions of others have discovered since, that a mastermind group can focus special energy on your efforts—in the form of knowledge, new ideas, a vast array of resources, and, most importantly, spiritual energy. And it's this spiritual aspect that Napoleon Hill wrote about extensively.

He said that if we are in tune with *the* mastermind—that is, God, the source, the universal power, or whatever term you use for the all-powerful creative life force—we have significantly more positive energy available to us, a power that can be focused on our success. Even the Bible talks about this:

For where two or three are gathered together in my name,
there am I in the midst of them.

MATTHEW 18:20
(King James Version of the Bible)

"Mastermind," therefore, is both the power that comes to us from each other and the power that comes to us from above.

A PROCESS FOR ACCELERATING YOUR GROWTH

The basic philosophy of a mastermind group is that more can be achieved in less time when people work together. A mastermind group is made up of people who come together on a regular basis—weekly, biweekly, or monthly—to share ideas, thoughts, information, feedback, and resources. By getting the perspective, knowledge, experience, and resources of the others in the group, not only can you move beyond your own limited view of the world but you can also advance your own goals and projects more quickly.

A mastermind group can be composed of people from your own industry or profession or people from a variety of walks of life. It can focus on business issues, personal issues, or both. But for a mastermind group to be powerfully effective, people must be comfortable enough with each other to tell the truth. Some of the most valuable feedback I have ever received has come from members of my mastermind group confronting me about overcommitting, selling my services too cheaply, focusing on the trivial, not delegating enough, thinking too small, and playing it safe.

Confidentiality is what allows this level of trust to build. Out in the world, we are usually managing our personal and corporate image. In a mastermind group, participants can let their hair down, tell the truth about their personal and business life, and feel safe that what is said in the group will stay in the group.

NEW THOUGHTS, NEW PEOPLE, NEW RESOURCES

When you form your mastermind group, consider bringing together people from different professional arenas and people that are "above" you and who can introduce you to a network of people you normally wouldn't have access to.

Though the benefits of masterminding with people outside your field may not seem obvious now, the truth is that we all tend to get stuck in our own field of expertise, doing things the same way everyone else in our industry does. But when you assemble people from different industries and professions, you get lots of different perspectives on the same subject.

Henry Ford was an assembly-line expert. Thomas Edison was an inventor. Harvey Firestone was a corporate management genius. So their mastermind group brought together diverse talent that could lend different perspectives to one another's challenges, whether they were legal, financial, or relational.

Members of my mastermind group include business strategist Marshall Thurber, Internet marketing expert Declan Dunn, CEO of OneWorldLive Liz Edlic, real-estate mogul and success strategist John Assaraf, and strategic coach and CEO of Empowered Wealth Lee Brower. Each one has different perspectives, life experiences, skills, and networks that the entire group benefits from. We meet every 2 weeks by phone and quarterly for 2 days in person with the stated purpose to help each other achieve our individual and corporate goals and contribute to the well-being of humanity.

Other mastermind groups have helped members start or salvage businesses, change jobs, become multimillionaires, become better parents, grow as teachers, become better advocates for social change, improve our environment, and more.

HOW TO ASSEMBLE A MASTERMIND GROUP

Regardless of its purpose, the key is to choose people who are already where you'd like to be in your life—or who are at least a level above you. If your goal is to become a millionaire and you're currently only making $60,000 a year, you will be better served by gathering together with people who are already making more than you. If you're concerned that people who are already achieving at a higher level than you might not want to be involved in a group with you, remember that you're the one facilitating the meeting. You are organizing, supporting, and building a forum for other people's growth and masterminding needs. Many people at a higher level will want to become involved simply because they'll get to play at a game they might never take the time to organize for themselves. They'd probably be delighted to mastermind with the other people you're going to invite—especially if some of the others are already playing at their level.

WHAT'S THE IDEAL SIZE FOR A MASTERMIND GROUP?

The ideal size of a mastermind group is five to six people. If it is any smaller, it loses its dynamics. If it is too much bigger, it gets unwieldy—meetings take longer, some people's needs may go unmet, and personal sharing is minimized. However, there are groups with as many as 12 people that meet for a whole day every month that operate very successfully.

CONDUCTING A MASTERMIND MEETING

Mastermind meetings should be conducted weekly or every other week with all members of the group in attendance. They can be conducted in person or over the phone. About 1 to 2 hours is an ideal length of time.

For the first few meetings, it's recommended that each member get the entire hour to familiarize the others with his or her situation, opportunities, needs, and challenges, while the other members brainstorm ways they can support that person. During later meetings, participants each get a small amount of time to update the others, ask for help, and get feedback.

Each meeting should follow the proven format below to ensure that each participant gets their needs met and therefore stays involved. Your group should also assign someone to be the timekeeper—either the same person each session or a different participant for each meeting—to ensure that all members adhere to their preapproved time to speak and receive attention.

Step 1: Ask for Spiritual Guidance by Delivering an Invocation

Ideally, mastermind meetings should start with a request for the group to be filled and surrounded with powerful spiritual energy. Members can trade off delivering the invocation. Using whatever spiritual belief structure the leader has, they ask the universal force to assist the group with each other's needs. A sample invocation that asks God or that higher power to be present might be:

We ask now to be filled and surrounded with light, and our hearts be open to receive guidance from the higher power.

Step 2: Share What's New and Good

A good way to bond with each other and keep excitement high is to each share a success story. Even small successes achieved since the last meeting give others in the group the feeling that the process is working and is something they need to stay involved with.

Step 3: Negotiate for Time

Although the normal weekly time allotment might be 10 to 15 minutes per person, there may be times when one participant needs extra time during that week's session to discuss a particularly difficult situation. During the step, they can ask for the amount of extra time they think they'll need. Others in the group may have their own challenges that week and need extra time, too. Still others may decide to give up their time entirely, as they do not have anything to discuss. Using the timekeeper as referee, each member negotiates for the amount of time he or she thinks is needed.

During the negotiating step, you'll often hear comments such as "I just lost my assistant and I need time to talk about that." . . . "I want to read you this new proposal I've written and get your feedback on it." . . . "I need to find a printing company in the Far East and I don't know the first thing about that."

Once the negotiation process is complete and everyone agrees to the schedule, the meeting begins in earnest, with the timekeeper ensuring that everyone stays on time and on focus. If some members don't get their needs met, the group will risk losing them as participants. Still others—the dominators or needy types—may monopolize the meeting or turn their brainstorming responses into a personal discourse.

Step 4: Individual Members Speak while the Group Listens and Brainstorms Solutions

What kinds of discussions can you expect during a mastermind meeting? "I need contacts." . . . "I need referrals." . . . "I'm lost at this new aspect of my business." . . . "I'm looking for an expert to help me develop this idea." . . . "I need you to open your Rolodex card files to me." . . . "I need to raise $40,000." . . . "I need advice on handling customer service."

After the allotted time of explanation, discussion, and brainstorming, the timekeeper says, "Time's up!" and the group moves on to the next member's needs.

Discussions can be personal or professional—it doesn't matter. As long as all members are getting value, they'll stay involved with the group. As long as you're giving value, everyone will want you to be there.

You'll find that groups tend to go through phases. They start out fairly businesslike, but as people get to know each other and begin to delve into personal challenges such as "My wife and I are having problems" or "I think my son is taking drugs" or "I just lost my job," they take on a special personal bond. You and the other members can use the group any way you want.

Step 5: Make a Commitment to Stretch

Once members have had their time to present, discuss, brainstorm, and gain feedback, the timekeeper asks each member in turn to commit verbally to a next action that will move him or her forward toward the achievement of his or her goals—something that the member will agree to accomplish before the next meeting. The commitment needs to be a stretch.

It could be a result of what the member heard from the group that day: "Okay, I'm going to make three calls to hire a new salesperson" or "I'm going to call John Deerfield at Consolidated and pitch our new service."

This commitment ensures that everyone is continually moving forward toward the completion of their goals, which is the ultimate benefit of a mastermind group.

Step 6: End with a Moment of Gratitude

Your meeting might end with a group prayer expressing gratitude. Or you might go around the table with each member saying one thing he or she appreciates about another person in the group. Or you might end with the "What I feel like saying" exercise described in Principle 49 ("Have a Heart Talk"), pages 330 through 335.

Step 7: Be Accountable

When members assemble the very next week, each member shares something related to the goal he set at the previous meeting. Did each member take action? Did they achieve their goal?

You'll find one of the real values of a mastermind group is the accountability factor—other members checking up on you to make sure you meet your stated commitments. People are more productive when they have a stated deadline and are held accountable to it. The reality is that if you know you're going to be asked next week about the commitment you made today, you'll take steps to accomplish it by next week's deadline. It's one way to ensure you'll accomplish a lot more.

ACCOUNTABILITY PARTNERS

Instead of a mastermind group, you might choose to work with what I call an accountability partner. The two of you agree to a set of goals that each is working toward and agree to talk regularly by phone to hold each other accountable for meeting deadlines, accomplishing goals, and making progress.

You agree to call each other every week or every other week to make sure you are both following through on your planned actions. Knowing that you'll be reporting to someone provides the extra motivation to get the job done. This is an especially useful relationship to develop if you're independent and work from home. Knowing that you'll be talking to your accountability partner on Thursday makes Wednesday an especially productive day.

You can also ask your partner to share ideas, information, contacts, and resources. You can pitch your partner on your latest idea and ask for feedback: "What's your opinion? How would you proceed?" Your partner might agree to make a call for you, give you a contact name, or e-mail you some information he or she has already collected on that subject.

An accountability partner can also provide enthusiasm when yours is waning because of obstacles, distractions, setbacks, or even better opportunities. The key to a successful accountability relationship is choosing someone who is as excited about reaching his or her goal as you are about reaching yours—someone who is committed to your success and theirs.

THREE MORE RESOURCES FOR
ENTREPRENEURS AND CEOS

A couple of other valuable organizations that provide opportunities to mastermind with other entrepreneurs are the Young Entrepreneurs Organization, TEC (originally founded as The Executive Committee), and the Young Presidents' Organization. They each provide local monthly support groups as well as regional and national meetings that are phenomenally educational and supportive. I have served as a resource to two of these organizations, and all of the members I have met are ecstatic about the benefits they have received—both personally and professionally. You can get information about them by going to the following Web sites: www.yeo.org, www.teconline.com, and www.ypo.org.

INQUIRE WITHIN

Brain researchers estimate that your unconscious data base
outweighs the conscious on an order exceeding ten million to one.
This data base is the source of your hidden, natural genius.
In other words, a part of you is much smarter than you are.
The wise people regularly consult that smarter part.

MICHAEL J. GELB
Author of *How to Think Like Leonardo da Vinci*

According to an ancient legend, there was a time when ordinary people had access to all the knowledge of the gods. Yet time and again, they ignored this wisdom. One day, the gods grew tired of so freely giving a gift the people didn't use, so they decided to hide this precious wisdom where only the most committed of seekers would discover it. They believed that if people had to work to find this wisdom, they would use it more carefully.

One of the gods suggested that they bury it deep in the earth.

No, the others said—too many people could easily dig down and find it.

"Let's put it in the deepest ocean," suggested one of the gods, but that idea was also rejected. They knew that people would one day learn to dive and thus would find it too easily.

One of the gods suggested hiding it on the highest mountaintop, but it was quickly agreed that people could climb mountains.

Finally, one of the wisest gods suggested, "Let's hide it deep inside the people themselves. They'll never think to look in there." And so it came to be—and so it continues today.

TRUST YOUR INTUITION

For most of us, our early education and training focused on looking outside of ourselves for the answers to our questions. Few of us have had any training on how to look inside, and yet most of the supersuccessful people I have met over the years are people who have developed their intuition and learned to trust their gut feelings and follow their inner guidance. Many practice some form of daily meditation to access this voice within.

Burt Dubin, then a successful real estate investor, now creator of the Burt Dubin Speaking Success System (serving Speakers Worldwide) knows all about trusting his intuition. For some time, he had been looking to buy a four-corner property in Kingman, Arizona. He knew it would be a good investment, but he had not been able to locate a property that was for sale. One night he went to bed as usual, only to be awakened at 3:00 AM with a clear inner message that he was to drive to Kingman, Arizona—now!

Burt found this strange because he had called a realtor in Kingman earlier that same day and was told there were no four-corner properties listed for sale. But having learned to trust his inner messages, Burt immediately got in his car and drove through the night, arriving at Kingman at 8:00 AM. He went to Howard Johnson's, bought a paper, and turned to the real estate section, where he saw a four-corner property for sale. He went directly to the real estate office at 9:00 and had the property in escrow by 9:15.

But how was this possible? He had called the day before to find no four-corner properties for sale. But at 4:30 the previous day, a property owner had called from New York to sell his property; he needed the money. Because it was too late to get the property into the multiple listings, but knowing that the weekly paper didn't close until 5:00 PM, the agent had called the paper and purchased an ad.

Because Burt had trusted his "still, small voice within," he managed to purchase this prime piece of real estate before anyone else even knew it was available.

When business magnate Conrad Hilton, founder of the Hilton Hotels Corporation, wanted to buy the Stevens Corporation at auction, he submitted a sealed bid for $165,000. When he awakened the next morning with the number 180,000 in his head, he swiftly changed his bid to $180,000, successfully securing the company and earning a $2 million profit. The next highest bid was $179,800!

Whether they are a real estate investor who hears a voice in the middle of the night, a detective who solves a dead-end case by following a hunch, an investor who just knows when to get out of the market, or a football linebacker who can sense what the quarterback's next play is going to be, successful people trust their intuition.

You, too, can use your intuition to make more money, make better decisions, solve problems more quickly, unleash your creative genius, discern people's hidden motives, envision a new business, and create winning business plans and strategies.

EVERYONE HAS INTUITION—IT'S JUST A MATTER OF DEVELOPING IT

All the resources we need are in the mind.

THEODORE ROOSEVELT
Twenty-sixth president of the United States

Intuition is not something relegated to certain people or to psychics. Everyone has it and everyone has experienced it. Have you ever been thinking about your old friend Jerry, and then the phone rings and it's Jerry on the line who was just thinking about you? Have you ever awakened in the middle of the night and knew something had happened to one of your children, only to find out later that it was the exact moment your son was in an automobile accident? Have you ever felt a burning sensation on the back of your neck, and then turned to see a man staring at you from across the room?

We've all experienced this kind of intuition. The trick is to learn how to tap into it at will to achieve greater levels of success.

USING MEDITATION TO ACCESS YOUR INTUITION

There is only one journey: going inside yourself.

RAINER MARIA RILKE
Poet and novelist

When I was 35, I attended a meditation retreat that permanently changed my life. For an entire week, we sat in meditation from 6:30 in the morning until 10:00 at night—with breaks only for meals and silent walks. Over the first few days, I thought I would go crazy. I would either fall asleep from years of not getting enough sleep, or my mind would race from one topic to another as I reviewed every experience of my past, planned how to improve my business, and wondered what I was doing sitting in a meditation hall while everyone else I knew was out enjoying life.

On the fourth day, an unexpected and wonderful thing happened. My mind became quiet and I moved into a place from which I could just witness everything that was occurring around me without judgment or attachment. I was aware of sounds, sensations in my body, and a profound sense of inner peace. Thoughts still came and went, but not at the same pace or of the same kind. The thoughts were deeper—what we might call insights, deeper understandings, and wisdom. I saw connections I had never seen before. I understood my motivations, fears, and desires at a deeper level. Creative solutions to problems that I had been facing in my life came into my consciousness.

I felt relaxed, calm, aware, and clearer than I had ever felt before. Gone were the pressures to perform, to prove myself, to explain myself, to measure up to some external standard, to meet the needs of others. Instead there was a deep sense of my self and my purpose in life. When I focused on my deepest, most heartfelt goals and desires, solutions would come pouring into my mind—clear thoughts and images of the steps I would need to take, the people I would need to talk to, and the ways to transcend any obstacles I might encounter. It was truly magical.

What I learned from this experience was that all the ideas I needed to complete any task, solve any problem, or achieve any goal were available inside me. I have used this valuable insight ever since.

REGULAR MEDITATION WILL DEEPEN YOUR INTUITION

The regular practice of meditation will help you clear out distractions and teach you to recognize subtle impulses from within. Think of parents sitting on a bench on the edge of a playground filled with children laughing and yelling at each other. In the midst of all this noise, the parents can pick out their own child's voice from all the other voices on the playground.

Your intuition works the same way. As you meditate and become more spiritually attuned, you can better discern and recognize the sound of your higher self or the voice of God speaking to you through words, images, and sensations.

The intellect has little to do on the road to discovery. There comes a leap in consciousness, call it intuition or what you will, and the solution comes to you, and you don't know how or why.

ALBERT EINSTEIN
Physicist and Nobel laureate

THE ANSWERS LIE WITHIN

When Mark Victor Hansen and I were nearing completion of our first *Chicken Soup for the Soul*® book, we still did not have a title for it. Because Mark and I both meditate, we decided to "inquire within." Every day for a week, we asked our internal guidance for a best-selling title. Mark went to bed every night repeating the phrase "mega-best-selling title" and would awaken every morning and immediately go into meditation. I simply asked God to give me the best title for the book, and then I would sit with my eyes closed in a state of relaxed expectancy, waiting patiently for an answer to come.

On the third morning, I suddenly saw a hand write the words *chicken soup* on a blackboard in my mind. My immediate reaction was, *What does chicken soup have to do with our book?*

I heard a voice in my head respond, *Chicken soup is what your grandmother gave you when you were sick as a child.*

But this book isn't about sick people, I thought.

People's spirits are sick, my inner voice replied. *Millions of people are depressed and living in fear and resignation that things will never get better. This book will inspire them and uplift their spirits.*

During the remaining minutes of that meditation, the title evolved from *Chicken Soup for the Spirit* to *Chicken Soup for the Soul* to *Chicken Soup for the Soul: 101 Stories to Open the Heart and Rekindle the Spirit.* When I heard *Chicken Soup for the Soul*, I got goose bumps. I have since learned that giving me goose bumps is one of the ways my intuition tells me I am on track.

Ten minutes later, I told my wife, and she got goose bumps, too. Then I called Mark and he got goose bumps. We were onto something right, and we all knew it.

HOW YOUR INTUITION COMMUNICATES WITH YOU

Your intuition can communicate with you in many ways. You may get a message from within as a vision or a visual image while you are meditating or dreaming. I often get images while I am lying in bed after I first wake up, while I'm meditating or getting a massage, or while sitting in a hot tub or taking a shower. It can come in a flash out of the blue or it can be a long, unfolding image like a movie.

Your intuition may speak to you as a hunch, a thought, or a voice actually telling you *yes, no, go for it*, or *not yet*. It might come as one resounding word, a short sentence, or a complete lecture. You may find you can dialogue with the voice for clarification or more information.

You may also receive a message from your intuition through your physical senses. If the message is one of *watch out* or *be careful*, you may experience it as a chill, the creeps, a sense of restlessness, discomfort in your gut, constriction in your chest, tightness or pain in your head, even a sour taste in your mouth. A positive or "yes" message might come in the form of goose bumps, a dizzy feeling, warmth, a sense of opening or expansiveness in the chest, a sense of relaxation, a feeling of relief, or a letting go of tension.

You may also experience intuitive messages through your emotions, such as a feeling of uneasiness, concern, or confusion. Or when information is of a positive nature, you may experience a feeling of joy, euphoria, or profound inner peace.

Sometimes it is just a sense of knowing. How many times have you heard someone say, "I don't know how I knew; I just knew" or "I knew it in my heart" or "in the depth of my soul"?

An indicator that the message is truly from your intuition is that it will often be accompanied by a sense of greater clarity, a feeling of *rightness* about the answer or the impulse. Another indicator that the message you are receiving is a correct one is an accompanying feeling of passion and excitement. If you are considering a plan of action or a decision, and it leaves you feeling drained, bored or enervated, that's a clear message saying *Don't go there*. On the other hand, if you feel energized and enthusiastic, your intuition is telling you to go ahead.

MAKE TIME TO LISTEN

It is important to make time to listen to your intuition. Your most valuable intuitive wisdom often comes when you are relaxed and open to receiving it. It may come through formal meditation—or through the many forms of informal meditation we engage in every day, such as sitting by a waterfall or stream, watching the ocean, watching the clouds float by, staring at the stars, sitting under a tree, feeling a soft breeze, staring into a fire, listening to inspiring music, jogging, yoga, prayer, listening to a bird sing, taking a shower, driving on the freeway, watching a child play, or writing in a personal journal.

Intuition isn't mystical.

DR. JAMES WATSON
Nobel laureate and codiscoverer of DNA

You can even do informal meditation in an abbreviated way during the middle of a hectic day. When you need help making a decision, take time to pause, take a deep breath, reflect on the question, and allow the intuitive impressions to come to you. Pay attention to any images, words, physical sensations, or emotions you experience. Sometimes you will find that intuitive insights will immediately come into your awareness. Other times, they may come later in the day when you least expect it.

ASK QUESTIONS

Your intuition can provide you with the answers to anything you need to know. Ask questions that begin with "Should I . . ." and "What should I do about . . . ?" and "How can I . . . ?" and "What can I do to . . . ?" You can ask your intuition questions such as

- Should I take this job?
- What should I do about the lack of morale in the company?
- What can I do to increase sales this year?
- What can I do to guarantee we get this account?
- Should I marry this person?
- What can I do to lower my time in the marathon?
- How can I achieve my ideal weight?
- What is the next step I need to take to achieve financial independence?
- What should I do next?

WRITE DOWN YOUR ANSWERS

Make sure to immediately write down any impressions you receive. Intuitive impressions are often subtle and therefore "evaporate" very quickly, so make sure to capture them in writing as soon as possible. Recent research in neuroscience indicates that an intuitive insight—or any new idea—*not* captured within 37 seconds is likely never to be recalled again. In 7 minutes, it's gone forever. As my buddy Mark Victor Hansen likes to say, "As soon as you think it, ink it!"

I always carry a digital voice recorder (I use an Olympus Digital Voice Recorder DM-1, which can hold up to 10 hours of notes and conversation) when I'm working, and some 3" × 5" cards and a pen in my coat or shirt pocket when I am not in work mode.

Many people have their greatest success accessing intuitive information through journal writing. Take any question that you need an answer to and just start writing about it. Write down the answers to your question(s) as quickly as they come to you. You will be amazed at the clarity that can emerge from this process.

TAKE IMMEDIATE ACTION

Pay attention to the answers you receive and act on the information as quickly as possible. When you act on the information you receive, you'll find that you get more and more intuitive impulses. After a while you will be living in the flow. It will all seem easy and effortless as the wisdom comes to you and you simply act on it. As you learn to trust yourself and your intuition more, it will become automatic.

Experts agree that your intuition works better when you trust it. The more you demonstrate faith in your intuition, the more you will see the results of it in your life.

I strongly encourage you to listen to your intuition, trust it, and follow it. Trusting your intuition is simply another form of trusting yourself, and the more you trust yourself, the more success you will have.

Remember, it's not what you think of; it's what you write down and take action on that counts.

SHE LISTENED AND TOOK ACTION

Madeline Balletta is a very spiritual person. For her, inquiring within means talking to God . . . and listening to His answers.

In 1984, Madeline's life—and her own success path—were dramatically changed when she and her fellow church members prayed for a solution to her fatigue and heard *fresh royal jelly*. Not understanding this clear directive, she investigated and discovered that royal jelly was the food substance worker bees fed to the queen in their hives—a wholesome and highly nourishing liquid that was just starting to be distributed in England as a nutritional supplement.

In time, Madeline started to get better. And soon, she began to pray about whether royal jelly was meant to do more than just help her.

Start a company was the response to her prayers. And so Madeline did.

Today, Bee-Alive is a multimillion-dollar company that has distributed nutritional products containing royal jelly to hundreds of thousands of people nationwide. And through it all, Madeline has prayerfully asked for guidance and listened attentively to the answers.

"I believe God gave me the vision, the inspiration, the strength, and the courage to see it all through," said Madeline.

For example, by her second year in business, Madeline's marketing efforts had produced few results. In fact, with only $450 left in her checking account, her accountant advised that she fold up shop and move on. Madeline returned from that meeting, locked herself in her room, and "cried and prayed and cried and prayed." On the third day, Madeline received the word *radio*, and decided to bet the farm—her remaining $450—on 10 radio commercials that cost $45 apiece. Within days she was making steady sales again. Impressed by her passionate commitment to her product, the radio station eventually interviewed her on one of their talk shows, and by the time she returned home from that interview, recording artist Pat Boone had called asking about royal jelly and how it might help his daughter. A few months later, Boone called back to tell her how pleased he was with the effects of the royal jelly. When he said, "If there's anything I can ever do for you, I'd be glad to," Madeline asked him to record three radio commercials. Boone agreed—and soon Bee-Alive was on 400 radio stations across America selling millions of dollars' worth of product.

What might happen when you inquire within? For Madeline Balletta, praying, listening quietly, and acting on what she heard meant the development of a successful company serving hundreds of thousands of satisfied customers, as well as the creation of an unimaginable lifestyle for her and her family.

FURTHER READING AND RESOURCES

In "Suggested Reading and Additional Resources for Success" (pages 441–451), you'll find excellent books to help further your ability to access your intuition more easily.

PART FOUR

Create
Successful
Relationships

Personal relationships are the fertile soil from which all advancement, all success, all achievement in real life grows.

BEN STEIN
Writer, actor, and game show host

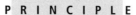

BE HEAR NOW

Listen a hundred times. Ponder a thousand times. Speak once.

SOURCE UNKNOWN

There's a big difference between *hearing*—that is, simply receiving communication—and truly *listening*, which is the art of paying thoughtful attention with a mind toward understanding the complete message being delivered. Unlike simply hearing someone's account, listening requires maintaining eye contact, watching the person's body language, asking for clarification, and listening for the unspoken message.

In the news reporting industry, journalists are trained in the art of active listening—an interview technique in which reporters listen and understand so well, they're able to ask intelligent, more in-depth questions about the information being delivered. Active listening is how good news stories are developed—and how many of us can improve our relationships, too. Not surprisingly, it also helps insure accuracy and fairness, two of the most important hallmarks of a journalist—and two important qualities of any relationship.

LISTENING PAYS OFF

Marcia Martin is an executive coach. One of her clients, a senior vice president at a major bank, asked her if she could help him make his team meetings more powerful. He complained that his direct team wasn't really operating the way he wanted it to in their meetings. They didn't bring the right things to the meeting, they weren't focused on the right things, and they didn't present properly.

When Marcia asked him what he did in his meetings and what the problems were, he said he always started off his meetings by telling them what the purpose of the meeting was, what he felt their breakdowns were, and what he wanted them to do. By the time he finished describing his meetings, she could tell the whole meeting was him just spitting out instructions to his team members.

Marcia told him, "I would advise you to start your meeting with just one sentence: 'The purpose of this meeting is for me to find out from you what you feel is going on in each of your departments, what you feel the breakdowns are, and what you need from me.' And then you should be quiet and just let them talk and talk and talk until they have totally talked themselves out. If they stop talking, just say, 'Well, what else?' and let them talk some more."

She explained that his people probably hadn't had a chance to really empty out their feelings, their viewpoints, their suggestions, or their questions. He was packing them with too much information and all of his opinions, and he wasn't really listening. She told him to allow 2 hours for the meeting and not to say anything during that whole time. He was just to listen, write down notes, and nod his head—be present and be interested, but not speak.

Three days later, he pulled Marcia aside to tell her that he had had the most fantastic, powerful meeting he'd ever had in his life. He had done exactly what she had asked him to do—he had listened in a way that he had never listened before. As a result his team members had talked and talked and talked, and he had learned more about what his people were going through, what his people needed, and what to do for them in that one meeting than he had in all of his previous executive experience.

ARGUE LESS AND LISTEN MORE

A New York photographer I once met traveled all over the world doing expensive location shoots for big-name clients like Revlon and Lancôme. At one point he shared with me how he would give clients exactly what they had asked for, then be mystified when they didn't like the end result. Even if it were the pyramids in Egypt, he said, they'd ask him to shoot it over.

It did no good to become defensive or argue with the clients, even though he had followed their specifications perfectly. Instead, he eventually learned—after losing several lucrative accounts—that all he had to do was say, "So let me see if I've got this right. You want more of this and less of that? Correct? Okay, I'll go reshoot it and bring it back so you can see if you like it."

In other words, he learned to argue less with the people who were paying the bills and to listen more—responding and adjusting to their feedback until they were satisfied.

BE *INTERESTED* RATHER THAN INTERESTING

Another way people fail to listen carefully is to be too concerned with being interesting themselves, rather than being *interested* in the person they're listening to. They believe the route to success is to constantly talk—showing off their expertise or intelligence with their words and comments.

The best way to establish rapport with people and to win them over to your side is to be truly interested in them, to listen with the intention of really learning about them. When the person feels that you are really interested in getting to know them and their feelings, they will open up to you and share their true feelings with you much more quickly.

Work to develop an attitude of curiosity. Be curious about other people, what they feel, how they think, how they see the world. What are their hopes, dreams, and fears? What are their aspirations? What obstacles are they facing in their lives?

If you want people to cooperate with you, to like you, or to open up to you, you must be *interested* . . . in them. Instead of focusing on yourself, start focusing on others. Notice what makes *them* happy or unhappy. When your thoughts are more on others than on yourself, you feel less stress. You can act and respond with more intelligence. Your production level increases and you have more fun. Additionally, when you are *interested*, people respond to your interest in them. They want to be around you. Your popularity increases.

A POWERFUL QUESTION

During my year of attending Dan Sullivan's "Strategic Coach Program,"[47] he taught me one of the most powerful communication tools I have ever learned. It is one of the most effective ways to establish rapport and create a feeling of connection with another person. I have used it in both my business and personal life. It is a series of four questions:

1. If we were meeting three years from today, what has to have happened during that three-year period for you to feel happy about your progress?

---

47. For information on the "Strategic Coach Program" or Dan's Sullivan's excellent books and audio programs, go to www.strategiccoach.com.

2. What are the biggest dangers you'll have to face and deal with in order to achieve that progress?

3. What are the biggest opportunities that you have that you would need to focus on and capture to achieve those things?

4. What strengths will you need to reinforce and maximize, and what skills and resources will you need to develop that you don't currently have in order to capture those opportunities?

About 1 week after I had learned these questions, I was meeting with my sister Kim, who is the coauthor of all of our *Chicken Soup for the Teenage Soul* books. I didn't feel like we were making much progress in getting connected, so I decided to try these new questions I had just learned and then really listen.

When I asked her the first question, it was as if I had magically opened a locked door. She proceeded to tell me about all of her hopes and dreams for her future. I think she must have talked for at least 30 minutes without interruption. Then I asked the second question. Off she went for another 15 minutes. I didn't say one word. Then I asked the third and fourth questions. Over an hour later, she stopped. She was grinning from ear to ear and looked unusually calm and relaxed. She smiled at me and said, "That's the best conversation I think we've ever had. I feel so clear and focused. I know exactly what I need to go and do now. Thank you."

It was amazing. I hadn't said a word—except for asking the four questions. She had taken herself through a process of clarification with those questions. She hadn't clearly addressed them before, and doing it with me had brought her great clarity and relief. I felt very connected to my sister, and she felt very connected to me. Up until then, I think I would have had a tendency at some point to jump in and tell her what I thought she should do, interrupting her own process of self-discovery by not listening.

Since that time I have used those questions with my wife, my children, my staff, my corporate clients, my coaching clients, prospective seminar participants, and several potential business partners. The results are always magical.

IT'S YOUR TURN

Take the time today to write those four questions on an index card and carry it with you. Practice each day asking someone these questions over lunch or dinner. Start with your friends and your family members, too. You will be surprised how much you will learn and how much closer you will feel afterward.

Use these questions with every potential business client or business colleague. Once they have answered, you'll know whether or not there is a basis for a business relationship. You'll know whether or not your products and services can help them achieve their goals.

If you find they don't want to answer these questions, then they are not people you want to do business with, because they are either unaware of their future and can't think ahead, which will make it hard for you to help them, or they are unwilling to tell you the answers, which means that there is no trust present, so you have nothing to build on—no basis for a relationship.

One final suggestion: Make sure to take yourself through the same four questions either alone on a piece of paper or verbally with a friend or mastermind partner. It's a valuable exercise.

49

HAVE A HEART TALK

Most communication resembles a Ping-Pong game in which people are merely preparing to slam their next point across; but pausing to understand differing points of view and associated feelings can turn apparent opponents into true members of the same team.

CLIFF DURFEE
Creator of the Heart Talk process

Unfortunately, in too many business, educational, and other settings, there is never an opportunity for feelings to be expressed and heard, so they build up to the point that people have no capacity to focus on the business at hand. There is too much emotional static in the space. It's like trying to put more water into a glass that is already full. There is nowhere for it to go. You must first pour out the old water to make room for the new water.

It is the same with emotions. People can't listen until they have been heard. They first need to get whatever is bothering them off their chest. Whether you are someone who has just come home from work, a parent looking at your child's report card with all C's, a salesperson attempting to sell a new car, or a CEO overseeing the merger of two companies, you first need to let the other people speak about their needs and wants, hopes and dreams, fears and concerns, hurts and pains, before you talk about yours. It opens up a space inside of them to be able to listen to and take in what you have to say.

WHAT IS A HEART TALK?

A Heart Talk is a very structured communication process in which eight agreements are strictly adhered to in order to create the safety for a deep level of communication to occur without the fear of condemnation, unsolicited advice, interruption, or being rushed. It is a powerful tool used to surface and release any unexpressed emotions that could otherwise get in the way of people being totally present to deal with the business at hand. It can be used at home, in business, in the classroom, with sports teams, and in religious settings to develop rapport, understanding, and intimacy.

WHEN TO USE A HEART TALK

Heart talks are useful

- Before or during a staff meeting
- At the beginning of a business meeting where two new groups of people are coming together for the first time
- After an emotionally stimulating event like a merger, a massive layoff, a death, a major athletic loss, an unexpected financial setback, or even a tragedy such as the terrorist attacks of September 11, 2001
- When there is a conflict between two individuals, groups, or departments
- On a regular basis at home, in the office, or in the classroom to create a deeper level of communication and intimacy

HOW TO CONDUCT A HEART TALK

A heart talk can be conducted with any size group of between 2 and 10 people. You'll want to break a group larger than 10 into smaller groups, because if the group is larger than that, the trust and safety factors tend to diminish, and it can also take up too much time.

The first time you conduct a Heart Talk, start by explaining that there is value in occasionally using a structure for communication that guarantees a deeper level of listening. The structure of a Heart Talk creates a safe, nonjudgmental space that supports the constructive—rather than the destructive—expression of feelings that if left unexpressed can block teamwork, synergy, creativity, and intuition, which are vital to the productivity and success of any venture.

GUIDELINES FOR A HEART TALK

Start by asking people to sit in a circle or around a table. Introduce the basic agreements, which include these:

- Only the person holding the heart talks.
- You don't judge or criticize what anyone else has said.
- You pass the object to the left after your turn.
- You talk about how you feel.
- You keep the information confidential.
- You don't leave the talk until it's declared complete.

If you have plenty of time, a Heart Talk completes naturally when the heart makes a complete circle without anyone having something to say.

Ask the group to agree to the guidelines, which are very important to make sure that the talk does not deteriorate and lose its value. Because no one is supposed to talk except for the person holding the object, it is often best to wait until the completion of the talk to remind people about certain agreements that need more attention. Another option is to have the agreements written down on paper or a whiteboard and to merely point to them if someone is getting too far off track. Go around the group at least once—with everybody getting one turn—or set a time frame (say 15 minutes to 30 minutes; longer for more emotionally intense issues) and keep going around the group until the time runs out or nobody has anything more to say.

You can use any object to pass around—a ball, a paperweight, a book, anything that can be seen by the other participants. I have seen everything from a stuffed animal (a hospital staff), a baseball (a college baseball team), and a football helmet (a state championship football team) to a Native American talking stick (on a corporate river rafting trip). I actually prefer to use the stuffed red velvet hearts that Cliff Durfee, the originator of the Heart Talk method, sells on his Web site[48] because they remind everyone that what we are hearing is coming from the other person's heart—and that we are trying to get to the heart of the matter at hand.

RESULTS YOU CAN EXPECT FROM A HEART TALK

You can expect the following results from a Heart Talk:

- Enhanced listening skills
- Constructive expression of feelings

---

48. For more complete information, I recommend that you visit www.livelovelaugh.com and obtain a copy of the *Heart Talk Book* for only $5.95. A bright-red card-stock heart is inserted in each book, with the eight key agreements printed on the back side for an easy reminder before having a Heart Talk. If you are an educator, there is also a complete classroom curriculum guide on this subject entitled *More Teachable Moments*.

- Improved conflict resolution skills
- Improved abilities to let go of resentments and old issues
- Development of mutual respect and understanding
- Greater sense of connection, unity, and bonding

One of the most valuable uses of the Heart Talk for me was in a weeklong training that I was conducting for 120 school administrators in Bergen, Norway. We were about to start our afternoon session when someone announced that one of the workshop participants had been killed in an automobile accident during the lunch break. There was massive shock and grief in the room. It would have been impossible to proceed with the scheduled agenda, so I divided the participants into groups of 6 and taught them the guidelines for a Heart Talk. I told them to just keep passing the heart around until everyone in the group said "I pass" twice in a row, meaning that there was nothing else to be said.

The groups talked and cried for over an hour. People talked about their grief, their own sense of mortality, how precious and fleeting life really is, how scary life can sometimes be, and how you need to live in the moment because your future is never guaranteed. We then took a short break and were able to proceed with the scheduled activities. Whatever emotions there were had been shared. The group was once again ready to focus on the material I was there to teach.

A HEART TALK SAVES THE FAMILY BUSINESS

James owned a small family business that had supported him and his family for years. His wife and two sons, both married with children, also worked as employees in the company. At least once a week, they would all gather together for a large meal, and James would do his best to unify this growing family. James hoped that when he retired, the family business would survive and continue to provide a living for everyone in the extended family.

Though it looked like an excellent plan on the surface, there had always been rivalry and competition between the two sons, and when both their wives started working in the business, things started coming apart at the seams. Resentments over little things were pushed down to supposedly keep the peace, but they would resurface later in sarcastic comments and unexpected outbursts of anger. When the two sons actually threw a couple of punches at each other, James realized they all needed to talk and clear the air. But he was afraid that the situation could become even more explosive unless there were some powerful ground rules present—so he decided to use the structure of a Heart Talk.

Sitting in a large circle after their weekly family meal, the group was unusually quiet, not knowing what to expect. James started by getting everyone to agree to the eight rules and the structure of the talk. At first the heart was passed without much to say. The second time around one of the sons expressed his anger, and when the heart reached the other son, even greater hostility surfaced—yet it was clear no one was going to violate the guidelines, stomp out of the room, or throw something.

It wasn't an easy talk, and there were times you could tell everyone would have preferred any other activity—even if it were doing the dishes. But as the heart kept going around the circle, everyone began to have the experience that he or she had been heard, and the hostility began to dissipate. Then one of the son's wives started crying and shared that she was at her wit's end. With all the friction in the family and in the business, she couldn't take it anymore. She said that something had to change. At that moment, something released, and there wasn't a dry eye in the group. As the heart continued around and around, the sadness was soon replaced by an acknowledgment of their love for each other and the things they were grateful for.

Though it will never be known for sure, James believes that that Heart Talk was most likely the key thing that saved his business, his family, and his sanity.

"WHAT I FEEL LIKE SAYING" SAVES MILLIONS OF DOLLARS

My friend Marshall Thurber is a trainer and management consultant who has been teaching people how to build and protect their wealth for over 30 years. Recently he has been working with Lee Brower of Empowered Wealth to help superwealthy families learn how to properly steward their money and consciously pass it on to the next generation. Marshall uses a simple variation of the Heart Talk, which he calls the "What I Feel Like Saying" exercise, with amazing effectiveness:

I start every business meeting by asking everyone present to first respond to this question: "What do you need to say in order to let go and be here?" One of the keys to the success of the process is that no one can comment on what is being said. Everyone must wait until the speaker is finished speaking, say "Thank you," and then move on to the next person in the group. I can tell by the energy if we need to go around a second time. Sometimes we may go around the group a couple of times. People can pass if they are already clear and present.

I have been working with a very wealthy family that has hundreds of millions of dollars but is totally dysfunctional. The children were not talking to their parents and were "punishing" them by not letting their children talk to their grandparents. The enmity, the absolute inability to communicate, and the lack of cooperation were costing the family tens of millions of dollars!

I sat them all down and said, "Look, it's clear that everyone has a lot of emotional baggage from the past, and there are a lot of important issues that are unresolved, but if we can't come together and resolve them in the present, there is no reason to go any further in trying to create a new and better future."

When I proposed that we do the "What I Feel Like Saying" exercise, everyone thought it was going to be a total waste of time, but I finally convinced them to do it . . . and we ended up doing it for four hours! And it wasn't just one round; it was round after round after round. But when those four hours were up, they were in love with each other, to the point where they have now agreed to work with the team at Empowered Wealth to create a new, more conscious way of working together with their family's wealth. It's far from perfect yet, but the family went from an absolute inability to communicate to getting totally present. And out of that level of total presence came two powerful family agreements—"family first" and "together we're better." That's all we did, but it took the entire day. If we hadn't done the "What I Feel Like Saying" exercise, there would have been no hope for this family. None whatsoever!

The miracle is that once you get present, underneath all of the anger, resentment, and distrust, there is nothing but love. And from a place of love, you can create anything.

TELL THE TRUTH FASTER

When in doubt, tell the truth.

MARK TWAIN
Author of several classic American works of fiction, including *Tom Sawyer*
and *The Adventures of Huckleberry Finn*

Most of us avoid telling the truth because it's uncomfortable. We're afraid of the consequences—making others feel uncomfortable, hurting their feelings, or risking their anger. And yet, when we don't tell the truth, and others don't tell us the truth, we can't deal with matters from a basis in reality.

We've all heard the phrase that "the truth will set you free." And it will. The truth allows us to be free to deal with the way things are, not the way we imagine them to be or hope them to be or might manipulate them to be with our lies.

The truth also frees up our energy. It takes energy to withhold the truth, keep a secret, or keep up an act.

WHAT HAPPENS WHEN YOU TELL THE TRUTH?

In my 4-day advanced seminar, I do a process called Secrets. It's a very simple exercise where we spend an hour or two telling the group our secrets—those things we imagine that if others knew, they surely wouldn't like us or approve of us. I invite participants to simply stand up and tell the group whatever it is they've been hiding and then sit down.

There is no discussion and no feedback, just sharing and listening. It starts out slowly as people test the water with "I cheated on my eighth-grade math exam" and "I stole a penknife from the five-and-dime when I was fourteen years old." But as people begin to realize that nothing bad is happening to anyone, people eventually open up and talk about deeper, more painful issues.

After there is no more to come out, I ask the group if they feel any less loving or accepting toward anyone in the group. In all these years, I have never had anyone answer yes.

Then I ask, "How many people feel relieved to have gotten this off their chest?"

Everyone says that they do.

And then I ask, "How many of you feel closer to the other people in the group?" and again all of the hands go up. People realize that the things they've been hiding aren't so horrible but in fact are usually shared by at least a few others in the group. They are not alone but rather are part of the human community.

But most astounding is what people report over the next few days.

Lifelong migraines disappear. Spastic colons relax and medication is no longer needed. Depression lifts and aliveness returns. People actually look younger and more vital. It's quite amazing. One participant actually reported losing 5 pounds of excess weight over the ensuing 2 days. He had indeed released more than just some withheld information.

This example tells us that it takes a lot of energy to hold back our truth, and that energy, when it is released, can be used to focus on creating greater success in all areas of our lives. We can become less cautious and more spontaneous, more willing to be our natural selves. And when this happens, information that is vital to making things work and to getting things done can be shared and acted on.

WHAT DO YOU NEED TO SHARE?

In every area of our lives, the three things that most need to be shared are resentments that have built up, the unmet needs and demands that underlie those resentments, and appreciations.

Underneath all resentments are unfulfilled needs and desires. Whenever you find yourself resenting someone, ask yourself, *What is it that I am wanting from him that I am not getting?* And then make the commitment to at least ask for it. As we have talked about earlier, the worst that you'll get is a no. You just might get a yes. But at least the request will be out in the open.

One of the most valuable practices and yet the hardest to do for most people is telling the truth when it is uncomfortable. Most of us are so worried about hurting other people's feelings that we don't share *our* true feelings. We end up hurting ourselves instead.

TELLING THE TRUTH PAYS DIVIDENDS

Shortly after I created the Foundation for Self-Esteem to take my work to the nonprofit world of education, prisons, social services, and other at-risk populations, my director, Larry Price, discovered a request for a proposal that had been issued by the Los Angeles County Office of Education. It turns out that more than 84% of the people going through the county's welfare-to-work orientation program never returned after the first day to start the job training portion. The county knew it needed an orientation program that would give people hope and motivate them to complete their job training and create a better life for themselves and their families.

We knew we could design a program that met the county's specifications, but we also knew it would not include enough contact hours and reinforcement to produce the results that the county was hoping for. It was clear that the way the county envisioned the program just wouldn't work.

Eager to land the $730,000 contract and provide the foundation with badly needed operating funds, however, we decided to create an extensive proposal and worked for months crafting a beautiful presentation. The night before it was due, we even stayed up all night finalizing, printing, and collating the numerous copies that were to be submitted.

It must have been a good proposal, because we were selected as one of the three finalists and were called into the county offices for a live interview and final presentation.

I can still remember standing in front of the county offices saying to Larry, "You know, I'm not sure I want to win this competition. No matter how good a program we put together, the way they want it structured can't possibly give them the results they want. I think we should tell them the truth. How were they to know how it needs to be structured? They're not the motivation experts. How could they ask for something they didn't fully understand?"

Our fear was that the county officers would feel somehow judged or criticized and award the contract to someone else. It was a huge risk, especially with the dollar figure involved. But we decided to tell the truth.

The reaction of the county officers surprised us. After listening to our point of view, they decided to hire us anyway *because we were willing to tell the truth*. After analyzing what we said, they agreed and felt we were the only ones who correctly understood the situation they were dealing with.

The results were so fantastic that eventually the program we developed—the GOALS Program—was adopted by other county welfare programs—plus the Housing and Urban Development Authority, Head Start, and as a prerelease program for San Quentin and several other prisons.[49]

THERE'S NO "PERFECT TIME" TO TELL
THE HARD TRUTH

As I discovered with the Los Angeles County Office of Education, telling the truth was the difference between winning that contract and losing it. We could have compromised our integrity, but we decided instead to tell the truth sooner rather than later.

Learning to speak your truth sooner is one of the most important success habits you will ever develop. In fact, as soon as you start asking yourself the question *I wonder when would be the best time to tell the truth*, that's actually the best time to do so.

Will it be uncomfortable? Probably. Will it create lots of reactions? Yes. But it is the right thing to do. Get into the habit of telling the truth faster. Ultimately, you want to get to the point where you say it as soon as you think it. That's when you become totally authentic. What you see is what you get. People will know where you stand. You can be counted on to speak your mind.

"I DON'T WANT TO HURT THEIR FEELINGS"

A lot of times people use the excuse that they don't want to hurt another person's feelings. This is always a lie. If you ever catch yourself thinking this, what's really happening is that you're protecting yourself from your own feelings. You're avoiding what you will feel when they get upset. It is the coward's way out, and it simply delays having all your cards on the table.

This includes telling the kids that you are getting a divorce, that the family is moving to Texas because Daddy got a new job, that you are going to have to lay off some staff members, that you aren't going to be taking a family vacation this year, that you have to put the family pet to sleep, that you aren't going to be able to deliver the order by the date you promised, or you lost the family nest egg in a bad stock deal.

Hiding the truth always backfires. The longer you withhold it, the more disservice you do to yourself and to the others involved.

---

49. For information on the GOALS Program, contact the Foundation for Self-Esteem, 6035 Bristol Parkway, Culver City, CA 90230. Phone: 310-568-1505.

YOU WON'T WANT TO HEAR THIS, BUT . . .

I don't want any yes-men around me. I want everybody to tell me
the truth even if it costs them their jobs.

SAMUEL GOLDWYN
Cofounder of Metro-Goldwyn-Mayer Studios

Marilyn Tam was working as a divisional manager overseeing the operations of 320 stores for Miller's Outpost in 1986 when a friend told her Nike was planning to open their own concept stores and CEO Phil Knight was interested in hiring her to oversee the project. Nike was frustrated because sports shoe stores like Foot Locker weren't displaying their clothing apparel in a way that properly portrayed their lifestyle image. Because Marilyn thought that working for Nike would be a great opportunity, she did some research prior to her meeting by visiting a number of different stores that carried Nike apparel so that she would be ready to make a proposal to Phil about how to create a store Nike would be proud to present to the world.

As she did her research, she discovered two things: The footwear was good. It was functional, durable, and priced well. But the apparel was a disaster. It was inconsistent in quality, sizing, and durability, and it was not integrated or color coordinated. She found out later that Nike's clothing line had been an afterthought in response to consumer demand for more Nike logo apparel. It had not been thought out in a coordinated way. Nike had simply gone out and bought stock goods and just put its own label on them. The company bought apparel from different manufacturers without any consistent standards in size, quality, or color. It was not an image that was really reflective of the brand.

Marilyn's dilemma was that her desire to work for Nike was in conflict with her professional judgment about the products. She was afraid that if she told Phil that the product wasn't consistent with the brand image and shouldn't be in stores, she wouldn't get the job.

When she finally met with Phil Knight in Oregon, the initial conversation about the potential of the new store concept was exciting. But as the conversation unfolded, Marilyn became more and more uncomfortable because she knew she needed to tell him the truth about the quality of the merchandise and her belief that the stores would fail if they went ahead without first creating a standardized and integrated product line. But she hesitated because she feared that in his haste to get the stores up and running, he'd just find someone else to do it. After 2 hours, she finally spoke up and told Phil that the Nike shoes were great, but if they were going to do a concept store based on apparel and accessories, even though apparel was a very small factor— only about 5% of the overall sales of the company—it would have been over half of the store's display. She told him that she thought the stores would fail because the products would not reflect what Nike stood for.

Just as she feared, her disclosure ended the conversation rather quickly. She flew back to California wondering if she had done the right thing. She felt that she had probably lost any chance of getting a job there, but she also felt good about having told the truth.

Two weeks later, Phil Knight called her and told her he had reconsidered what she had said, had done his own research on the quality of the merchandise, and agreed with her assessment of the situation. He offered her the job as the first vice president of apparel and accessories. He told her, "You come, fix the goods; then we open the stores."

As you probably know, the rest is history. Though the decision to wait held up the opening of the Nike stores by about 2 years, the apparel division has had huge growth, and the concept stores have helped Nike continue to expand and take even greater hold on the American imagination.[50]

---

50. I highly recommend Marilyn's inspirational book *How to Use What You've Got to Get What You Want* (New York: SelectBooks, 2004). In it, she shares her extraordinary life and the principles of success she has learned from her birth into a traditional family in Hong Kong to her meteoric rise through the executive ranks of the international business world with such world-class companies as Aveda, Reebok, and Nike.

SPEAK WITH IMPECCABILITY

Impeccability of the word can lead you to personal freedom,
to huge success and abundance; it can take away all fear and
transform it into joy and love.

DON MIGUEL RUIZ
Author of *The Four Agreements*[51]

For most of us, our words are spoken without consciousness. We rarely stop to think about what we are saying. Our thoughts, opinions, judgments, and beliefs roll off our tongues without a care for the damage or the benefits they can produce.

Successful people, on the other hand, are the master of their words. They know that if they don't take dominion over their words, their words will take dominion over them. They're conscious of the thoughts they think and the words they speak—both about themselves and others. They know that to be more successful, they need to speak words that will build self-esteem and self-confidence, build relationships, and build dreams—words of affirmation, encouragement, appreciation, love, acceptance, possibility, and vision.

To speak with impeccability is to speak from your highest self. It means that you speak with intention and with integrity. It means that your words are in alignment with what you say you want to produce—your vision and your dreams.

---

51. I wish to express my gratitude to Don Miguel Ruiz, author of *The Four Agreements*, for the insights on the impeccability of the word contained in this chapter. For more information, I strongly encourage you to read his book.

YOUR WORD HAS POWER

When you speak with impeccability, your words have power not only with yourself but also with others. To speak with impeccability is to speak only words that are true, that uplift, and that affirm other people's worth.

As you learn how to speak with impeccability, you'll discover that words are also the basis of all relationships. How I speak *to you* and *about you* determines the quality of our relationship.

WHAT YOU SAY *TO OTHERS* CREATES A RIPPLE EFFECT IN THE WORLD

Let no corrupt communication proceed out of your mouth,
but that which is good to the use of edifying,
that it may minister grace unto the hearers.

EPHESIANS 4:29
(King James Version of the Bible)

Successful people speak words of inclusion rather than words of separation, words of acceptance rather than words of rejection, and words of tolerance rather than words of prejudice.

If I express love and acceptance to you, you will experience love for me. If I express judgment and contempt for you, you will judge me back. If I express gratitude and appreciation for you, you will express gratitude and appreciation back to me. If I express words of hatred toward you, you will most likely hate me back.

The truth is, your words put out a certain energy or message that creates a reaction in others—a reaction that is usually returned to you multiplied. If you are rude, impatient, arrogant, or hostile, you can expect negative conduct to be returned to you.

Everything you say produces an effect in the world. Everything you say to someone else produces an effect in that person. Know that you are constantly creating something—either positive or negative—with your words.

Always ask yourself: Is what I am about to say going to advance the cause of my vision, mission, and goals? Will it uplift the hearer? Will it inspire, motivate, and create forward momentum? Will it dissolve fear and create safety and trust? Will it build self-esteem, self-confidence, and a willingness to risk and take action?

STOP LYING

As with negative conduct, when you lie, you not only separate yourself from your higher self but you also run the risk of being found out and eroding others' trust even more.

For the *Chicken Soup for the Soul®* series, we have a policy that except for poems and stories that are clearly parables or fables, all the stories we print in *Chicken Soup* books are true. This is important to us because if the story is inspiring, we want readers to be able to say, *If they can do it, then I can do it, too.*

Occasionally, we find out that a contributor fabricated a story—simply made it up. Every time we learn that, we end up not using any more of that writer's stories. We no longer trust such writers. Their word is no longer impeccable.

In reality, lying is the product of low self-esteem—the belief that you and your abilities are somehow not enough to get what you want. It is also based on the false belief that you can't handle the consequences of people knowing the truth about you—which is simply another way of saying *I am not enough.*

When you speak ill of another to anyone else, it may temporarily bond you to that other person, but it creates a lasting impression in the other that you are the kind of person who gossips negatively about others. That other person will always be wondering—even if unconsciously—when you will turn that verbal poison against them. It will erode their sense of deep trust in you.

WHAT YOU SAY *ABOUT* OTHERS
MATTERS EVEN MORE

If we look back through history, all the world's highest and most respected beings and spiritual teachers have warned us against gossip and judgment of others. It's because they knew how damaging untruth really is. Wars have been started over words. People have been killed because of words. Deals have been lost because of words. Marriages have been destroyed because of words.

Not only that, but gossip and judgment affect you, too, because you end up releasing a poison into the river of energy that is set up to bring you that which you truly want.

Even without any words being spoken, others can pick up your negative, judgmental, and critical energy toward them. Then, what you say about others has a way of finding its way back to the person you are talking about. Many times, people who care about me will call to say that someone I know has said something negative about me. What does that do to my relationship with them? It creates a subtle crack.

Additionally, I have had to learn the hard way that when I gossip about another person, it (1) brings me down in the moment, (2) focuses my attention on what I *don't* want in my life—rather than creating more of what I *do* want, and (3) it literally wastes my breath. I've learned that I could be using my mental and verbal powers to create more of what I *do* want by focusing the power of my words on abundance instead.

To speak with more impeccability when addressing others,

- Make a commitment to be impeccable in your speech when talking to others.
- Make an effort to appreciate something about every person you interact with.
- Make a commitment to tell the truth, as best you can, in all of your interactions and dealings with others. Make a commitment to do it for 1 day, then 2 days in a row, then a whole week. If you falter, start over. Keep building that muscle.
- Make it the intention of every interaction with others that you uplift them in some small way. Notice how you feel when you do that.

Often, we use words in a damaging way not because we are bad people but simply because we are not paying attention. No one ever taught us how powerful words really are.

IDLE GOSSIP

I learned how powerful idle gossip is during my first year of teaching high school in 1968. On the first day of school, I walked into the teachers' lounge before school started. One of the older teachers approached me and said, "I see you have Devon James in your American history class. I had him last year. He is a real terror. Good luck!"

You can imagine what happened when I walked into class and saw Devon James. I was examining his every move. I was waiting for him to show signs of the terror he was promised to be. Devon didn't have a chance. He was already typecast. I already had an image of him before he ever opened his mouth. No doubt I was even sending him a sort of unconscious signal: *I know you are a troublemaker.* That is the definition of *prejudice*—prejudging a person before you ever really get a chance to know them.

I learned never to let another teacher—or anyone, for that matter—tell me what someone else was going to be like before I met the person. I learned to rely on my own observations. I also learned that if I treated all people with respect and signaled them through my speech and actions that I had high expectations for them, they almost always lived up to that positive expectation.

The biggest cost of gossiping, of course, is that it robs you of a clear mind. People who are impeccable see the world more clearly. They think more clearly and thus can be more effective in their decisions and actions. In *The Four Agreements*, Don Miguel Ruiz likens the process of gossiping to releasing a computer virus into your mind, causing it to think a little less clearly every time.

Here are some practical ways to stop yourself and discourage others from gossiping:

1. Change the subject.
2. Say something positive about the other person.
3. Walk away from the conversation.
4. Keep quiet.
5. Clearly state that you no longer want to participate in gossiping about others.

CHECK YOUR THOUGHTS
AND YOUR FEELINGS

How do you know when you have been impeccable with your word? When you feel good, happy, joyful, calm, and at peace. If you're not feeling these things, check your thoughts, your self-talk, and your verbal and written communication with others.

When you begin to be more impeccable with your word, you will begin to see changes happening in all areas of your life.

WHEN IN DOUBT,
CHECK IT OUT

There may be some substitute for hard facts, but if there is,
I have no idea what it can be.

J. PAUL GETTY
Author of *How to Be Rich*

Too many people waste valuable time and precious resources wondering what other people are thinking, intending, or doing. Rather than just asking them for clarification, they make assumptions—usually assuming against themselves—and then make decisions based on those assumptions.

Successful people, on the other hand, don't waste time assuming or wondering. They simply check it out: "I'm wondering if . . ." or "Would it be okay to . . . ?" or "Are you feeling . . . ?" They are not afraid of rejection, so they ask.

PEOPLE ALWAYS IMAGINE THE WORST WHEN THEY DON'T KNOW WHAT IS TRUE

What's the fundamental problem with assuming anything? It's that people are usually the most afraid of that which they don't know. Instead of checking into things, they assume facts that may not exist, then build prejudices around those assumptions. They make bad decisions based on these assumptions, on rumors, or on other peoples' opinions.

Consider the difference when you know all the facts—the *actual* facts— about a situation, person, problem, or opportunity. Then you can make decisions and take actions on the basis of what is real rather than what you are making up.

I remember a seminar I once conducted where one attendee—sitting in the back of the room—looked like he just didn't want to be there. He looked hostile and withdrawn. He had his arms crossed over his chest. He had what looked like a permanent scowl on his face and looked like he hated every-thing I had to say. I knew if I wasn't careful, I'd end up focusing on him and his apparent hostility, to the detriment of everyone else in the room.

As you can imagine, no speaker wants to hear that an audience member was forced to come to the seminar by his boss or that he is unhappy with the material or—even worse—that he dislikes the speaker himself. Given this participant's body language, it would have been easy to assume one of these things to be the case.

Instead, I checked it out.

I approached him during the first break and said, "I can't help but notice you don't look like you're in a really good space. I was wondering if maybe the workshop's not working for you. Or maybe you were sent here by your boss against your will and you really don't want to be here. I'm just really concerned."

At that point, his entire demeanor shifted. He said, "Oh no. I'm loving everything you're saying. But I feel like I'm coming down with the flu. I didn't want to stay home and miss this, because I knew how good it would be. It's taking every ounce of my concentration just to be here, but it's worth it because I'm getting so much out of it."

Wow. If I hadn't asked, I could have ruined my whole day assuming the worst.

How many times do *you* make assumptions—good or bad—without checking them out?

Do you assume without checking when a special project is due that all parties will deliver on time? Do you assume without checking that what you're providing is what everybody needs? Do you assume without checking at the end of a meeting that everyone is clear on who is responsible for getting which action items done by which date?

Imagine how much easier it would be to *not* assume—and instead say, "John, you're going to complete the report by next Friday. Right? And Mary, you're going to get a quote from the printer by Tuesday at five. Right?"

WE USUALLY HESITATE THE MOST WHEN IT MIGHT BE BAD NEWS

It's usually when we assume the worst that we don't want to check it out. We're simply afraid of what the answer might be. If I arrive home from work and my wife has a scowl on her face, it's easy to assume that she's mad at me. And though I could start walking around on tiptoes, thinking I've done something wrong and anticipating a blowup, imagine how much better it would be for our relationship if I simply said, "You don't look happy. What's going on?"

The moment you begin to check it out, two things happen.

First, you find out the real facts. Did you really do something wrong—or did she just get a nasty phone call from her sister that you don't know about? Second, you have the option to do something about it—to help her shift her mood—if you know what is really going on.

This goes the same for things that might improve your quality of life. Perhaps you assume there's no way to get a ticket to the rock concert at this late date or that you'll never be accepted into that arts program or that you can't afford that antique buffet that would look great in the dining room.

It's so much simpler just to ask. Check it out, using phrases such as *"I'm wondering if . . ."* and *"Would it be okay if . . ."* and *"Are you feeling . . ."* and *"Is there a possibility of getting . . ."* and *"What do I have to do in order to . . ."* and *"What would have to happen for you to be able to . . . "* and so on.

DO YOU MEAN . . . ?

Another way to check out assumptions is to use a technique I teach in my couples training sessions that can help improve communication in your relationships.

I call it the "Do You Mean" technique.

Let's say that my wife asks me to help her clean out the garage on Saturday. "No," I say.

Now, my wife could instantly assume, *Jack's mad at me. He doesn't care about my needs. He doesn't care that my car no longer fits in the garage*, and so on. But with the "Do You Mean" technique, she assumes nothing but *asks* what I'm really thinking instead.

"Jack, do you mean that you're not ever going to help me with this task, that you want me to do it all myself?"

"No, I don't mean that."

"Do you mean that you would rather be doing something else?"

"No, I don't mean that either."

"Do you mean that you're busy Saturday and you have something else planned that I don't know about?"

"Yes, that's exactly what I mean. I'm sorry I hadn't told you yet. It slipped my mind."

Sometimes, people don't immediately tell the reasons behind their answers. They just say no, with no explanation for their position. Men are more likely to respond like this. Whereas women will often give you all kinds of reasons why their answer is no, men more often will just give you the bottom line, not the details. Asking "Do you mean . . . ?" will get you a lot more clarity, so that you aren't left wondering what is really going on.

CHECKING IT OUT CONTRIBUTES
TO YOUR SUCCESS

Checking out your assumptions improves your communication, your relationships, your quality of life, and most especially your success and productivity in the workplace. You start getting better results. You don't show up with parts missing. You don't make assumptions about what people were going to do that they didn't do. Whenever you have the inkling that Barbara's not going to finish that on time, you call Barbara. You check it out.

W. Edwards Deming, the brilliant systems expert who helped post–World War II Japan manufacture automobiles, electronics, and other goods better than almost any other country on the planet, once said the first 15% of any project is the most important. This is where you need to get clear, gather data, check things out.

For example, when you get into a business relationship, you determine in the beginning—in the first 15%—how you'll work together, how you'll resolve conflicts, what the exit strategy is if someone wants to leave, what the criteria are for determining if one of the people is not living up to his or her side of the bargain, and so on. Most of the conflicts that arise later in relationships are because people made erroneous assumptions without checking them out. They failed to get clear up front. They failed to get clear on their agreements.

Deming also said that at the beginning of any project, too many people rush in without the facts—without even knowing how to measure success. How will you know when you've won? Are you building a business to simply make money, to accomplish some social goal, to eventually sell the business and cash out for a huge profit and an early retirement, to use it as a political platform, to solve a certain problem in the world? What is your purpose? What are your core values? What is your exit strategy?

SPACE BETWEEN THE RULES

Of course, the 15% rule also applies to any personal goal you might pursue as well. Remember Tim Ferriss, the kickboxer who won the national championship with just 6 weeks of training? The story behind that story is that he didn't assume *anything* about the rules of kickboxing but instead checked them out thoroughly. He learned from his research that if you threw your opponent out of the ring twice in one round, you won the match.

Now, in kickboxing, most people think of kicking and boxing. Ferriss, on the other hand, was a wrestler by training. So he told his coach, "Don't teach me how to knock someone out. Teach me how to throw my opponent out of the ring while not getting knocked out myself." That's how he won the championship. He determined the difference between what the rules *actually* were and what people *assumed* the rules were.

In life, there are a lot of instances where there is space to maneuver between the rules. If you don't ask and simply assume you can't accomplish something, it may be that you *could* have easily succeeded through some loophole or other hidden fact that is revealed only when you research it— when you *check it out*.

53

PRACTICE UNCOMMON
APPRECIATION

*There is more hunger for love and appreciation
in this world than for bread.*

MOTHER TERESA
Winner of the Nobel Peace Prize

*I have yet to find a man, however exalted his station,
who did not do better work and put forth greater effort
under a spirit of approval than under a spirit of criticism.*

CHARLES SCHWAB
Founder of Charles Schwab & Co., a financial services empire

A recent management study revealed that 46% of employees leaving a company do so because they feel unappreciated; 61% said their bosses don't place much importance on them as people, and 88% said they do not receive acknowledgment for the work they do.

An example of how powerful appreciation can be and what a difference it can make is illustrated in the e-mail below. On the tenth anniversary of *Chicken Soup for the Soul®*, our publisher, Health Communications, Inc., held a party and featured a slide show of the most memorable highlights from the past decade. Randee Zeitlin Feldman at HCI created the slide show, and I sent her flowers to appreciate her for the superb job she had done. Here's the e-mail I received in return. The subject line read "I have never felt so appreciated."

Hi, Jack,

Thank you so much for the beautiful flowers I received today. I was so touched and couldn't believe this amazing bouquet was for me. It has been such a privilege and an honor to work with you for the last 8 years.

I think it's wonderful that I have been a part (however small) of one of the most successful book series ever. It has been so much fun over the years and I have really enjoyed every minute of it. I feel lucky and blessed and I want to thank you again for thinking of me.

The flowers have made quite a hit with everyone who has walked by my office. Most people want to know exactly what I had to do for such beautiful flowers . . . I tell them it was all about love!

Thanks again.

Love,
Randee

I've never known anyone to complain about receiving too much positive feedback. Have you? In fact, just the opposite is true.

Whether you are an entrepreneur, manager, teacher, parent, coach, or simply a friend, if you want to be successful with other people, you must master the art of appreciation.

Consider this: Every year, a management consulting firm conducts a survey with 200 companies on the subject of what motivates employees. When given a list of 10 possible things that would most motivate them, the employees always list *appreciation* as the number-one motivator. When asked to rank-order that same list, the managers and supervisors ranked *appreciation* number eight. This is a major mismatch, as the chart below so clearly shows.

---

10 WAYS TO REALLY MOTIVATE AN EMPLOYEE

Employees	Supervisors
Appreciation	Good wages
Feeling "in" on things	Job security
Understanding attitude	Promotion opportunities
Job security	Good working conditions
Good wages	Interesting work
Interesting work	Loyalty from management
Promotion opportunities	Tactful discipline
Loyalty from management	*Appreciation*
Good working conditions	Understanding attitude
Tactful discipline	Feeling "in" on things

It's interesting to also note that the top three motivators from an employee's perspective—appreciation, feeling "in" on things, and an understanding attitude—do not cost anything in terms of money, just a few moments of time, respect, and understanding.

THREE KINDS OF APPRECIATION

It's valuable to make a distinction between three different kinds of appreciation—auditory, visual, and kinesthetic. These are the three different ways that the brain takes in information, and everybody has a dominant type they prefer.

Auditory people need to hear it, visual people need to see it, and kinesthetic people need to feel it. If you give visual feedback to an auditory person, it doesn't have the same effect. The person might say, "He sends me letters and cards and e-mails, but he never takes the time to walk over and tell me to my face."

Visual people, on the other hand, like to receive something they can see, perhaps even hang on their refrigerator. They love letters, cards, flowers, plaques, certificates, pictures—gifts of any kind. They can see it and keep the memory of it around forever. We can tell who these people are by their bulletin boards, refrigerators, and walls. They are covered with reminders that they are loved and appreciated.

Kinesthetic people need to feel it—a hug, a handshake, a pat on the back, or actually doing something with them, such as the gift of a massage, taking them out to lunch or dinner, taking them to a baseball game, going for a walk, or going out dancing.

If you want to be a real pro at appreciation, you want to learn which kind of feedback makes the most impact on the person you are delivering it to. One easy way is to ask the person to remember the time they felt most loved in their life. Then ask them to describe it to you. You can ask some follow-up questions such as "Was it something they said, something they did, the way they touched you? Was it the look in their eyes (visual), the tone of their voice (auditory), the tenderness of their touch, or the way they held you as you were dancing (kinesthetic)?" Once you determine if the person is primarily auditory, visual, or kinesthetic, then you can purposely direct your feedback that way.

I know that my wife, Inga, is primarily a kinesthetic person. She majored in physical education, was a massage therapist, personal trainer, and yoga teacher for many years. She loves to go hiking, horseback riding, running on the beach, swimming, body surfing, and dancing. She loves to take long baths, get massages, and practice yoga. These things make her *feel* good. When she picks her clothes, how they feel to the touch is more important to her than how they look.

The best way to express appreciation to my wife is with a hug, a kiss, or a foot massage. She feels most loved when I go for a walk with her. If I am going to give her verbal feedback, she wants me to sit down opposite her, look her in the eye, and *hold her hands*. Just lying in bed holding hands is enough to make her feel loved and appreciated. If I go off on a long-winded appreciation of her, she will usually interrupt me at some point with "Blah, blah, blah; just hold my hand."

On the other hand, Patty Aubery, the president of my company, is auditory. She loves to talk on the phone, listen to the radio, or enjoy the peace and quiet of an empty house. She is really sensitive to the tone of my voice. She loves it when I speak in a caring and compassionate tone of voice. A brief phone call to say thank you works wonders with Patty.

I am visual. I love to receive presents, cards, letters, and e-mails from people whose lives I have touched. I have a wall full of plaques, pictures, book covers, cartoons about *Chicken Soup for the Soul®*, magazine covers that feature our books, and my children's art. I love things to be aesthetic, neat, and orderly—pleasing to the eye. I pick my clothes by how they look. I have two banker's boxes full of letters and newspaper clippings. I call them my Warm Fuzzy Boxes. Just taking out the items and looking at them can get me into a very elevated mood.

Bringing me a simple gift that says "Thank you; I appreciate you" goes a long way with me. My wife will bring me a single rose in a bud vase in the morning and put it on my desk, and I can look at it all day and know that she loves me. My *Chicken Soup* coauthor, Mark Victor Hansen, recently brought me back a small statue from one of his trips to Asia. He said, "I thought of you when I saw it and I wanted you to have it." Every time I look at it, I feel acknowledged, appreciated, and cared about.

THE PERFECT COMBINATION

When in doubt, use all three types of communication—auditory, visual, and kinesthetic. Tell them, show them, and give them a pat on the back. You can take a person's hands in yours, look them directly in the eyes, and in a sincere and expressive way tell them that you appreciate them and their efforts. Then give the person a card or a gift to keep as a reminder. Or you can put your arm around your son or daughter as you walk down the beach together, telling your child how much you appreciate him or her, and then follow up later with a card. You are sure to make your point.

HANG IN THERE UNTIL YOU GET IT RIGHT

I once took a couples workshop with Dr. Harville Hendricks, the coauthor of *Getting the Love You Want: A Guide for Couples*, in which he told the story about learning exactly how his wife wanted to be told she was loved and appreciated. Because she always gave other people flowers as gifts of appreciation, he figured that that was what she would also want. So one day he sent her a dozen roses. When he came home from work, he was expecting to get what he called his reward—a big, gracious thank-you from his wife.

When he walked in, she didn't even mention it. When he asked her if she had received the roses, she said yes. "Didn't you like them?" he asked.

"Not particularly."

"I don't understand. You always give other people flowers. I thought you loved flowers."

"Not really that much."

"Well, what do you like to get?"

"Cards," she replied.

Okay, he thought. So the next day he went to the card store and bought her a huge, oversize Snoopy card with a funny inscription inside and placed it where she would find it during the day. That night when he came home, he was once again expecting his reward.

No reward. He was so disappointed. He asked, "Did you find the card?"

"Yes."

"Didn't you like it?"

"Not really."

"Well, why not? I thought you liked to get cards."

"I do, but not funny cards. I like the kind of cards that you get at the art museums that have a piece of beautiful art on the front and then a really sweet and romantic message on the inside."

Okay.

The next day he went to the Metropolitan Museum of Art and bought a beautiful card and wrote a sweet, romantic inscription on the inside. The next day he placed it where his wife would find it. When he returned home, she met him at the door and smothered him with kisses and appreciation for the perfect card.

Out of his commitment to make sure that she knew he loved her, he finally found the perfect medium for his message.

WHO CARES?

If asked, could you name the five wealthiest people in the world or five people who have won the Nobel Prize or the last five Academy Award winners for best actor and actress? The point is, none of us remembers the headliners of yesterday. When the applause dies, the awards tarnish, and achievements are forgotten, no one cares about who won which award.

But if I asked you to list five teachers or mentors who believed in you and encouraged you, five friends who have helped you through a difficult time, five people who have taught you something worthwhile, or five people who have made you feel appreciated and special—that's much easier to do, isn't it? That's because the people who make a difference in your life aren't the ones with the most credentials, the most money, or the most awards. *They're the ones who care.* If you want to be remembered for being important to someone else's life, make them feel appreciated.

APPRECIATION AS A SECRET OF SUCCESS

Another important reason for being in a state of appreciation as often as possible is that when you are in such a state, you are in one of the highest vibrational (emotional) states possible. When you are in a state of appreciation and gratitude, you are in a state of abundance. You are appreciating what you do have instead of focusing on and complaining about what you don't have. Your focus is on what you have received, and you always get more of what you focus on. And because the law of attraction states that like attracts like, you will attract more abundance—more to be thankful for—to you. (The more you are in a state of gratitude, the more you will attract to be grateful for.) It becomes an upward-spiraling process of ever-increasing abundance that just keeps getting better and better.

Think about it. The more grateful people are for the gifts we give them, the more inclined we are to give them more gifts. Their gratitude and appreciation reinforces our giving. The same principle holds as true on a universal and spiritual level as it does on an interpersonal level.

KEEPING SCORE

When I first learned about the power of appreciation, it made total sense to me. However, it was still something that I forgot to do. I hadn't yet turned it into a habit. A valuable technique that I employed to help me lock in this new habit was to carry a 3" × 5" card in my pocket all day, and every time I acknowledged and appreciated someone, I would place a check mark on the card. I would not allow myself to go to bed until I had appreciated 10 people. If it was late in the evening and I didn't have 10 check marks, I would appreciate my wife and children, I would send an e-mail to several staff people, or I would write a letter to my mother or stepfather. I did whatever it took until it became an unconscious habit. I did this every single day for 6 months—until I no longer needed to carry the card to remind me.

TAKE TIME TO APPRECIATE YOURSELF, TOO

David Casstevens, formerly of the *Dallas Morning News*, tells a story about Frank Szymanski, a Notre Dame center in the 1940s, who had been called in as a witness in a civil suit in South Bend, Indiana.

"Are you on the Notre Dame football team this year?" the judge asked.

"Yes, Your Honor."

"What position?"

"Center, Your Honor."

"How good a center?"

Szymanski squirmed in his seat, but said firmly: "Sir, I'm the best center Notre Dame has ever had."

Coach Frank Leahy, who was in the courtroom, was surprised. Szymanski had always been modest and unassuming. So when the proceedings were over, he took Szymanski aside and asked why he had made such a statement. Szymanski blushed.

"I hated to do it, Coach," he said. "But, after all, I was under oath."

I want you to be under oath for the rest of your life and own the magnificent being you are, the positive qualities you have, and the wonderful accomplishments you have achieved.

PRINCIPLE

54

KEEP YOUR AGREEMENTS

Your life works to the degree you keep your agreements.

WERNER ERHARD
Founder of the est Training and Landmark Forum

Never promise more than you can perform.

PUBLILIUS SYRUS

It used to be that one's word was one's bond. Agreements were made and kept with a minimum of fanfare. People thought carefully about whether they could deliver on their promises before agreeing to anything. It was that important. Today, keeping one's agreements seems to be a hit-or-miss affair.

THE HIGH COST OF NOT KEEPING
YOUR AGREEMENTS

In my seminars, I ask participants to agree to a list of 15 ground rules that include things like being on time, sitting in a different chair after every break, and no alcoholic beverages until after the training is over. If they will not agree to play by the ground rules, I do not allow them to take the training. I even have them sign a form in their workbook that says, "I agree to keep all these guidelines and ground rules."

On the morning of the third day, I ask everyone who has broken one of the ground rules to stand up. We then look at what we can learn from the experience. What becomes apparent is how casually we give our word—and then how casually we break it.

But what's even more interesting is that most people know they are going to break at least one of the guidelines *before agreeing to them*. And yet they agree to them anyway. Why? Most people want to avoid the discomfort of questioning the rules. They don't want to be the focus of attention. They don't want to risk confrontation of any kind. Others want to take the training without really following the rules, so they appear to agree, but they don't really intend to follow through.

The real problem is not that people give and break their word so easily; it's that they don't realize the psychological cost of doing so.

When you don't keep your agreements, you pay both external and internal costs. You lose trust, respect, and credibility with others—your family, your friends, your colleagues, and your customers. And you create messes in your own life and in the lives of those who depend on you for getting things done—whether it's showing up on time to leave for the movies, getting a report done on time, or cleaning the garage.

After a few weeks of not following through on your promise to take the kids to the park on the weekend, they begin not to trust you to keep your word. They realize they can't count on you. You lose authority with them. Your relationship deteriorates.

EVERY AGREEMENT YOU MAKE IS WITH YOURSELF

More importantly, every agreement you make is ultimately with yourself. Even when you are making an agreement with someone else, your brain hears it and registers it as a commitment. You are making an agreement with yourself to do something, and when you don't follow through, you learn to distrust yourself. The result is a loss of self-esteem, self-confidence, and self-respect. You lose faith in your ability to produce a result. You weaken your sense of integrity.

Let's say that you tell your spouse you're going to get up at 6:30 in the morning and do some exercise before going to work. But after 3 days of hitting the snooze alarm, your brain knows better than to trust you. Of course, *you* may think sleeping late is no big deal, but to your unconscious it is a very big deal. When you don't do what you say you will, you create confusion and self-doubt. You undermine your sense of personal power. It's not worth it.

YOUR INTEGRITY AND SELF-ESTEEM ARE WORTH MORE THAN A MILLION DOLLARS

When you realize how important your integrity and self-esteem really are, you will stop making casual agreements just to get someone off your back. You won't sell your self-esteem for a little bit of momentary approval. You won't make agreements you don't intend to keep. You will make fewer agreements, and you will do whatever it takes to keep them.

To illustrate this in my seminars, I ask attendees, "If you knew you would get a million dollars if you made it to the end of the seminar without breaking one ground rule, could you have done it?" Most agree that they could.

Often there is still one holdout who says, "No way. I just couldn't do it. I'm not responsible for the traffic jam I encountered on the way to the seminar this morning." Or "How am I supposed to be on time when my ride was late picking me up?"

I then ask, "What if the person whom you love most in the world would have to die if you didn't keep all the ground rules for the training? Would you have done anything differently then?"

Now the person who says the traffic made them late finally gets it and acknowledges, "Oh, yes. If my son's life were at stake, I wouldn't even have left this room. I would have slept on the floor in the conference room rather than take the risk of being late."

Once you realize how important keeping your word is, you realize you have the ability to do it. It's simply a matter of realizing what you are giving up. The personal power that you get from keeping your agreements is worth a whole lot more than a million dollars. If you want more self-esteem, self-confidence, self-respect, personal power, mental clarity, and energy, then you'll make keeping your word more important. If you want to have the respect and trust of others, which is critical to accomplishing anything big and important in life (including making a million dollars), then you will take keeping your agreements more seriously.

SOME TIPS ON MAKING AND KEEPING AGREEMENTS

Here are some tips for making fewer agreements and for keeping the ones you make.

1. **Make only agreements that you intend to keep.** Take a few seconds before making an agreement to see if it is really what you *want* to do. Check in with yourself. How does your body feel about it? Don't make an agreement just because you are looking for someone's approval. If you do, you'll find yourself breaking these commitments.

2. **Write down all the agreements you make.** Use a calendar, daily planning book, notebook, or computer to record all of your agreements. In the course of a week, you might enter into dozens of agreements. One of the big reasons we don't keep our agreements is that with the daily press of all of our activities, we forget many of the agreements that we have made. Write them down, and

then review your list every day. As I have stated before, a new finding from brain research is that when we don't write something down or make some effort to store it in long-term memory, the memory can be lost in as little as 37 seconds. You may have great intentions, but if you forget to do what you agreed to do, the result is the same as your *choosing* not to keep your agreements.

3. **Communicate any broken agreement at the first appropriate time.** As soon as you know you are going to have a broken agreement—your car won't start, you are caught in traffic, your child is sick, your babysitter can't make it, your computer crashes—notify the other person as soon as possible, and then renegotiate the agreement. This demonstrates respect for others' time and their needs. It also gives them time to reschedule, replan, make other arrangements, and limit any potential damage. If the first appropriate time is after the fact, still let them know that you have a broken agreement, clean up any consequences, and decide whether to recommit to the agreement.

4. **Learn to say no more often.** Give yourself time to think it over before making any new agreements. I write the word *no* in yellow highlighter on all my calendar pages as a way to remind myself to really consider what else I'll have to give up if I say yes to something new. It makes me pause and think before I add another commitment to my life.

THE RULES OF THE GAME

One of the most powerful trainings I ever took was one called "Money and You," created by Marshall Thurber in the late 1970s. It radically changed how I related to money, business, and relationships.

Everything that you want to accomplish requires relationships—with your friends, family, staff, vendors, coaches, bosses, board of directors, clients, customers, partners, associates, students, teachers, audience, fans, and others. For those relationships to work, you need to set up what my friend John Assaraf calls "the rules of engagement," what Marshall Thurber, D.C. Cordova, and the other folks at Excellerated Business Schools call "the rules of the game."

How are we going to play together? What are the ground rules and guidelines for the relationship going to be? Marshall taught us the following guidelines, which I have endeavored to live by ever since. If you and all the people you interacted with were to agree to the following rules, your level of success would soar.

1. Be willing to support our purpose, values, rules, and goals.
2. Speak with good purpose. If it doesn't serve, don't say it. No making people wrong, justifying, or defending.
3. If you disagree or do not understand, ask clarifying questions. Don't make the other person wrong.
4. Make only agreements you are willing and intend to keep.
5. If you can't keep an agreement, communicate as soon as practical to the appropriate person. Clear up any broken agreement at the first appropriate opportunity.
6. When something is not working, first look to the system for corrections and then propose a system-based solution to the person who can do something about it.
7. Be responsible. No blaming, no defending, no justifying, and no shaming.

UPPING THE ANTE

If you want to really take it to the max in terms of keeping your commitments to yourself, you can use this technique that my friend Martin Rutte taught me. Set up consequences (such as writing a large check to a person or an organization that you don't like or shaving off all of your hair) that are greater than the payoffs (such as the comfort and the safety of not having to take a risk) you get for not keeping your word. The cost of having to deliver on the consequences is too expensive not to follow through on the commitment.

Martin used this technique to motivate himself to follow through on his commitment to learn how to dive off a diving board. To make sure that he wouldn't back out of his commitment, he declared to his friends that if he didn't learn to dive by a certain date, he would write a check for $1,000 to the Ku Klux Klan. Being Jewish, Martin was not a big fan of the Klan. Obviously, he didn't want to write that check. That would have been more painful than confronting his fear of diving. So as challenging as it was for him, Martin learned how to dive.

What is so important in your life that you don't want to give yourself an out? Make a public declaration of a consequence that you would find painful to pay, and you'll use the power of motivating yourself to take the action that you say you want to take but that you have been procrastinating.

BE A CLASS ACT

*In every society, there are "human benchmarks"—certain
individuals whose behavior becomes a model for everyone else—
shining examples that others admire and emulate.
We call these individuals "class acts."*

DAN SULLIVAN
Cofounder and president of The Strategic Coach, Inc.

I've already mentioned my friend and colleague Dan Sullivan, the creator of
"The Strategic Coach Program." One of the groups he coaches is for high-
achievers earning over $1 million a year. Though I routinely earn many times
that, I still seek out coaches of Dan's caliber to help me fine-tune my success
skills, so I joined Dan's coaching group in Chicago.

While I was in the program Dan taught me a success principle that works
for so many of the superachievers I've met and studied that I'm surprised I didn't
recognize it earlier as an important discipline we should all come to master.

Simply stated, it's "Be a class act."

That's it. Strive to become the kind of person who acts with class, who
becomes known as a class act, and who attracts other people with class to his
or her sphere of influence.

The sad truth in society today is that there don't seem to be as many class
acts around as there used to be. I think everyone would agree that actor
Jimmy Stewart was a class act. Tom Hanks is a class act. So are Paul Newman
and Denzel Washington. Coretta Scott King and former president of South
Africa Nelson Mandela are both class acts. Herb Kelleher, president of
Southwest Airlines, is a class act.

But how can you differentiate yourself as a class act in a world where
most people are unconscious and "unspecial"? The answer is that you have to
consciously work to become free from the many fears, worries, and anxieties
that diminish the imaginations and ambitions of the vast majority of people

and operate outside the world of conventionality in a world of expanding awareness, creativity, and accomplishment. But to do this, you need a model of class act behavior to guide your own thinking and behavior. Dan has identified the following characteristics of a class act to serve as your guide[52]:

- **Live by your own highest standards.** Class acts liberate themselves by establishing personal standards of thinking and behavior that are more demanding and exacting than those of conventional society. They are consciously *chosen*, established, and applied.
- **Maintain dignity and grace under pressure.** There are three aspects of this characteristic. The first is imperturbability in the face of chaos. Because you are used to leading yourself by living by your own highest standards, you are able to lead others as well. The second is a calmness that gives courage. Your calmness gives others hope that things will turn out all right. The third is a quality of certainty. The greatest twentieth-century example of this characteristic of a class act was Winston Churchill, who in World War II almost single-handedly saved Western civilization from defeat at the hands of Nazi Germany, by his ability to stay calm and provide confident and courageous leadership that focused the resolve of both the British and the Americans.
- **Focus and improve the behavior of others.** Because a class act individual is a good role model, other people around them begin thinking and acting at a level that surprises both themselves and others. Someone who best exemplifies this third characteristic of a class act is Larry Bird, the great all-star, Hall of Fame basketball player who played on three championship teams with the Boston Celtics. To a person, the other players on those teams have said they were able to play at such a high level only because of Larry Bird's example and leadership.
- **Operate from a larger, inclusive perspective.** Because class acts are in touch with their own humanity, they have a deeper understanding and compassion for the humanity of others. They feel inextricably linked to others, are compassionate about human failures, and are courteous in the midst of conflict.
- **Increase the quality of every experience.** Class act individuals have the ability to transform seemingly insignificant situations into something enjoyable, meaningful, and memorable because of their

---

52. For a brilliant presentation of Dan's Class Act Model, purchase "The Class Acts Model" (module 3 of the "Always Increase Your Confidence" series) by going to www.strategiccoach.com. It is a valuable resource that I highly encourage you to get and work with. If you fully embrace the characteristics of a class act, you will be light-years ahead of 99% of the rest of the world in terms of creating success and making a difference in the world.

conscious thinking and actions. They are creators rather than merely consumers, and they constantly enrich the lives of others by introducing greater beauty, significance, uniqueness, and stimulation into every experience. How you are treated at a Four Seasons Hotel is a good example of this characteristic.

- **Counteract meanness, pettiness, and vulgarity.** The hallmarks of this characteristic are courtesy, respect, appreciation, gratitude, and generosity of spirit. One of my favorite examples of this characteristic of a class act is Pat Riley, the former coach of the Los Angeles Lakers and the New York Knicks and current coach of the Miami Heat. What makes him a class act in my mind is his grace in the face of loss off the court. When Pat was coaching the Miami Heat in the NBA playoffs against the New York Knicks, he invited the entire opposing team and its coach to his home for a barbeque and personally spoke to each player, congratulating all for a great season and wishing them the best. Though Pat could have been competitive and aggressive, he acted instead in a way that elevated and acknowledged others. That's a class act.

- **Take responsibility for actions and results.** Class act individuals are accountable when others hide; they tell the truth about their failures; and they transform defeats into progress.

- **Strengthen the integrity of all situations.** Class act individuals are always establishing and achieving larger goals that require them to constantly grow and develop as well as add increasing value to the world.

- **Expand the meaning of being human.** Class act individuals approach everyone, including themselves, uniquely, and as a result constantly find new ways to make life better for themselves and others. In pushing boundaries for themselves, they do the same for others by giving them new freedom to express their uniqueness in the world.

- **Increase the confidence and capabilities of others.** Class acts are energy creators rather than energy drainers. Class acts build confidence in themselves by consciously choosing their governing ideas and ideals and creating structures that support the fulfillment of their aspirations and capabilities. These new structures also support others in their full expression by creating environments that encourage greater creativity, cooperation, progress, and growth.

In giving me the above list, Dan has taught me a lot about what it truly means to be a class act. But more importantly, he's taught me the benefits of being recognized as a class act by others.

HOW TO BECOME KNOWN AS A CLASS ACT

When people mention the great former UCLA basketball coach John Wooden, they agree that he's a class act. John has become known as a class act because, frankly, he acts like one. He takes time to acknowledge others, and he conducts himself with an eye toward improving and expanding the world. He says to people, "You're special. You count."

One of the hardest parts of any coach's job is making the final cut—deciding who makes the team and who doesn't. Most coaches just put up a list of who made the team on a bulletin board in the gym. You either made it or you didn't. Manifesting his deep respect and love for all people, Wooden did it differently. Instead of simply posting a list of names on the wall, Coach Wooden sat down with each player, one at a time, and told them what other sports at UCLA he felt they could be successful at. He shared what he saw as their strengths, discussed their weaknesses, and—on the basis of their strengths—identified what they could do to improve their athletic careers. He took the time to acknowledge their strengths and boost their self-esteem, leaving prospective athletes motivated and encouraged rather than feeling emotionally devastated.

Simply choose to live by a higher set of standards, and watch people respond enthusiastically toward you. Soon, you'll notice the effect that it evokes: "Wow, that's someone I want to be friends with, be in business with, and be connected with."

WHY BEING A CLASS ACT HELPS YOU SUCCEED

In fact, that's one of the major benefits of being a class act: People want to do business with you or become involved in your sphere of influence. They perceive you as successful and someone who can expand their possibilities. They trust you to act with responsibility, integrity, and aplomb.

Perhaps that's why the easiest way to spot class acts is by looking at the people class acts attract. Look at the people they do business with, the people they socialize with. Class acts tend to attract people who are at the top of their game.

Have you taken a good look lately at your friends, your colleagues, your partners, clients, and contacts? Are they class acts? If not, consider that disparity as a mirror reflecting your status back to you. Make the decision now to re-create yourself as a class act, and see what kind of people you start attracting. Do fewer things, but do them better. Raise the quality of your attitude and change your behaviors for the better.

At my office, for example, we noticed we were using paper cups when we could easily have chosen to use crystal glassware, thereby supporting the environment by not using up as many trees and by reducing unnecessary landfill. Plus, we would be improving our office environment and sending a message to our staff, clients, and guests that we think highly of them.

Similarly, my wife and I used to throw several parties a year that frankly weren't all that great. Now, we throw one big party every year or so, but we create it as an event that nobody can forget. People enjoy gourmet food in an elegant setting with an array of interesting and important guests and entertainment. Everyone feels privileged, esteemed, nurtured, and loved. It's important to me to treat my guests with high regard and value.

This is not to say that we never have a pizza and beer out by the pool with our closest friends and family, but when it comes to business and our larger social network, we continually strive to be class acts.

CLASS ACTS TEACH OTHERS TO TREAT THEM WITH ESTEEM

Of course, one of the first people you should treat with respect and esteem is yourself. My friend Martin Rutte is a class act. He always dresses well, eats well, and conducts himself at all times with refinement and style. In addition, he treats everyone around him with love, dignity, and respect. Consequently and by example, he's taught everyone around him to also treat him well—simply because he treats himself and others with such thoughtfulness and care.

If you're sloppy, always late, and don't care how you conduct yourself, you're going to be met with people who treat you in a sloppy, always-late, don't-care manner.

When I know Martin's coming over, what's my first reaction? I make sure we have a good bottle of wine, a nice piece of fresh fish, some simple but exceptional vegetables, and fresh raspberries for dessert (even if they're out of season and we have to buy the expensive imported ones from New Zealand), because that's how Martin has "trained" me to treat him.

If a head of state, the pope, or the Dalai Lama were coming to visit your home, wouldn't you have the house-cleaners in there for a week? Wouldn't you buy the best food? Well, why don't you do that for yourself? You're just as important!

The bottom line is that certain people command a certain level of respect not only because of how they treat others but, more importantly, because of how they treat themselves. When you establish a higher level of personal standards, not only do you get better treatment from those around you but suddenly you also begin attracting others with the same elevated standards. You get invited to places where those standards exist. You get to enjoy the activities that people in the upper echelons enjoy. All by becoming a class act.

PART FIVE

Success
and Money

There is a science of getting rich, and it is an exact science, like algebra or arithmetic. There are certain laws which govern the process of acquiring riches, and once these laws are learned and obeyed by anyone, that person will get rich with mathematical certainty.

WALLACE D. WATTLES
Author of *The Science of Getting Rich*

DEVELOP A POSITIVE
MONEY CONSCIOUSNESS

*There is a secret psychology to money. Most people don't know
about it. That's why most people never become financially
successful. A lack of money is not the problem; it is merely
a symptom of what's going on inside you.*

T. HARV EKER
Multimillionaire and president of Peak Potentials Training

Like everything else I've discussed in this book, financial success also starts in
the mind. You have to first decide what you want. Next, you have to believe it's
possible and that you deserve it. Then you must focus on it by thinking about it
and visualizing it as if it were already yours. And finally, you have to be willing
to pay the price to get it—with disciplined effort and perseverance over time.

But most people never get to even the first stages of accumulating wealth.
Too often, they are limited by their own beliefs about money and by the
question of whether or not they deserve it.

IDENTIFY YOUR LIMITING BELIEFS ABOUT MONEY

To become wealthy, you'll need to surface, identify, root out, and replace any
negative or limiting beliefs you may have about money. Though it may seem
odd that anyone would have a negative predisposition toward wealth, often
we hold these beliefs in our subconscious from childhood. Perhaps when you
were young, you heard:

Money doesn't grow on trees.
There's not enough money to go around.
You have to have money to make money.

Money is the root of all evil.
People with money are evil, bad, and unethical.
People with a lot of money are selfish and self-centered.
Everyone can't be a millionaire.
You can't buy happiness.
Rich people only care about money.
If you are rich, you can't be spiritual.

These messages from early childhood can actually sabotage and dilute your later financial success, because they subconsciously emit a vibration that's contrary to your conscious intentions.

What did your parents, grandparents, teachers, religious leaders, friends, and coworkers teach you about money as you were growing up and as a young adult?

My father taught me that rich people got rich by exploiting the working classes. He constantly told me he wasn't made of money, that money didn't grow on trees, and that money was hard to come by. One Christmas my father decided to sell Christmas trees. He rented a lot, worked hard every night from Thanksgiving to Christmas Eve, and just broke even after a month of hard labor. As a family, we were left with the belief that no matter how hard you work, you never get ahead.

Anne was in her midthirties when she attended one of my seminars in Australia. She had inherited a lot of money, but she hated it. She was ashamed of her wealth, hid it, and wouldn't spend it. When the subject of money came up in the seminar, she began screaming about how money had destroyed her family. Her father, who had made a lot of money, was never home. He was either out working hard to make money or out jet-setting around the world spending it. As a result, her mother drank excessively, causing constant fighting and screaming in their household. Not surprisingly, Anne's childhood had been a miserable experience. But instead of identifying her father's greed and workaholism as the actual cause of her pain, Anne had decided as a child that money was the culprit. Because childhood decisions made during times of intense emotional upset tend to stay with us longer—and remain stronger over time—Anne had retained her negative beliefs around money for over 20 years.

There are many other limiting decisions you can make about money that can keep you from making or enjoying the amount of money you deserve or want. For example:

It's Not Okay to Make More Money Than My Father

Scott Schilling, the vice president of sales and marketing of Pulse Tech Products Corporation in Dallas, Texas, was attending one of my seminars where we were working on identifying and releasing limiting beliefs.

As I asked the participants to review their childhood for the source of a limiting belief, Scott remembered a day in 1976. He was 18 and had just finished his first month as a life insurance agent—earning a commission check of $1,856. His father, who was in his forty-sixth year with the same insurance company and only one month away from retirement, received his own paycheck that day—for $1,360.

Scott said, "When I showed my check to my father, he never said a word, but the look on his face told me he was deeply hurt. I thought, *How could I do that to my dad? How could I make such a great and noble man question himself and his value?*"

Scott had made a subconscious decision not to earn more money than his father—in order to avoid causing his father the shame and embarrassment Scott imagined he felt that day in 1976. But less than a month after releasing this decision in my seminar, Scott told me he received a contract to do a week's worth of sales training for a fee equal to one fifth of his previous year's total salary.

Becoming Rich Would Violate the Family Code

I grew up in a working-class family. My father was a florist and he worked "for the rich." Somehow the rich were not to be trusted. They stepped on the little people. They took advantage of the common worker. To become rich would have meant becoming a traitor to my family and my class. I didn't want to become one of the "bad guys."

If I Become Wealthy, I Will Be a Burden

My friend Tom Boyer is a business consultant who felt like he had hit a plateau in terms of his income. With some brilliant assistance from our friend Gay Hendricks, he discovered the following childhood decision had put a cap on his success:

> I grew up in a decidedly middle-class family in Ohio. We never wanted for food or anything, but my dad made lots of financial sacrifices so that I could pursue my dream of playing the clarinet.

I started out playing on my dad's old metal clarinet, but soon graduated to a Leblanc, a very middle-of-the-road wooden instrument. When I began to really excel, my clarinet teacher, Mrs. Zielinski, went to my parents and said, "Your son has real talent. He deserves a very, very fine instrument. He deserves a Buffet clarinet." Now understand, there are only two great clarinets on the planet—the Buffet and the Selmer—and in 1964, a Buffet cost $300, which is about $1,500 today. Though that was a lot of money in my family, nevertheless, it was agreed that Mrs. Zielinski would pick out the clarinet for me, and that was going to be my Christmas present.

On Christmas morning I went downstairs, unwrapped the package, opened the case, and discovered this unbelievably gorgeous clarinet with its polished grenadilla wood body and bright shiny silver keys, sitting in its regal blue velvet case. It was the most beautiful thing I'd ever seen in my life. I have since seen King Faruk's crown jewels, and they didn't compare to that Buffet clarinet sitting in that blue velvet case when I opened it up that Christmas morning.

I turned to thank my parents and didn't even get the thank-you out of my mouth before my mom said, "We never would've been able to afford that if your sister had lived." (My sister Carol had suddenly died of encephalitis when I was seven years old.)

And in that moment I took on the subconscious belief that the greater a success I am, the greater a burden I will be to those who love me—not only financially, but emotionally.

I now realize this subconscious belief had held me back from attaining the level of success I consciously wanted. I had convicted myself of the crime of being a burden, and now I was punishing myself by not allowing myself the level of success I truly deserve.

You must begin to understand, therefore, that the present state of your bank account, your sales, your health, your social life, your position at work, etc., is nothing more than the physical manifestation of your previous thinking. If you sincerely wish to change or improve your results in the physical world, you must change your thoughts, and you must change them IMMEDIATELY.

BOB PROCTOR
Author of *The Power to Have It All*

THREE STEPS TO TURN AROUND YOUR
LIMITING BELIEFS ABOUT MONEY

You can change this early programming using a simple yet powerful three-step technique that replaces your limiting beliefs with more positive and empowering ones. While this exercise can be done on your own, it's usually more powerful—and more fun!—to do it with a partner or a small group of people.

1. Write down your limiting belief.
Money is the root of all evil.

2. Challenge, make fun of, and argue with the limiting belief.
You can do this by brainstorming a list of new beliefs that challenge the old ones. The more outrageous and fun you make them, the more powerful the resulting shift in your consciousness will be.

Money is the root of all philanthropy.
Money is the root of great vacations!
Money might be the root of evil for someone who is evil,
but I am a loving, generous, compassionate, and kind
person who will use money to create good in the world.

You can even write out your new money beliefs on 3" × 5" index cards and add them to your stack of affirmations to be read out loud with enthusiasm and passion every day. This kind of daily discipline will go a long way toward helping you manifest success in the arena of money.

3. Create a positive turnaround statement. The last step is to create a new statement that is the opposite of the original belief. You want this "turnaround statement" to be one that sends shivers of delight through your body when you say it. Once you have it, walk around the room for a few moments repeating the new statement out loud with energy and passion. Repeat this new belief several times a day for a minimum of 30 days and it will be yours forever.[53] Try one like

---

53. Strong emotions actually facilitate the growth of hundreds of thousands of new little microscopic hairlike filaments on the ends of the dendrites of the neurons in your brain. These little dendrite spiny protuberances actually create more connections in the brain that will support the installment of the new belief and the creative fulfillment of your new financial goals. It's not magic; it's brain science! For more information on the brain science that supports this, see all of the resources at Doug Bench's fabulous Web site at www.scienceforsuccess.com. Doug is a fanatic about staying up on the latest brain research and its relation to creating more success in your life.

When it comes to me, money is the root of love, joy, and good works.

Remember, ideas about financial success never form by themselves! You have to keep thinking the thoughts that build the "thought form" of prosperity. You have to take time each day and focus on thoughts of prosperity and images of financial success. When you intentionally focus on these thoughts and images, they will eventually crowd out the limiting thoughts and images and begin to dominate your thinking. If you want to accelerate reaching your financial goals, you need to practice saying positive money affirmations every day. Here are a few more that I have used with great success:

- God is my infinite supply, and large sums of money come to me quickly and easily for the highest good of all concerned.
- I now have more money than I need to do everything I want to do.
- Money comes to me in many unforeseen ways.
- I am making positive choices about what to do with my money.
- Every day, my income increases whether I am working, playing, or sleeping.
- All my investments are profitable.
- People love to pay me money for what I most enjoy doing.

Remember, you can plant any idea into the subconscious mind by repetition of thought infused with a positive expectancy and the emotion associated with already having it.

USE THE POWER OF RELEASING TO ACCELERATE YOUR MILLIONAIRE MIND-SET

Whenever you are doing your money affirmations—or any affirmation, for that matter—it is not uncommon to become aware of competing thoughts (objections), such as *Who are you kidding? You're never going to be rich. How many times do I have to tell you? You have to have money to make money.* When this occurs, first write the objection down. Then you can close your eyes and just release the thought and the emotions that accompany it.

Here is a simple technique for releasing that is a version of the Sedona

Method as taught by Hale Dwoskin. I am a big fan of this work, teach it in my workshops, and recommend people take the weekend Sedona Method Class, purchase the *Sedona Method Home Study* audio program, or read *The Sedona Method* by Hale Dwoskin.[54]

The Basic Releasing Questions

Our tendency is to resist or ignore these thoughts and feelings, but that just keeps them around even longer. All you have to do is let yourself fully experience the accompanying feeling and then release it. Though you can do this with your eyes open or closed, most people find that closing their eyes helps them to focus more clearly on their feelings. Letting be and letting go is a choice. It is much easier than you think.

Just take yourself through this little process whenever a negative or limiting belief or feeling about money comes up.

What am I feeling right now?
Focus on whatever feeling arises as you experience your negative limiting belief.

Could I welcome and allow it?
Just welcome the feeling and let it be as best you can.

Could I let it go?
Ask yourself the question *Could I let this go?*
Yes and *no* are both acceptable answers.

Would I let it go?
Ask yourself, *Am I willing to let this go?*
If the answer is no, or if you are not sure, ask yourself,
Would I rather have this feeling, or would I rather be free?
Even if you would rather have the feeling, go on to the next question.

When?
Ask yourself, *When?*
This is just an invitation to let it go now. Remember that letting go is a decision you can make anytime you choose.

---

54. *The Sedona Method*, by Hale Dwoskin (Sedona, Ariz.: Sedona Press, 2003). For more information on workshops, audio programs, and other resources on the Sedona Method, go to www.sedona.com or call 1-888-282-5656. If you used this process every time a negative thought or feeling arose, you could literally release your way to success.

Just keep repeating the preceding steps as often as needed until you feel free of that particular feeling.

VISUALIZE WHAT YOU WANT AS IF YOU ALREADY HAVE IT

Remember to also include money in your daily visualizations, seeing all your financial goals as already accomplished. See images that affirm your desired level of income such as paychecks, rent checks, royalty checks, dividend statements, and people handing you cash. See images of your ideal bank statements, stock reports, and real estate portfolios. See images of the things you would be able to buy, do, and contribute to if you had already met all of your financial goals. Make sure to add the kinesthetic and olfactory dimensions to your visualization—feel the smooth texture of the world's finest silk against your skin, feel the relaxing feeling of a luxurious massage in the world's finest spas, and smell the fragrance of your favorite cut flowers filling your home or the delicate scent of your favorite imported perfume. Next, add in the auditory dimension such as the sound of the surf lapping up on the beach in front of your vacation home or the gentle hum of the finely tuned engine of your new Porsche.

Finally, remember to add in the feeling of appreciation and gratitude for already having these things. This feeling of abundance is part of what will actually attract more abundance to you.

Constantly fill your mind with images of what you want and picture yourself already having them.

YOU GET WHAT
YOU FOCUS ON

If you don't put a value on money and seek wealth, you most
probably won't receive it. You must seek wealth for it to seek you.
If no burning desire for wealth arises within you, no wealth
will arise around you. Having definiteness of purpose
for acquiring wealth is essential for its acquisition.

DR. JOHN DEMARTINI
Self-made multimillionaire and consultant on financial and life mastery

It's been said that in life, you get what you focus on. This rule applies to getting a new job, building a business, winning an award—but most especially to acquiring money, wealth, and a rich lifestyle.

YOU MUST *DECIDE* TO BE WEALTHY

One of the first requirements of becoming wealthy is to make a conscious decision to do so.

When I was in graduate school, I decided to become wealthy. Though I didn't quite know at the time what that meant, "being wealthy" seemed as if it would provide many of the things I wanted in life—the ability to travel and attend any workshops I wanted and the resources to accomplish my goals and underwrite my hobbies. I wanted to be able to do whatever I wanted, whenever I wanted, wherever I wanted, for as long as I wanted.

If you want wealth, too, you must decide now from the deepest place in your heart to have wealth in your life—without worrying yet if it's possible or not.

NEXT, DECIDE WHAT *WEALTHY* MEANS TO YOU

Do you know how much wealth you want? Some of my friends want to retire as millionaires, whereas others want to retire with $30 million or even $100 million. Two friends want to become megarich because of the philanthropic ability it would give them. There is no right financial goal to have. But you do have to decide what *you* want.

If you haven't yet determined your vision from Principle 3 ("Decide What You Want")—including defining what your financial goals are—take time to do so now. Make sure to include written goals like these:

I will have a net worth of $ _____ by the year _____.
I will earn at least $ _____ next year.
I will save and invest $ _____ every month.
A new financial habit I will develop starting now is _____.
To become debt free, I will _____.

FIND OUT WHAT IT COSTS TO FINANCE YOUR DREAM LIFE . . . NOW AND LATER

When creating wealth in your life, remember that there is the life you want to live now and the life you want to live in the future.

The life you are currently living is the result of the thoughts you have thought and the actions you have taken in the past. The life you live in the future will be the result of today's thoughts and actions. To get the kind of life you want 1 to 2 years from now, as well as the kind of lifestyle you want when you "retire," decide exactly how much money you'll need to live the lifestyle of your dreams. If you don't know, research how much it would cost you to do and buy everything you want over the course of the next year. This could include rent or mortgage, food, clothes, medical care, automobiles, utilities, education, vacations, recreation, insurance, savings, investments, and philanthropy.

For each category, visualize those items or activities in your life, then write down what you would need to spend to get them. Imagine eating in fine restaurants, driving your dream car, going on your dream vacation—even refurbishing your home or moving into a new one. Don't let your mind tell you that these things are impossible or crazy. For the moment, just do the research and find out exactly what it will cost to fund your dream life—whatever that is.

GET REAL ABOUT YOUR RETIREMENT

Determine, too, how much you'll need to maintain your current lifestyle once you retire and stop working. Though I don't ever plan to stop working, if retirement is in your plans, Charles Schwab suggests that for every $1,000 in monthly income you'll want during retirement, you'll need to have $230,000 invested when you stop working. If you have $1 million invested with a 6% yield, that will give you a taxable income of about $4,300 a month.

Whether that's enough will depend on a number of factors, such as whether your house is paid for, how many people you'll be supporting, how much you will be receiving from Social Security, and what level of lifestyle you expect to live. At any rate, today $4,300 a month may not be enough to support the extravagant lifestyle you may be envisioning for yourself. If you are hoping to travel and have an active life, it may not even be adequate. With inflation, it may be less than adequate.

BECOME CONSCIOUS ABOUT YOUR MONEY

Most people are unconscious when it comes to their money. For instance, do you know your net worth—your total assets minus your total liabilities? Do you know how much money you have in savings? Do you know exactly what your fixed and variable monthly expenses are? Do you know the total amount of debt you are carrying and the amount of money you are spending a year on interest payments? Do you know if you are adequately insured? Do you have a financial plan? Do you have an estate plan? Do you have a will? Is it up to date?

If you want to be financially successful, you have to get conscious. Not only do you have to know precisely where you are but you also need to know exactly where you want to go and what's required to get you there.

Step 1: Determine Your Net Worth

If you don't know your net worth, you can

1. Work with an accountant or a financial planner to calculate it.
2. Join an organization such as the Avedis Group (a network marketed financial services organization that consults with average

REAL LIFE ADVENTURES by Gary Wise and Lance Aldrich

According to your latest figures, if you retired today, you could live very, very comfortably until about 2 p.m. tomorrow.

people who want to become financially literate and financially independent). They'll help you determine your net worth and provide other financial services for a lot less than most financial planners charge.[55]

3. Purchase some software, such as Personal Financial Statement, which is available at www.myfinancialsoftware.com.

Step 2: Determine What You Need to Retire

Next, calculate what your financial needs will be when and if you retire. Be aware that retirement by its very nature requires that you be financially independent. A good financial planner can tell you how much in savings and investments would be required to produce enough in interest, dividend, rental, and royalty income to live your current lifestyle without having to work.

Financial independence frees you up to pursue your passions, travel, engage in philanthropic endeavors and service projects—or do whatever you wish.

---

55. For information on how to join the Avedis Group, go to www.thesuccessprinciples.com.

Step 3: Become Aware of What You're Spending

*The number one problem in today's generation and economy
is the lack of financial literacy.*

ALAN GREENSPAN
Chairman of the Federal Reserve Board

Most people aren't aware of what they really spend in a month. If you've never tracked your expenditures, start by writing down all your normal *fixed* monthly expenses such as your mortgage or rent, your car payment, any other installment or loan payments, insurance bills, cable bill, Internet provider, health club, and so on. Then go back over the last 6 to 12 months and calculate *average* monthly expenditures that fluctuate—utilities, phone bills, food bills, clothing expenditures, auto maintenance, medical expenses, and so on.

Finally, keep a record for 1 month of *everything* you spend money on during that month, no matter how big or small—from gas for your car to coffee at Starbucks. Add up everything at the end of the month so that you are consciously aware—rather than unaware—of what you're spending. Check off those items you must pay for and those things you have discretion over. This exercise will get you conscious of what you're currently spending and where you could cut back if you chose to.

Step 4: Become Financially Literate

*We were not taught financial literacy in school. It takes a lot of work
and time to change your thinking and to become financially literate.*

ROBERT KIYOSAKI
Coauthor of *Rich Dad, Poor Dad*

Not only should you stay conscious around money by reviewing your financial goals every day and tracking your spending every month, but I recommend that you also proactively learn about money and investing by reading at least one good financial book every month for the next year. To get started, see pages 450–451 in "Suggested Reading and Additional Resources for Success" or go to www.thesuccessprinciples.com for a list of many of the best titles.

Another way to become financially literate is to seek out professionals who can teach you the money skills you'll need to grow a healthy financial future. You can invest your money in stocks and bonds, which pay you in interest, or you can invest in income-producing real estate, which pays you in positive cash flow from rental income that is greater than your mortgage payments.

Like most baby boomers in their midfifties, Mark and Sheila Robbins were locked into the employee mind-set. They didn't talk about creating a life of wealth and abundance. They just worked hard—Sheila for 35 years as a flight attendant for United Airlines, and Mark as the manager of a car dealership—and put money in their 401(k) accounts.

After losing about half of their retirement funds in a declining stock market, they decided there had to be a better way. That's when they joined a network marketed financial services organization called The Avedis Group, and started taking the courses they offered. As a result of reading the *Rich Dad, Poor Dad* books and playing the Cash Flow Game, their conversations began to include the language of money and their minds embraced the idea of becoming real estate investors. They sought out a realtor who specialized in the types of properties they were interested in, and over the summer they went shopping. Only 1 short year later, they have 15 single-family rental properties worth over $2 million, all of which are generating positive cash flow.

If that weren't enough, they also now own their own successful Chrysler/Dodge/Jeep dealership, and another home-based business. Because they were willing to take the time and money to invest in their financial education and implement the principles they learned, their lives have dramatically changed and will never be the same again.

To find out more information about Avedis and other organizations that can help you learn about these kinds of wealth-building tools, go to www.thesuccessprinciples.com.

WEALTH HAS MANY ASPECTS

Lee Brower, the founder of Empowered Wealth and a member of my mastermind group, has developed a model to teach people how to deal with all of their wealth—not just their financial wealth. If you'll look at the chart that appears below, you'll see that you possess four different kinds of assets.

The first are your human assets. These include your family, your health, your character, your unique abilities, your heritage, your relationships, your habits, and your ethics, morals, and values.

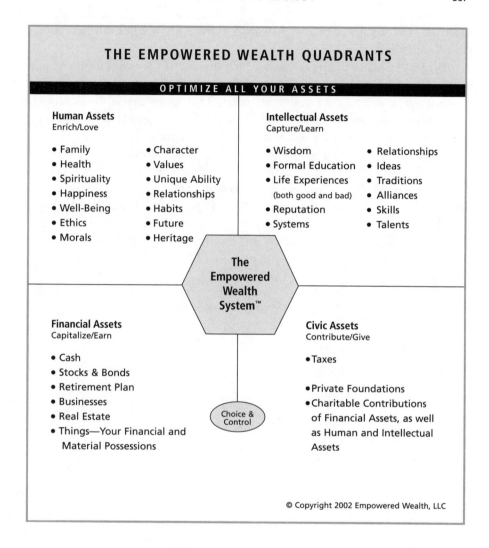

THE EMPOWERED WEALTH QUADRANTS

OPTIMIZE ALL YOUR ASSETS

Human Assets
Enrich/Love

- Family
- Health
- Spirituality
- Happiness
- Well-Being
- Ethics
- Morals

- Character
- Values
- Unique Ability
- Relationships
- Habits
- Future
- Heritage

Intellectual Assets
Capture/Learn

- Wisdom
- Formal Education
- Life Experiences
  (both good and bad)
- Reputation
- Systems

- Relationships
- Ideas
- Traditions
- Alliances
- Skills
- Talents

The Empowered Wealth System™

Financial Assets
Capitalize/Earn

- Cash
- Stocks & Bonds
- Retirement Plan
- Businesses
- Real Estate
- Things—Your Financial and
  Material Possessions

Choice & Control

Civic Assets
Contribute/Give

- Taxes

- Private Foundations
- Charitable Contributions
  of Financial Assets, as well
  as Human and Intellectual
  Assets

© Copyright 2002 Empowered Wealth, LLC

The second are your intellectual assets, which include your skills and talents, your wisdom and your education, your life experiences (both good and bad), your reputation, the systems you've developed, your ideas, the traditions you've inherited or established, and the alliances you've built over the years.

The third are your financial assets, which include cash, stocks and bonds, money in your retirement plan, real estate, any businesses you own, and any other possessions you might have, such as your antiques collection.

The fourth are what Lee calls civic assets, which may include only the taxes you pay (and the services and infrastructure they provide). It can also include the tax money that you "redirect" through contributions to worthy charities, and if you are one of the superwealthy, you might even have a private foundation.

When Lee asks wealthy families which quadrants they would pick if they could pass on assets from only two of the four quadrants, they universally say the human assets and the intellectual assets. They know that if their children have those, they can always make more money. If they only have the money and not the other two, they will ultimately lose the money. What Lee and his team at Empowered Wealth do is teach wealthy families how to maximize and pass on the assets in all four quadrants of their model to the next generation.

I invite you to start thinking about how to build and optimize your assets in all four sectors of the Empowered Wealth Quadrants. If you do, then you will create real wealth in a balanced and integrated way. And you will keep money in its proper perspective. It is just a tool to be used for higher purposes.

PAY YOURSELF FIRST

*You have a divine right to abundance, and if you are anything less
than a millionaire, you haven't had your fair share.*

STUART WILDE
Author of *The Trick to Money Is Having Some!*

In 1926, George Clason wrote a book called *The Richest Man in Babylon*—one
of the great success classics of all time. It's the fabled story of a man named
Arkad, a simple scribe who convinces his client, a money lender, to teach him
the secrets of money.

The first principle the money lender teaches Arkad is: "A part of all you
earn must be yours to keep." He goes on to explain that by first putting aside
at least 10% of his earnings—and making that money inaccessible for
expenses—Arkad would see this amount build over time and, in turn, start
earning money on its own. Over an even longer time, it would grow into a
lot, because of the power of compound interest.

Many people have built their fortunes by paying themselves first. It's as
true and effective today as it was in 1926.

A TELLING STORY

As easy as this 10% formula is, I'm always shocked at how unwilling people
are to hear it. Just the other night, I was taking a limo from the airport back to
my home in Santa Barbara. The 28-year-old limo driver, after realizing who I
was, asked me to share with him some principles of success he could apply to
his own life. When I told him he should invest 10% of every dollar he earned,
and then keep reinvesting the dividends, I could tell the information was
falling on deaf ears. He was looking for a get-rich-quick scheme.

But though opportunities that can earn you money faster are always
something to watch for, I believe your future must initially be built on the

Investments
and Financial Planning

GLASBERGEN

"I retire on Friday and I haven't saved a dime.
Here's your chance to become a legend!"

solid bedrock of a long-term investment plan. The earlier you start, the more quickly you can build your safety net of a million dollars.

Sit down with a financial planner or go to one of the myriad sites on the Internet where you can enter the amount of your current net worth and your financial goals for retirement, and then calculate how much you need to save and invest from this point forward to make your goal amount by the time you retire.[56]

THE EIGHTH WONDER OF THE WORLD

Compound interest is the eighth natural wonder of the world and the most powerful thing I have ever encountered.

ALBERT EINSTEIN
Winner, Nobel Prize for Physics

If you are new to the idea of compound interest, here's how it works: If you invest $1,000 at a 10% rate of interest, you'll earn $100 in interest and at the

56. One that will help you calculate how long it will take to become a millionaire is at www. armchairmillionaire.com/calculator.

end of the first year have a total investment of $1,100. If you leave both your original investment and the earned interest in the account, the next year you'll earn 10% interest on $1,100, which is $110. The third year, you'll earn 10% on $1,210—and so on, for as long as you leave it there. At this rate, your money would actually double every 7 years. That's how it eventually turns into a huge amount over time.

Of course, the best news is, time is your friend when it comes to compound interest. The sooner you start, the greater the result. Consider the following example. Mary starts investing at age 25 and stops when she reaches 35. Tom doesn't start investing until the age of 35 but keeps investing until he retires at 65. Both Mary and Tom invest $150 per month, with a rate of return of 8% per year compounding interest. But look at the surprising result when they both retire at age 65. Mary invested only $18,000 over 10 years and ended up with $283,385, whereas Tom contributes $54,000 over 30 years and ends up with only $220,233. The person who contributed for only 10 years has more than the person who invested for 30 years but started later! The sooner you start saving, the longer you have for compounding interest to work its powerful magic.

MAKE SAVING AND INVESTING A PRIORITY

The world's most aggressive savers make investing money as central a part of their money management as they do paying their mortgage.

To get in the habit of saving *some* money every month, immediately take a predetermined percentage of your paycheck and put it in a savings account that you don't allow yourself to touch. Keep building that account until you've saved enough to move it into a mutual fund or bond account or to invest it in real estate—including the purchase of your own home. The amount of money that is wasted paying rent without building any equity in a home is a tragedy for many people.

Investing just 10% or 15% of your income will help you eventually amass a fortune. Pay yourself first, then live on what is left. This will do two things: (1) it will force you to start building your fortune and (2) if you still want to buy more or do more, it will force you to find ways to earn more money to afford it.

Never dip into your savings to fund your bigger lifestyle. You want your investments to grow to the point that you could live off of the interest, if necessary. Only then will you be truly financially independent.

HE PAID HIMSELF FIRST

Dr. John Demartini is a chiropractor who now conducts seminars for other chiropractors on how to grow themselves personally and their practices financially. He is one of the wealthiest and most abundant people I know—in spirit, friends, and adventure, as well as in money. John told me:

> When I first got into practice years ago, I paid everybody first and took whatever was left over. I didn't know any better. Then I noticed that people who had only been working for me less than 6 months were all getting paid on time. I realized that their pay was fixed and mine was variable. That was kind of crazy. The most important person—me—was the one under the stress, while the others had all the stability. I decided to turn that around and pay myself first. I paid my taxes second, my lifestyle budget third, and my bills fourth.
>
> I arranged for *automatic* withdrawals, and they've completely changed my financial situation. I don't waver. If bills pile up and money doesn't come in, I don't stop the withdrawals. My staff is forced to find a way to book more seminars and collect more money. Under the old system, if they didn't book or collect, it was on my back. But now, it's the other way around. If they want to get paid, they figure out ways to make more money.

THE 50/50 LAW

Another rule John suggests is that you never spend more than you save. John puts 50% of every dollar he earns into savings. If he wants to increase his personal expenditures by $45,000, he first has to earn an additional $90,000. Let's say you want to buy a car for $40,000. If you can't put an extra $40,000 into savings, you don't buy the car. Either buy a cheaper car, make do with what you have right now, or go out and make more money. The key is that you don't raise your lifestyle until you've earned the right to raise it by putting the same amount into savings. If you *do* raise your savings by $40,000, you know you've earned the right to raise your lifestyle by that same amount.

The 50/50 Law will get you rich very quickly. It was the core of billionaire Sir John Marks Templeton's strategy for building wealth.

DON'T TELL ME YOU CAN'T DO IT!

Most people wait to start saving until they have some extra money lying around—a comfortable surplus. But it doesn't work like that. You have to start saving and investing for the future *now*! And the more you invest, the sooner you will reach financial independence. Sir John Marks Templeton started out working for $150 a week as a stockbroker. He and his wife, Judith Folk, decided to invest *50%* of their income in the stock market *while still making tithing a priority*. That left the two of them only 40% of his income to live on. But today, John Templeton is a billionaire! He has kept the practice up his whole life and now gives away $10 for every dollar he spends to individuals and organizations that support spiritual growth.

WHO WANTS TO BE A MILLIONAIRE?

According to government figures, in 1980 there were 1.5 million millionaires in the United States. By 2000 there were 7 million. The number is expected to grow to approximately 50 million by the year 2020. It has been estimated that someone in America becomes a millionaire every 4 minutes. With a little planning, self-discipline, and effort, one of these millionaires can be you.

MILLIONAIRE DOESN'T MEAN "CELEBRITY"

Although you might think—judging from Donald Trump, Britney Spears, and Oprah Winfrey—that most millionaires are celebrities, the truth is more than 99% of millionaires are hardworking, methodical savers and investors.

These folks typically make their fortune in one of three ways: From entrepreneurship, which accounts for 75% of all the millionaires in the United States; as an executive at a major corporation, about 10% of millionaires; or as a professional practitioner (doctor, lawyer, dentist, certified public accountant, architect). Additionally, about 5% become millionaires through sales and sales consulting.

Indeed, most of U.S. millionaires are regular folks who worked hard, lived within their budgets, saved 10% to 20% of all their income, and invested it back into their businesses, real estate, and the stock market. They are the people who own the dry cleaning business, the car dealership, the restaurant chain, the bread company, the jewelry store, the cattle ranch, the trucking company, and the plumbing supply store.

However, people from any walk of life can become millionaires if they learn the discipline of saving and investing and start early enough. You no doubt read or heard about Oseola McCarty of Hattiesburg, Mississippi, who had to drop out of school in the sixth grade to take care of her family, and spent some 75 years of her life washing and ironing other people's clothes. She lived a frugal life and saved what she could from the little money she made. In 1995, she donated $150,000, the bulk of her $250,000 life savings, to the University of Southern Mississippi to provide scholarships for needy students. And here's the interesting part: Had Oseola invested her savings, which is estimated to have been about $50,000 in 1965, in an S&P 500 index fund, which earns on average 10.5% a year, her money would have grown to not $250,000, but $999,628—virtually a million dollars, four times as much.[57]

HOW TO BECOME AN "AUTOMATIC MILLIONAIRE"

The simplest way to implement the pay yourself first plan is to have a plan that is totally "automatic"—that is, set up so a percentage of your paycheck is automatically deducted and invested as you direct.

Financial planners will tell you, from their extensive experience with hundreds of clients, that very few—if any—follow through with a plan to pay themselves first, if it is not automatic. If you're an employee, check with your company to see if they have self-directed retirement accounts such as 401(k) plans.

You can arrange for the company to automatically deduct your contribution to the plan from your paycheck. If it's deducted before you receive your check, you'll never miss it. More important, you won't have to think about your investments—you won't have to exercise self-discipline. It doesn't depend on your mood swings, household emergencies, or anything else. You make the commitment once and it's a done deal. Another advantage of these kinds of plans is that they are free of most taxes until you withdraw the money. So instead of having 70 cents working for you, you have an entire dollar working for you—compounding year after year.

Some companies will even match a portion of your contribution. If you work for such a company, get on board *now*! Check with the employee benefits office of your company and find out how to sign up. When you do, make

---

57. See "The Oseola McCarty Fribble," by Selena Maranjian, September 5, 1997, on the Motley Fool Web site, at www.fool.com/Fribble/1997/Fribble970905.htm.

sure to make the largest percentage contribution you are allowed by law, but at least 10%. If you absolutely cannot bring yourself to do 10%, then do the largest percentage you can. After a few months, reassess and then see if you can't increase it. Get creative about where you can cut costs and how you can increase your income through some other source.

If you don't have a company retirement plan, you can open an individual retirement account (IRA) at a bank or a brokerage firm. With an IRA, you make a financial contribution of up to $3,000 a year ($3,500 if you're 50 or older). Ask the bank, the brokerage firm, or a financial advisor to help you decide if you want a traditional IRA or a Roth IRA. The paperwork to start an IRA takes about the same amount of time as opening a checking account. And to keep it automatic, you can arrange for an automatic deduction from your checking account.

For a much more detailed explanation of how to benefit from an automatic investment program, I strongly recommend that you read *The Automatic Millionaire: A Powerful One-Step Plan to Live and Finish Rich*, by David Bach (New York: Broadway Books, 2004). David has done a superb job of providing you with everything you need to know, as well as a host of resources for putting these recommendations into action—even including phone numbers and Web sites so you can do all of this from the comfort of your own home.

BUILD ASSETS RATHER THAN LIABILITIES

Rule One. You must know the difference between an asset and a liability and buy assets. Poor and middle class acquire liabilities, but they think they are assets. An asset is something that puts money in my pocket. A liability is something that takes money out of my pocket.

ROBERT T. KIYOSAKI
Coauthor of *Rich Dad, Poor Dad*

Far too many people run their financial lives by their expenditures and whims. For most people, their "investment" model looks like this:

Your Income	**100%** →	Your Expenses & Liabilities	**$0** →	Your Assets $0

But take a look at how wealthy people approach their investments. They take the money they earn and invest a large portion of it in income-producing assets—real estate, small businesses, stocks, bonds, gold, and so on. If you want to become wealthy, follow their lead. Start approaching your financial activities like this:

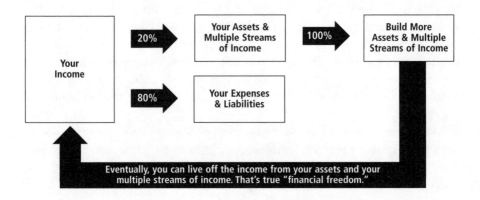

ONCE YOUR NEST EGG STARTS TO GROW

As your money begins to grow, you'll want to educate yourself further about the best way to invest your money. Eventually, you'll probably want to find a good financial advisor. The way I found mine was to ask successful friends who they used, then listen for the same name to come up more than once or twice. That's exactly what happened.

If you don't have friends who are using a financial advisor or you don't get anyone that several people agree on, a good place to go for more information on how to pick a financial advisor is www.finishrich.com. Click on the "Find a Financial Advisor" button under the "Resources Section" on the Web site. There is a wealth of information there that can help you.

PROTECT WHAT IS YOURS WITH INSURANCE

It's a sad reality today that many wealthy people are targets of frivolous lawsuits, claims, and other complaints—often for no legitimate reason. Additionally, mistakes and accidents can always occur, which is why it's important to protect your financial assets through a good insurance policy. This is even more important if you operate a small business.

Locate a good insurance broker the same way you would find a financial planner or asset management company.

PROTECT WHAT'S YOURS WITH A PRENUPTIAL OR COHABITATION AGREEMENT

If you are getting married later in life or bringing a lot of assets to the marriage, most financial advisors will tell you to get a prenuptial agreement. I know it may feel like you're introducing a negative matter to an experience that should be one of love and bliss, but these days, such agreements have become almost a necessity. I have watched way too many people—both men and women—lose what rightfully should have been theirs because they were afraid to get a prenuptial agreement.

When I got remarried, my wife-to-be was more than willing to get a prenuptial agreement. "I don't want to ever take away from you what you rightfully owned when we came together," she said. "You've worked hard for what you have, and I want you to feel safe knowing that it's still yours if we don't make it."

It's exactly that attitude that lets me know we will make it because she loves *me*, and not my money. I admire that she is a levelheaded, rational person who is not out to take advantage of me or my company.

If you can't talk openly about a prenuptial agreement, you probably aren't going to be able to talk openly about other difficult emotional issues when they come up. That doesn't bode well for the quality or the longevity of the relationship. Find a good marriage counselor and a couple of good lawyers— whose prenuptial agreements have stood up in court—and work out an agreement you both feel good about. It can be a very clarifying personal growth experience for both of you.

MASTER THE
SPENDING GAME

*Too many people spend money they haven't earned, to buy things
they don't want, to impress people they don't like.*

WILL ROGERS
American humorist, actor, and writer

When I was shopping with my 13-year-old son Christopher recently, I saw a
book near the checkout called *How to Absolutely Save Money: The Only Guide
You'll Ever Need.* Opening it up to read what it said, I saw there were the same
three words on every page: *Spend less money.* Pretty sage advice!

HOW MUCH DID YOU SPEND LAST YEAR?

Spending too much can wreak havoc with your financial goals. It keeps you
in debt, prevents you from saving as much as you could, and turns your focus
to consumption, rather than to wealth creation and accumulation.

If you can't seem to curb your spending, try this exercise. Go through
every closet, drawer, and cabinet in your house and take out everything you
haven't used in the past year. This includes clothes, shoes, jewelry, utensils,
electronics, sheets, towels, blankets, sporting equipment, audiocassettes,
CDs, videos, games, toys, auto accessories, and tools—anything and everything you spent money on *but didn't use in the last year.* Gather it all together in
one place, such as your living room, family room, or garage. Then add up the
price you paid for each and every item.

I've encountered people who found expensive clothes with the tags still
attached, shopping bags containing housewares they never unboxed, and expensive tools and equipment they literally used once, perhaps 3 or 4 years ago.

The truth is that with the exception of tuxedos, evening gowns, ski boots,
and snorkel gear you may use only once every few years, you probably never

really needed all those things in the first place. Yet you spent money on them. And when you add up what these items cost, you may find the total will be more than your current credit card debt.

START PAYING CASH FOR VIRTUALLY EVERYTHING

One way to curb spending is to start paying cash for everything. Cash is more immediate. It makes you think about what you're buying. You'll probably find yourself spending less than you would if you used credit cards. Every potential purchase will be considered more carefully, "necessary" incidentals will become less necessary, and large purchases will probably be put off, forcing you to think about how you can make do without them.

REDUCE THE COST OF YOUR RICH LIFESTYLE

Another way to master the spending game is to live the lifestyle you want yet pay a whole lot less for it. I know many people who do this all the time yet still maintain an aggressive saving and investment program, with a few simple changes in the way they spend and buy.

Let's look at a few examples.

A woman I know regularly purchases $685 season tickets to the opera for just $123. She sees the same world-class tenors, hears the same thunderous music, and hobnobs with the same art patrons as those who pay more to be there—but she gets her tickets at 82% off what other people pay. How does she do it? When the mailing for season ticket subscribers arrives in March, she selects the operas she wants to see, disregards those she doesn't like, and sends in her payment with instructions for her "Design-Your-Own" series—simply assuming the order will be accepted (which, of course, it always is). Because she is perfectly happy to sit in the balcony, she gets an entire season's worth of "champagne" experiences for less than the cost of a month's worth of gas for her car.

Another friend is a collector of vintage cars—not just any cars, but convertible Cadillacs. He buys them in January when no one would ever think of purchasing a convertible and saves literally tens of thousands of dollars off the cost of his purchases. As a result of this strategy and other savvy purchasing ideas, he can afford to own several rental properties and put the positive cash flow they produce into saving himself rich.

Another woman I know likes to wear expensive designer fashions but feels morally bound to purchase them at the consignment store, where she selects from racks and racks of virtually new or never-been-worn cast-offs, paying pennies on the dollar to look like a movie star.

Other people barter for goods and services, ask for discounts even when they're not offered, ask how they can buy the item cheaper, call four or five vendors and take bids for the same identical item, shop at ultra-budget stores for the things that don't matter so that they can spend on the ones that do—in short, routinely squeeze every dime they can out of the cost of living the extravagant lifestyle they want.

To these people—who are all aggressive savers—living this kind of lifestyle on as little money as possible is almost like a game.

TAKE STEPS NOW TO BECOME DEBT FREE

Another big part of mastering the spending game is to simply get out of debt. Stop paying high credit card interest rates and assume a less consumptive lifestyle.

It's amazing that as a population, we've amassed as much personal debt as we have. Credit card, mortgage, and auto payments are staggering for many people. Savings and financial security suffer. If this is your situation, take steps now to start living life debt free using these strategies:

1. **Stop borrowing money.** As simple as this may sound, borrowing money is one of the main reasons why people don't get out of debt. While they're paying down existing debt, they're still using their credit cards, taking out new loans, and so on. This is madness. Why? Because the cost of borrowing is actually more staggering than most people know. The numbers below show you how much you actually pay when you purchase an item with borrowed money.

Amount borrowed	$10,000
Interest rate	10%
Months financed	60 months
Total interest paid	$3,346.67
Total interest as a percentage of item purchased	33.5%

    If you wouldn't pay $13,346 for the item you've just borrowed $10,000 for, find a way to pay cash for it, purchase a similar item for less money, or decide whether you really need that item at all.

2. **Don't get a home equity loan to pay off credit card debt.** When you "consolidate" all your monthly payments into a lower-rate loan, you actually make your situation worse. Why? Because you start back at the beginning of the amortization scale where

interest is the highest portion of each month's payment. At the beginning of any loan, very little of your new monthly payment goes to pay down the principal, whereas the consumer loans you were paying on before may have had most or even all of your monthly payment going toward reduction of the principal.

3. **Pay off your smallest debts first.** When you pay off your smallest debt first, you achieve a major success breakthrough—even if it doesn't seem that way. For one thing, you experience a huge boost in your self-esteem whenever you accomplish any goal. Why not start with the smallest goal that's the easiest to achieve?

4. **Slowly increase your debt payments.** Once you've paid off a smaller debt, simply take the monthly payment you were making on that debt and use it to increase your payments on your next debt. For example, if by paying $300 a month on your credit card you reduce your balance to zero, take that same $300 next month and add it to the amount you would normally make on your car loan. This saves you thousands of dollars in interest by paying off your car loan early, plus it keeps you from expanding your lifestyle by that $300 a month.

5. **Pay off your home mortgage and credit cards early.** Many mortgage lenders offer what's called a biweekly mortgage. That means you pay half your monthly mortgage amount every other week, instead of making one big payment at the beginning of the month. Because these loans often reamortize with every payment, it has the effect of turning a 30-year mortgage into a 23-year loan. This results in staggering savings on mortgage interest and gets you out of debt faster than you ever thought possible. If your lender doesn't offer such a loan, why not make one extra payment a year or pay a small extra sum on your own every month? It will still reduce the number of years on the loan and save you years' worth of interest. You can also make extra payments on your credit cards.

THE POWER OF FOCUS

As you commit to becoming debt free and saving more, you'll encounter an almost miraculous force working in your life. As you change your focus from spending and consuming to enjoying the things you already have and putting money aside, you'll progress at an almost unexplainable rate.

Even if you don't believe you'll survive every month, once you commit to a debt-reduction and savings plan, you'll be surprised at your ability to manage and arrive at your goal faster than you had planned.

You may go through a profound transformation. You'll see your values and priorities change. Suddenly, you'll measure your success in terms of debts paid off rather than goods purchased. And as your investment portfolio grows, you'll begin to weigh *all purchases* against your goal to be financially secure and debt free.

Regardless of where you are in life—even if you're in what appears to be a hopeless situation—stay the course and allow this miracle to accelerate you to your goal.

PRINCIPLE

60

TO SPEND MORE,
FIRST MAKE MORE

*Whatever may be said in praise of poverty, the fact remains
that it is not possible to live a really complete or
successful life unless one is rich.*

WALLACE D. WATTLES
Author of *The Science of Getting Rich*

In the final analysis, there are really only two ways to end up with more money for investing or additional luxuries—either spend less money in the first place or simply make more of it. Personally, I'm a fan of making more. I would rather make more and have more to spend than to always be denying myself things I want for some distant future gain.

The fact is that making more money means you can both invest more *and* spend more on the things you want—travel, clothes, art, concerts, fine food, quality medical care, world-class entertainment experiences, quality transportation, education, hobbies, and all sorts of time- and labor-saving devices and services.

This is common sense.

HOW TO MAKE MORE MONEY

The first step to making more money is to decide how much more you want to make. I've talked extensively about using the power of affirmations and visualization to see yourself as already in the possession of that money. Not surprisingly, story after story exists in the world about superrich individuals who have used these daily habits to bring more abundance into their lives.

The second step is to ask yourself, *What product, service, or additional value can I deliver to generate that money?* What does the world, your employer, your community, fellow businesspeople, fellow students, or your customers need that you could provide?

Finally, the third step is simply to develop and deliver that product, service, or extra value.

MORE MONEY IDEA #1: BECOME AN INTRAPRENEUR

Today, many of America's smartest companies are cultivating entrepreneurship amongst their employees and executives. If one of these companies is your employer—or if you can convince your boss to give you a percentage of the newfound money you generate from overlooked areas of revenue, you can almost instantly increase your income.

Perhaps your employer has a customer list it isn't selling additional goods and services to. Perhaps your workgroup is so good at managing projects, its members have extra time that they could "hire out" to other departments for extra pay. Maybe there's a piece of machinery, a vendor relationship, an overlooked marketing idea, or other unusual asset your employer isn't using to full advantage. You can create a plan to turn this asset into cash and approach your employer with a proposal to work on the asset-maximizing project off-hours for extra pay. It may even garner you a well-deserved promotion.

MORE MONEY IDEA #2: FIND A NEED AND FILL IT

I never perfected an invention that I did not think about in terms of the service it might give others. . . . I find out what the world needs, then I proceed to invent.

THOMAS A. EDISON
America's most successful inventor

Many of the most successful people throughout history have identified a need in the marketplace and provided a solution for it, yet most of us have never asked what's needed—or even what's possible.

If your dream is to earn more money—either with your own business or in addition to your job—identify a need that isn't being met and determine how to meet it.

Whether it's starting a Web site for a particular group of collectors, providing a unique education for people who need rare or unusual skills, or developing new products or services to address emerging trends you see in society, there are always needs you can find to create a business or a service around. Many of these former "met needs" are inventions and services we now take for granted. But the fact remains that people discovered something they needed in their own life or stumbled on the needs of others, then created the gadgets and services we enjoy today:

- The Baby Jogger was invented by a man who wanted to go jogging but had child care responsibilities. What he created for himself was soon in demand by nearly everyone who saw it.
- eBay, the world's largest online auction service, was born in 1995 when founder Pierre Omidyar engineered a way to help his fiancée trade PEZ candy dispensers.
- Avon decided that its direct-selling approach was ideal for the newly emerging Russian democracy, where Avon representatives could not only act as personal beauty consultants to Russian women who were unaccustomed to wearing cosmetics but could also serve as delivery outlets at a time when retail infrastructures were practically nonexistent.
- Internet dating services were invented when smart entrepreneurs matched the desires (and busy schedules) of single people with the computer technology that was sitting in front of them 8 to 12 hours a day.

What need could you identify? Need is literally everywhere you look. It doesn't matter whether you are a college student seeking a summer income, a housewife wanting to earn an extra $500 a month to make ends meet, or an entrepreneur looking for the next big business opportunity—there is always a need that could be your opportunity to make some serious money.

A Fresh Idea Makes Mike Milliorn a Multimillionaire

In the 1980s, Mike Milliorn was a salesman for a label company who needed to make a few more dollars a month. One of his biggest customers was the TGI Friday's restaurant chain, a sophisticated operation looking for a fail-safe way to mark their stock and ensure that employees used the oldest perishable foods first—a process called food rotation. Before meeting Mike, they used masking tape and markers, or they bought colored dots at an office supply store and posted a chart on the wall that said "Red dot equals Wednesday."

Their biggest problem? The adhesive didn't stick in their walk-in coolers.

So Mike invented Daydots for food rotation—a fail-proof system of colored dots with the day of the week imprinted right on the cold-temperature label.

He realized that if TGI Friday's needed the dots, other restaurants probably needed them, too. He began marketing Daydots to as many restaurants as he could economically afford to reach.

Like most people with a new idea, Mike kept his day job. "With three kids, a mortgage, and two car payments, it was too big of a risk to quit and devote full time to Daydots. I had zero money, so I had to figure out how to take my idea to market economically and without quitting my job. That's where the mail-order idea came up."

Mike produced a simple one-page flyer that explained the Daydots system and financed it with a $6,000 loan against his wife's Chevy station wagon, and then mailed it to the handful of restaurants for which he could afford the postage. He got just enough orders from that first mailing to encourage him to do another mailing, then another. For 4 years, he and his wife kept their day jobs and worked out of their house.

Today, Mike's company mails 3 million catalogues a year and prints over 100 million Daydots a week. Mike saw a need, and—with the help of his wife, kids, and employees—he worked diligently to fill it.

Daydots has even evolved into a manufacturer and distributor of food safety products—as well as cold-temperature, dissolvable, and "SuperRemovable" dots and labels.

Thirteen years later, Mike was approached by a $4 billion Fortune 500 company, which purchased Daydots for tens of millions of dollars. What started out as a simple enterprise to earn a few extra dollars to "get his kids through school" ended up earning Mike enough to do all that—and more. Mike Milliorn noticed a need and found a creative, economical way to fill it.

We the People

In the early 1990s, Linda and Ira Distenfield began looking for the next adventure in their lives. They'd been successful in civil service jobs but wanted to make a change. And after looking at the marketplace—at all the products and services available—the one service they couldn't find was budget-priced legal work.

It was no wonder they couldn't find it, of course.

In those days, attorneys still had the upper hand and charged thousands of dollars for simple documents that might take just a few minutes to produce. A typical bankruptcy cost $1,500, and a simple divorce might run as high as $2,000 to $5,000.

But what about a service, the Distenfields thought, where everyday folks could get help with simple legal forms for $399 or less? What about a service that would demystify the legal process and explain a customer's options in everyday, nonlegal language?

In a small storefront in Santa Barbara, the Distenfields began doing just that. Their company, We the People, was born.

Today, the husband-and-wife team have more than 150 offices in 30 states and have served more than 500,000 customers in the last 10 years with as many as 60 different kinds of legal services—all at prices that won't break the bank. That's definitely finding a need and filling it.

But perhaps the most telling proof that they've found a need and filled it is the story of one satisfied customer in New York who raved about We the People to New York City's former corporation counsel, Michael Hess. Within days, Hess had checked them out and passed along his findings to former New York City mayor Rudolph Giuliani. As a former U.S. Attorney himself, Mayor Giuliani was intrigued by a people-oriented legal service that simplifies the process and charges lower fees. Today, he's a partner in We the People, bringing tremendous credibility to the Distenfields' dream and the industry they created.

We the People has become so successful, in fact, that a major corporate powerhouse recently contacted the couple about buying them out and taking We the People to the next level. The Distenfields' commitment to providing an affordable service to their community has now paid them back handsomely.

Chicken Soup for the Soul®

When Mark Victor Hansen and I wrote the first *Chicken Soup for the Soul®* book, we unwittingly met a huge need that at first, we had only a hint about. We knew people wanted to be inspired by positive and uplifting stories; that's why we wrote the first book. What we didn't know was how deep the need truly was. We realized we were onto something bigger than we had anticipated when we started to receive between 50 and 300 stories a day—in the mail, over the fax, and by e-mail. Everyone had a story to tell, and everyone wanted to read other people's stories.

When the first book hit the stands and eventually went on to sell 8 million copies, the bookstores and our publisher came clamoring for a sequel. We were ready, and we have been filling that need ever since with as many as 10 books a year.[58]

---

58. For a complete list of the books in the *Chicken Soup for the Soul®* series, go to www.chickensoup.com.

The Possibilities Are Endless

Do you see a similar need in your own life? What about a longing or aspiration in the lives of others around you?

Is there something that needs to be provided, solved, addressed, or eliminated? Is there something you find annoying that could be alleviated if there were some gadget or service to solve that particular problem? Do you share a common goal or ambition with others in your industry or social circle that you could achieve if only someone gave you a system or process for achieving it? Do you enjoy certain activities that could be made even more enjoyable with a new invention or service?

Look at your own life and ask what is missing that would make it easier or more fulfilling.

MORE MONEY IDEA #3: THINK OUTSIDE THE BOX

When Dave Liniger, founder and CEO of RE/MAX, was a successful young real estate agent, like everyone else he grumbled about paying 50% of his commissions to the broker whose office he worked in. Experienced and an out-of-the-box thinker, he began to look for an alternative—a better way to sell homes and keep more of what he earned at the same time.

Not long after, Dave happened upon a simple, independent rent-a-desk real estate office that—for $500 a month—provided a desk, a receptionist, and limited other services to real estate agents who were experienced enough to find their own customers and do their own marketing. Like Dave, these agents didn't need the backing of a big-name entity to be successful. But unlike more professionally managed real estate brokerages, the rent-a-desk idea didn't offer outstanding management, a large brand name, lots of offices, and the ability to share expenses across thousands of agents.

Why not create a hybrid? Dave mused. *Why not create a firm that offers more independence to agents, that lets them keep more than 50% of their sales commission but still provides more support than going it alone?*

Real Estate Maximums—RE/MAX for short—was born. And since its inception in 1973, because of Dave's commitment to the vision and his dogged determination not to give up during the very challenging first 5 years, RE/MAX has become the fastest-growing, largest network of real estate agents in the world, with more than 92,000 agents in 50 countries who share overhead, enjoy expense control, and are part of a bigger entity but who also remain independent enough to determine their own advertising budget and decide how much of their income they want to keep after their expenses.

Because Liniger's out-of-the-box idea was backed up with hard work, perseverance, and passion, and because it met a need for thousands of real estate agents, the dream has grown into an almost billion-dollar-a-year business.

How far might you go if you were willing to do some out-of-the-box thinking?

MORE MONEY IDEA #4: START A BUSINESS ON THE INTERNET

As an income generation specialist, Janet Switzer works with countless Internet entrepreneurs, helping them earn more money from their online businesses. Today, an Internet business is one of the easiest to start and operate—even while you keep your current job. You can find a need and fill it for a very narrow market, yet still reach thousands and even millions of people with that interest all over the world.

You can even sell e-books, audio files, software, training materials, special reports, how-to courses, and other information products that are downloadable—meaning that you never have to ship a single box or send an envelope. Of course, other items are equally easy to sell, too. It's simply a matter of finding out who needs what, how best to reach them, and how to convince them to buy.

Additionally, the good news is the Internet is now a mature marketplace. Hundreds of other Web sites, newsletters, and clubs already have visitors, subscribers, and members who could be perfect prospective customers for you, once you offer a percentage to the other Web site owner, or affiliate. One of the best resources I've found for setting up these joint-venture affiliate programs is Yanik Silver's *Instant Internet Profits*, available at www.instantinternetprofits. com. One client of Janet's modeled this affiliate system and got 578,667 new visitors to his Web site in just 90 days. Many of those people bought products and services on an ongoing basis from the Web site owner.

Once you learn how to market on the Internet, you can also market other people's products online. A man in Florida approached his local jeweler and asked him if he had ever thought about selling his jewelry on the Internet. The jeweler replied that he had thought about it but had never had the time to get around to actually doing it. He offered to build the Web site and drive traffic to it for a percentage of the profits. The jeweler readily agreed. It was a win-win for both of them.

In July 2001, Shane Lewis, a medical student in Virginia, decided to create an Internet business to cover the cost of supporting his family while he was attending medical school at George Washington University. With the help of StoresOnline.com, he looked around for a product he could market and found a rapid urine drug test that parents and others could use to administer drug tests with immediate results. He is making well over $100,000 a year from this and two other drug- and alcohol-testing products. He told me, "My first month I only had a few orders, but by the third month we were doing really well and exceeded my initial goals. Today we earn enough for my wife to stay home with our children while I attend school. Thanks to our Internet business, we are virtually debt free and no longer have to rely on student loans to make ends meet."

MORE MONEY IDEA #5: JOIN A NETWORK MARKETING COMPANY

There are more than 1,000 companies who sell their products and services through network marketing—certainly one or more you can get passionate about. From health and nutrition products to cosmetics, cookware, toys, educational materials, and phone services—even low-cost legal and financial services—there is something for everyone. A little research on the Internet will yield a host of opportunities. A list of 500 company addresses is available at www.onlinemlm.com/500List.html. Another list of companies is available at www.mlminsider.com/Companies_List.html#I. Or you can visit the Web sites of the Direct Selling Association and the Direct Selling Women's Alliance at www.dsa.org and www.mydswa.org, respectively.

Tony and Randi Escobar decided to join forces with Isagenix, a newly created network marketing company specializing in nutrition for life, internal cleansing, weight loss, and skin care products. Because of their passion for health and wellness, their desire to succeed, their love for people, their love of the products, and their commitment to work hard, Tony, an Australian immigrant who had been working in the copper mines of Superior, Arizona, only a few short years before, and his wife, together facing bankruptcy just prior to their joining Isagenix, created an income of nearly $2,000,000 a year in less than 2 years. Although the speed at which they achieved this level is exceptional, millions of people are adding thousands of dollars a month to their incomes by participating in network marketing companies—and many are becoming millionaires. In fact, it has been reported that network marketing has produced over 100,000 millionaires since the mid-1990s in the United States alone!

Because many network marketing companies do not last, make sure you get solid advice about the company and its products before you get involved.

Find a company that has been around for a while and has a great reputation. Try the products and make sure you love them. If you are passionate about the product and passionate about people, you can make a lot of money through the leverage that building a downline provides you. There are very few businesses where you can capitalize on such a huge opportunity for such a small financial investment.[59]

MONEY FLOWS TO VALUE

Wherever you decide to put your energies, the key is to become more valuable to your current employer, customers, or clients. You do that by getting better at solving their problems, delivering products, and adding services that they want and need.

You may need to get more training, develop new skills, create more relationships, or put in extra time. But the responsibility for getting better at what you do and how you do it is totally yours. Always seek out opportunities for more training and self-development. If you need an advanced degree or some kind of certification to move up in your chosen trade or profession, quit talking about it and go get it.

CREATE MULTIPLE SOURCES OF INCOME

The best way to enjoy greater income *and* develop economic security in your life is to create several sources of income. This protects you from any one of those sources—usually your job—from drying up and leaving you without any cash flow. I have always had several sources of income. Even when I was a therapist in private practice, I also gave speeches, ran workshops for educators, and wrote magazine articles and books.

You, too, can find all kinds of additional ways to make money if you merely start looking for them. You can work up from simple ways such as hauling trash with your truck on the weekends, tutoring someone, or giving music lessons to investing in rental properties, consulting, or marketing on the Internet.

---

59. If you choose to pursue network marketing as a career or as a source of supplemental income, read the following two books to quickly learn the important basics. I consider these must-reads: *Your First Year in Network Marketing*, by Mark Yarnell and Rene Reid Yarnell (Roseville, Calif.: Prima Publishing, 1998), and *Secrets of Building a Million Dollar Network Marketing Organization from a Guy Who's Been There Done That and Shows You How to Do It Too*, by Joe Rubino (Charlottesville, Va.: Upline Press, 1997).

There are endless possibilities for multiple income sources. If you are a voracious reader, you could create an e-zine that includes reviews of the books you have read, with links to Amazon.com, which will pay you a percentage of every book that is sold through your link. You can sell something on e-Bay. You can buy and sell art. One of my friends whose main source of income is professional speaking loves Oriental art. Twice a year, he travels to China and Japan and purchases art very inexpensively. He keeps what he likes and sells the rest for a handsome profit to a growing list of collectors he has cultivated. His travel and his own art is in essence free, plus he makes a handsome profit off of the art that he sells. I know the principal of a private school who does the same thing during his summer vacation with antique Chinese furniture, which he then sells out of his home and garage.

My sister Kim started stringing beads as a hobby when she was in her twenties, and by the time she was 35 she had created Kimberly Kirberger Designs and was selling her jewelry to Nordstrom and Barneys as well as a host of local boutiques and the cast of the television series *Beverly Hills 90210*.

AN IMPORTANT DISTINCTION

When you are building multiple sources of income, do your best to focus on creating businesses that require very little time and money to start and operate. Your ultimate goal is to set things up so that you're free to work when and where you want—or to take time off to pursue leisure. Too many scattered streams mean that you run the risk of losing your main source of income.

The two best resources I know for really understanding and mastering multiple sources of income are *Multiple Streams of Income: How to Generate a Lifetime of Unlimited Wealth*, second edition, and *Multiple Streams of Internet Income: How Ordinary People Make Extraordinary Money Online*, both by Robert G. Allen.

And remember to apply everything you have learned so far to creating multiple sources of income. Make it part of your vision and your goals, visualize and affirm that you are making money from your multiple income sources, and start reading books and articles about it and talking with your friends about it. You will start attracting all kinds of opportunities and ideas. Then just act on the ones that feel most right for you.

61

GIVE MORE TO GET MORE

Bring the full tithes into the storehouse, that there may be food
in my house; and thereby put me to the test, says the Lord of hosts,
if I will not open the windows of heaven for you and pour down
for you an overflowing blessing.

MALACHI 3:10
(Revised Standard Version of the Bible)

Tithing—that is, giving 10% of your earnings to the work of God—is one of the best guarantees of prosperity ever known. Many of the world's richest individuals and most successful people have been devout tithers. By tithing regularly, you, too, can put into motion God's universal force, bringing you continual abundance.

Not only does it serve others but it serves you as the giver, too. The benefits cross all religious boundaries and serve those of every faith—because the simple act of giving both creates a spiritual alliance with the God of abundance, and fosters the mind-set of love for others. Tithing proves in a compelling way that abundant wealth is something God wants for His children. In fact, He created a world where the more successful you are, the more wealth there is for everyone to share. An increase in wealth for an individual almost always represents an increase in wealth for society at large.[60]

THE TITHING PLAN THAT
CHICKEN SOUP COOKED UP

Tithing has certainly played a huge part in my success and the success of the *Chicken Soup for the Soul®* series. Ever since the first book in the series, we

---

60. See *God Wants You to Be Rich: How and Why Everyone Can Enjoy Material and Spiritual Wealth in Our Abundant World*, by Paul Zane Pilzer (New York: Fireside, 1997).

have tithed a portion of the profits to nonprofit organizations that were dedicated to healing the sick, feeding the hungry, housing the homeless, empowering the disempowered, educating the uneducated, and saving the environment.

Along with our publisher and coauthors, we've given away millions of dollars to more than 100 organizations including the Red Cross, the YWCA, and the Make-A-Wish Foundation. Since 1993 we've planted over 250,000 trees at Yellowstone National Park with the National Arbor Day Foundation, underwritten the cost of building homes for the homeless with Habitat for Humanity, fed the hungry of the world with Feed the Children, and prevented thousands of teen suicides through Yellow Ribbon International. We feel so blessed by all that we have been given that we want to give back. We also strongly believe that everything we give away comes back multiplied many times over.

We also tithe a portion of our personal income to our churches and other spiritual missionary and service organizations that uplift humanity through doing God's work.

One of the most exciting projects we've been involved in was the distribution of 100,000 free copies of *Chicken Soup for the Prisoner's Soul* to people incarcerated in our prisons. The book was never intended for distribution in the general population, but it was so successful that soon we received thousands of requests from family members, correctional officers, and prison ministries to make copies of the book available for them. What started out strictly as a philanthropic endeavor turned into another successful *Chicken Soup* book in the bookstores—and another example of how good works come back to you multiplied.

THERE ARE DIFFERENT TYPES OF TITHING

There are two different kinds of tithing. *Financial tithing* is best explained as contributing 10% of your gross income to the organization from whence you derive your spiritual guidance or whose philanthropic work you want to support.

Time tithing is volunteering your time to serve your church, temple, or synagogue or any charity that could use your help. There are currently more than 18,000 charities in the United States alone that need volunteers.

HIS LIFE TURNED AROUND AS SOON AS HE
STARTED TITHING

Nature gives all, without reservation, and loses nothing;
man or woman, grasping all, loses everything.

JAMES ALLEN
Author of *Path of Prosperity*

Robert Allen, best-selling author of *Nothing Down* and *The One Minute Millionaire*, didn't always tithe. But after he'd lost everything and was down to zero, he said to himself, *Wait a second. I've had so much money in my life. I'm supposed to be the guru who teaches people how to become rich. Where's it all gone? I must have done something wrong.*

Eventually Bob worked his way back to prosperity. But along the way, he learned a valuable lesson: *Either I believe in tithing,* he said to himself, *or I don't. If I believe it, I'm going to tithe every week. I'm going to figure out what our income is that week and write my check that week.*

As he became a dedicated tither, suddenly a whole new world opened up for him. Though his debts were almost insurmountable, he became more grateful for what he had. Soon, new opportunity started flowing to him. Today, Bob says, he has so much opportunity it would take him 10 lifetimes to tap into it. He believes it's that way for all dedicated tithers.

But even more telling than his own story is how he inspires others to tithe. He recalls one woman who approached him and complained, "My husband and I can't tithe. We can barely make our mortgage payment. Our lifestyle costs us $5,000 a month. There's not enough money left over at the end of the month."

Bob admonished her, saying, "You don't tithe because you want to get something. You tithe because you've already gotten it. You're so blessed already, there's no way in the world you'll be able to repay it. There are six billion people on the face of the Earth who would give their left lung to trade places with you. You tithe out of the gratitude you feel for the unbelievable blessings and lifestyle you have."

Bob never expects a thing when he tithes, because he now realizes the windows of heaven have already been opened to him. He tithes because he's already received the blessings.

CORPORATE GIVING

Corporations, too, can reap the rewards of giving back. William H. George, the Chairman and CEO of Medtronic, recently revealed to a Minneapolis conference on philanthropy how his company had committed to giving 2% of their pretax profits. Although these "tithes" amounted to only $1.5 million in the beginning, the company's 11-year growth streak of 23% per year enabled them to boost their giving to $17 million in 1 year alone.

Perhaps the most impressive recent acts of giving have been the $1 billion grant by Ted Turner to the United Nations and the $7 billion in grants made by Bill and Melinda Gates through the Bill and Melinda Gates Foundation. However, you don't have to be a corporation or superwealthy to give back to the community. Any contribution, whether it is in time or in money, will make a difference to the recipients and to you, both in the good feelings you'll experience and in expanded flow of abundance streaming into your life.

SHARE THE WEALTH

Money is like manure. If you spread it around it does a lot of good.
But if you pile it up in one place it stinks like hell.

JUNIOR MURCHISON

When you engage others in your success—when you share the wealth with them—more work gets done, greater success is achieved, and ultimately everyone benefits more. The key to the success of the *Chicken Soup for the Soul®* series was our decision to involve more coauthors in the process. Though Mark and I each received smaller royalties—30 or 40 cents a book instead of 60 cents—it allowed us to complete more titles, get more media coverage, and sell more books. There is no way the two of us could have compiled, edited, written, and promoted 80 books by ourselves.

What started out as the collaboration of 2 authors and 2 secretaries grew to a staff of 12 with 2 editors, several consulting editors, 2 editorial assistants, a permissions specialist, a marketing director, a licensing director, a new projects director, several secretaries, and a group of 75 coauthors and almost 7,000 contributors, including over 50 cartoonists. We have always done our best to fairly compensate everybody involved. Our staff salaries have been higher than normal for the publishing industry, and we have a generous pension plan and an equally generous bonus plan. All of our staff members get 6 weeks of vacation time every year. We have paid out over $4 million in permission fees to contributors and donated millions of dollars to charity. It is our firm belief that this willingness to share the wealth has produced more wealth than we could have ever produced on our own. Trying to hang on to it all would have just constricted the flow of wealth.

FIND A WAY TO SERVE

*It is one of the beautiful compensations of this life that no man
can sincerely try to help another without helping himself.*

RALPH WALDO EMERSON
American essayist and poet

The greatest levels of contentment and self-satisfaction are experienced by
those who have found a way to serve others. In addition to the true inner joy
that is created by serving others, it is a universal principle that you cannot
serve others without it coming back multiplied to yourself.

DECIDE WHAT IS IMPORTANT TO *YOU*

Take some time to determine what causes and groups of people are important
to you. What issues call out to you? What organizations make your heart sing?
Do you care more about the homeless or the arts?

If you love art and think that the schools are woefully lacking in art education, you might decide to volunteer to raise funds for art supplies, volunteer to
teach an art class, or become a docent at your local art museum. If you were an
only child and really missed having your father or mother around, you might
want to volunteer for Big Brothers or Big Sisters. Perhaps you love animals
and would rather help find homes for abandoned pets. If you love books, you
could volunteer to read a book for the Recording for the Blind & Dyslexic.

VOLUNTEER YOUR SKILLS

There are many nonprofit organizations that could use your business skills—
management, accounting, marketing, volunteer recruitment, fund-raising,
and so on.

If you have organizational talent, consider working on charitable events. If you can easily convince others of the value of your cause, consider becoming a fund-raiser for local charities who need your help. If you are a skilled executive, consider serving on the board of a nonprofit organization.

YOU'LL GET MORE THAN YOU GIVE

When you volunteer, you will get back a whole lot more than you give. Research on volunteerism shows that people who volunteer live longer, have stronger immune systems, have fewer heart attacks, recover from heart attacks faster, have higher self-esteem, and have a deeper sense of meaning and purpose than those who don't volunteer. The research also shows that people who volunteer in their younger years are more likely to end up in more prestigious and higher-paying jobs than their nonvolunteering counterparts. Volunteering is a powerful way of networking and often leads to business and career opportunities.

Volunteering is also a way to develop important success skills. Many large corporations have come to realize this and actually encourage their employees to volunteer. Many companies, such as SAFECO and the Pillsbury Company, actually build volunteerism into their employee development programs and make it part of their annual review process. SAFECO's Building Skills through Volunteerism Program helps employees identify skills they would like to work on. Employees can go to the "Volunteer @ SAFECO" intranet, where they'll find a guide to the types of volunteer activities that help build competency in the areas the employee chose. They then have a discussion with their supervisor about adding the volunteer opportunity to their personal development plan.

Many prospective employers also report that when they are interviewing candidates for hire, they now look to see if the candidates have engaged in volunteer work. So volunteering your time could well have a positive payoff by helping you land a future job.

Additionally, one of the keys to success is building a huge network of relationships, and volunteering lets you meet all kinds of people you would never meet otherwise. Better yet, they're often the people—or the spouses of the people—who make things happen in your profession and in your community.

UNEXPECTED CAREER AND BUSINESS REWARDS

Dillanos Coffee Roasters has a policy of sponsoring a Christian Children's Fund child for every employee in the company. As a way to give back to the countries that make their business possible, they sponsor children only in coffee-growing countries from which they buy beans, such as Guatemala, Colombia, and Costa Rica. Dillanos pays the $35 monthly sponsorship fee, and the individual employees correspond with their child, send birthday and Christmas gifts, and maintain a relationship with the child. In addition to making a difference in the world, the sponsorship program has proven to be a great boost for employee morale.

And while the motivation to sponsor these children was purely philanthropic, it has also had a positive impact on the company's bottom line. All the pictures of the children they sponsor are posted along the wall of one of the hallways in the company. A prospective client was being given a tour of the company and asked about the origin of the pictures. When it was explained that the pictures were of children being supported by the company through the Christian Children's Fund, the woman was so touched that before she even tasted Dillanos' coffee, she decided that she wanted to do business with a company that cared so much for children and for their employees.

CHICKEN SOUP FOR THE SOUL®

When Mark and I were writing and compiling stories for the first *Chicken Soup for the Soul®* book, we realized we needed 30 more stories than we had to make it a complete book. Because we had spent so many years serving others through our volunteer work, making our presentations at professional conferences, and doing work that uplifted and empowered others, people were more than willing to support us in return by giving us one or more stories to use in the book. Nobody even asked to be compensated for the use of his or her story. They all just wanted to serve us and serve the readers by inspiring them to become all that they could be.

When you spend a lot of time serving with people who serve, you build up a network of generous, caring people who love to give and make a difference. When you know a lot of people who are into service, you can get a lot done in the world.

SERVICE ALWAYS COMES BACK MULTIPLIED

Serving others can also consist of focusing your company's mission on producing products and services that are beneficial to mankind. Sir John Marks Templeton studied more than 10,000 companies over a 50-year period and discovered that the best long-term results flowed to those who focused on providing increasingly beneficial products and services.

"Whatever one does," Templeton said, "he first should ask, *In the long run, is this really useful to the public?* If so, he is serving as a minister. I think those in business can assure each other that if one tries to give his best when serving the community, his business will not languish but prosper."[61]

Think about the possibility that when you choose to do work that uplifts and serves, that brings people "increasingly beneficial" products and services, when your efforts are focused on giving rather than getting, then you are going to eventually receive back more than you have given.

The world responds to givers more positively than to takers. We naturally want to support the givers. Simply stated, givers get.

I am convinced that the huge monetary rewards that have come to us as a result of the *Chicken Soup for the Soul*® books were partially because of our hard work, but more importantly because of our deep desire to be of service, to give as much as we can to as many as we can through our books. I truly believe that our stories are contributing to the healing of the world one story and one person at a time.

An old proverb teaches that if you feed a man a fish, you feed him for a day, and if you teach a man to fish, you feed him for a lifetime. He will become prosperous and probably teach others to fish as well. We have devoted our lives to teaching people how to fish by empowering them with the principles and skills to create greater levels of success for themselves. That is also what the programs I have developed for welfare recipients, prisoners, and inner-city high school students were all designed to do—teach people the skills of self-sufficiency so that they can support themselves. This is, in a way, a form of ministry, using one's talents to uplift and empower others. And as Zig Ziglar, one of America's greatest teachers of success principles, is fond of saying, "You can get anything in life you want if you will just help enough other people get what they want."

---

61. Excerpted from *Religion and Liberty* (November–December 2000, volume 10, number 6), a publication of the Acton Institute for the Study of Religion and Liberty, 161 Ottawa NW, suite 301, Grand Rapids, MI 49503. Phone: 616-454-3080; fax: 616-454-9454; info@acton.org.

PART VI

Success
Starts Now

*No amount of reading or memorizing
will make you successful in life. It is
the understanding and application
of wise thought which counts.*

BOB PROCTOR
Author of *You Were Born Rich*

START NOW!...JUST DO IT!

Many people die with their music still in them. Why is this so?
Too often it is because they are always getting ready to live.
Before they know it, time runs out.

OLIVER WENDELL HOLMES
Former U.S. Supreme Court justice

There is no perfect time to start. If you are into astrology and you want to contact your astrologer about an auspicious date to get married, open your store, launch a new product line, or begin a concert tour, okay—that's fine. I can understand that. But for everything else, the best strategy is just to jump in and get started. Don't keep putting things off waiting for 12 doves to fly over your house in the sign of a cross before you begin. Just start.

You want to be a public speaker? Fine. Schedule a free talk for a local service club, school, or church group. Just having a date will put the pressure on you to start researching and writing your speech. If that's too big of a stretch, then join Toastmasters or take a speech class.

You want to be in the restaurant business? Go get a job in a restaurant and start learning the business. You want to be a chef? Great! Enroll in a cooking school. Take action and get started—today! You do not have to know everything to get going. Just get into the game. You will learn by doing.

First you jump off the cliff and you build wings on the way down.

RAY BRADBURY
Prolific American author of science fiction and fantasy

Don't get me wrong here. I am a big proponent of education, training, and skill building. If you need more training, then go and get it. Sign up for that class or that seminar now. You may need a coach or a mentor to get where you want to go. If so, then go get one. If you're afraid, so what? Feel the fear and do it anyway. The key is to just get started. Quit waiting until you are *perfectly* ready. You never will be.

I started out my career as a history teacher in a Chicago high school. I was far from the perfect teacher on my first day of teaching school. I had a lot to learn about classroom control, effective discipline, how to avoid getting conned by a slick student, how to confront manipulative behavior, and how to motivate an unmotivated student. But I had to start anyway. And it was in the process of teaching that I learned all of those other things.

Most of life is on-the-job training. Some of the most important things can only be learned in the process of doing them. You do something and you get feedback—about what works and what doesn't. If you don't do anything for fear of doing it wrong, poorly, or badly, you never get any feedback, and therefore you never get to improve.

When I started my first business, a retreat and conference center in Amherst, Massachusetts, called the New England Center for Personal and Organizational Development, I went to a local bank to get a loan. The first bank I went to told me I needed to have a business plan. I didn't know what that was, but I went and bought a book on how to write a business plan. I wrote one up and took it to the bank. They told me there were a bunch of holes in my plan. I asked what they were, and they told me. I went back and rewrote the plan, filling in the areas I had left out or that were unclear or unconvincing. I then went back to the bank. They said the plan was good, but they wanted to pass. I asked them who might be willing to fund the plan. They gave me the names of several bankers in the area they thought might respond favorably. Again I went off to the bank. Each one gave us more feedback until I had honed the plan and my presentation to the point where I did finally obtain the $20,000 loan that we needed.

When Mark Victor Hansen and I first released *Chicken Soup for the Soul*®, I thought it would be a good idea to sell the book in bulk quantity to some of the larger network marketing companies, thinking they could give them or resell them to their sales force to motivate them to believe in their dreams, take more risks, and therefore achieve greater success in selling. I got a list of all the companies that belonged to the Direct Marketing Association, and I started cold-calling the sales directors of the larger companies. Sometimes I couldn't get the sales director to take my call. Other times I was told, "We're not interested." Several times I was actually hung up on! But eventually, after getting better at getting through to the right decision maker and properly discussing the book's potential benefits, I made several significant sales. A few of the companies liked the book so much they later hired me to speak at their national conventions.

Was I a little scared making cold calls? Yes. Did I know what I was doing when I started? No. I had never tried to sell mass quantities of books to anyone before. I had to learn as I went. But the most important point is that I just got started. I got into communication with the people I wanted to serve; found out what their dreams, aspirations, and goals were; and explored how our book might help them in achieving their objectives. Everything unfolded because I was willing to take a risk and jump into the ring.

You, too, have to begin—from wherever you are—to start taking the actions that will get you to where you want to be.

HOW TO GET STARTED

A journey of 1,000 miles must begin with one step.
ANCIENT CHINESE PROVERB

The key to success is to take what you have learned (or relearned) in this book and put it into action. You can't do everything at once, but you can begin. There are 64 principles in this book. If you're not careful, that could feel a bit overwhelming to you. So here is all you have to do:

Go back to Section I and start working through each principle one at a time, in the order they are presented—take 100% responsibility for your life and your success, clarify your life purpose, decide what you want, set specific and measurable goals for all the parts of your personal vision, break them down into specific action steps you can take, create affirmations for each one of your goals, and begin the practice of visualizing your completed goals every day. If you're smart, you'll also enroll someone to be your accountability partner, or you'll start a mastermind group to do these first steps with you.

Then begin *taking action* on your most important goals *every day except your R & R Days*. Pay the price by doing whatever it takes, ask for whatever you need with no fear of rejection, ask for and respond to feedback, commit to never-ending improvement, and persist in the face of whatever obstacles may come up. Now you're up *and running* toward the completion of your major goals.

Next, to build and maintain momentum, create a program for cleaning up your incompletes, work on transforming your limiting beliefs, pick a habit to work on developing for the next quarter, commit to reading one of the books in "Suggested Reading and Additional Resources for Success" (and then another and another), and purchase a motivational audio program to listen to in your car or when you are exercising. Then schedule a vacation with your spouse or some friends, and enroll in a personal development seminar to be completed sometime in the next 6 months. Start saying no to the people and things that distract you from your major goals, and find a mentor or hire a coach to advise you and keep you on track.

Finally, work on developing your money consciousness. Make sure you set up a procedure for automatically investing 10% *or more* of every paycheck in an investment account, and some portion of your time and money to your religious or favorite nonprofit organization. Analyze and cut back on your spending, and begin figuring out how to make a fortune rather than a living by becoming more valuable to your employer or your clients.

You can't do everything at once. But if you keep adding a little progress every day, over time you will have built a whole new set of habits and self-disciplines. Remember, anything valuable takes time. There are no overnight successes. It took me years to learn and implement all of the principles in this book. I have mastered some and am still working on mastering others.

Though it will take you some time, it shouldn't have to take you as long as it took me. I had to discover all of these principles on my own over a period of many years and from many different sources. I am passing them all on to you in one large package. Take advantage of my having gone before and blazed a trail for you. Everything you need is here to take you to the next level.

Granted, there are things you'll need to learn that are unique to your specific situation, profession, career, and goals that are not covered in this book, but the fundamental principles needed to succeed in *any* venture have been covered throughout the preceding chapters. Make the commitment to start now and get on with using them to create the life of your dreams.

PRECESSIONAL EFFECTS

Scientist, inventor, and philosopher Buckminster Fuller talked about the precessional effects that issue from just getting started in the service of humanity. Fuller explained precession by pointing out that the honeybee's seemingly primary objective is to obtain nectar to make honey, but while going after the nectar, the honeybee is unwittingly involved in a much bigger purpose. As it flies from flower to flower in search of more nectar, it picks up pollen on its wings and thus ends up cross-pollinating all the rooted botanicals in the world. It's an unintended by-product of the bee's nectar-seeking activity. Think of yourself as a speedboat moving through the water. To the sides of you and behind you is a wake of activity caused by the sheer force of your forward motion. Life is like that, too. As long as you are actively in motion in the pursuit of your goals, you will create precessional effects that will turn out to be far more important than you initially were capable of understanding or intending. You just begin, and the path of opportunities just keeps unfolding in front of and to the side of you.

None of the wealthy and successful people I know (both my closest friends and the more than 70 people I interviewed for this book) could have possibly planned or predicted the exact sequence of events that unfolded over the course of their lives. They all started with a dream and a plan, but once they started, things unfolded in unexpected ways.

Look at my own example. Mark Victor Hansen and I never predicted that *Chicken Soup for the Soul*®, the title of our first book, would evolve into a brand name and would become a household phrase in North America and numerous other countries around the globe. Nor could we have ever predicted that we would have a line of Chicken Soup for the Pet Lover's Soul™ dog and cat foods, a line of greeting cards, a television show, a syndicated column, or a syndicated radio show. All of these things just evolved out of our initial commitment to write a book and be of service.

When Dave Liniger decided to leave the biggest real estate agency in Denver and start his own agency, he had no idea that 30 years later his company, RE/MAX, would become the largest real estate agency in the United States, a billion-dollar business with 92,000 agents in 50 countries around the world.

When Donald Trump built his first building, he wasn't aware that he would eventually own casinos, golf courses, a resort, the Miss USA contest, and the number-one reality show on American television. He just knew he wanted to build magnificent buildings. The rest unfolded along the way.

Carl Tarcher started with a rolling hot dog stand in downtown Los Angeles. As he made a little money, he bought another one and then another one until he could buy a real restaurant. That one restaurant evolved into Carl's Junior.

When Paul Orfalea started out with a single copy shop to serve local college students, little did he know it would evolve into a chain of over 1,800 Kinko's stores and net him $116 million when he later sold it.

All of these people may have had a set of goals and a detailed plan as best as they could conceive it at the time, but each new success opened up new unforeseen possibilities. If you just aim in the direction you want to go, start, and keep moving forward, all kinds of unforeseen opportunities will grow out of that forward motion.

MEETING VIN DI BONA

When the first *Chicken Soup for the Soul*® book hit the best seller lists, our publisher asked us if we would start working on a sequel. He also asked us if we would be willing to create a cookbook of chicken soup recipes. Though that seemed like too limiting a focus for a book—how many chicken soup recipes can one person use?—the idea of creating a cookbook interested us. One of our close friends, Diana von Welanetz Wentworth, is an award-winning cookbook author who had already dedicated her life to making a difference in the world. The idea for a book of stories written by famous people, celebrated cookbook authors, chefs, and restaurateurs, accompanied by a recipe that tied into the story, did intrigue us. And so we asked Diana to collaborate with us on such a book. Together we gathered moving stories that centered on a meaningful experience with food accompanied with the recipe for that food.

The best part of the project was that Diana would prepare each recipe to make sure that it actually worked and tasted good. Then every couple of weeks, Mark and I would go to Diana's house and eat the results as we selected which of the hundreds of stories and recipes we would include in the book. (I don't remember losing any weight during that project!)

A year later, Mark and I began thinking all the stories we had been collecting would make good material for a television show. Other than being interviewed on a lot of talk shows and news programs to promote our books, Mark and I had no experience in the world of television. We didn't know any producers, directors, or programming executives at the networks. But we began to get the sense that television was a next step we should be exploring. Once we added a *Chicken Soup for the Soul®* television show to our goal list and started affirming and visualizing *Chicken Soup* on TV, it wasn't more than a couple of weeks before Diana called us and said, "You know, I've been thinking that I should introduce you to Vin Di Bona. He's the producer of *America's Funniest Home Videos*. He used to produce a cooking show that Paul and I did, and I think he might be interested in doing something on television with *Chicken Soup for the Soul®*."

Sure enough, through Diana's connection, we secured a meeting with Vin Di Bona and his company's vice president, Lloyd Weintraub. It turned out Lloyd was a big fan of *Chicken Soup*. He took over the meeting and totally sold Vin on the idea. A year later, we were in production with a series of 16 shows that aired on PAX TV and later on ABC, with such actors as Jack Lemmon, Ernest Borgnine, Martin Sheen, Stephanie Zimbalist, Teri Garr, Rod Steiger, and Charles Durning starring in each week's episodes.

Once you start moving and producing results, all manner of things begin to happen that will take you further and faster than you ever imagined.

AN OLYMPIC DREAM TURNS INTO A PROFESSIONAL SPEAKING CAREER

When Ruben Gonzalez finally realized his dream of competing in the winter Olympics for the third time, he returned home to Texas, where his 11-year-old neighbor reminded him of his promise to be his show-and-tell story at the local elementary school. After Ruben regaled Will's fifth-grade class with the tales of his struggles to achieve his Olympic dream, Will's teacher asked Ruben if he would be willing to address an assembly of the whole school. So Ruben stayed for another hour and talked to all 200 kids.

At the end of his talk, several teachers told him that they often hired speakers to come speak to the kids, and he was easily better than anyone they had previously hired. They told him that he had a natural gift as a speaker. Encouraged by this feedback, Ruben began calling up other schools in the Houston area, and soon had so many bookings that he quit his job as a copier salesman.

Everything went well until June, when to Ruben's surprise school let out for the summer and there were no more speaking engagements until the fall. Spurred on by the need to feed himself and his wife, Ruben began calling up local businesses. Little by little, he established a toehold in the corporate world around Dallas and, as word grew about his incredibly motivational talks, Ruben's career took off. Just under 2 years later, Ruben made as much money in the first 2 months of the year as he had made all year in his previous job as a copier salesman.

Placing thirty-fifth in the world in luge, a sport most people have never even heard of, was a step toward a career as a world-class speaker, but it was not something he was planning when he was plummeting down the ice track at 90 miles an hour at the U.S. Olympic Training Center in Lake Placid, New York. It was one of those precessional effects that Buckminster Fuller was talking about.

GO GET STARTED!

I have done my best to give you the principles and the tools you need to go and make all of your dreams come true. They have worked for me and for countless others, and they can work for you as well. But this is where the information, motivation, and inspiration stop, and the perspiration (provided by you) begins. You and you alone are responsible for taking the actions to create the life of your dreams. Nobody else can do it for you.

You have all of the talent and the resources you need to start right now and eventually create anything you want. I know you can do it. You know you can do it . . . so go out there and do it! It's a lot of fun as well as a lot of hard work. So remember to enjoy the journey!

Everyone who got to where they are had to begin where they were.

RICHARD PAUL EVANS
Best-selling author of *The Christmas Box*

64

EMPOWER YOURSELF BY EMPOWERING OTHERS

If your actions create a legacy that inspires others to dream more,
learn more, do more, and become more,
then you are an excellent leader.

DOLLY PARTON
Songwriter, singer, actor, entrepreneur, Oscar nominee,
Country Music Association Award winner, and Grammy winner
who currently oversees a $100 million media empire

I want to encourage you to read this book over and over several times. Underline the things that are most important to you and reread what you have underlined. You will discover that with each rereading, you will not only reinforce what you already know but you will also discover something new, some concept that perhaps didn't register during the first time through. It takes a while to absorb and assimilate all of these new ideas. Give yourself that time.

I also want to suggest you give several copies of this book to your teenage and college-age children, to your employees, team members, and managers. You'll be amazed at how radically you can change a family, a team, or a business simply by having everyone using the same principles at the same time.

The greatest gift you can give anyone is a gift of empowerment and love. What could be more loving than helping people you care about get free from their limiting beliefs and ignorance about success, and empowering them to create the life that they truly want from the depths of their soul?

So many Americans currently live in a state of resignation or despair. It is time to turn that around. We all have the power within us to create the life we want, the life we dream about, the life we were born to live. We all deserve to fulfill our full potential and manifest our true destiny. It is our birthright, but it must be claimed. It must be earned through hard work, and part of that work is first learning and then living by the time-tested and ageless principles that are guaranteed to bring about our desired results. Most of us did not learn these principles in school or at church, and only a few of us learned them at home.

They have been passed down from person to person by mentors, teachers, coaches, and, more recently, in books, seminars, and audio programs. Now you have the core of those principles in your hands. First use them to liberate your own life and the lives of those whom you care about most and those whose activities most impact your life.

What if all members of your family gave up complaining, took full responsibility for themselves and their lives, and started creating the lives of their dreams? What if all employees in your company practiced these principles? What if all members of your softball team approached life this way? What if all the high school students in the United States knew these principles and put them into practice in class, on the playing field, and in their social lives? What if all men and women in prison were to learn these valuable principles before they were released back into society? It would be a very different world.

People would take 100% responsibility for their lives and the results they produce or don't produce. They would be clear about their visions and their goals. Nobody would fall victim to the criticism and abuse of others. Everyone would persevere in the face of hardship and challenge. Men and women would band together in teams to support each other to become all that they could be. People would ask for what they need and want and feel free to say no to the requests of others when it is not right for them to respond with a yes. People would stop whining and complaining and get on with creating the life that they want. People would tell the truth and listen to each other with compassion because they know that peace, joy, and prosperity flourish when they do.

In short, the world would work!

The greatest contribution you can make to the world is to grow in self-awareness, self-realization, and the power to manifest your own heartfelt dreams and desires. The next greatest thing you can do is to help others do the same. What a wonderful world it would be if we were all to do that.

It is my intention that this book would contribute to creating that kind of world. If it does, I will have fulfilled my purpose of inspiring and empowering others to live their highest vision in a context of love and joy.

If you would thoroughly know anything, teach it to others.

TYRON EDWARDS
American theologian

One of the most powerful ways to learn anything is to teach it to others. It forces you to clarify your ideas, confront inconsistencies in your own thinking, and more closely walk your talk. But most importantly, it requires you to read, study, and speak the information over and over again. The resulting repetition reinforces your own learning.

One of the great benefits to me of researching and teaching the principles of success is that I am constantly reminding myself about the principles and how important it is to use them. As my staff members read the chapters of this book as I finished them, it helped all of us recommit to the ones we were not fully using. And whenever I conduct seminars around the country, I find that I become more diligent in implementing the principles in my own life.

TEACH THESE PRINCIPLES TO OTHERS

Think about whom you might teach these principles to. Could you teach a seminar at your church? Offer a class at the local high school or community college? Teach a seminar at work? Facilitate a 6-week study group that meets once a week over lunch? Lead a discussion group with your family?

If you would like to, you can go to www.thesuccessprinciples.com and download a free study guide for teaching the basic principles in this book to others. Though you'll definitely be helping the others you teach, you'll be helping yourself even more.

You don't have to be a master of these principles to lead a discussion group. You just have to be willing to facilitate a discussion of the principles. The study guide will tell you everything you need to say and do to lead a productive discussion and help people implement the principles at work, at school, and at home.

Imagine a family, group, club, religious group, office, sales team, or company where the people were all working together to support each other in actively living these principles. The results would be miraculous. And you could be the person who makes that happen. If not you, then who? If not now, then when?

WHEN YOU LIFT UP OTHERS,
THEY WILL LIFT UP YOU

And here's another major benefit—the more you help other people succeed in life, the more they will want to help you succeed. You might wonder why all the people who teach success strategies are so successful. It's because they have helped so many people get what they want. People naturally support those who have supported them. The same will be true for you.

One of my spiritual teachers once taught me to be a student to those above me, a teacher to those below me, and a fellow traveler and helpmate to those on the same level. That's good advice for all of us.[62]

HELP US START A MOVEMENT

If you think you're too small to have an impact, try going to bed with a mosquito in the room.

ANITA RODDICK
Founder of the Body Shop (with 1,980 stores serving over 77 million customers) and a prominent human rights activist and environmentalist

I envision a world where all people are inspired to believe in themselves and their abilities and are empowered to reach their full potential and realize all their dreams. I want these principles taught in every school and university and practiced in every small business and large corporation.

I have trained other trainers and speakers, developed curricula for schools,[63] created video-based training programs for welfare programs and corporations,[64] written books, created audio and video programs,[65] conducted seminars and online courses, and developed coaching and telecoaching programs for the general public. I've created a syndicated column, helped produce a television series, and appeared on countless radio and television programs sharing these ideas with others.

I'd love to have you join me in spreading the word. If you'd like to be part of the Success Principles Team, visit www.thesuccessprinciples.com, register by clicking on the Success Principles Team link, and we'll let you know how you can join us in reaching and teaching others.

---

62. If you are interested in deepening your own understanding of these principles and learning how to teach these principles in the form of an interactive workshop, you might also want to attend my annual 7-day summer training. It will accelerate your own growth and teach you valuable leadership skills and instructional methods. For more information, go to www.jackcanfield.com.

63. See *Self-Esteem in the Classroom: A Curriculum Guide*, by Jack Canfield. Available from Self-Esteem Seminars, P.O. Box, 30880, Santa Barbara, CA 93130. Web site: www.jackcanfield.com.

64. Information on these programs—the GOALS Program and the STAR (Success Through Action and Responsibility) Program—is available from the Foundation for Self-Esteem, 6035 Bristol Parkway, Culver City, CA 90230. Phone: 310-568-1505.

65. For a complete listing of my books, audio and video programs, seminars, and coaching programs, go to www.thesuccessprinciples.com and click on the link for "Jack's Success Resources."

Take your success to the next level . . .

Download
The Success Principles
FREE SUCCESS TOOLS™
at www.thesuccessprinciples.com/tools.htm

FREE One-Year Planning Guide . . . to help you plan your activities, to-do list, action items, success reading, Breakthrough Results time-management schedule, and more. Includes page after page of colorful daily checklists, notes pages, goal-setting pages, reading lists, personal journal entries, inspirational and thought-provoking messages from Jack and Janet . . . and more.

FREE Victory Log . . . for your three-ring binder or other victory log format. These letter-size pages are colorful, inspiring, and designed to empower you with daily successes you create. When times are tough, remind yourself how successful you really are—with your own Victory Log pages designed to coordinate with *The Success Principles* Audio Program.

FREE Mastermind Strategy Guide . . . designed specifically for mastermind groups, this free strategy guide helps your group with activities, ideas, and thought-provoking messages that can help any group break through to a higher level of success!

The Success Principles
ANNUAL SUCCESS CHALLENGE™

Every year, Janet and I select individuals from more than a dozen categories who demonstrate a significant increase in their personal or professional success. Perhaps you've overcome a substantial obstacle . . . discovered a new purpose . . . pursued a new path.

You could win **The Success Challenge** when you read and apply *The Success Principles* to your life. Find out how by visiting www.thesuccessprinciples.com!

The Success Principles
FREE SUCCESS STRATEGIES COURSE™

In this powerful, FREE online course—delivered to your e-mail address—you'll discover easy-to-use strategies that will help you decide what you want . . . and get it. Register today at www.the successprinciples.com.

BRING THE POWER OF CHANGE TO YOUR ORGANIZATION: *THE SUCCESS PRINCIPLES*™ WORKSHOP

Positive and profound changes are the result when your employees, managers, members, and students experience *The Success Principles* live group workshop.

Not only will your team be inspired and motivated to achieve greater success but they'll also learn how to up-level all their efforts, strategic alliances, relationships, attitudes, and behaviors.

The Success Principles™ Workshop will empower them with strategies that make them more productive with less effort . . . that help put more money in their paychecks . . . that help them function better within their workgroups . . . and that help them respond more effectively and productively to everyday events.

The Success Principles™ Workshop includes success tools, plus highly customized program materials, for each participant. Long-term training or remote training can also be designed for your organization. *The Success Principles*™ Workshop is ideal for groups such as

- Independent sales professionals
- Small-business owners
- Managers and executives
- Trade association memberships
- Corporate workgroups and new hires
- Work-at-home employees and telecommuters
- Students and educators
- School business officials and administrators
- Nonprofit employees and managers
- Professional practitioners and their staffs
- Employees facing layoff or transfer
- Government employees
- Military and civilian personnel

YOUR EMPLOYEES AND MEMBERS BENEFIT WHEN YOU PURCHASE *THE SUCCESS PRINCIPLES*™ AUDIO PROGRAM IN QUANTITY . . .

Now your employees, managers, members, and students can experience this revolutionary system for accomplishing any goal, living any dream, and becoming successful in any area when you purchase *The Success Principles*™ Audio Program in bulk. You'll enjoy substantial discounts off the regular retail price—plus, your team will discover powerful new habits that bring astonishing opportunities and extraordinary results.

Let *The Success Principles* give your group the day-by-day written exercises that will help them incorporate these new attitudes and behaviors into their compelling new lives. Then, watch as unexplained benefits come their way . . . important new contacts approach them with opportunities . . . and the world opens its bounty and riches to them—all because they, too, have made the journey through exercises and success principles like these:

- Articulating your unique appeal so the world's resources will gravitate toward you
- Accessing powerful mentors and friends who'll open doors for you as you seek success
- Saying no to the good so that you'll have room in your life to say yes to the great
- Completing past projects, relationships, and hurts so that you can embrace the future
- Telling the truth sooner to save you from disaster as you move forward to success
- Changing the outcome of any event, simply by changing your reaction to it
- Preparing and being instantly ready when opportunity comes knocking
- Using the unique time management system that ensures that you'll have time to focus on success

To purchase *The Success Principles*™ Audio Program, visit www .thesuccessprinciples.com. To arrange for an in-house workshop, call 805-563-2935, extension 41.

SUGGESTED READING AND ADDITIONAL RESOURCES FOR SUCCESS

*You are the same today as you'll be in five years except for
two things, the books you read and the people you meet.*

CHARLIE "TREMENDOUS" JONES
Member of the National Speakers Hall of Fame

Remember, I recommend that you read for an hour a day. That should add up to one or two books a week. The list below contains 120 books—enough to keep you busy for at least 2 years. I suggest you read through the list and see which books jump out at you and start with those. Follow your interests, and you'll find that each book you read will lead you to other books.

There are also 27 audio programs I suggest you listen to and 12 training programs I encourage you to attend. There's even a success-oriented summer camp for your kids.

For a more extensive and continually updated list of books, audio programs, and trainings in all of these areas, go to www.thesuccessprinciples.com.

I. THE FUNDAMENTALS OF SUCCESS

The Science of Success

The Power of Focus: How to Hit Your Business, Personal and Financial Targets with Absolute Certainty, by Jack Canfield, Mark Victor Hansen, and Les Hewitt. Deerfield Beach, Fla.: Health Communications, 2000.

The Aladdin Factor: How to Ask for and Get Anything You Want in Life, by Jack Canfield and Mark Victor Hansen. New York: Berkley, 1995.

The Art of Possibility: Transforming Personal and Professional Life, by Rosamund Stone Zander and Benjamin Zander. New York, Penguin, 2000.

The DNA of Success: Know What You Want . . . To Get What You Want, by Jack M. Zufelt. New York: Regan Books, 2002.

The Science of Success: How to Attract Prosperity and Create Life Balance Through Proven Principles, by James A. Ray. La Jolla, Calif.: SunArk Press, 1999.

The Success System That Never Fails, by W. Clement Stone. Englewood Clifffs, N.J.: Prentice-Hall, 1962.

Success Through a Positive Mental Attitude, by Napoleon Hill and W. Clement Stone. Englewood Cliffs, N.J.: Prentice-Hall, 1977.

Think and Grow Rich, by Napoleon Hill. New York: Fawcett Crest, 1960.

Napoleon Hill's Keys to Success: The 17 Principles of Personal Achievement, edited by Matthew Sartwell. New York: Plume, 1997.

Think and Grow Rich: A Black Choice, by Dennis P. Kimbro, Ph.D. New York: Ballantine, 1997.

What Makes the Great Great: Strategies for Extraordinary Achievement, by Dennis P. Kimbrow, Ph.D. New York: Doubleday, 1997.

The 7 Habits of Highly Effective People, by Stephen R. Covey. New York: Fireside, 1989.

The 100 Absolutely Unbreakable Laws of Business Success, by Brian Tracy. San Francisco: Berret-Koehler, 2000.

Play to Win: Choosing Growth Over Fear in Work and Life, by Larry Wilson and Hersch Wilson. Austin, Tex.: Bard Press, 1998.

Master Success: Create a Life of Purpose, Passion, Peace and Prosperity, by Bill Fitzpatrick. Natick, Mass.: American Success Institute, 2000.

The Traits of Champions: The Secrets to Championship Performance in Business, Golf, and Life, by Andrew Wood and Brian Tracy. Provo, Utah: Executive Excellence Publishing, 2000.

The Great Crossover: Personal Confidence in the Age of the Microchip, by Dan Sullivan, Babs Smith, and Michel Néray. Chicago and Toronto: The Strategic Coach, 1994.

Extreme Success, by Richard Fettke. New York: Fireside, 2002.

The Power of Positive Habits, by Dan Robey. Miami: Abritt Publishing Group, 2003.

Unlimited Power, by Anthony Robbins. New York: Simon & Schuster, 1986.

The Official Guide to Success, by Tom Hopkins. Scottsdale, Ariz.: Champion Press, 1982.

Create Your Own Future, by Brian Tracy. New York: John Wiley & Sons, 2002.

The Street Kid's Guide to Having It All, by John Assaraf. San Diego: The Street Kid, LLC, 2003.

Peak Performance: Mental Training Techniques of the World's Greatest Athletes, by Charles A. Garfield, with Hal Z. Bennett. Los Angeles: Jeremy P. Tarcher, 1984.

Peak Performers: The New Heroes of American Business, by Charles Garfield. New York: William Morrow, 1986.

How to Use What You've Got to Get What You Want, by Marilyn Tam. San Diego: Jodere, 2003.

You Were Born Rich, by Bob Proctor. Willowdale, Ontario, Canada: McCrary Publishing, 1984.

The Magic of Believing, by Claude M. Bristol. New York: Simon & Schuster, 1991.

The Magic of Thinking Big, by David Schwartz. New York: Fireside, 1987.

Work Less, Make More, by Jennifer White. New York: John Wiley & Sons, 1998.

Ask and It Is Given: Learning to Manifest Your Desires, by Esther and Jerry Hicks. Carlsbad, Calif.: Hay House, 2004.

50 Success Classics, by Tom Butler-Bowdon. Yarmouth, Maine: Nicholas Brealey Publishing, 2004.

See You at the Top (2nd revision), by Zig Ziglar. New York: Pelican, 2000.

Entrepreneurial Success

All You Can Do Is All You Can Do But All You Can Do Is Enough!, by A. L. Williams. New York: Ivy Books, 1988.

The E-Myth Revisited: Why Most Small Businesses Don't Work and What to Do About It, by Michael Gerber. New York: HarperBusiness, 1995.

E-Myth Mastery: The Seven Essential Disciplines for Building a World Class Company, by Michael Gerber. New York: HarperBusiness, 2004.

Mastering the Rockefeller Habits, by Verne Harnish. New York: Select Books, 2002.

1001 Ways to Reward Employees, by Bob Nelson. New York: Workman Publishing, 1994.

The One Minute Manager, by Kenneth Blanchard and Spencer Johnson. New York: Berkley Books, 1983.

Start Small, Finish Big: Fifteen Key Lessons to Start—and Run—Your Own Successful Business, by Fred DeLuca with John B. Hayes. New York: Warner Books, 2000.

Corporate Success

Built to Last: The Successful Habits of Visionary Companies, by Jim Collins and Jerry I. Porras. New York: HarperBusiness, 1997.

Execution: The Discipline of Getting Things Done, by Larry Bossidy and Ron Charan. New York: Crown Business, 2002.

Good to Great: Why Some Companies Make the Leap . . . and Others Don't, by Jim Collins. New York: HarperCollins, 2001.

The Five Temptations of a CEO: A Leadership Fable, by Patrick M. Lencioni. San Francisco: Jossey-Bass, 1998.

Jack: Straight from the Gut, by Jack Welch. New York: Warner, 2001.

The Goal: A Process of Ongoing Improvement (2nd edition), by Eliyahu M. Goldratt. Great Barrington, Mass.: North River Press, 1992.

The One Minute Manager, by Kenneth Blanchard and Spencer Johnson. New York: William Morrow, 1982.

The Spirit to Serve: Marriott's Way, by J.W. Marriott Jr. New York: HarperCollins, 2001.

Who Says Elephants Can't Dance? Inside IBM's Historic Turnaround, by Louis V. Gerstner Jr. New York: HarperBusiness, 2002.

Scorekeeping for Success

The Game of Work: How to Enjoy Work as Much as Play, by Charles A. Coonradt. Park City, Utah: Game of Work, 1997.

Managing the Obvious: How to Get What You Want Using What You Know, by Charles A. Coonradt, with Jack M. Lyons and Richard Williams. Park City, Utah: Game of Work, 1994.

Scorekeeping for Success, by Charles A. Coonradt. Park City, Utah: Game of Work, 1999.

Inspiration and Motivation

Chicken Soup for the Soul®, by Jack Canfield and Mark Victor Hansen. Deerfield Beach, Fla.: Health Communications, 1993.

Chicken Soup for the Soul at Work, by Jack Canfield, Mark Victor Hansen, Martin Rutte, Maida Rogerson, and Tim Clauss. Deerfield Beach, Fla.: Health Communications, 1996.

Chicken Soup for the Soul: Living Your Dreams, by Jack Canfield and Mark Victor Hansen. Deerfield Beach, Fla.: Health Communications, 2003.

Dare to Win, by Jack Canfield and Mark Victor Hansen. New York: Berkley, 1994.

It's Not Over until You Win, by Les Brown. New York: Simon & Schuster, 1997.

Rudy's Rules for Success, by Rudy Ruettiger and Mike Celizic. Dallas, Tex.: Doddridge Press, 1995.

Health and Fitness

8 Minutes in the Morning, by Jorge Cruise. New York: HarperCollins, 2001.

The 24-Hour Turnaround: The Formula for Permanent Weight Loss, Antiaging, and Optimal Health—Starting Today! by Jay Williams, Ph.D. New York: Regan Books, 2002.

Body for Life: 12 Weeks to Mental and Spiritual Strength, by Bill Phillips. New York: HarperCollins, 1999.

The Mars and Venus Diet and Exercise Solution, by John Gray, Ph.D. New York: St. Martin's Press, 2003.

Stress Management Made Simple, by Jay Winner, M.D. Santa Barbara, Calif.: Blue Fountain Press, 2003.

Ultimate Fit or Fat, by Covert Bailey. Boston: Houghton Mifflin Company, 2000.

II. TRANSFORM YOURSELF FOR SUCCESS

Time Management and Getting Things Done

First Things First, by Stephen Covey, A. Roger Merrill, and Rebecca R. Merrill. New York: Fireside, 1995.

Getting Things Done: The Art of Stress-Free Productivity, by David Allen. New York: Viking, 2001.

Getting Things Done, by Edwin C. Bliss. New York: Charles Scribner's Sons, 1991.

Doing It Now, by Edwin C. Bliss. New York: Macmillan, 1983.

The 10 Natural Laws of Successful Time and Life Management: Proven Strategies for Increased Productivity and Inner Peace, by Hyrum W. Smith. New York: Warner Books, 1994.

The Procrastinator's Handbook: Mastering the Art of Doing It Now, by Rita Emmett. New York: Walker Publishing, 2000.

Personal Awareness, Human Potential, Inner Peace and Spirituality

Loving What Is: Four Questions That Can Change Your Life, by Byron Katie. New York: Harmony Books, 2002.

The Sedona Method: Your Key to Lasting Happiness, Success, Peace and Emotional Well-being, by Hale Dwoskin. Sedona, Ariz.: Sedona Press, 2003.

The Four Agreements: A Practical Guide to Personal Freedom, by Don Miguel Ruiz. San Rafael: Amber-Allen, 1999.

The Power of Full Engagement, by Jim Loehr and Tony Schwartz. New York: Free Press, 2002.

Don't Sweat the Small Stuff . . . and It's All Small Stuff: Simple Ways to Keep the Little Things from Taking Over Your Life, by Richard Carlson. New York: Hyperion, 1997.

The Six Pillars of Self-Esteem, by Nathaniel Branden. New York: Bantam, 1994.

Life After Life, by Raymond A. Moody Jr., M.D. New York: Bantam, 1975.

Life Strategies: Doing What Works, Doing What Matters, by Phillip C. McGraw, Ph.D. New York: Hyperion, 1999.

Power vs. Force: The Hidden Determinants of Human Behavior, by David R. Hawkins, M.D., Ph.D. Carlsbad, Calif.: Hay House, 2002.

The Power of Now: A Guide to Spiritual Enlightenment, by Eckhart Tolle. Novato, Calif.: New World Library, 1999.

Eliminating Stress, Finding Inner Peace, by Brian Weiss, M.D. Carlsbad, Calif.: Hay House, 2003.

The Seven Spiritual Laws of Success, by Deepak Chopra. San Rafael, Calif.: Amber-Allen, 1994.

The Spirituality of Success: Getting Rich with Integrity, by Vincent M. Roazzi. Dallas: Brown Books, 2002.

The Way of the Spiritual Warrior (audio cassette), with David Gershon. Available from his Web site at www.empowermenttraining.com.

Audio Programs

The Success Principles: Your 30-Day Journey from Where You Are to Where You Want to Be, by Jack Canfield and Janet Switzer, is a 30-day course with 6 CDs and a 90-page workbook that is a great supplement to this book. It contains numerous worksheets and exercises to help you integrate the material presented here. You can also listen to the CDs in the car to reinforce your new learning. To order, go to www.thesuccessprinciples.com or www.jackcanfield.com or call 1-800-237-8336.

The following are the other motivational and educational audio programs I most recommend. All are available from Nightingale-Conant (www.nightingale.com) except one, which is indicated:

Action Strategies for Personal Achievement, by Brian Tracy
A View from the Top, by Zig Ziglar

The Aladdin Factor, by Jack Canfield and Mark Victor Hansen
The Art of Exceptional Living, by Jim Rohn
The Automatic Millionaire, by David Bach
Get the Edge, by Anthony Robbins
Goals, by Zig Ziglar
Guide to Everyday Negotiating, by Roger Dawson
Jump and the Net Will Appear, by Robin Crow
Live with Passion, by Anthony Robbins
Magical Mind, Magical Body, by Deepak Chopra
Maximum Confidence, by Jack Canfield
Multiple Streams of Income, by Robert Allen
The New Dynamics of Winning, by Denis Waitley
The New Psycho-Cybernetics, by Maxwell Maltz and Dan Kennedy
The One Minute Millionaire System, by Mark Victor Hansen and Robert Allen
The Power of Purpose, by Les Brown
The Power of Visualization, by Dr. Lee Pulos
The Psychology of Achievement, by Brian Tracy
The Psychology of Selling, by Brian Tracy
Pure Genius, by Dan Sullivan
Rich Dad Secrets, by Robert Kiyosaki
The Secrets to Manifesting Your Destiny, by Wayne Dyer
The 7 Habits of Highly Effective People, by Stephen Covey
Self-Esteem and Peak Performance, by Jack Canfield (CareerTrack)
The Weekend Millionaire's Real Estate Investing Program, by Roger Dawson and Mike Summey
Think and Grow Rich, by Napoleon Hill

Human Potential and Self-Development Training

Canfield Training Group, P.O. Box 30880, Santa Barbara, CA 93130. Phone: 805-563-2935. Toll-free: 1-800-237-8336. Fax: 805-563-2945. www.jackcanfield.com. Throughout the year, I conduct day-long, weekend, and weeklong training programs that focus on Living the Success Principles, Living Your Highest Vision, the Power of Focus, Self-Esteem and Peak Performance, Maximum Confidence, and the Training of Trainers Program.

Global Relationship Centers, 25555 Pedernales Point Drive, Spicewood, TX 78669. Phone: 512-264-3333. Fax: 512-264-2913. www.grc333.com. Larry Price, the executive director of my foundation—the Foundation for Self-Esteem—took their Understanding Yourself and Others program and received tremendous value from it.

The Hendricks Institute, 402 W. Ojai Avenue, suite 101, PMB 413, Ojai, CA 93023. Phone: 1-800-688-0772. www.hendricks.com. Gay and Katie Hendricks offer a variety of courses, both live and online, on relationships and conscious living. My wife and I have both benefited deeply from their work.

Hoffman Institute, 223 San Anselmo Avenue, suite 4, San Anselmo, CA 94960. Phone: 415-485-5220. Toll-free: 1-800-506-5253. www.hoffmaninstitute.org. This powerful weeklong training helps you make peace with your parents and overcome the limiting beliefs and reactive behavior patterns that you developed as a child. My partner Mark Victor Hansen recently took it, as did Martin Rutte and Tim Claus, coauthors of *Chicken Soup for the Soul at Work*. My son Oran, now 30, also took it, and it radically changed his life.

Human Awareness Institute. Phone: 1-800-800-4117; international: +1-650-571-5524. www.hai.org. Offers workshops on opening the heart, creating intimate relationships, and for individuals and couples. The institute has offices in Australia and the United Kingdom, as well as throughout the United States.

Insight Seminars, 2101 Wilshire Boulevard, suite 101, Santa Monica, CA 90403. Phone: 310-315-9733. Fax: 310-315-9854. www.insightseminars.org. A single weekend seminar provides an opportunity to transform your life, experience a deeper connection with your true self, and create greater balance and personal fulfillment. The advanced courses assist you in letting go of fears and limiting behaviors, cultivate greater ability to access your wisdom, intuition, and inner magnificence, and live your life in greater alignment with your spiritual values.

Landmark Education—The Forum, 353 Sacramento Street, suite 200, San Francisco, CA 94111. Phone: 415-981-8850. Fax: 415-616-2411. www.landmarkeducation.com. This powerful weekend training takes you out of fear into living a dynamic, intentional life of contribution and fulfillment. You can expect greater self-esteem, more fulfilling relationships, greater financial success, and more balance in your life.

Money and You Program of the Excellerated Business School for Entrepreneurs, 4878 Pescadero Avenue, suite 204, San Diego, CA 92107. Phone: 619-230-1888. www.excellerated.com. Conducts breakthrough, transformational workshops on money and business for entrepreneurs.

Peak Potentials Training, 1651 Welch Street, North Vancouver, BC, Canada, V7P 3G9. Phone: 604-983-3344. www.peakpotentials.com. I strongly recommend Harv Eker's Millionaire Mind weekend. It is his core training. Sign up for a free Millionaire Mind Evening Teleseminar on the Web site to get more information. There are also many graduate seminars you can take on a variety of topics, including a powerful training-of-trainers course.

PSI Seminars, 11650 High Valley Road, Clearlake Oaks, CA 95423. Phone: 707-998-2222). www.psiseminars.com. The company offers a series of powerful, transformational seminars.

Sedona Training Associates, 60 Tortilla Drive, Sedona, AZ 86336. Phone: 928-282-3522. Fax: 928-203-0602. www.sedona.com. The Sedona Method is one of the easiest and most powerful tools for self-improvement and spiritual growth that I have ever experienced. I have been amazed at the simplicity of the method and the powerful effect it has had on my life. It focuses on releasing emotions so that you come back into touch with the deepest part of your nature. Life gets easier. There is less resistance to everything. It helps you release anxiety and fears, eliminate stress, manage anger, overcome depression, improve relationships, enjoy more energy, sleep more soundly, achieve more radiant health, and find lasting inner peace, joy, and love.

The Breakthrough Experience with Dr. John Demartini, Demartini Seminars, 2800 Post Oak Boulevard, suite 5250, Houston, TX 77056. Phone: 713-850-1234. Toll-

free: 888-DEMARTINI. www.drdemartini.com. John is a master facilitator and a
truly wise and profound being.

Therapy and Counseling

The resources below can help you find a practitioner in your area. Finding a good
therapist is a lot like dating. You may need to test-drive a few before you find one you
like. A good therapist should make you feel safe but also a little uncomfortable. The
therapist should be loving and confrontive at the same time.

The following three approaches to therapy are my favorite in terms of impact.
There are many fine therapists who do not use these approaches, but if you find a
practitioner who does use one of these, you're likely to be in good hands.

Gestalt therapy: For information on Gestalt therapy and for a directory of Gestalt
therapists in all regions of the United States, go online to the Gestalt Therapy Page at
www.gestalt.org. Then scroll down to the entry that says: *If the reason for your visit to
The Gestalt Therapy Page is to find a Gestalt therapist in your locale for personal therapy, click
here.* This will take you directly to the only comprehensive, worldwide guide to
Gestalt therapists in private practice. Then click on the state you live in and scroll
down to your closest city,

Psychosynthesis: To find a directory of psychosynthesis centers and practitioners, go to www.chebucto.ns.ca/Health/Psychosynthesis/. Click on *Centers and Practitioners.*

Neurolinguistic Programming (NLP): NLP is a powerful system of thinking that can
accelerate the achievement of your personal and professional goals—in fact, it's the
methodology that much of Tony Robbins's work is based on. To find a directory of
NLP practitioners, trainers, and centers, go to www.nlpinfo.com. Some of my favorite trainers are Robert Dilts and Judith DeLozier (408-336-3457) at the NLP University in California, Tad James (808-596-7765) at Advanced Neuro Dynamics in
Hawaii, and Steve Andreas (303-987-2224) and the folks at NLP Comprehensive in
Colorado. They've trained hundreds of people who live all over the United States and
Canada.

III. BUILD YOUR SUCCESS TEAM

*How to Say No Without Feeling Guilty: And Say Yes to More Time and What Matters Most to
    You,* by Patti Breitman and Connie Hatch. New York: Broadway, 2001.
When I Say No, I Feel Guilty, by Manuel J. Smith. New York: Bantam, 1975.
*Coach Yourself to Success: 101 Tips from a Personal Coach for Reaching Your Goals at Work
    and in Life,* by Talane Miedaner. Lincolnwood, Ill.: Contemporary Books, 2000.
Take Yourself to the Top: The Secrets of America's #1 Career Coach, by Laura Berman Fort-
    gang. New York: Warner, 1998.
The Portable Coach: 28 Sure Fire Strategies for Business and Personal Success, by Thomas J.
    Leonard. New York: Scribner, 1998.

COACHING PROGRAMS

For information on The Success Principles Coaching Program, which is designed to personally help you integrate these principles into your life, career, relationship, and finances, visit www.thesuccessprinciples.com/coaching.htm.

These are my other two favorite coaching programs:

The Strategic Coach Program was created by Dan Sullivan. Contact the organization toll-free at 1-800-387-3206, call 416-531-7399, or visit www.strategiccoach.com. Dan also has a host of books, audios, and other media based on core Strategic Coach concepts and tools.

Achievers Coaching Program was created by Les Hewitt (who coauthored *The Power of Focus* with Mark Victor Hansen and me) and has offices in four countries. Contact the organization by writing Achievers Canada, suite 220, 2421 37th Avenue, Calgary, Alberta T2E 6Y7 Canada; calling 403-295-0500; or visiting www.thepoweroffocus.ca.

To find a personal coach, contact

The International Coach Federation. Call toll-free at 888-423-3131 or visit www.coachfederation.org.

Coach U. Call toll free 1-800-482-6244 or visit www.coachinc.com. Click on *Find a Coach*.

Other coaches—especially those that specialize in a specific industry or business how-to training—have Web sites that can be found with a simple Internet search like "real estate coaching." One of the best in that category, by the way, is Mike Ferry's Real Estate Coaching at www.mikeferry.com.

Developing Your Intuition

Divine Intuition: Your Guide to Creating a Life You Love, by Lynn A. Robinson. New York: Dorling Kindersley, 2001. Also check out Lynn's Web site at www.lynnrobinson.com.

PowerHunch, by Marcia Emery. Hillsboro, Ore.: Beyond Words Publishing, 2001.

Practical Intuition, by Laura Day. New York: Broadway Books, 1997.

Practical Intuition for Success, by Laura Day. New York: HarperCollins, 1997.

The Corporate Mystic, by Gay Hendricks and Kate Ludeman. New York: Bantam Books, 1997.

The Executive Mystic, by Barrie Dolnick. New York: HarperBusiness, 1999.

IV. CREATE SUCCESSFUL RELATIONSHIPS

Conscious Loving: The Journey to Co-Commitment, by Gay Hendricks and Kathlyn Hendricks. New York: Bantam Books, 1992.

Lasting Love: The 5 Secrets of Growing a Vital, Conscious Relationship, by Gay Hendricks and Kathlyn Hendricks. New York: Rodale, 2004.

Men Are from Mars, Women Are from Venus: A Practical Guide for Improving Communication and Getting What You Want in Your Relationships, by John Gray, Ph.D. New York: HarperCollins, 1993.

Real Moments: Discover the Secret for True Happiness, by Barbara DeAngelis. New York: Doubleday, 1994.

Feel Alive with a Heart Talk, by Cliff Durfee. San Diego: Live, Love, Laugh, 1979.

How to Talk So Kids Will Listen & Listen So Kids Will Talk, by Adele Faber and Elaine Mazlish. New York: Avon Books, 1980.

Communicate with Confidence, by Dianna Booher. New York: McGraw Hill, 1994.

How to Say It at Work: Putting Yourself Across with Power Words, Phrases, Body Language and Communication Secrets, by Jack Griffin. Englewood Cliffs, N.J.: Prentice-Hall, 1998.

Boundaries: When to Say Yes, When to Say No to Take Control of Your Life, by Dr. Henry Cloud and Dr. John Townsend. Grand Rapids, Mich.: Zondervan, 1992.

Radical Honesty: How to Transform Your Life by Telling the Truth, by Brad Blanton. New York: Dell, 1996.

Practicing Radical Honesty, by Brad Blanton. Stanley, Va.: Sparrowhawk Publishing, 2000.

The Truth Option, by Will Schutz. Berkeley, Calif.: Ten-Speed Press, 1984.

V. FINANCIAL SUCCESS AND MONEY

Cash Flow Quadrant, by Robert Kiyosaki. New York: Warner Books, 2000.

Multiple Streams of Income, by Robert G. Allen. New York: John Wiley & Sons, 2000.

Multiple Streams of Internet Income, by Robert Allen. New York: John Wiley & Sons, 2001.

Rich Dad, Poor Dad, by Robert Kiyosaki with Sharon L. Lecter. Paradise Valley, Ariz.: Tech Press, 1997.

The Courage to Be Rich: Creating a Life of Material and Spiritual Abundance, by Suze Orman. New York: Riverhead Books, 1999.

The Dynamic Laws of Prosperity, by Catherine Ponder. New York: DeVorss, 1988.

The Automatic Millionaire: A Powerful One-Step Plan to Live and Finish Rich, by David Bach. New York: Broadway Books, 2003.

The Armchair Millionaire, by Lewis Schiff and Douglas Gerlach. New York: Pocket Books, 2001.

The Millionaire Course, by Mark Allen. Novato, Calif.: New World Library, 2003.

The Millionaire in You, by Michael LeBoeuf. New York: Crown Business, 2002.

The Millionaire Mind, by Thomas J. Stanley. Kansas City: Andrews McMeel Publishing, 2000.

The Millionaire Mindset: How Ordinary People Can Create Extraordinary Income, by Gerry Robert. Kuala Lumpur, Malaysia: Awesome Books, 1999.

The Millionaire Next Door, by Thomas J. Stanley and William D. Danko. New York: Pocket Books, 1996.

The Miracle of Tithing, by Mark Victor Hansen. Newport Beach, Calif.: Mark Victor Hansen & Associates, 2003. Call 1-800-433-2314 to order.

The One Minute Millionaire: The Enlightened Way to Wealth, by Mark Victor Hansen and Robert G. Allen. New York: Harmony Books, 2002.

The Science of Getting Rich, by Wallace D. Wattles. Tucson, Ariz.: Iceni Books, 2001. (Reprint of original book, which was published in 1910.)

The 21 Success Secrets of Self-Made Millionaires, by Brian Tracy. San Francisco: Berrett-Koehler, 2001.

The Wealthy Barber, 3rd edition, by David Chilton. Roseville, Calif.: Prima Publishing, 1998.

Secrets of the Millionaire Mind: Mastering the Inner Game of Wealth, by T. Harv Eker. New York: HarperCollins, 2005.

CASHFLOW® 101 is a fun educational game developed by Robert Kiyosaki that teaches accounting, finance, and investing as you learn how to get out of the rat race and onto the fast track, where your money works for you instead of you working hard for your money. The game is appropriate for anyone 10 and older. You can purchase it online at www.richdad.com.

ADDITIONAL RESOURCES

The ededge book club, which was mentioned in Principle 36 ("Learn More to Earn More"), is a powerful way to stay on the cutting edge of breakthrough business success books. To enroll in the service, go www.ededge.com.

AdvantEdge is a new magazine focused on providing the world's most powerful success information and is published by Nightingale-Conant. Subscribe at www.nightingale.com or by calling 1-800-560-6081.

SuperCamp is a truly transformational experience that will give your kids a head start on the success track. Check out www.quantumlearning.com for a possible 10-day summer experience for kids aged 9 to 18. What their graduates have accomplished is truly awesome.

Chicken Soup's Daily Serving (www.chickensoup.com) is a free daily e-mail of a heartwarming, inspirational story from the best-selling *Chicken Soup for the Soul®* series.

ABOUT THE AUTHORS

Jack Canfield has been a successful author, professional speaker, seminar leader, corporate trainer, and entrepreneur. After graduating from Harvard University, Jack started his career as a high school teacher in Chicago's inner city. Jack quickly became obsessed with learning how to motivate his unmotivated students. In this quest, he discovered self-made Chicago millionaire and success guru W. Clement Stone. Stone was the publisher of *Success Magazine*, the president of Combined Insurance Corporation, the author of *The Success System That Never Fails*, and coauthor, with Napoleon Hill, of *Success Through a Positive Mental Attitude*.

Jack went to work at the W. Clement & Jessie V. Stone Foundation with the charge to take these success principles into the schools and Boys Clubs of the greater Chicago area—and later the entire Midwest. Wanting to understand these achievement motivation principles even more clearly, Jack returned to graduate school at the University of Massachusetts, where he received his master's degree in psychological education. After graduating, Jack embarked on a career of conducting seminars for schoolteachers, counselors, psychotherapists, and—later—corporate leaders, managers, salespeople, and entrepreneurs, teaching the principles of self-esteem, peak performance, achievement motivation, and success.

Along the way, Jack wrote and coauthored such books as *100 Ways to Enhance Self-Esteem in the Classroom*, *Dare to Win*, *The Aladdin Factor*, *Heart at Work*, and *The Power of Focus: How to Hit All Your Personal, Business and Financial Goals with Absolute Certainty*, as well as the best-selling 85-book *Chicken Soup for the Soul*® series, which has currently sold over 80 million copies in 39 languages around the world. Jack has also shared his principles for success, self-esteem, and happiness in his best-selling CareerTrack audio album *Self-Esteem and Peak Performance* and his Nightingale-Conant albums *Maximum Confidence* and *The Aladdin Factor*.

Because he's in demand more days each year than he could possibly speak and do seminars, Jack has also created two video-based training programs: the STAR Program, which is his basic self-esteem and peak performance training for corporations and schools, and the GOALS Program, which are the same principles presented for at-risk populations such as welfare recipients and prisoners.

Organizations and corporations that have sought Jack out to share these principles with their members and employees include Virgin Records, Sony Pictures, Merrill Lynch, Monsanto, ITT Hartford Insurance, GlaxoSmith-Kline, Scott Paper, The Million Dollar Forum, Coldwell Banker, RE/MAX, FedEx, Campbell's Soup, TRW, Society of Real Estate Professionals, the Million Dollar Roundtable, American Society of Training & Development, Ameritech, NCR, Young Presidents' Organization, Chief Executives Organization, GE, Income Builders International, U.S. Department of the Navy, Siemens, Cingular Wireless, Southern Bell, Domino's Pizza, Accenture, Bergen Brunswig Pharmaceuticals, Children's Miracle Network, UCLA, University of Michigan, the Council for Excellence in Government, and hundreds of others.

Jack has given speeches and conducted workshops in all 50 states in the United States, as well as in Canada, Mexico, Europe, Asia, Africa, and Australia. He has also appeared on over 600 radio shows and 200 television shows, including *20/20*, *Inside Edition*, the *Today* show, *Oprah*, *Fox and Friends*, *CBS Evening News*, *NBC Nightly News*, *Eye to Eye*, and CNN's *Talk Back Live!* and on PBS and QVC.

Jack conducts one-day and weekend workshops that focus on Living the Success Principles, the Power of Focus, Self-Esteem and Peak Performance, and Maximum Confidence, as well as an annual 7-day Breakthrough to Success: Living the Success Principles training in which he teaches the principles of success in a powerful, life-changing workshop. His trainings are designed for businesspeople, managers, entrepreneurs, salespeople, sales managers, managers, educators, counselors, coaches, consultants, ministers, and others who are interested in maximizing their personal and professional success.

To find out more about Jack's workshops and training, books, and audio and video training programs or to inquire about Jack's availability as a speaker or trainer, you can contact his office at

The Jack Canfield Companies
P.O. Box 30880, Santa Barbara, CA 93130

Phones: 805-563-2935 and 1-800-237-8336; fax: 805-563-2945
Web site: www.thesuccessprinciples.com

Janet Switzer, from her first job as campaign coordinator for a member of Congress at age 19 to building an international publishing company with over $10 million in assets by age 29, epitomizes the personal achievement and professional accomplishment that comes from applying these proven principles of success.

Today, she's the marketing genius and business growth expert of choice for some of the world's top success gurus: peak performance expert Jack Canfield, master motivator Mark Victor Hansen, marketing icon Jay Abraham, Internet income expert Yanik Silver, and *Jesus CEO* author Laurie Beth Jones, among others. Additionally, Janet has counseled more than 50,000 companies and entrepreneurs worldwide in leveraging their intangibles and information assets for untold millions in potential windfall revenue. She's the author of the Instant Income® series of small-business marketing resources designed to help entrepreneurs not only create immediate cash flow for their business but develop lucrative new profit centers, too. For details, visit www.instantincome.com.

Janet is an internationally recognized keynote speaker and founder and editor of *Leading Experts* magazine—as well as a columnist with *Training Magazine Asia* and numerous newswires and press syndicates.

She regularly speaks to thousands of entrepreneurs, independent sales professionals, corporate employees, and industry association members on the principles of success and income generation. Additionally, she helps achievers who are experts in their field attain worldwide status and million-dollar incomes by building publishing empires around their business strategies, training concepts, industry expertise, and unique market posture. Her multimedia short course "How Experts Build Empires: The Step-By-Step System for Turning Your Expertise into Super-Lucrative Profit Centers" is the industry's definitive work on the subject of developing and marketing information products.

Janet makes her home in Thousand Oaks, California, where she belongs to Calvary Community Church and works with young people as a local 4-H Club project leader—a role she's enjoyed for nearly 20 years.

To bring Janet to your next event, call 805-499-9400 or visit www.janetswitzer.com. To subscribe to *Leading Experts e-Magazine*, visit www.leadingexperts.net.

PERMISSIONS

INDEX